PICTORIAL
PRICE GUIDE
TO AMERICAN ANTIQUES

and Objects Made for the American Market

1998-1999 EDITION

PICTORIAL PRICE GUIDE TO AMERICAN ANTIQUES
and Objects Made for the American Market

ILLUSTRATED AND PRICED OBJECTS

By

Dorothy Hammond

PENGUIN STUDIO
Published by the Penguin Group
Penguin Putnam Inc., 375 Hudson Street,
New York, New York, 10014, U.S.A.

Penguin Books Ltd, 27 Wrights Lane,
London W8 5TZ, England

Penguin Books Australia, Ltd, Ringwood,
Victoria, Australia

Penguin Books Canada Ltd, 2801 John Street,
Markham, Ontario, Canada L3R 1B4

Penguin Books (N.Z.) Ltd, 182-90 Wairau Road,
Auckland 10, New Zealand

Penguin Books Ltd, Registered Offices:
Harmondsworth, Middlesex, England

First published by Penguin Studio, a member of Penguin Putnam Inc.

First printing, January 1998
10 9 8 7 6 5 4 3 2 1

ISBN: 0-14-027017-5

CONTENTS

INTRODUCTION

Now in its Nineteenth Edition, Pictorial Price Guide to American Antiques and Objects Made for the American Market, is recognized by collectors throughout the country as one of the most authoritative and up-to-date references on the market. The format is designed to provide the collector and antiques dealer with an accurate market value of items sold at auction galleries from September 1996 through September 1997. A selection of more than 5,000 illustrated items has been chosen for this edition. Entries are keyed to the auction house where an item was actually sold. A state abbreviation has been included for the reader's convenience because prices vary in different regions of the country. The year and the month the item sold has also been included.

Auction houses have enjoyed another great year with very healthy and diversified buyer response. In the first month of 1997, the same enthusiastic response was characteristic of 1996 endeavors. Art Glass, Lamps, Arts & Crafts, Art Deco, Fine Period Furniture, Porcelain, Early Glass, Samplers Toys and Art Pottery were no exception. And because good early antiques in fine condition are so incredibly scarce, values of quality English furniture have set records during the past twelve months. Furniture manufactured from the 1920s well into the 1950s continues to make the transition from tacky to trendy these days...and household items produced during this period remained very popular.

Although most auction houses give detailed catalog descriptions of items sold, others do not, therefore, every effort has been made to include as much information as possible with each entry illustrated. When comparing similar pieces, the reader must always take into consideration that fluctuations in the market as well as the quality of an object, the region in which it sold, as well as demand, determine the auction price.

Most auction houses charge a buyer's premium which is a surcharge on the hammer or final bid price at auction. For the reader's convenience the buyer's premium has been included with each auction house in acknowledgments.

Every effort has been made to record prices accurately and describe each item in the space allotted to our format. However, the writer cannot be responsible for any clerical or typographical errors that may occur.

— Dorothy Hammond

ACKNOWLEDGMENTS

Many persons have generously helped in assembling the materials for this book. I would like to express my gratitude to the following auction galleries and their staff members for their help in making this edition a reality. American Stoneware Auction, 10%, Bay Head, NJ; Aston Auctioneers & Appraisers, 10%, Endwell, NY; Bill Bertoi Auctions, 10%, Vineland, NJ; David Rajo Auctions, Inc., 10%, Lambertville, NJ; DeCaro Auction Sales, Inc., 15%, Easton, MD; Early Auction Company, 10%, Milford, OH; Robert C. Eldred Company, Inc., 10%, East Dennis, MA; Ken Farmer Auctions, 10%, Radford, VA; Garth's Auctions, Inc., 10%, Delaware, OH; Gene Harris Auction Center, 10%, Marshalltown, IA; Glass Works, 10%, Greenville, PA; Horst Auction Center, Ephrata, PA; Jackson's Auctioneers & Appraisers, 10%, Cedar Falls, IA; James D. Julia Inc., 15%, Fairfield, ME; Maritime Auctions, 10%, York, ME; Northeast Auctions, 15%, Hampton, NH; Pook & Pook, Inc., 10%, Downingtown, PA; Richard Opfer Auctioneering, Inc., 10%, Timonium, MD; Skinner, Inc., 15%, Bolton & Boston, MA; Thomas Hirchak Company, 10%, Morrisville, VT; and Woody Auction, Douglass, KS.

I am especially indebted to Steve Philip, President of S.A. Philip, Co., and his staff for their assistance with the varied details in organizing for photographic reproduction the many entries in order that deadlines could be met.

ABBREVIATIONS USED IN THIS BOOK AND THEIR MEANINGS

Am. . . . . .American	illus. . . . . . . .illustrated/illustration	pcs. . . . . .pieces
attrib. . . . . .attributed	imper. . . . . .imperfections	prob. . . . . .probably
batt. . . . . .battery	impr. . . . . .impressed	prof. . . . . .professional
blk. . . . . .black	int. . . . . .interior	Q.A. . . . . .Queen Anne
br. .brown	irid. . . . . .iridescent	reconst. . . . . .reconstructed
C. . . . . .century	lrg. . . . . .large	ref. . . . . .refinished/refinishing
ca. .circa	L . . . . .length/long	repr. . . . . .repair/repaired
compo. . . . . .composition	lt. .light	repl. . . . . .replaced
const. . . . .constructed/construction	litho. . . . . .lithograph	replm. . . . . .replacement
dk. .dark	L .long	repro. . . . . .reproduction
dec. . . . . .decorated/decoration	mah. . . . . .mahogany	rev. . . . . .reverse
diam. . . . . .diameter	mfg. . . . . .manufactured	sgn. . . . . .signed
emb. . . . . .embossed	mkd. . . . . .marked	sm. . . . . .small
Eng. . . . . .England	mech. . . . . .mechanical/mechanism	sq. . . . . .square
engr. . . . . .engraved	mono. . .monogram/monogrammed	T . . . . .tall
escut. . . . . .escutcheon	N.E. . . . . .New England	unmkd. . . . . .unmarked
Euro. . . . . .Europe/European	opal. . . . . .opalescent	unsgn. . . . . .unsigned
ext. . . . . .exterior	oper. . . . . .operate	W .wide
Fed. . . . . .Federal	ora. . . . . .orange	w/ .with
Fr. . . . . .France/French	orig. . . . . .original	wrt. . . . . .wrought
gal. . . . . .gallon	pr. .pair	yel. . . . . .yellow
Ger. . . . . .German/Germany	pat. . . . . .patent	
gr. .green	patt. . . . . .pattern	The common and accepted abbreviations are used for states.
H . . . . .high	pc. .piece	

A-PA Mar. 1997   Bill Bertoi Auctions

Dairy Wagon Mechanical Bank,
Sheffield Farms, Rich Toys, wood const.,
blk. paint & heavily decaled $385.00

A-PA Mar. 1997   Bill Bertoi Auctions

Supply Wagon Mechanical Bank,
wood const., yel. overall w/ stenciling, red
backrests, felt covered horses . . .$523.00

A-PA Mar. 1997   Bill Bertoi Auctions

Hen & Chick Mechanical Bank, J & E
Stevens Co., pat. 10/1/1901 . . .$4,020.00

A-PA Mar. 1997   Bill Bertoi Auctions

Owl Turns Head Mechanical Bank,
J & E Stevens Co., pat. 9/28/1880 . . .$413.00
Owl Turns Head Mechanical Bank,
J & E Stevens Co., pat. 9/28/1880,
missing one eye $3,520.00

A-PA Mar. 1997   Bill Bertoi Auctions

Jonah & Whale Mechanical Bank, Shep-
.ard Hardware Co., pat. 1890 . . .$1,705.00

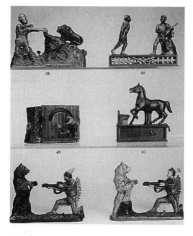

A-MA Sept. 1996   Skinner, Inc.

Row 1, Left to Right

Cast Iron Mechanical Banks
Lion Hunter Bank, J. &E. Stevens Co.,
pat. Aug. 22, 1911, some darkening,
10⅞" L $8,050.00
Darktown Batt. Bank, J.E. Stevens
Co., pat. Jan. 17, 1888, red & blue pitcher's uniform, some darkening &
scratches, 9⅞" L $2,300.00

Row 2, Left to Right

Leap Frog Bank, Shepard Hardward
Co., pat. Sept. 15, 1891, losses to top of
stump & base, 7½" L $1,610.00
Trick Pony Bank, Shepard Hardware
Co., pat. June 2, 1885, orig. key, finish
darkened, 7¹⁄₃₂" L $920.00

Row 3, Left to Right

Indian & Bear Bank, J.&E. Stevens Co.,
ca. 1900, br. bear, missing trap, Indian head
no longer moves, 10⁵⁄₁₆" L $1,150.00
Indian & Bear Bank, J.&E. Stevens Co.,
pat. Jan. 7, 1883, white bear, finish shel-
lacked, good condition, 10½" L .$1,725.00

A-PA Mar. 1997   Bill Bertoi Auctions

Bull Dog Bank Mechanical Bank, J & E
Stevens Co., pat. 4/27/1880 . . .$1,320.00

A-PA Mar. 1997   Bill Bertoi Auctions

Trick Dog Bank Mechanical Bank,
Hubley Mfg. Co., yel. & br. base . .$798.00

A-PA Mar. 1997   Bill Bertoi Auctions

Uncle Sam Mechanical Bank, Shepard
Hardware Co., pat. 6/8/1886 . .$3,300.00

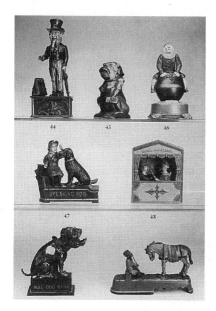

A-MA Sept. 1996   Skinner, Inc.

Cast Iron Mechanical Banks

Row 1, Left to Right

Uncle Sam Bank, Shepard Hardware
Co., pat. June 8, 1886, finish darkened,
minor chipping, 4⅞" L $1,150.00
General Butler Still Bank, J.&E.
Stevens Co., ca. 1884, chipping to top
of head & chin, 6½" H $2,185.00
Clown on Globe Bank, J.&E. Stevens
Co., tan base, minor wear & scratches,
9" H $6,325.00

Row 2, Left to Right

Speaking Dog Bank, Shepard Hardware
Co., pat. Oct. 20, 1885, maroon base, minor
chips on girl's dress, 7⅛" L $1,610.00
Punch & Judy Bank, Shepard Hardware Co., pat. July 22, 1884, sm. chip
in bottom plate, 7½" H $1,610.00

Row 3, Left to Right

Bull Dog Bank, J.&E. Stevens Co., pat.
April 27, 1880, br. dog, blue carpet, miss-
ing eye, jaw inoperable, 5⁵⁄₁₆" L .$6,325.00
I Always Did 'Spize a Mule, J.&E.
Stevens, pat. April 27, 1897, missing
trap, 10¹⁄₁₆" L $3,737.50

A-MA Sept. 1996 Skinner, Inc.

Cast Iron Mechanical Banks

Row 1, Left to Right

Artillery Bank, Shepard Hardware Co., pat. May 31, 1892, nickel plated cast iron, 8" L . . . . .N/S
Frog On Round Base, J.&E. Stevens Co., pat. Aug. 20, 1872, fair condition, base 4⁷⁄₁₆" diam. $345.00
Toad on Stump Bank, J.&E. Stevens Co., ca. 1880, 4" L . N/S

Row 2, Left to Right

Elephant Pull-Tail Bank, Hubley, 1930's, 9" L . . .$316.25
Elephant No Stars Bank, mfg. unknown, 8" L . . . . .N/S
Owl Slot in Head Bank, Kilgore, ca. 1930, missing trap, 5¾" H $230.00

Row 3, Left to Right

U.S. & Spain Bank, book of knowledge repro., 8" L . . .$143.75
Tammany Bank, J.&E. Stevens Co., pat. June 8, 1875, gray pants, blk. coat, overall wear, 5¾" H $230.00
Try Your Weight & Save Money Bank, Ger., ca. 1906, litho. tin weight scale, 6½" H $517.50
The Record Money Bank, Ger., ca. 1906, litho. tin weight scale, 6½" H $517.50

A-PA Mar. 1997 Bill Bertoi Auctions

Circus Mechanical Bank, Shepard Hardware Co., pat. 2/8/1887, Hegarty Collection $11,550.00
Clown on Globe Mechanical Bank, J & E Stevens Co., pat. 5/20/1890 . . . .$1,540.00
Trick Dog Mechanical Bank, Shepard Hardware Co., red & lt. gr. base $2,970.00
Elephant & Clowns Mechanical Bank, J & E Stevens Co., pat. 8/28/1883, cracked at base $1,320.00
Trick Dog Mechanical Bank, Hubley Mfg. Co., ca. 1906 . . . .$825.00

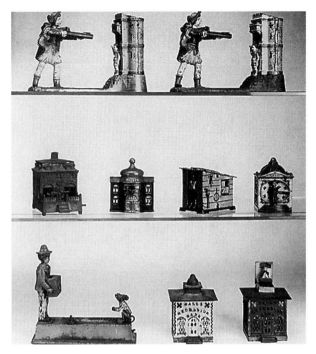

A-MA Sept. 1996 Skinner, Inc.

Cast Iron Mechanical Banks

Row 1, Left to Right

William Tell Bank, J.&E. Stevens Co., pat. June 23, 1896, 10½" L $431.25
William Tell Bank, J.&E. Stevens Co., pat. June 23, 1896, 10½" L $431.25

Row 2, Left to Right

Dog on Turntable Bank, Judd Mfg. Co., ca. 1880, copper-bronze plated, 5½" L $460.00
Presto Bank, possibly Kyser & Rex Co., ca. 1894, red doors & roof, gold striping, 4¼" H $690.00
Cabin Bank, J.&E. Stevens Co., pat. June 2, 1885, yel., some darkening, 4³⁄₁₆" L $747.50
Hull's Liliput Bank, J.&E. Stevens Co., pat. April 24, 1877, lt. gr. building w/ tin tray, some darkening, 4½" H .$920.00

Row 3, Left to Right

Monkey Bank, Hubley, 1920s, medium gr. base, 8¹³⁄₁₆" L $460.00
Hall's Excelsior Bank, J.&E. Stevens Co., pat. Dec. 2, 1869, white building, red & blk. trim, gray roof, darkening, cashier missing arms, 5¼" H $316.25
Hall's Excelsior Bank, J.&E. Stevens Co., pat. Dec. 21, 1869, red building w/ white & blk. trim, darkening, cashier missing arms, 5¼" H $345.00

A-PA Mar. 1997 Bill Bertoi Auctions

Professor Pug Frog Mechanical Bank, J & E Stevens & Co., ca. 1886, spring mechanism missing $6,820.00
Humpty Dumpty Mechanical Bank, Ohio Mfg. Co., . .$550.00
Jonah & Whale Mechanical Bank, Shepard Hardware Co., pat. 7/15/1890 . . . .$3,960.00
Pelican Mechanical Bank, J & E Stevens Co., pat. 1878 . . . .$2,200.00

A-MA Feb. 1997   Skinner

Row 1, Left to Right

J. & E. Stevens Mech. Bank, "I Always Did Spise a Mule", pat. April 22, 1879, painted cast iron, br. base, finish very good, 10¼" L $1,495.00
J. & E. Stevens Bank, "Bear Hunt" trade card, early 20th C., small tear $57.50
J. & E. Stevens Mech. Bank, Indian & Bear, pat. Jan. 17, 1888, painted cast iron, br. bear, Indian's head inoperative, 10⁵⁄₁₆" L $2,415.00

Row 2, Left to Right

J. & E. Stevens Mech. Bank, Eagle & Eaglets, pat., painted cast iron gr. grass version, 6½" L $2,185.00
J. & E. Stevens Mech. Bank, Eagle & Eaglets, pat. Jan. 23, 1883, gray grass, one eaglet & nest damaged, 6¹¹⁄₁₆" L $488.75
J. & E. Stevens Magic Bank, pat. Mar. 7, 1876, painted cast iron, yel. building, red roof, blue & red striping, br. door, 4¾" L . . . .N/S

Row 3, Left to Right

J. Barton Smith Bank, "Fidelity Trust Vault" Safe, ca. 1890, cast iron, br. asphaltum finish, wear to clock face, 6" W, 5½" D, 6" H $460.00
Hubley Bank, or A.C. Williams Rooster Still, painted cast iron, gold, red wattle, 4⅞" H $172.50
J. & E. Stevens Mech. Bank, "Darktown Battery", pat. Jan. 17, 1888, cast iron, completely overpainted, 10" L $805.00

A-PA Mar. 1997   Bill Bertoi Auctions

Punch & Judy Mechanical Bank, Shepard Hardware Co., pat. 7/15/1884 . . . .$2,860.00
Picture Gallery Mechanical Bank, Shepard Hardware, ca. 1885 . . . .$13,750.00
Punch & Judy Mechanical Bank, Shepard Hardware Co., pat. 7/15/1884 . . . .$2,090.00
Humpty Dumpty Mechanical Bank, Shepard Hardware Co., pat. 6/17/1884 . . . .$2,750.00

A-PA April 1997   Pook & Pook Inc.

Row 1, Left to Right

Mech. Banks
Cabin, good condition $425.00
Eagle & Eaglets, cast iron, good condition $475.00
Chief Big Moon, cast iron, w/ red base $800.00
Boy on Trapeze, repairs $1,000.00
Uncle Sam, minor retouching & repr. $1,300.00
Bulldog Savings Bank, fine condition $12,000.00
Clown on Globe, minor retouching $900.00
Owl, possible restoration $650.00

Row 2, Left to Right

Organ, dog possibly restored $600.00
Little Joe, eyes retouched or repl. $200.00
Artillery Bank, good cond. $1,400.00
Mammy Feeding Child, spoon repl. $3,500.00
Speaking Dog Bank, possible restoration to base . . .$1,000.00
Trick Dog, w/ 6 pc. base, fine condition $1,100.00
Santa Claus, fine cond. $4,500.00

Row 3, Left to Right

Weedens Plantation, very good condition $300.00
Jolly Blk. Man, good cond. $450.00
Frog Bank, repl. leg $750.00
Lion & 2 Monkeys, sm. monkey & arm repl. $300.00
Dinah, repainted $350.00
Bulldog Bank, coin on nose, excellent condition $3,000.00

A-MA Sept. 1996   Skinner
Row 1, Left to Right

Mech. Banks
Speaking Dog Bank, J.&E. Stevens Co., ca. 1900, good condition, 7⅛" L $316.25
Trick Dog Bank, Hubley, ca. 1920's, good condition, some darkening, 8¾" L $747.50
Tammany Bank, J.&E. Stevens Co., pat. Dec. 23, 1873, good condition, 5¾" H $230.00
Row 2, Left to Right

Tammany Bank, J.&E. Stevens Co., pat. Dec. 23, 1873, fin. darkened, 5¾" $172.50
Elephant Pull Tail Bank, Hubley, 1930s, 8½" L .$258.75
Lion on Wheels Still Bank, Arcade, gold, rubber wheels, 4½" L $130.00

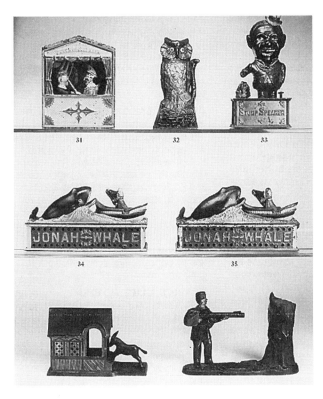

A-MA Sept. 1996   Skinner, Inc.

Row 1, Left to Right

Cast Iron Mechanical Banks
Punch & Judy Bank, J.&E. Stevens Co., pat. July 22, 1884, losses to Punch's face & edges, 6⅛" L $1,265.00
Owl Bank, J.&E. Stevens Co., pat. Sept. 28, 1880, 3⅞" L . . $575.00
Stump Speaker Bank, J.&E. Stevens Co., pat. Nov. 16, 1886, blk. face, missing trap door, cracked base, 4⅞" L $1092.50

Row 2, Left to Right

Jonah & The Whale Bank, Shepard Hardware Co., pat. July15, 1890, some paint loss to figures, 10½" L . . .$2875.00
Jonah & The Whale Bank, Shepard Hardware Co., pat. July 15, 1890, scratches, 10¼" L $1,495.00

Row 3, Left to Right

Mule Entering Barn Bank, J.&E. Stevens Co., pat. January 6, 1880, crack in back of barn, 8½" L $517.50
Creedmoor Bank, J.&E. Stevens Co., pat. January 6, 1877, fair condition, 8⅛" L $287.50

A-PA Mar. 1997   Bill Bertoi Auctions

Hen & Chick Mechanical Bank, J & E Stevens, pat. 10/1/1901 . . . .$2,145.00
Magic Mechanical Bank, J & E Stevens Co., pat. 3/7/1886 . . . .$1,870.00
Mule Entering Barn Mechanical Bank, J & E Stevens Co., pat. 1/6/1880 . . . .$2,860.00
Speaking Dog Mechanical Bank, maroon base, Shepard Hardware Co., pat. 10/20/1885 . . . .$2,530.00

A-PA April 1997   Pook & Pook Inc.

Row 1, Left to Right

Mechanical Banks
Horse Race, one arch recast $3,500.00
Punch & Judy, small letter version $4,500.00
Bad Accident, restored to paint/parts $375.00
Girl Skipping Rope, repr. or repaint on inside cover of wheel in yellow/red $19,000.00
Leapfrog Bank, gr. base restored/broken mech. .$550.00
Dk. Town Battery, fine condition $6,250.00

Row 2, Left to Right

Jonah & the Whale, some repaint $1,400.00
Mason Bank, excellent condition $3,750.00
Tammany Bank, gray pants, fine condition $600.00
I Always Did Spize a Mule, possible restoration $275.00
Creedmore, repainted $150.00
Trick Pony $1,700.00

Row 3, Left to Right

William Tell, some repaint $650.00
Indian Shooting Bear, feathers restored $2,250.00
Uncle Tom, restored, possible marriage $275.00
I Always Did Spize a Mule $750.00
Mule Entering Barn, excellent condition $2,500.00

A-PA Mar. 1997   Bill Bertoi Auctions

Rabbit in Cabbage Mechanical Bank, Kilgore Mfg. Co., ca. 1925 . . . .$275.00
Frog Mechanical Bank, J & E Stevens Co., ca. 1870's, red lattice base $688.00
Jolly Figure Mechanical Bank, aluminum, blue shirt, red bow tie, white pants, possibly Austrian $3,850.00
Dinah Mechanical Bank, John Harper & Co., Ltd., registered 3/29/1911 . . . .$633.00
Vending Mechanical Bank, Hartwig & Vogel, Ger., litho. tin, gr. w/ gold highlights $193.00
Cat and Mouse Mechanical Bank, J & E Stevens Co., designed by James H. Bowen, pat. 4/21/1891, excellent condition $4,290.00

ABC PLATES — Alphabet plates were made especially for children as teaching aids. They date from the late 1700s and were made of various material including porcelain, pottery, glass, pewter, tin and ironstone.

AMPHORA ART POTTERY was made at the Amphora Porcelain Works in the Teplitz Tum area of Bohemia during the late 19th and early 20th centuries. Numerous potteries were located there.

ANNA POTTERY — The Anna Pottery was established in Anna, IL, in 1859 by Cornwall and Wallace Kirkpatrick, and closed in 1894. The company produced utilitarian wares, gift wares and pig-shaped bottles and jugs with special inscriptions, which are the most collectible pieces.

BATTERSEA ENAMELS — The name "Battersea" is a general term for those metal objects decorated with enamels, such as pill, patch, and snuff boxes, doorknobs, and such. The process of fusing enamel onto metal—usually copper—began about 1750 in the Battersea District of London. Today the name has become a generic term for similar objects—mistakenly called "Battersea."

BELLEEK porcelain was first made at Fermanagh, Ireland, in 1857. Today this ware is still being made in buildings within walking distance of the original clay pits according to the skills and traditions of the original artisans. Irish Belleek is famous for its thinness and delicacy. Similar type wares were also produced in other European countries as well as the United States.

BENNINGTON POTTERY — The first pottery works in Bennington, Vermont, was established by Captain John Norton in 1793; and, for 101 years, it was owned and operated by succeeding generations of Nortons. Today the term "Bennington" is synonymous with the finest in American ceramics because the town was the home of several pottery operations during the last century—each producing under different labels. Today items produced at Bennington are now conveniently, if inaccurately, dubbed "Bennington." One of the popular types of pottery produced there is known as "Rockingham." The term denotes the rich, solid brown glazed pottery from which many household items were made. The ware was first produced by the Marquis of Rockingham in Swinton, England—hence the name.

BESWICK — An earthenware produced in Staffordshire, England, by John Beswick in 1936. The company is now a part of Royal Doulton Tableware, Ltd.

BISQUE — The term applies to pieces of porcelain or pottery which have been fired but left in an unglazed state.

BLOOR DERBY — "Derby" porcelain dates from about 1755 when William Duesbury began the production of porcelain at Derby. In 1769 he purchased the famous Chelsea Works and operated both factories. During the Chelsea-Derby period, some of the finest examples of English porcelains were made. Because of their fine quality, in 1773 King George III gave Duesbury the patent to mark his porcelain wares "Crown Derby." Duesbury died in 1796. In 1810 the factory was purchased by Robert Bloor, a senior clerk. Bloor revived the Imari styles which had been so popular. After his death in 1845, former workmen continued to produce fine porcelains using the traditional Derby patterns. The firm was reorganized in 1876 and in 1878 a new factory was built. In 1890 Queen Victoria appointed the company "Manufacturers to Her Majesty" with the right to be known as Royal Crown Derby.

BUFFALO POTTERY — The Buffalo Pottery of Buffalo, New York, was organized in 1901. The firm was an adjunct of the Larkin Soap Company, which was established to produce china and pottery premiums for that company. Of the many different types produced, the Buffalo Pottery is most famous for its "Deldare" line which was developed in 1905.

CANARY LUSTER earthenware dates to the early 1800s, and was produced by potters in the Staffordshire District of England. The body of this ware is a golden yellow and decorated with transfer printing, usually in black.

CANTON porcelain is a blue-and-white decorated ware produced near Canton, China, from the late 1700s through the last century. Its hand-decorated Chinese scenes have historical as well as mythological significance.

CAPO-di-MONTE, originally a softpaste porcelain, is Italian in origin. The first ware was made during the 1700s near Naples. Although numerous marks were used, the most familiar to us is the crown over the letter N. Mythological subjects, executed in either high or low relief and tinted in bright colors on a light ground, were a favorite decoration. The earlier wares had a peculiar grayish color as compared to the whiter bodies of later examples.

CARLSBAD porcelain was made by several factories in the area from the 1800s and exported to the United States. When Carlsbad became a part of Czechoslovakia after World War I, wares were frequently marked "Karlsbad." Items marked "Victoria" were made for Lazarus & Rosenfeldt, Importers.

CASTLEFORD earthenware was produced in England from the late 1700s until around 1820. Its molded decoration is similar to Prattware.

CELEDON — Chinese porcelain having a velvet-textured greenish-gray glaze. Japanese and other oriental factories also made celedon glazed wares.

CHELSEA — An early soft paste porcelain manufactured at Chelsea in London from around 1745 to 1769. Chelsea is considered to be one of the most famous of English porcelain factories.

CHELSEA KERAMIC ART WORKS — The firm was established in 1872, in Chelsea, MA, by members of the Robertson family. The firm used the mark CKAW. The company closed in 1889, but was reorganized in 1891, as the Chelsea Pottery U.S. In 1895, the factory became the Dedham Pottery of Dedham, MA, and closed in 1943.

CHINESE EXPORT PORCELAIN was made in quantity in China during the 1700s and early 1800s. The term identifies a variety of porcelain wares made for export to Europe and the United States. Since many thought the product to be of joint Chinese and English manufacture, it has also been known as "Oriental" or "Chinese Lowestoft."

As much as this ware was made to order for the American and European market, it was frequently adorned with seals of states or the coat of arms of individuals, in addition to eagles, sailing scenes, flowers, religious and mythological scenes.

CLARICE CLIFF POTTERY — Clarice Cliff (1899–1972) was a designer who worked at A.J. Wilkinson, Ltd.'s Royal Staffordshire Pottery at Burslem, England. Cliff's earthenwares were bright and colorful Art Deco designs which included squares, circles, bands, conical shapes and simple landscapes incorporated with the designs. Cliff used several different printed marks, each of which incorporated a facsimile of her signature—and generally the name of the pattern.

CLEWS POTTERY — (see also, Historical Staffordshire) was made by George Clews & Co., of Brownhill Pottery, Tunstall, England, from 1806–1861.

CLIFTON POTTERY — William Long founded the Clifton Pottery in Clifton, NJ, in 1905. Pottery was simply marked CLIFTON. Long worked until 1908, producing a line called Crystal Patina. The Cheasapeake Pottery Company made majolica marked Clifton Ware, which oftentimes confuses collectors.

COALPORT porcelain has been made by the Coalport Porcelain Works in England since 1795. The ware is still being produced at Stroke-on-Trent.

COORS POTTERY — Coors ware was made in Golden, CO, by the Coors Beverage Company from the turn of the century until the pottery was destroyed by fire in the 1930s.

COPELAND-SPODE — The firm was founded by Josiah Spode in 1770 in Staffordshire, England. From 1847, W.T. Copeland & Sons, Ltd., succeeded Spode, using the designation "Late Spode" to its wares. The firm is still in operation.

COPPER LUSTER — See Lusterwares.

CORDEY — Boleslaw Cybis was one of the founders of the Cordey China Company, Trenton, NJ. Production began in 1942. In 1969, the company was purchased by the Lightron Corporation, and operated as the Schiller Cordey Company. Around 1950, Cybis began producing fine porcelain figurines.

COWAN POTTERY — Guy Cowan produced art pottery in Rocky River, OH, from 1913 to 1931. He used a stylized mark with the word COWAN on most pieces. Also, Cowan mass-produced a line marked LAKEWARE.

CROWN DUCAL — English porcelain made by the A.G. Richardson & Co., Ltd. since 1916.

CUP PLATES were used where cups were handleless and saucers were deep. During the early 1800s, it was very fashionable to drink from a saucer. Thus, a variety of fancy small plates was produced for the cup to rest in. The lacy Sandwich examples are very collectible.

DAVENPORT pottery and porcelain were made at the Davenport Factory in Longport, Staffordshire, England, by Joan Davenport from 1793 until 1887 when the pottery closed. Most of the wares produced there—porcelains, creamwares, ironstone, earthenwares and other products—were marked.

DEDHAM (Chelsea Art Works) —The firm was founded in 1872 at Chelsea, Massachusetts, by James Robertson & Sons, and closed in 1889. In 1891 the pottery was reopened under the name of The Chelsea Pottery, U.S. The first and most popular blue underglaze decoration for the desirable "Cracqule Ware" was the rabbit motif—designed by Joseph L. Smith. In 1893 construction was started on the new pottery in Dedham, Massachusetts, and production began in 1895. The name of the pottery was then changed to "Dedham Pottery," to eliminate the confusion with the English Chelsea Ware. The famed crackleware finish became synonymous with the name. Because of its popularity, more than 50 patterns of tableware were made.

DELFT — Holland is famous for its fine examples of tin-glazed pottery dating from the 16th century. Although blue and white is the most popular color, other colors were also made. The majority of the ware found today is from the late Victorian period and when the name Holland appears with the Delft factory mark, this indicates that the item was made after 1891.

DORCHESTER POTTERY was established by George Henderson in Dorchester, a part of Boston, Massachusetts, in 1895. Production included stonewares, industrial wares, and, later, some decorated tablewares. The pottery is still in production.

DOULTON — The pottery was established in Lambeth in 1815 by John Doulton and John Watts. When Watts retired in 1845, the firm became known as Doulton & Company. In 1901 King Edward VII conferred a double honor on the company by presentation of the Royal Warrant, authorizing their chairman to use the word "Royal" in describing products. A variety of wares has been made over the years for the American market. The firm is still in production.

DRESDEN — The term identifies any china produced in the town of Dresden, Germany. The most famous factory in Dresden is the Meissen factory. During the 18th century,

English and Americans used the name "Dresden china" for wares produced at Meissen which has led to much confusion. The city of Dresden which was the capital of Saxony, was better known in 18th century Europe than Meissen, which was fifteen miles away. Therefore, Dresden became a generic term for all porcelains produced and decorated in the city of Dresden and surrounding districts including Meissen. By the mid-19th century, about thirty factories in the city of Dresden were producing and decorating porcelains in the style of Meissen. Therefore, do not make the mistake of thinking all pieces marked Dresden were made at the Meissen factory. Meissen pieces generally have crossed swords marks and are listed under Meissen.

FLOWING BLUE ironstone is a highly glazed dinnerware made at Staffordshire by a variety of potters. It became popular about 1825. Items were printed with patterns (Oriental) and the color flowed from the design over the white body so that the finished product appeared smeared. Although purple and brown colors were also made, the deep cobalt blue shades were the most popular. Later wares were less blurred, having more white ground.

FRANKOMA — The Frank Pottery was founded in 1933, by John Frank, Sapulpa, Ok. The company produced decorative wares from 1936-38. Early wares were made from a light cream-colored clay, but in 1956 changed to a red brick clay. This along with the glazes helps to determine the period of production.

FULPER — The Fulper mark was used by the American Pottery Company of Flemington, NJ. Fulper art pottery was produced from approximately 1910 to 1930.

GALLE — Emile Galle was a designer who made glass, pottery, furniture and other Art Nouveau items. He founded his factory in France in 1874. Ceramic pieces were marked with the initials E.G. impressed, Em. Galle Faiencerie de Nancy, or a version of his signature.

GAUDY DUTCH is the most spectacular of the gaudy wares. It was made for the Pennsylvania Dutch market from about 1785 until the 1820s. This softpaste tableware is lightweight and frail in appearance. Its rich cobalt blue decoration was applied to the biscuit, glazed and fired—then other colors were applied over the first glaze—and the object was fired again. No luster is included in its decoration.

GAUDY IRONSTONE was made in Staffordshire from the early 1850s until around 1865. This ware is heavier than gaudy Welsh or gaudy Dutch, as its texture is a mixture of pottery and porcelain clay.

GAUDY WELSH, produced in England from about 1830, resembles gaudy Dutch in decoration, but the workmanship is not as fine and its texture is more comparable to that of spatterware. Luster is usually included with the decoration.

GOUDA POTTERY — Gouda and the

surrounding areas of Holland have been one of the principal Dutch pottery centers since the 17th century. The Zenith pottery and the Zuid-Hollandsche pottery, produced the brightly colored wares marked GOUDA from 1880 to about 1940. Many pieces of Gouda featured Art Nouveau or Art Deco designs.

GRUEBY — Grueby Faience Company, Boston, MA, was founded in 1897 by William H. Grueby. The company produced hand thrown art pottery in natural shapes, hand molded and hand tooled. A variety of colored glazes, singly or in combinations were used, with green being the most prominent color. The company closed in 1908.

HAEGER — The Haeger Potteries, Inc., Dundee, IL, began making art wares in 1914. Their early pieces were marked with the name HAEGER written over the letter "H." Around 1938, the mark changed to ROYAL HAEGER.

HAMPSHIRE — In 1871 James S. Taft founded the Hampshire Pottery Company in Keene, NH. The company produced redware, stoneware, and majolica decorated wares in 1879. In 1883, the company introduced a line of colored glazed wares, including a Royal Worchester-type pink, blue, green, olive and reddish-brown. Pottery was marked with the printed mark or the impressed name HAMPSHIRE POTTERY or J.S.T. & CO., KEENE, N.H.

HARKER — The Harker Pottery Company of East Liverpool, OH, was founded in 1840. The company made a variety of different types of pottery including yellowware from native clays. Whiteware and Rockinghamtype brown-glazed pottery were also produced in quantities.

HISTORICAL STAFFORDSHIRE — The term refers to a particular blue-on-white, transfer-printed earthenware produced in quantity during the early 1800s by many potters in the Staffordshire District. The central decoration was usually an American city scene or landscape, frequently showing some mode of transportation in the foreground. Other designs included portraits and patriotic emblems. Each potter had a characteristic border which is helpful to identify a particular ware, as many pieces are unmarked. Later transfer-printed wares were made in sepia, pink, green and black but the early cobalt blue examples are the most desirable.

HULL — In 1905, Addis E. Hull purchased the Acme Pottery Company in Crooksville, OH. In 1917, Hull began producing art pottery, stoneware and novelties including the Little Red Riding Hood line. Most pieces had a matte finish with shades of pink and blue or brown predominating. After a flood and fire in 1950, the factory was reopened in 1952 as the Hull Pottery Company. Pre-1950 vases are marked HULL USA or HULL ART USA. Post-1950 pieces are simply marked HULL in large script or block letters. Paper labels were also used.

HUMMEL — Hummel items are the original creations of Berta Hummel, born in 1909 in Germany. Hummel collectibles are made by W. Goebel Porzellanfabrik of Oeslau, Germany, now Rodenthal, West Germany. They were first made in 1934. All authentic Hummels bear both the signature, M.I. Hummel, and a Goebel trademark. However, various trademarks were used to identify the year of production.

IRONSTONE is a heavy, durable, utilitarian ware made from the slag of iron furnaces, ground and mixed with clay. Charles Mason of Lane Delft, Staffordshire, patented the formula in 1823. Much of the early ware was decorated in imitation of Imari, in addition to transfer-printed blue ware, flowing blues and browns. During the mid-19th centruy, the plain white enlivened only by embossed designs became fashionable. Literally hundreds of patterns were made for export.

JACKFIELD POTTERY is English in origin. It was first produced during the 17th century; however, most items available today date from the last century. It is a red-bodied pottery, often decorated with scrolls and flowers, in relief, then covered with a black glaze.

JASPERWARE — A very hard, unglazed porcelain with a colored ground, varying from blues and greens to lavender, red, yellow or black. White designs were generally applied in relief to these wares, and often times reflect a classical motif. Jasperware was first produced by Wedgwood's Etruria Works in 1775. Many other English potters produced jasperware, including Copeland, Spode and Adams.

JUGTOWN POTTERY — This North Carolina pottery has been made since the 18th century. In 1915 Jacques Busbee organized what was to become the Jugtown Pottery in 1921. Production was discontinued in 1958.

KING'S ROSE is a decorated creamware produced in the Staffordshire district of England during the 1820-1840 period. The rose decorations are usually in red, green, yellow and pink. This ware is often referred to as "Queen's Rose."

LEED'S POTTERY was established by Charles Green in 1758 at Leed, Yorkshire, England. Early wares are unmarked. From 1775 the impressed mark "Leeds Pottery" was used. After 1880 the name "Hartly, Green & Co." was added, and the impressed or incised letters "LP" were also used to identify the ware.

LIMOGES — The name identifies fine porcelain wares produced by many factories at Limoges, France, since the mid-1800s. A variety of different marks identify wares made there including Haviland china.

LIVERPOOL POTTERY — The term applies to wares produced by many potters located in Liverpool, England, from the early 1700s, for American trade. Their print-decorated pitchers—referred to as "jugs" in England—have been especially popular. These featured patriotic emblems, prominent men, ships, etc., and can be easily identified as nearly all are melon-shaped with a very pointed lip, strap handle and graceful curved body.

LONHUDA — In 1892, William Long, Alfred Day, and W.W. Hunter organized the Lonhuda Pottery Company of Steubenville, OH. The firm produced underglaze slip-decorated pottery until 1896, when production ceased. Although the company used a variety of marks, the earliest included the letters LPCO.

LOTUS WARE — This thin Belleek-like porcelain was made by the Knowles, Taylor & Knowles Company of Easter Liverpool, OH, from 1890 to 1900.

LUSTERWARE — John Hancock of Hanley, England, invented this type of decoration on earthenwares during the early 1800s. The copper, bronze, ruby, gold, purple, yellow, pink and mottled pink luster finishes were made from gold painted on the glazed objects, then fired. The latter type is often referred to as "Sunderland Luster." Its pinkish tones vary in color and pattern. The silver lusters were made from platinum.

MAASTRICHT WARE — Petrus Regout founded the De Sphinx pottery in 1835 at Maastricht, Holland. The company specialized in transfer painted earthenwares.

MAJOLICA — The word MAJOLICA is a general term for any pottery glazed with an opaque tin enamel that conceals the color of the clay body. It has been produced by many countries for centuries. Majolica took its name from the Spanish island of Majorca, where figuline (a potter's clay) is found. This ware frequently depicted elements in nature: birds, flowers, leaves and fish. English manufacturers marked their wares and most can be identified through the English Registry mark, and/or the potter-designer's mark, while most continental pieces had an incised number. Although many American potteries produced majolica between 1850 and 1900, only a few chose to identify their wares. Among these were the firm of Griffen, Smith, and Hill; George Morely; Edwin Bennett; Cheaspeake Pottery Company; and the new Milford-Wannoppe Pottery Company.

MARBLEHEAD — This hand thrown pottery had its beginning in 1905 as a therapeutic program by Dr. J. Hall for the patients of a Marblehead, MA, sanitarium. Later, production was moved to another site and the factory continued under the management of A.E. Baggs until it closed in 1936. The most desirable pieces found today are decorated with conventionalized designs.

MATT-MORGAN — By 1883 Matt morgan, an English artist, was producing art pottery in Cincinnati, OH, that resembled Moorish wares. Incised designs and colors were applied to raised panels, then shiny or matte glazes were applied. The firm lasted only a few years.

McCOY POTTERY — The J.W. McCoy Pottery was established in 1899. Production of art pottery began after 1926 when the name was changed to Brush McCoy.

MEISSEN — The history of Meissen porcelain began in Germany in 1710, when Frederich August I established the Royal Saxon Porcelain Manufactory. The company was first directed by Johann Boettger, who developed the first truly white porcelain in Europe. The crossed swords mark of the Meissen factory was adopted in 1723.

METTLACH, Germany, located in the Zoar Basin, was the location of the famous Villeroy & Boch factories from 1836 until 1921 when the factory was destroyed by fire. Steins (dating from about 1842) and other stonewares with bas relief decorations were their specialty.

MINTON — Thomas Minton established his pottery in 1793 at Stroke-on-Trent, Hanley, England. During the early years, Minton concentrated on blue transfer painted earthenwares, plain bone china, and cream colored earthenware. During the first quarter of the 19th century, a large selection of figures and ornamental wares were produced in addition to their tableware lines. In 1968, Minton became a member of the Royal Doulton Tableware group, and retains its reputation for fine quality hand painted and gilted tablewares.

MOCHAWARE — This banded creamware was first produced in England during the late 1700s. The early ware was lightweight and thin, having colorful bands of bright colors decorating a body that is cream colored to very light brown. After 1840 the ware became heavier in body and the color was often quite light—almost white. Mochaware can easily be identified by its colorful banded decorations—on and between the bands—including feathery ferns, lacy trees, seaweeds, squiggly designs and lowly earthworms.

MOORCROFT — William Moorcroft established the Moorcroft Pottery, in Burslem, England in 1913. The majority of the art pottery wares were hand thrown. The company initially used an impressed mark, MOORCROFT, BURSLEM, with a signature mark, W.MOORCROFT, following. Walker, William's son, continued the business after his father's death in 1945, producing the same style wares. Contemporary pieces are marked simply MOORCROFT with export pieces also marked MADE IN ENGLAND.

NEWCOMB — William and Ellsworth Woodward founded Newcomb Pottery at Sophie Newcomb College, New Orleans, LA, in 1896. Students decorated the high quality art pottery pieces with a variety of designs that have a decidedly southern flavor. Production continued through the 1940s. Marks include the letters NC and often have the incised initials of the artist as well. Most pieces have a matte glaze.

NILOAK POTTERY with its prominent swirled, marbelized designs, is a 20th century pottery first produced at Benton, Arkansas, in 1911 by the Niloak Pottery Company. Production ceased in 1946.

NIPPON porcelain has been produced in quantity for the American market since the late 19th century. After 1891, when it became obligatory to include the country of origin on all imports, the Japanese trademark "Nippon" was used. Numerous other marks appear on this ware identifying the manufacturer, artist or importer. The hand-painted Nippon examples are extremely popular today and prices are on the rise.

NORSE POTTERY was founded in 1903 in Edgerton, WI. The company moved to Rockford, IL, in 1604, where they produced a black pottery which resembled early bronze items. The firm closed in 1913.

OHR POTTERY was produced by George E. Ohr in Biloxi, Mississippi, around 1883. Today Ohr is recognized as one of the leading potters in the American Art Pottery movement. Early work was often signed with an impressed stamp in block letters—G.E. OHR, BILOXI. Later pieces were often marked G.E. Ohr in flowing script. Ohr closed the pottery in 1906, storing more than 6,000 pieces as a legacy to his family. These pieces remained in storage until 1972.

OLD IVORY dinnerware was made in Silesia, Germany during the late 1800s. It derives its name from the background color of the china. Marked pieces usually have a pattern number on the base, and the word "Silesia" with a crown.

OTT & BREWER — The company operated the Etruria Pottery in Trenton, NJ, from 1863 to 1893. A variety of marks were used which incorporated the initials O & B.

OWENS — The Owens Pottery began production in Zanesville, OH, in 1891. The first art pottery was made after 1896, and pieces were usually marked with a form of the name OWENS. Production of art pottery was discontinued about 1907.

PAUL REVERE POTTERY — This pottery was made at several locations in and around Boston, MA, between 1906 and 1942. The company was operated as a settlement house program for girls. Many pieces were signed S.E.G. for Saturday Evening Girls. The young artists concentrated on children's dishes and tiles.

PETERS & REED Pottery Company of Zanesville, Ohio, was founded by John D. Peters and Adam Reed about the turn of the century. Their wares, although seldom marked, can be identified by the characteristic red or yellow clay body touched with green. This pottery was best known for its matte glaze pieces—especially one type, called Moss Aztec, combined a red earthenware body with a green glaze. The company changed hands in 1920 and was renamed the Zane Pottery Company. Examples marked "Zaneware" are oftentimes identical to earlier pieces.

PEWABIC — Mary Chase Perry Straton founded the Pewabic Pottery in 1903 in Detriot, MI. Many types of art pottery was produced here including pieces with matte green glaze and an iridescent crystaline glaze. Operations ceased after the death of Mary Stratton in 1961, but the company was reactivated by Michigan State University in 1968.

PISGAH FOREST POTTERY — The pottery was founded near Mt. Pisgah in North Carolina in 1914 by Walter B. Stephen. The pottery remains in operation.

QUIMPER — Tin-glazed, hand-painted pottery has been produced in Quimper, France, dating back to the 17th century. It is named for a French town where numerous potteries were located. The popular peasant design first appeared during the 1860s, and many variations exist. Florals and geometrics were equally as popular. The HR and HR QUIMPER marks are found on Henriot peices prior to 1922.

REDWARE is one of the most popular forms of country pottery. It has a soft, porous body and its color varies from reddish-brown tones to deep wine to light orange. It was produced in mostly utilitarian forms by potters in small factories, or by potters working on their farms, to fill their everyday needs. The most desirable examples are the slip-decorated pieces, or the rare and expensive "sgraffito" examples which have scratched or incised line decoration. Slip decoration was made by tracing the design on the redware shape with a clay having a creamy consistency in contrasting colors. When dried, the design was slightly raised above the surface.

RED WING ART POTTERY AND STONEWARE — The name includes several potteries located in Red Wing, MN. David Hallem established his pottery in 1868, producing stoneware items with a red wing stamped under the glaze as its mark. The Minnesota Stoneware Co. began production in 1883. The North Star Stoneware company began production in 1892, and used a raised star and the words Red Wing as its mark. The two latter firms merged in 1892, producing stoneware until 1920, when the company introduced a pottery line. In 1936, the name was changed to Red Wing Potteries. The plant closed in 1967.

RIDGWAY — Throughout the 19th century the Ridgway family, through partnerships held positions of importance in Shelton and Hanley, Staffordshire, England. Their wares have been made since 1808, and their transfer-design dinner sets are the most widely known product. Many pieces are unmarked, but later marks include the initials of the many partnerships.

RIVIERA — This dinnerware was made by the Homer Laughlin Company of Newell, WV, from 1938 to 1950.

ROCKINGHAM — See Bennington Pottery.

ROOKWOOD POTTERY — The Rookwood Pottery began production at Cincinnati, Ohio, in 1880 under the direction of Maria Longworth Nichols Storer, and operated until 1960. The name was derived from the family estate, "Rookwood," because of the "rook" or "crows" which inhabited the wooded areas. All pieces of this art pottery are marked, usually bearing the famous flame.

RORSTRAND FAIENCE — The firm was founded in 1726 near Stockholm, Sweden.

Items dating from the early 1900s and having an "art noveau" influence are very expensive and much in demand these days.

ROSE MEDALLION ware dates from the 18th century. It was decorated and exported from Canton, China, in quantity. The name generally applied to those pieces having medallions with figures of people alternating with panels of flowers, birds and butterflies. When all the medallions were filled with flowers, the ware was differentiated as Rose Canton.

ROSE TAPESTRY — See Royal Bayreuth.

ROSEVILLE POTTERY — The Roseville Pottery was organized in 1890 in Roseville, Ohio. The firm produced utilitarian stoneware in the plant formerly owned by the Owens Pottery of Roseville, also producers of stoneware, and the Linden Avenue Plant at Zanesville, Ohio, originally built by the Clark Stoneware Company. In 1900 an art line of pottery was created to compete with Owens and Weller lines. The new ware was named "Rozane," and it was produced at the Zanesville location. Following its success, other prestige lines were created. The Azurine line was introduced about 1902.

ROYAL BAYREUTH manufactory began in Tettau in 1794 at the first porcelain factory in Bavaria. Wares made there were on the same par with Meissen. Fire destroyed the original factory during the 1800s. Much of the wares available today were made at the new factory which began production in 1897. These include Rose Tapestry, Sunbonnet Baby novelties and the Devil and Card items. The Royal Bayreuth blue mark has the 1794 founding date incorporated with the mark.

ROYAL BONN — The tradename identifies a variety of porcelain items made during the 19th century by the Bonn China Manufactory, established in 1755 by Elmer August. Most of the ware found today is from the Victorian period.

ROYAL CROWN DERBY — The company was established in 1875 in Derby, England, and has no connection with the earlier Derby factories which operated in the late 18th and early 19th centuries. Derby porcelain produced from 1878 to 1890 carry the standard crown printed mark. From 1891 forward, the mark carries the "Royal Crown Derby" wording, and during the present century, "Made in England" and "English Bone China" were added to the mark. Today the ocmpany is a part of Royal Doulton Tableware, Ltd.

ROYAL DOULTON wares have been made from 1901, when King Edward VII conferred a double honor on the Doulton Pottery by the presentation of the Royal Warrant, authorizing their chairman to use the word "Royal" in describing products. A vadriety of wares has been produced for the American market. The firm is still in production.

ROYAL DUX was produced in Bohemia during the late 1800s. Large quantities of this decorative porcelain ware were exported to the United States. Royal Dux figurines are especially popular.

ROYAL RUDOLSTADT — This hard paste ware was first made in Rudolstadt, Thuringen, East Germany, by Ernt Bohne in 1854. A second factory was opened in 1882 by L. Straus & Sons, Ltd. The ware was never labeled "Royal Rudolstadt" originally, but the word "Royal" was added later as part of an import mark. This porcelain was imported by Lewis Straus and Sons of New York.

ROYAL WORCESTER — The Worcester factory was established in 1751 in England. This is a tastefully decorated porcelain noted for its creamy white lusterless surface. Serious collectors prefer items from the Dr. Wall (the activator of the concern) period of production which extended from the time the factory was established to 1785.

ROYCROFT POTTERY was made by the Roycrofter community of East Aurora, New York, during the late 19th and early 20th centuries. The firm was founded by Elbert Hubbard. Products produced included pottery, furniture, metalware, jewelry and leatherwork.

R.S. GERMANY porcelain with a variety of marks was produced at the Tillowitz, Germany, factory of Reinhold Schlegelmilch from about 1869 to 1956.

R.S. PRUSSIA porcelain was produced during the mid-1800s by Erdman Schlegelmilch in Suhl. His brother, Reinhold, founded a factory in 1869 in Tillowitz in lower Silesia. Both made fine qualtiy porcelain, using both satin and high gloss finishes with comparable decoration. Additionally, both brothers used the same R.S. mark in the same colors, the initials being in memory of their father, Rudolph Schlegelmilch. It has not been determined when production at the two factories ceased.

RUSKIN is a Brittish art pottery. The pottery, located at West Smethwick, Birmingham, England, was started by William H. Taylor. His name was used as the mark until around 1899. The firm discontinued producing new pieces of pottery in 1933, but continued to glaze and market their remaining wares until 1935. Ruskin pottery is noted for its exceptionally fine glazes.

SAMPSON WARE dates from the early 19th century. The firm was founded in Paris and reproduced a variety of collectible wares including Chelsea, Meissen and Oriental Lowestoft, with marks which distinguish their wares as reproductions. The firm is still in production.

SATSUMA is a Japanese pottery having a distinctive creamy crackled glaze decorated with bright enamels and often with Japanese figures. The majority of the ware available today includes the mass-produced wares dating from the 1850s. Their quality does not compare to the fine early examples.

SEWER TILE — Sewer tile figures were made by workers at sewer tile and pipe factories during the late nineteenth and early twentieth centuries. Vases and figurines with added decorations are now considered folk art by collectors.

SHAWNEE POTTERY — The Shawnee Pottery Company was founded in 1937 in Zanesville, OH, The plant closed in 1961.

SHEARWATER POTTERY — was founded by G.W. Anderson, along with his wife and their three sons. Local Ocean Springs, MS, clays were used to produce their wares during the 1930s, and the company is still in business.

SLEEPY EYE — The Sleepy Eye Milling Company, Sleepy Eye, MN, used the image of the 19th century Indian chief for advertising purposes from 1883 to 1921. The company offered a variety of premiums.

SPATTERWARE is a softpaste tableware, laboriously decorated with hand-drawn flowers, birds, buildings, trees, etc., with "spatter" decoration chiefly as a background. It was produced in considerable quantity from the early 1800s to around 1850.

To achieve this type of decoration, small bits of sponge were cut into different shapes—leaves, hearts, rosettes, vines, geometrical patterns, etc.—and mounted on the end of a short stick for convenience in dipping into the pigment.

SPONGEWARE, as it is known, is a decorative white earthenware. Color—usually blue, blue/green, brown/tan/blue, or blue/brown—was applied to the white clay base. Because the color was often applied with a colorsoaked sponge, the term "spongeware" became common for this ware. A variety of utilitarian items were produced—pitchers, cookie jars, bean pots, water coolers, etc. Marked examples are rare.

STAFFORDSHIRE is a district in England where a variety of pottery and porcelain wares has been produced by many factories in the area.

STICKSPATTER — The term identifies a type of decoration that combines hand-painting and transfer-painted decoration. "Spattering" was done with either a sponge or brush containing a moderate supply of pigment. Stickspatter was developed from the traditional Staffordshire spatterware, as the earlier ware was time consuming and expensive to produce. Although most of this ware was made in England from the 1850s to the late 1800s, it was also produced in Holland, France and elsewhere.

TEA LEAF is a lightweight stone china decorated with copper or gold "tea leaf" sprigs. It was first made by Anthony Shaw of Longport, England, during the 1850s. By the late 1800s, other potters in Staffordshire were producing the popular ware for export to the United States. As a result, there is a noticeable diversity in decoration.

TECO POTTERY is an art pottery line made by the Terra Cotta Tile works of Terra Cotta, Illinois. The firm was organized in 1881 by William D. Gates. The Teco line was first made in 1885 but not sold commercially until 1902 and was discontinued during the 1920s.

UHL POTTERY — This pottery was made in Evansville, IN, in 1854. In 1908 the pottery was moved to Huntingburg, IN, where their stoneware and glazed pottery was made until the mid-1940s.

UNION PORCELAIN WORKS — The company first marked their wares with an eagle's head holding the letter "S" in its beak in around 1876; the letters "U.P.W." were sometimes added.

VAN BRIGGLE POTTERY was established at Colorado Springs, Colorado, in 1900 by Artus Van Briggle and his wife, Anna. Most of the ware was marked. The first mark included two joined "As," representing their first two initials. The firm is still in operation.

VILLEROY & BOCH — The pottery was founded in 1841 at Mettlach, Germany. The firm produced many types of pottery including the famous Mettlach steins. Although most of their wares were made in the city of Mettlach, they also had factories in other locations. Fortunately for collectors, there is a dating code impressed on the bottom of most pieces that makes it possible to determine the age of the piece.

VOLKMAR pottery was made by Charles Volkmar, New York, from 1879 to around 1911. Volkmar had been a painter, therefore many of his artistic designs often look like oil paintings drawn on pottery.

WALRATH — Frederick Walrath worked in Rochester, NY, New York City, and at the Newcomb Pottery in New Orleans, LA. He signed his pottery items "Walrath Pottery." He died in 1920.

WARWICK china was made in Wheeling, WV, in a pottery from 1887 to 1951. The most familiar Warwick pieces have a shaded brown background. Many pieces were made with hand painted or decal decorations. The word ILGA is sometimes included with the Warwick mark.

WEDGWOOD POTTERY was established by Josiah Wedgwood in 1759 in England. A tremendous variety of fine wares has been produced through the years including basalt, lusterwares, creamware, jasperware, bisque, agate, Queen's Ware and others. The system of marks used by the firm clearly indicates when each piece was made.

Since 1940 the new Wedgwood factory has been located at Barleston.

WELLER POTTERY — Samuel A. Weller established the Weller pottery in 1872 in Fultonham, Ohio. In 1888 the pottery was moved to Piece Street in Putnam, Ohio—now a part of Zanesville, Ohio. The production of art pottery began in 1893 and by late 1897 several prestige lines were being produced including Samantha, Touranda and Dicken's Ware. Other later types included Weller's Louwelsa, Eosian, Aurora, Turada and the rare Sicardo which is the most sought after and most expensive today. The firm closed in 1948.

WHEATLEY — Thomas J. Wheatley worked with the founders of the art pottery movement in Cincinnati, Ohio. He established the Wheatley Pottery in 1880, which was purchased by the Cambridge Tile Manufacturing Company in 1927.

A-OH Jan. 1997   Garth's Auctions

Spatterware

Row 1, Left to Right

Cup & Saucer, red handleless, peafowl in red, blue yel. & blk., chip $385.00
Sugar Bowl, red, tulip in yel., gr. & blk., lid repr., 4¾" H $302.50
Cup & Saucer, red & gr. handleless, re-enameled, chip $1,045.00

Row 2, Left to Right

Cup & Saucer, red handleless, peafowl in blue, gr., red & blk. w/ gr. tree, ...$1,705.00
Waste Bowl, blue w/ house in red, yel., blk. & gr., 5¾" diam. 3" H $1,375.00
Cup & Saucer, br. handleless, thistle in red, gr. & blk. $1,320.00

Row 3, Left to Right

Pitcher, blue, fort in gray, blk., red & gr., damage & yellowed repairs, 7⅜" H . $385.00
Waste Bowl, blue, fort in gray, blk., red & gr., repr., stains & sm. chips, 5⅝" diam., 3½" H $302.50
Creamer, blue, fort in gray, blk., red & gr., repr. & hairlines, 4½" H$192.50
Vegetable Dish, blue, fort in gray, blk., red & gr., repr., 10 ½" L .$550.00

A-MA Mar. 1997   Eldred's

Row 1, Left to Right

Canton Sugar Bowl, covered, w/ entwined handles, 6" H $440.00
Canton Curry Dish, 10½" L $605.00
Canton Creamer, 3½" H $88.00

Row 2, Left to Right

Canton Tray, lozenge-form, 5" W, 6¾" H $101.00
Canton Serving Dish, rectangular, 6¾" L, 8¾" W, 1½" H $357.50
Canton Tile, octagonal, 6¼" sq. $32.50

A-OH Jan. 1997   Garth's Auctions

Spatterware

Row 1, Left to Right

Cup & Saucer, blue handleless, rooster in red, blue, yel. ochre & blk., pinpoint flake $880.00
Cup & Saucer, blue handleless, rooster in red, blue, yel. ochre & blk., repr. $357.50
Cup & Saucer, blue handleless, tulip in blue, yel., red, gr. & blk., minor wear, pinpoint flake $302.50
Cup & Saucer, blue handleless, peafowl in red, blue, yel. & blk., minor glaze flakes $660.00

Row 2, Left to Right

Sugar Bowl, red & blue rainbow rim & lid, peafowl in red, blues, yel., gr. & blk., repairs & crow's foot, 4⅞" H $330.00
Vegetable Dish, open, blue, Adam's Rose in red, gr. & blk., 8⅜" L .$247.50
Sugar Bowl, red & gr. rainbow, wear, stains crow's foot, lid repr., 5¼" H $275.00

Row 3, Left to Right

Plate, red w/ tulip in purple, gr., blk. & yel. ochre, 8½" diam. $605.00
Paneled Pitcher red & blue rainbow, minor stain, 6⅝" H $770.00
Plate, blue w/ petal flower in maroon, blue & green, 8⅜" diam. $495.00

A-OH Jan. 1997   Garth's Auctions

Pitcher, canary w/ silver luster trim, blk. transfer, wear, minor hairlines & repr., 5½" H $110.00
Mocha Cup, canary w/ gr. band, br. stripes & earthworm in yel. & br., flakes through yel. glaze into blue undercoat $1,045.00

A-MA Mar. 1997   Eldred's

Left to Right

Rockingham Spittoon, 19th C., 9" diam. $33.00
Bennington Toby Bottle, 19th C., man astride a cask, br. glaze, 9½" H . N/S
Rockingham Milk Basin, 19th C., 12" diam., 3½" H $99.00
Rockingham Pitcher, Bennington-type, 19th C., w/ dec. of a hunger & his dog, 9" H . . . . .N/S

A-MA Mar. 1997   Eldred's

Row 1, Left to Right

Dedham Plate, pottery, in Azalea patt., minor foot chip, 8½" diam. $88.00
Dedham Bowl, pottery, in Rabbit patt., 8¾" diam., 3¾" H $434.50
Dedham Plate, pottery, in Rabbit patt., minor rim chips, 8⅜" diam. $110.00

Row 2, Left to Right

Dedham Bowl, pottery, in Rabbit patt., 6¾" diam., 3¾" H $330.00
Dedham Cup, pottery, handleless, in Rabbit patt., 2" H $660.00

A-MA Mar. 1997   Eldred's

Left to Right

Imari Plates, pr., 19th C., w/ scalloped edges, 10½" H $412.50
Cylinder-form Vase, rose medallion, 19th C., 9½" H $495.00
Fenestrated Basket & Undertray, oval rose medallion, w/ matching undertray, 19th C., 11" L, 9½" W, 4" H .$990.00

A-OH Jan. 1997   Garth's Auctions

Oriental Exports

Row 1

Six Cups, set, polychrome enameled, oriental figures $330.00

Row 2, Left to Right

Creamer, w/ lid, polychrome enameled Euro. scene, mismatched lid, 3½" H . .$38.50
Tray, grisaille, rim w/ owls & hunting scene, salmon red enameled highlights, 5" L $137.50
Saucer, grisaille, scene of man w/ goblet, woman & child, worn gilt, 4¾" diam. $93.50
Flat Dish, w/ table ring, Armorial eagle in br.gilt, minor stains, 4⅛" diam ...$165.00
Creamer, w/ lid, polychrome enameled, scene of two men & dog, floral trim & gilt, 3½" H plus lid ...$192.50

Row 3, Left to Right

Creamer, w/ lid, underglaze blue grisaille ship & flowers, 4⅜" H plus lid ..$385.00
Plate, enameled oriental scene in sepia w/ gilt, 1780-1851, NY, 6" diam. .$55.00
Gr. Fitzhugh, leaf like dish, 7⅝" L .$385.00
Creamer, w/ lid, grisaille armorial design, worn gilt, sm. flake, 4⅝" H plus lid ..$110.00

A-OH Jan. 1997   Garth's Auctions

Spatterware

Row 1, Left to Right

Plate, peafowl in red, blue, gr. & blk., 8¾" diam. $1,100.00
Cup & Saucer, blue handleless, blk. dots $3,245.00
Teapot, red w/ peafowl in blue, yel., gr. & blk., chips, repr. 7¼" H $1,650.00
Cup & Saucer, gr. handleless, peafowl in blue, yel., red & blk., glaze incomplete $550.00
Soup Plate, rainbow w/ Adam's Rose in red, gr. & blk., glaze wear, 9" diam. $495.00

Row 2, Left to Right

Plate, purple w/ rose & blue bud, chip, 8⅝" diam. $577.50
Pitcher, lt. blue, house in purple w/ br. & gr., leaf handle, pinpoint flakes, 5⅛" H $3,080.00
Plate, rainbow w/ bull's eye, red & gr., 7⅜" diam. $440.00
Cup & Saucer, gr. handleless, peafowl on bar in blk., red, blue gr. & yel. ochre, chip $1,595.00
Plate, blue w/ peafowl in red, gr., blk. & yel., minor glaze wear & stains, 8¼" diam. $495.00

A-MA Mar. 1997   Eldred's

Cups & Saucers, seven, Chinese export, handled, w/ salmon & br. floral dec. $495.00

A-MA Mar. 1997   Eldred's

Row 1, Left to Right

Canton Serving Dish, sq., 8½" sq., 1¼" H $275.00
Canton Charger, 14½" diam. $605.00
Canton Dish, 10¼" diam. ...$302.50

Row 2, Left to Right

Canton Tray, 7½" L, 5½" W .$121.00
Canton Fenestrated, oval basket & undertray, 8¾" L $715.00
Canton Dish, leaf-form, 7½" L......................$258.50

A-MA Jan. 1997   Skinner

Staffordshire Tea Service, 16-pc., blue & white transfer dec., Eng. second qtr. 19th C., two teapots, 6" & 7", covered sugar, creamer & six cups & saucers, some imper. $1,610.00

A-MA Mar. 1997   Eldred's

Left to Right

Spatterware, five pcs., peafowl variant, cup & saucer & three handleless cups $302.50
Spatterware, peafowl cup & saucer, w/ blue ground, age crack in cup, some toning $165.00

A-OH Jan. 1997   Garth's Auctions

Spatterware

Row 1, Left to Right

Cup & Saucer, mini. blue rainbow handleless, two tone blue flower $742.50
Cup Plate, blue, rose in red, gr. & blk., 4" diam. $220.00

Cup Plate, purple, blue transfer eagle & shield, 3⅞" diam. $302.50
Cup & Saucer, gr. mini., peafowl in red, blue, yellow & black., pinpoints $330.00

Row 2, Left to Right

Cup Plate, red, gr. transfer, 3½" diam. $192.50
Cup Plate, red, purple transfer, 3½" diam. $440.00
Cup Plate, gr., purple transfer, hairlines, 3½" diam. $55.00
Cup Plate, red, blk. transfer, 3½" diam. $192.50

Row 3, Left to Right

Creamer, red & gr. rainbow, wear & minor stains, 4⅛" H $275.0
Creamer, gr. w/ peafowl in red, blue, yel. & blk., minor edge wear & sm. spout repr., 4" H $1,045.00

A-OH Jan. 1997 Garth's Auctions

Spatterware *Row 1, Left to Right*
Cup & Saucer, handleless, star flower in blue, gr. & blk., minor stains & sm. flakes $880.00
Cup & Saucer, red handleless, Hollyberry in red, gr. & blk., minor stains . $550.00
Cup & Saucer, pr., blue handleless, sprig of flowers in red, gr. & blk., pinpoints on cup $440.00
Cup & Saucer, red handleless, dahlia in red, gr., blue & blk., chips & hairline $275.00
Cup & Saucer, red handleless, cock's comb in blue, gr. & blk., lt. stains & chip $990.00

Row 2, Left to Right
Purple Plate, twelve sided, hollyberry in red, gr. & blk., glazed over hairline, 8⅝" diam. $82.50
Blue Plate, primrose in red, gr., yel. & blk., 8⅝" diam. $495.00
Purple Creamer, Adam's Rose in red, gr. & blk., minor stains & crazing, 5⅛" H $302.50
Blue Plate, ten sided, primrose in red, gr., yel. & blk., sm. flakes, 7⅝" diam. .$423.50
Red Plate, w/ flowers in blue, yel., gr. & br., blk. transfer lion & unicorn mark, wear & minor glaze flakes, 8⅝" diam. .$385.00

A-MA Jan. 1997 Skinner

Left to Right
Leeds Creamer & Sugar, surface covered granite, Eng., early 19th C., imper., edge repair, 4¾" H, & 5" H $546.25
Leeds Pitcher, surface agate, Eng., early 19th C., repr. spout & rim, hairlines, 6¾" H $805.00
Leeds Creamer & Sugar, surface covered granite, Eng., early 19th C., imper., edge repair, 4¾" H, & 5" H $546.25

A-OH Jan. 1997 Garth's Auctions

Row 1, Left to Right
Green Plate, feather edge, pearlware w/ Leeds peafowl in yel., ora., blue, gr. & br., minor stains, 6¼" $660.00
Mocha Waste Bowl, gr. molded rib rim & marbelized dec. in blue, white, blk. & tan, broken & glued, 6¼" diam. 2¾" H $55.00
Mocha Mustard, blue & blk. stripes & seaweed, lid brownish gray w/ blk. stripes, wear & sm. chips, 2⅞" H $330.00
Pearlware Pitcher, w/ silver luster, blk. transfer w/ polychrome enamel, stains, chips & glued spout, 5⅝" H $220.00

Row 2, Left to Right
Cup & Saucer, pearlware oversize handleless, Leeds peafowl in blue, yel., ora., gr. & dk. br. $1,155.00
Pearlware Plate, blue feather edge, Leeds peafowl in blue, yellow, orange, green & dark brown, sm. flakes & chips, 9⅛" diam. $632.50
Cup & Saucer, pearlware oversize handleless, Leeds peafowl in blue, yellow, orange, green & dark brown, saucer has repr. $440.00

A-MA Jan. 1997 Skinner

Row 1, Left to Right
Slipware Plate, N.E., early 19th C., minor glaze wear, rim chips, 12¼" diam. $805.00
Slipware Plate, early 19th C., inscribed "Susan Toste", rim chips, 12" diam. $747.50

Row 2, Left to Right
Redware Plate, slip dec., Am., 19th C., minor rim chips, glaze wear, 9⅛" diam. $546.25
Redware Plates, two slip dec., Am., 19th C., chips, glaze wear, 9⅛" - 10¼" diam. $747.50

A-OH Jan. 1997 Garth's Auctions

Spatterware

Row 1, Left to Right
Cup & Saucer, rainbow handleless, red, blue & gr., impr. "Adams" . .$550.00
Cup & Saucer, red handleless, yel. center, ...$1,595.00
Cup & Saucer, gr. handleless, twenty six dots $330.00
Cup & Saucer, blue handleless, tulip in blue, red, gr. & blk., anchor mark, stains & flakes, chips on cup .$467.50
Cup & Saucer, blue handleless, four petal flower in red & gr. 632.50

Row 2, Left to Right
Blue Plate, w/ gr. leaf, 9¼" diam. $385.00
Waste Bowl, red, acorn in br., shades of gr. & blk., repr., 6" diam. 3¼" H . .$557.50
Blue Plate, w/ bull's eye, impr. "J. & G. Meakin", 8⅝" diam. $192.50
Sugar Bowl, gr. w/ rainbow design in red, yel., gr. & blk., lid has repr., stains, 4⅛" H $1,045.00
Blue Plate, Adam's Rose in red, gr. & blk., lt. stains, 9⅛" diam. $220.00

A-OH Nov. 1996 Garth's Auctions

Row 1, Left to Right
Creamware Tea Caddies, two, w/ similar dec. in red & gr. enamel, wear & sm. chips, flake, 5¼" H . .$1,402.50
Creamware Teapot, w/ molded acanthus spout & ribbed handle, sm. flakes, 4¾" H $385.00

Row 2, Left to Right
Leeds Creamware Teapot, polychrome enameled portraits of Prince of Orange, lid restored, sm. flakes & enamel wear, 5" H $440.00
Leeds Creamware Teapot, molded floral ends, flower finial, polychrome enameled rose, sm. flakes, 4¾" H $3,025.00

Spatterware

Row 1, Left to Right

Cup & Saucer, blue handleless, dove in blue, blk., yel. & gr. $836.00
Red Saucer, w/ school house in red, gr. & blk., repr., 6" diam. $247.50
Red Cup, handleless, school house in blue & yel. w/ br. & gr., repr. $275.00
Cup & Saucer, red handleless, peafowl in gr., yel., blue & blk., mismatch, colors vary, saucer impr. "F.W. & Co. Stoneware", touch-up repr. $192.50
Cup & Saucer, yel. handleless, thistle in red & gr., repr. $1,045.00
Cup & Saucer, handleless, festoon & ball in blue, purple & gr., mismatched & colors vary, cup is red, has repr. & saucer has minor hairlines . .$330.00

Row 2, Left to Right

Rainbow Plate, bull's eye center, blue & purple, 8⅜" diam. $330.00
Blue Plate, w/ peafowl in blue, ora., red & blk., sm. area unglazed, 8¼" diam. $550.00
Red Plate, w/ peafowl in blue, yel., gr. & blk., wear & crazing w/ stains on back, 8⅛" diam. $440.00
Gr. Plate, w/ peafowl in blue, green, red & blk., worn glaze & flaked, 8¼" diam. $495.00

Left to Right

Stoneware Cooler, incised cobalt dec. four-gallon, Leonard, Benjamin & Clark Chase, Somerset, MA, 1845-82, dec. w/ foliate devices, minor chips, cracks, 15" H $345.00
Stoneware Crock, cobalt dec. six-gallon, J. Norton & Co., Bennington, Vermont, mid-19th c., dec. w/ a basket of flowers, minor chips, 13¼" H $488.75

Spatterware *Row 1, Left to Right*
Cup Plate, rainbow w/ bull's eye center, blue & purple, 4¹/₁₆ diam. .$214.50
Blue Mug, w/ flower in pink & gr., 1⅞" H $1,100.00
Cup Plate, rainbow w/ bull's eye center, blue & purple stains, 4⅛" diam. . .$214.50

Row 2, Left to Right

Creamer, red & gr., Adam's Rose in red, gr. & blk., repr., 4" H . . .$522.50
Creamer, gr. w/ blk. edge stripe & peafowl in blk., yel. ochre & blue, leaf handle, 3¾" H $495.00
Creamer, blue & purple, Adam's Rose in red, gr. & blk., repr. & edge wear, 4" H $110.00

Row 3, Left to Right

Cup & Saucer, rainbow handleless, gr. & blk., cup has wear . . .$3,905.00
Sugar Bowl, plaid in blue, red & gr., repr., stains, 4⅜" H $247.50
Creamer, purple w/ blue star, minor stains, 4½" H $770.00
Cup & Saucer, rainbow mini., red & gr. $275.00

Spatterware

Row 1, Left to Right

Cup & Saucer, rainbow handless in blue & red, Adam's Rose in gr. & blk., impr. "Adams", colors darker on cup . .$440.00
Cup & Saucer, blue handleless w/ flower in red & gr., impr. mark, cup repr., mismatch $137.50
Waste Bowl, gr., Adam's Rose in red, gr. & blk., 5" diam. 2¾" H . . .$550.00
Cup & Saucer, blue handleless, Adam's Rose in red, gr. & blk., colors vary $385.00
Cup & Saucer, blue handleless, Adam's Rose in red, gr. & blk., colors vary, stains $330.00

Spatterware w/ Transfer Dec.

Row 1, Left to Right

Blue Teapot, horses in blue, sm. edge flakes, 6¼" H $247.50
Cup & Saucer, maroon handleless, eagle & shield in blue, color varies, short hairline in cup $137.50
Blue Plate, eagle in brown, 9" diam. $357.50
Blue Creamer, horses & cowboy in blue, leaf handle, 3⅞" H $93.50
Blue Teapot, horses & cowboy in blue, slight hairline, edge flakes, 6⅝" H $225.50

Row 2, Left to Right

Red Plate, cowboy in red, minor stains & crazing, 9½" diam. . .$71.50
Blue Pitcher, eagle & shield in blue, stains, hairlines & wear, 6¼" H .$286.00
Purple Teapot, eagle in brownish blk., lid slightly darker, repr., 9" H $357.50
Blue Creamer, eagle & shield in brownish blk., repairs, 5¾" H $176.00
Blue Plate, scene of bird in fountain in blue, minor stains, 10⅜" diam. . . .$104.50

Row 2, Left to Right

Cup & Saucer, handleless, red & gr. rainbow w/ red dot center, chip, colors vary $385.00
Cup & Saucer, red handleless w/ Adam's Rose in red & gr. $440.00
Cup & Saucer, blue handleless, multipointed star border, chip $220.00
Cup & Saucer, red handleless, Adam's Rose in red & green, stains $357.50
Cup & Saucer, rainbow handleless, red & gr. w/ center dot, mismatch $302.50

Row 3, Left to Right

Cup & Saucer, green handleless, multi-point star border, minor edge wear $550.00
Cup & Saucer, blue handleless w/ thistle in red & gr., sm. chips on cup $715.00
Cup & Saucer, purple handleless w/ thistle in red & gr., lighter cup colors $935.00
Cup & Saucer, red handleless w/ thistle in red & gr., darker saucer colors $1,540.00
Cup & Saucer, red handleless multipoint star border $440.00

A-MA Mar. 1997   Skinner

Row 1, Left to Right

Pitcher, yel. glaze transfer dec., Eng., 19th C., minor chips, glaze wear, 4¾" H $632.50

Plate, yel. glazed, Fr., second quarter 19th C., impr. "L.L. & T", knife marks, chips, glaze wear, 8¹¹⁄₁₆" diam. $172.50

Row 2, Left to Right

Children's Mug, yel. glazed transfer dec., Eng., second quarter 19th C., "A rocking horse for John", minor chips, glaze wear, 2½" H $460.00

Children's Mug, yel. glazed transfer dec., Eng., second quarter 19th C., "A new doll for Margaret", minor chips, glaze wear, 2⅜" H $488.75

Children's Mugs, two, yel. glazed transfer dec., Eng., second quarter 19th C., "Keep thy shop & thy shop will keep thee," minor chips, glaze & transfer wear, 2⅛" H & 2¼" H $345.00

Children's Mugs, two, yel. glazed transfer dec., Eng., second quarter 19th C., "A rabbit for William' & one dec. w/ reserve of two sheep, luster rim, chips, glaze wear, 1¾" H & 2⅛" H $460.00

Children's Mugs, two, yel. glazed transfer dec., Eng., second quarter 19th C., dec. w/ a reserve of a townscape w/ bridge, minor chips, glaze & transfer wear, 1¾" H & 2⅛" H . .$345.00

A-MA May 1997   Skinner

Left to Right

Fulper Pottery Lamp, striated butterscotch glaze, vertical mark, 6" diam., 15½" H $517.50

Fulper Pottery Vase, coiled form w/ mottled gr. glaze, vertical mark, 6½" diam., 6" H $287.50

Fulper Pottery Vase, coiled form w/ two handles under a mottled gr. glaze, 5" diam., 9" H $345.00

A-MA May 1997   Skinner

Row 1, Left to Right

Pottery Items, two, Saturday Evening Girls, mug dec. in dk. br. w/ the word "Veritas" mkd. S.E.G., 5½" W, 5" H, sm. covered vase w/ blue glaze, Paul Revere paper label, cracked lid, 3¾" diam., 3" H . . .N/S

Pottery Items, three, Saturday Evening Girls, vase w/ deep gr. glaze, mkd. S.E.G., 4¼" H, vase w/ blue glaze, Bowl shop paper label, glaze nicks, 8" H, bowl w/ gr. glaze, impr. Paul Revere, 5½" diam., 2½" H $230.00

China Painted Bowl, dec. w/ lobsters & turtles, Limoges mark & artist initials A.K., Chicago, 8" diam. $402.50

Vases, two, Saturday Evening Girls, dec. w/ blue & white mottled glazes, impr. Paul Revere mark, 4½" diam., 5" H, & S.E.G. mark, 5" diam., 4½" H $230.00

Row 2, Left to Right

Pottery Items, two, Saturday Evening Girls, mug dec. in dk. br. w/ the word "Veritas" mkd. S.E.G., 5½" W, 5" H, sm. covered vase w/ blue glaze, Paul Revere paper label, cracked lid, 3¾" diam., 3" H . . . . .N/S

Bowl, Saturday Evening Girls, dec. w/ yel. & blue drips on a blue ground, S.E.G. mark, 7½" diam., 3" H .$172.50

Bowl & Underplate, Saturday Evening Girls, lt. blue & white glaze w/ incised blk. dec., & the name "Jamies", chip, 7½" diam., 2¼" H $373.75

Pottery Items, three, Saturday Evening Girls, vase w/ deep gr. glaze, mkd. S.E.G., 4¼" H, vase w/ blue glaze, Bowl shop paper label, glaze nicks, 8" H, bowl w/ gr. glaze, impr. Paul Revere, 5½" diam., 2½" H . . .$230.00

Vases, two, Saturday Evening Girls, dec. w/ blue & white mottled glazes, impr. Paul Revere mark, 4½" diam., 5" H, & S.E.G. mark, 5" diam., 4½" H $230.00

A-MA Mar. 1997   Skinner

Row 1, Left to Right

Nanking Platter, China, 19th C., chips, 12¾" L $402.50

A-OH Nov. 1996   Garth's Auctions

Row 1, Left to Right

Cup & Saucer, blue spatterware, peafowl in red, blue, gr. & blk., chips, ...$165.00

Waste Bowl, rainbow spatterware, red, blue & gr., hairlines, stains & chips, 5⅜" diam. $159.50

Creamer, Eng. porcelain, dec. in underglaze blue, polychrome enamel & gilt, mkd. "Spode", 5½" L . .$121.00

Cup & Saucer, red spatterware, peafowl in blue, yel., gr. & blk., mismatched, hairlines $148.50

Row 2, Left to Right

Sunderland Luster, three pcs., plate 6⅝"; mug, 2¾" H; footed salt, sm. flakes, 3⅛" diam., 2⅛" H, all have minor wear $132.00

Wedgwood, two pcs., blk. basalt bowl w/ chips, & spill holder, white glaze & dec. in blue & mauve, 4" H, both impr. "Wedgwood" $60.50

Staffordshire Plate, dk. blue "Catskill House, Hudson", impr. "Wood", minor wear & stains, 6½" diam. . . .$522.50

Row 3, Left to Right

Octagonal Teapot, pearlware w/ oriental transfer w/ polychrome enamel, edge flakes, repr., 5¾" H . .$412.50

Pitchers, two, copper w/ white banks, red & purple dec., 6" H, & silver, not pictured, 4⅞" H $192.50

Gaudy Teapot, Dutch, extensive repr., 5¾" H $82.50

Canton Milk Pitcher, China, 19th C., minor chips, 6⅛" H $575.00

Canton Platters, two, China, 19th C., rim chips, knife marks, 18⅜", 18½" L . .$1,265.00

Row 2, Left to Right

Canton Tureen, w/ undertray, China, 19th C., mismatched lid & undertray, cracks, chips, tureen 12½" L .$805.00

Canton Fish Platter, China, 19th C., glaze roughness, 13½" L . . .$1,265.00

Canton Fruit Basket, China, 19th C., undertray possibly mismatched, 10½" L $1,092.50

A-OH Jan. 1997   Garth's Auctions

Row 1, Left to Right

Delft Plate, Bristol, polychrome oriental scene, red, blue, yel., gr. & manganese, rim chips, 8¾" diam. .$297.00
Canton Pieces, three, blue & white, posset cup w/ mismatched lid, 3¼" H, & two similar egg cups, 2½" H $220.00
Canton Dish, w/ scalloped rim, high foot, rim chip, 13⅜" L $605.00
Delft Plate, blue & white w/ flowers, birds & insects, from Hudson River Valley family, minor chips, 9" diam., 4" H $330.00

Row 2, Left to Right

Canton Cake Plate, 10" diam., 3¾" H
. . . .$165.00
Canton Pieces, two, oval dish w/ boar's head handles & mismatched lid, 6¾" L, & creamer, 3¼" H $412.50
Canton Cups, four & saucers $71.50
Canton Tray, oval w/ reticulated rim, sm. rim chips, 10⅞" L $467.50
Canton Pieces, five, sm. tray, pictured, short hairline, 4½" x 6⅝"; two later tea bowls; a mismatched saucer & sauce w/ glued handle . . .$220.00

A-OH Nov. 1996   Garth's Auctions

Row 1, Left to Right

Whieldon Tea Caddy, cauliflower, no lid w/ gr. & clear glaze, wear & lt. stains, 4¼" H $550.00
Whieldon Sugar, cauliflower w/ lid, gr. & clear glaze, wear, stains & edge chips, 4⅜" diam., 3⅝" H . . .$3,245.00
Whieldon Creamer, cauliflower w/ applied handle, gr. & clear glaze, old yellowed repr., wear, stains & edge damage, 4¼" H $385.00

Row 2, Left to Right

Jackfield Pitcher, blk. w/ applied handle, traces of enameling w/ bird, initials & "1763", wear & sm. flakes, 6½" H $110.00
Whieldon Coffee Pot, br. tortoise shell glaze w/ blue & gr., mismatched lid & old repr., 7½" H, plus lid $467.50

A-MA May 1997   Skinner

Row 1, Left to Right

Owens Vase, dec. w/ florals in lt. matte glaze, impr. Owen, 5¼" W, 9¾" H . .$230.00
Arts & Crafts Scarab Planter, dec. w/ six finely detailed scarabs under matte gr. glaze, 7½" diam., 5" H $460.00

Row 2, Left to Right

Keramics Vase, gold, white & gr. raised glaze, mkd., hairline, 6" diam., 7¼" H .N/S
Cabinet Vase, Pewabic pottery, jet blk. glaze on mottled yel. irid. ground, impr. mark, 2½" diam., 3" H .$175.50
Clifton Pottery Pitcher, design in blk. & br. colors, incised marks, 7" W, 4" H .N/S
Clewell Pottery Vase, good patina, int. hairlines, 4¼" diam., 8¾" H $276.00
Keramics Ewer, dec. foliate design in gold, red & gr., 5" W, 13" H . . . . .N/S

A-MA May 1997   Skinner

Row 1, Left to Right

Fulper Pottery Vase, striated blue, gr. & cream color glaze, vertical mark, 7" diam., 5½" H $345.00
Fulper Pottery Vase, flared rim & foot under a striated mirror blade glaze, incised vertical mark, 4½" diam., 11¾" H .$287.50
Fulper Pottery Vase, cylindrical form under a lavender to pink glaze, vertical mark, 6" diam., 9¼"H $345.00
Fulper Pottery Vase, corset form w/ striated blk. glaze on a gr. ground, vertical mark, 5" diam., 10" H . . .$172.50

Row 2, Left to Right

Fulper Pottery Vase, intertwining handles under a striated matte gr. glaze, vertical mark, 8½" diam., 4¾" H $345.00
Fulper Pottery Vase, w/ dripping blue Chinese glaze, vertical mark, 5" diam., 8¼" H $287.50
Fulper Pottery Vase, tapering form, two handles under a striated gr., lavender & pink glaze, vertical mark, 6" W, 4¼" H $230.00

A-MA May 1997   Skinner

Left to Right

Van Briggle Vase, early, w/ incised foliate design, gr. glaze, incised AA logo, glazed bottom, 5½" diam., 4½" H $1,495.00
Van Briggle Vase, w/ three Indian heads, br. & gr. glaze, incised AA logo, Colorado Springs, minor glaze nicks, 5¼" diam., 11¼" H $172.50
Van Briggle Vase, w/ dragonflies, br. & gr. glaze, incised AA logo, Colorado Springs, 3¼" diam., 6½" H . . .$258.75

A-MA May 1997   Skinner

Left to Right

Fulper Pottery Vase, w/ lamp mount, mottled blue/green glaze, vertical mark, vase not drilled, 8½" W, 6¾" H $546.25
Fulper Pottery Lamp Base, striated blue & gr. glaze, base drilled, w/ leaded glass shade damaged, 8" diam., 17½" H $258.75

A-MA June 1997   Skinner

231-Staffordshire Plate, wigwam br. & pale gr. spatterware, ca. 1840, 8½" diam. $460.00
224A-Staffordshire Cup & Saucer, ca. 1840, rooster dec. in blue, crimson, & yel. w/ overall blue spatter dec. $1,150.00
141-Staffordshire Plate, ca. 1840, red banded border w/ red schoolhouse, dk. br. & gr. field, 7½" diam. . .$1,955.00
236A-Staffordshire Pottery, group, ca. 1840, incl. two pitchers, child's cream pot, three cups, one saucer, & plate, all w/ blue spatter ground, castle dec. in blk., red & gray w/ gr. spatter foliage, repairs, cream pot 5" H $977.50
251A-Staffordshire Plate, ca. 1840, red band, yel. & purple tulip blossom, 8" diam., w/ blue sunburst spatter plate, gr., blue & pink star center, repr., 9¼" diam. $747.50

Row 2, Left to Right

246A-Staffordshire Plate, pr., ca. 1840, one w/ band of blue spatter w/ red & yel. schoolhouse, 8" diam., gr. spatterware plate w/ red schoolhouse on gr. field, 8¼" diam. $2,530.00

273A-Staffordshire Pieces, four pcs., ca. 1840, incl. teacup, plate & saucer w/ blue spatter, a teacup w/ yel. & red spatter, ea. w/ castle polychromed in br., crimson & yel., edge roughness $862.50
250-Staffordshire Teapot & Plate, ca. 1840, bands of red & gr., plate w/ central ring dec., 9½" diam., 5¼" H $1,380.00
265A-Staffordshire Items, three, blue spatterware, ca. 1840, incl. parrot pot, missing cover, a parrot mini. teacup & a peafowl pitcher $546.25
288-Staffordshire Cup & Saucer, gr. spatterware, mid 19th C., gr. spatter ground on cup & saucer, saucer has br. transfer & spatter deer, 5½" diam. $1,495.00
246A-Staffordshire Plate, pr., one blue spatterware, ca. 1840, one w/ band of blue spatter w/ red & yel. schoolhouse, 8" diam., gr. spatterware plate w/ red schoolhouse on gr. field, 8¼" diam. $2,530.00

Row 3, Left to Right

253-Leeds Charger & Plate, spatterware, early 19th C., w/ blue edge, dinner plate w/ gr. border, both w/ polychrome peafowl, 9" diam., & 12" $2,070.00
236-Staffordshire Teapot, red & purple spatterware, Townhouse Child's Teapot, ca. 1840, overall crimson spatter dec., repairs, 3¼" H $1,265.00
229-Staffordshire Plates, two, bird a tree, ca. 1840, 9½" diam. & 9" diam. $690.00
265-Staffordshire Child's Tea Service, spatterware, ca. 1840, incl. covered teapot, covered sugar, cream pot, saucer & three cups, dec. w/ central peafowl in blue, yel., & crimson w/ gr. spatter field, all edged in ochre, repairs $977.50
229-Staffordshire Plates, two, bird in a tree, ca. 1840, 9½" diam. & 9" diam. $690.00
276-Staffordshire Child's Tea Service, partial, ca. 1840, incl. covered teapot, two cups & saucers, peafowl on yel., blue & crimson w/ gr. spatter foliage, some repairs $373.75
253-Leeds Charger & Plate, spatterware, early 19th C., w/ blue edge, dinner plate w/ gr. border, both w/ polychrome peafowl, 9" diam., & 12" $2,070.00

A-MA June 1997   Skinner

Row 1, Left to Right

238-Staffordshire Cream Pot, red & purple spatterware, Townhouse Child's Cream Pot, ca. 1840, repairs, 2½" H $2,530.00
236-Staffordshire Teapot, red & purple spatterware, Townhouse Child's Teapot, ca. 1840, repairs, 3¼" H $1,265.00
265-Staffordshire Tea Service, child's peafowl spatterware, ca. 1840, incl. covered teapot & sugar, cream pot, saucer & three cups, dec. w/ central peafowl in blue, yel. & crimson w/ field of gr., repairs . .$977.50

251-Staffordshire Child's Coffee Set, mid 19th C., incl. coffee pot, no lids, a cream pot, a covered sugar, five cups & saucers, two plates, & one lrg. bowl, minor staining & damage . . . . .N/S
244A-Staffordshire Pottery, late 18th C., pr. of peafowl child's cups, sauce tureen & undertray w/ blue edging & pearlware plate w/ polychrome floral dec., minor chips . .$690.00
267-Staffordshire Child's Plate, spatterware, ca. 1840, crimson spatter border w/ crimson schoolhouse on br. & gr. spatter ground, 5" diam. $4,140.00

Row 2, Left to Right

Staffordshire Pottery, group of blue spatterware, ca. 1840, incl. two pitchers, child's cream pot, three cups, one saucer, & plate, all w/ blue spatter ground, castle dec. in blk., red & gray w/ gr. spatter foliage, repairs, cream pot 5" H $977.50
290A-Spatterware Cup & Plate, yel. glazed, dec. w/ polychrome bird perched on branch w/ gr. spatter foliage, 4¼" diam. $316.25
Staffordshire Mini. Cup & Saucer, gr. spatterware w/ blue, yel. & red gooney bird, w/ mini. cup & saucer w/ red & yel. schoolhouse $1,265.00
Staffordshire Child's Tea Service, partial, ca. 1840, incl. covered teapot, two cups & saucers, peafowl on yel., blue & crimson w/ gr. spatter foliage, some repairs $373.75

A-MA June 1997　　　　　　　　　　　　Skinner

239A-Staffordshire Cup & Saucer, thistle red & yel. spatterware, ca. 1840 w/ bands of red & yel. spatter centering red blossom, 6" diam. $1,840.00
261-Staffordshire Plates, five, red spatterware, ca. 1840, wigwams flanked w/ spatter, trees, 8½" diam. . . . $1,380.00
289-Staffordshire Platter, blue spatterware, ca. 1840, central dec. of br. & blk. fort, 13½" W, 10½" H $2,300.00
231A-Staffordshire Plate, schoolhouse red, ca. 1840, red spatterware band, br. field, 8" diam. $862.50
272-Staffordshire Bowl, ca. 1840, blue spatter ground w/ gray, blk. & red castle, 7" diam. $460.00

Row 2, Left to Right
254-Staffordshire Pitcher, rainbow spatterware, ca. 1840, blue & red bands, 7¾" H $1,380.00
259-Staffordshire Sugar Bowl, covered, ca. 1840, blue & gr. spatter, castle dec. in gray, blk. & red, 5" H $517.50
254A-Pearlware Mug, blue & br. spatterware, Eng., ca. 1820, blue w/ scroll handle, 4¾" H $1,840.00
224-Staffordshire Sugar Bowl, red & blue spatterware w/ cover, ca. 1840, red & gr. parrot on blk. branch, crimson & blue spattered border, 4½" H $402.50
258-Leeds Covered Sugar & Saucer, spatterware, early 19th C., peafowl on ora., yel., blue & blk. w/ overall gr. spatter dec., similar sauce, 5¼" diam., 5¼" H $575.00
279A-Leeds Pearlware Cream Pot, early 19th C., peafowl dec. in yel., blue, & ora., overall pale blue overglaze, sm. chips, 4¼" H $862.50
287-Staffordshire Sugar Bowl, gray & yel. spatterware, covered, ca. 1840, central dec. of red thistle, repr., 5" H $1,840.00

Row 3, Left to Right
247-Staffordshire Compote, spatterware rainbow, ca. 1840, blue & red bands w/ central star dec., 11½" diam. $1,725.00
222-Staffordshire Tureen, blue spatterware, ca. 1840, dec. in blk., crimson & yel. w/ gr. spatter trees & foreground, overall blue spatter, crack to base, 9¼" diam., 8" H $4,600.00
246-Staffordshire Bowl & Pitcher, ca. 1840, pitcher w/ blk., gr., yel., red & blue spatter striping, repr., 8" H, bowl w/ red & gr. spatter striping, 12" diam. $1,840.00
246B-Staffordshire Bowl, blue spatterware, ca. 1840, red & yel. schoolhouse, gr. spatter on blk. field, hairline, 6½" diam.$1,150.00
259A-Staffordshire Sugar Bowl, cluster of red & gr. buds, ca. 1840, w/ red spatterware cup & saucer, & blue & gr. cream jug, damaged $1,840.00

A-OH Nov. 1996　　　　　　　Garth's Auctions

Rockingham

Row 1, Left to Right
Tub, molded cherub heads, br. & blue variegated glaze, wear, 6⅜" diam., 4" H $192.50
Bottle, shoe, 6½" H $99.00
Pitcher, molded swan cattails, 7" H. $126.50
Bottle, monkey on chamber pot, 5½" H $220.00
Cuspidor, w/ molded eagles, sm. chips, 6" diam. $650.00

Row 2, Left to Right
Pitcher, molded corn, 9½" H $121.00
Toby, woman w/ flask & cup, cup chipped, has lid, 8½" H $650.00
Toby, man w/ spout, has lid, 10¼" H $192.50
Pitcher, molded deer, br. & gr. variegated glaze, 9" H $192.50

A-MA Mar. 1997　　　　　　　　　Skinner

Left to Right
Liverpool Jug, creamware, Eng., early 19th C., transfer printed, minor glaze wear, 9½" H $805.00
Liverpool Jug, creamware, Eng., 19th C., transfer printed, inscribed "Josh Edge Caldon Grange", ext. repairs, 9⅝" H .$345.00
Creamware Mugs, two, Eng., early 19th C., transfer printed, handpainted polychrome enamels, cracks & darkening, 5⅛" H & 5½" H $345.00
Liverpool Jug, creamware, Eng., early 19th C., transfer printed w/ portrait of Thomas Jefferson, chips & some glaze wear, 10" H $21,850.00
Creamware Mugs, two, Eng., early 19th C., transfer printed, handpainted polychrome enamels, cracks & darkening, 5⅛" H & 5½" H $345.00
Liverpool Jug, creamware, Eng., early 19th C., transfer printed, "The Greenwich Pensioner", repairs, 8¾" H $460.00

A-MA May 1997　　　　　　　　　Skinner

Row 1, Left to Right
Roseville Pottery
Bonita Vase, w/ gr. glazed ground, paper label, 8" diam., 10" H $1,035.00
Apple Blossom Vase, apple red glaze, raised mark, 8¾" W,15½" H $488.75
Fuchsia Vase, two handles, impr. mark, 8" W, 12¼" H $402.50

Row 2, Left to Right
Apple Blossom Vase, blue glaze w/ pink, white, gr. & br. flowers, raised mark, 6¼" diam., 12¼" H $345.00
Pine Cone Centerpiece, branch handle, int. w/ flower holder under deep blue/gr. glaze, impr. mark, 9½" W, 8" H . . .$460.00
Jonquill Vase, two handles, paper label, 6½" W, 9½" H $402.50
Blackberry Vase, w/ two handles, crisp detail, unmkd., 6" W, 4" H $373.75
Vista Vase, 5¾" diam., 9¾" H . . .$460.00
Iris Vase, pink glaze w/ gr. white & yel. flower, impr. mark, 7" W, 12½" H .$373.75

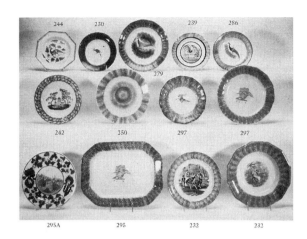

A-MA June 1997   Skinner

Row 1, Left to Right

244-Leeds Plate, octagonal spatterware peafowl, ca. 1820, gr. border w/ ora., yel. & blue peafowl, age crack, 7½" diam.$230.00
230-Staffordshire Plate, blue spatterware, blue border w/ gr. & red paint, minor crack, 7¼" diam. $345.00
279-Staffordshire Dinner Plate, ca. 1840, blue spatter ground & border w/ peafowl on gr., yel. & crimson, 9½" diam. . .$690.00
239-Staffordshire Plate, ca. 1840, blue spatter border w/ blk. banding, 7½" diam. $488.75
286-Staffordshire Luncheon Plate, ca. 1840, red spatter border w/ peafowl dec. in crimson, gr. & blue, 7½" diam. . . .$575.00

Row 2, Left to Right

242-St. Clement Bowl, Fr., early 19th C., blue & red border w/ yel. br. & blk. castle, gr. spatter landscape, crack, 8½" diam. .N/S
250-Staffordshire Plate, & teapot, not shown, ca. 1840, bands of red & gr., plate w/ central ring dec., 9½" diam., 5¼" H . .$1,380.00
297-Staffordshire Collection, blue spatterware, eagle & shield transfer dec. pottery, mid 19th C., incl. bowl & three plates, one plate w/ sepia transfer dec. eagle in flight, plate diam. 10¼" & 8¼", bowl 6½" diam. $862.50

Row 3, Left to Right

295A-Staffordshire Dinner Plates, five, late 19th C., cut sponge & polychrome floral dec. 9¼" diam. $1,380.00
295-Staffordshire Platters, two, blue spatterware, eagle & shield transfer dec., mid 19th C., one w/ sepia dec. one w/ blue transfer dec. pcs., lg. 13¾" & 15½" $920.00
232-Staffordshire Items, four, blue spatterware, ca. 1840, "Children at Play" plate & cup, & red transfer dec. "Arab w/ Horse" & blue transfer "Chinoiserie Transfer", 9" diam. & 23" $143.75

A-MA June 1997   Skinner

Row 1, Left to Right

272A-Staffordshire Bowl, gr. spatterware, ca. 1840, gr. band above a red schoolhouse on a br. field, 5¾" diam., 3" H $4,887.50
236A-Staffordshire Pottery, group of blue spatterware, ca. 1840, incl. two pitchers, child's cream pot, three cups, one saucer, & plate, all w/ blue spatter ground, castle dec. in blk., red & gray w/ gr. spatter foliage, repairs, cream pot 5" H $977.50
287A-Staffordshire Collection, blue spatterware eagle & shield transfer dec. pottery, mid 19th C., incl. pitcher, cup & saucer, a saucer, & a faceted cup & saucer, age crack in creamer $747.50
298B-Pearlware Bowl, Eng. ca. 1820, w/ blue & yel. lined edge, ext. of blue, rust & yel. peafowl dec. hairline, 7½" diam. $690.00
223-Staffordshire Sugar Bowls, two, red spatterware, parrot footed, ca. 1840, red & gr. parrot on blk. branch w/ crimson spatter border, no covers, 5½" H . . . . .N/S

Row 2, Left to Right

282-Staffordshire Teacup & Saucer, red & purple spatterware, ca. 1840, peafowl dec. in crimson, yel. & blue, 5¾" diam. $862.50
280-Staffordshire Cup & Saucers, one cup, ca. 1840, three saucers w/ red spatter ground, one saucer & cup w/ blue ground, peafowls dec. in polychrome, minor damage $460.00
269-Staffordshire Cups & Saucers, two, ca. 1840, overall crimson spatter ground w/ peafowls in yel., gr. & blue, one repaired chip $345.00
268-Staffordshire Cups & Saucers, two, spatterware, ca. 1840, both w/ blue spatter ground, yel., blk. & red castle, assembled set . . . . .N/S

A-PA Apr. 1997   Horst Auction Center

Spatterware Cups & Saucers, set of six matching Peafowl patt., white ground, yel. body, blue neck, red tail & crest, impr. rosette-type mark on bottoms, saucers 6" diam., cups 4⅛" diam., 2⅝" H $2,300.00

A-PA Apr. 1997   Horst Auction Center

Spatterware

Left to Right

Plate, blue w/ cut-sponge floral design border of red w/ gr. leaves, impr. "J, F8", 8¹¹⁄₁₆" diam., minor glaze wear, some discoloring $170.00
Soup Plate, blue w/ cut-sponge floral sprig designs in center, blue border, unmkd., 8¾" diam. $130.00

A-PA Apr. 1997   Horst Auction Center

Redware Bank, PA, dated 1893, ornately dec., inscribed "Olive Winifred Browne 1893", horizontal coin slot on top, approx. 4⅛" diam., 5" H$1,900.00

A-MA May 1997   Skinner

Row 1, Left to Right

Hampshire Pottery Vase, organic form w/ leaves in relief & plant-like handles, impr. marks, 7¾″ diam., 5½″ H . . .$287.50
Grueby Pottery Vase, monumental, feathered matte gr. glaze, impr. marks, remnant of orig. paper label, 8½″ diam., 18″ H . . . . .N/S
Hampshire Pottery Vase, mottled matte gr. glaze w/ hints of br., yel. & white, impr. marks, 5″ diam., 7″ H $345.00

Row 2, Left to Right

Hampshire Pottery Vase, molded leaf & flower form under smooth matte gr. glaze, impr. marks, 4″ diam., 6¾″ H $546.25
Merrimac Pottery Vase, ruffled rim under a mottled br. glaze, Merrimac paper label, 3¾″ diam., 5″ H . . . .N/S
Grueby Pottery Vase, leaves in relief under matte gr. glaze w/ unusually lrg. glaze skips, impr. mark, 3¼″ diam., 6¼″ H $460.00
Hampshire Pottery Candlestick, dec. w/ matte gr. glaze, Hampshire Pottery stamp mark, hairline, 4½″ W, 6¾″ H . . . . .N/S
Grueby Pottery Vase, leaves in relief under a lt. matte gr. glaze, impr. marks, imper., 4¼″ diam., 6½″ H $920.00

A-PA Apr. 1997   Horst Auction Center

Spatterware

Left to Right

Plate, yel. Peafowl patt., overall yel. spatter ground, unmkd. chip on underside of rim, 7½″ diam. $2,250.00
Cup & Saucer, blue Holly Berries patt., impr. asterisk-type mark on saucer, minor glaze flakes, 5⅞″ diam., cup 3⅞″ diam., 3″ H $260.00
Cup & Saucer, blue Dove patt., saucer w/ slight chips, 5⅝″ diam., cup w/ slight fracture & minor glaze wear, 3⅞″ diam., 2¼″ H $400.00
Plate, red Peafowl patt., gr. ground, unmkd., chip on rim, 8⅝″ diam. . .$600.00

A-MA May 1997   Skinner

Row 1, Left to Right

Teco Pottery Vases, two, one w/ two handles under a vibrant blue glaze, chips, 4¾″ W, 9″ H, other w/ smooth blue glaze, impr. Teco, 3¾″ diam., 8½″ H, ...N/S
Teco Pottery Tile, dec. w/ an incised frog under matte gr., butterscotch & blue glaze, impr. Teco, minor nicks, 8″ sq. .$2,990.00

Row 2, Left to Right

Teco Pottery Vase, tapering form w/ flared rim, blue glaze, impr. mark, 4½″ diam., 11″ H . . . . .N/S
Teco Pottery Candlesticks, circular form w/ sq. handles w/ blue glaze, impr. Teco, 5″ diam. $431.25
Fountain Frog, Weller Coppertone, gr. mottled glaze, openings for water tube, minute glaze nick, 7″ W, 5½″ H . .$690.00
Iris Vase, two handles, pink glaze w/ gr. white & yel. flower, impr. mark, 7″ W, 12½″ H $373.75

A-OH Nov. 1996   Garth's Auctions

Row 1, Left to Right

Cowan Pottery Jar, gray mat glaze w/ sage highlights, hairlines, 5⅛″ H $121.00
St. Cloud Pottery Jar, Eng., gr. w/ yel. shamrock, 5½″ H $82.50

Row 2, Left to Right

Rockwood Vase, tan pebble glaze, mkd. 1920, dated 1925, int. residue, 9⅜″ H $214.50
Wheeling Peachblow Vase, shades of yel. to cranberry to magenta to mah. w/ dk. br. at neck & lip, cased in white, 7¼″ H $660.00
Porcelain Vase, handpainted, shades of yel., blk. on rust red & gr. ground, yel. neck & lip, 8½″H $137.50

A-MA Oct. 1996   Skinner, Inc.

Left to Right

Stoneware Items, three, cobalt blue dec., Fort Edwards, N.Y., one-gallon two-handle crock w/ bird dec., two-gallon two-handle crock w/ floral dec., two-gallon jug w/ leaf dec., imp. N/S
Stoneware Crocks, three cobalt dec., Am. 19th c., incl. two-gallon, Edward & Luman P. Norton, Bennington, Vermont, 1858-81; two-gallon, Frank B. Norton & Co., Worcester, MA, 1865-80; & a three gal., L. Norton & Son, cracks, chips, one lacking lid, 9¼″ H-13½″ H .N/S
Stoneware Water Cooler, cobalt dec., late 19th c., dec. w/ vines & flowerhead, on tripod base, minor chips, repr. to one foot, 9½″ H, 13″ L $287.50
Stoneware Jug & Crock, cobalt blue dec., jug impr. A.B. Wheeler & Co. 60 Broad Street Bosston, Mass," w/ flyion onion, 14½″ H; & crock impr. "New York Stoneware Co." w/ bird, 9″ H . . N/S
Stoneware Crock, cobalt dec., three-gallon, J. Norton & Co., Bennington, Vermont, mid-19th c., dec. w/ a foraging game bird, cracks, minor chips, firing blemishes, 10⅝″ H $402.50

A-PA Apr. 1997   Horst Auction Center

Spatterware

Row 1, Left to Right

Teapot, red & blue rainbow, w/ lid, unmkd., lid w/ chip, prof. repr., pot w/ minor glaze wear, 7½″ H $650.00
Plate, gr. & blue rainbow, unmkd., minor glaze nick, 9⁷⁄₁₆″ diam. . .$650.00

Row 2, Left to Right

Pitcher, red & gr. rainbow, unmkd., minor glaze nick & two chips, 10⅜″ H .$650.00
Toddy Plate, red & blue rainbow, 14-sided, unmkd., 5¼″ diam. . . .$475.00
Plate, purple & blk. rainbow, unmkd., 8⁵⁄₁₆″ diam. $1,150.00

A-MA Oct. 1996   Skinner, Inc.

Row 1, Left to Right

Staffordshire Platter, blue & white, Eng., second quarter 19th c., depicting figures w/ cows in foreground, waterfalls & ruins in background, minor glaze chips, minor edge roughness, knife marks, 16¾" L $488.75
Staffordshire Platters, two blue & white, Eng., second quarter 19th c., including "The Dam & Waterworks Philadelphia.," boat w/ side wheel, & Clews, Cobridge 1819-36, "the Escape of the Mouse from Wilkies Designs," mkd. on base, minor chip, edge wear, knife marks, 10" Diam. $460.00

Row 2, Left to Right

Staffordshire Low Bowl, historic blue & white, John & Richard Riley, Burslem, Eng., 1814-28, beaded edge w/ floral & scroll borders, impr. "Riley", minor chips, hairlines, knife marks, 10⅝" diam. . . . . . .N/S
Staffordshire Vegetable Dish, covered blue, Eng., second quarter 19th c., lrg. chips & hairlines, 12" L $230.00
Staffordshire Teapot, historic blue & white, Enoch Wood & Sons, Burslem, Eng., 1819-46, Lafayette at Franklin's Tomb, cracks, minor chips, 8" H .N/S
Staffordshire, three pcs., blue & white, Eng., 19th c., including a hot water dish, Spode, 1812-15, the Tower patt., impr. "Spode 1" on base; a covered two-handled bowl w/ undertray, Wild Rose patt. & a plate, Enoch Wood & Sons, c. 1820, "Landing of the Fathers at Plymouth," impr. on base, cracks, minor chips, staining, dish 9¾" Diam. $373.75
Staffordshire Soup Plates, set of six blue & white, Eng., 2nd qtr.19th c., minor chips, edge roughness, knife marks, staining, 10" Diam. . .$345.00

A-PA Apr. 1997   Horst Auction Center
Spatterware Cup Plate, gr. Peafowl patt., yel. body, blue neck, red tail & crest, slight nick & chip, unmkd., 3¾" diam. $525.00

A-OH Nov. 1996   Garth's Auctions

Row 1, Left to Right

Cup & Saucer, blue handleless spatterware, mismatched, hairline & $93.50
Staffordshire Inkwells, two, polychrome swan, repr., 3½" H, & chicks, 2¾" H $275.00
Pearlware Cups, two miniature, gaudy design in red, gr. & purple, repr., 2¼" H, handleless, blue & gr., wear, flakes $104.50
Staffordshire Mugs, two, red transfer "Reward of Merit", stains & flakes, 2⅝" H, blk. transfer "School", polychrome enamel, 2⅞" H $220.00
Cup & Saucer, blue spatterware handleless, flower in red & gr., rprs. $93.50

Row 2, Left to Right

Staffordshire Plate, blk. man w/ sledge hammer, blk. transfer w/ ora. luster, 5⅝" diam. $126.50
Staffordshire Plates, "ABC" w/ blk. transfer & polychrome enamel, "Stilt Walking", 5⅜" diam. & "Franklin's Provs:...", 5⅜" diam., both w/ stains, impr. "Meakin" $264.00
Toddy Plates, two King's Rose oyster patt., repr., 5⅜" diam.; polychrome & blk., "A Trifle for Margaret" impr. "Wood", minor flakes, 5⅜" diam. $357.50

Row 3, Left to Right

Staffordshire, two pcs., blue transfer, toddy w/ "U.S. Constitution", stains & hairlines, 6" diam.; mug w/ "Franklin Maxims", hairline & chip, 2¾" H $159.50
Staffordshire Dog, w/ pups, white sanded w/ cobalt blue base & gilt, 7⅛" H $330.00
Staffordshire Girl, riding goat, polychrome, crazing & damage, 5⅛" H$302.50
Staffordshire Pcs., two w/ polychrome enamel, mug, blk. transfer "A" & "B", hairlines & chip, 2¾" H, toddy w/ blue transfer center,chips, 6⅛" diam. $192.50

A-PA Apr. 1997   Horst Auction Center
Pearlware Toddy Plate, blue shell edge 2-color polychrome dec., emb. fish, slight chip on underside, 4¼" diam. $700.00

A-OH Nov. 1996   Garth's Auctions
Rockingham

Row 1, Left to Right

Five Pieces, milk pitcher, some gr., hairlines, 4½" H; two sm. bowls, pictured, 4¼" & 5½" diam.; sm. cuspidor, damaged, 4" diam., & sugar bowl w/ incised name & date "1866", 4⅝" H, damage & no lid, not pict. . . .$214.50
Bowls, four w/ mottled gr. & br. glaze, three nest, 4¼", 5¼" & 6¼" diam., larger bowl, 8¼" diam. $286.00
Custard Cups, five various, one is pictured & two have damage $60.50
Shallow Bowls, three, one is pictured & largest damaged, 8½", 10" & 10½" diam. $137.50
Bowls, nine similar, hairlines, 5" diam. $170.50

Row 2, Left to Right

Covered Jars, two w/ molded peacocks, hanging salt jar, chips & hairline, 6½" H, & jar 6½" diam., 5" H $181.50
Bowls, two, chips, 10¾" & 11¾" diam. $104.50

Row 3, Left to Right

Pitchers, two, molded fish, badly chipped, filled repairs & lid mismatched, 9¼" H; one w/ cherub, hairline crack, 8¼" H $170.50
Pie Plates, two, wear, chips, 10¼" diam. $143.00

A-PA Apr. 1997   Horst Auction Center

Left to Right

Spatterware Plate, blue Bulls-Eye patt., blue flowers in center w/ red leaves, 9¹⁵⁄₁₆" diam. $200.00
Plate, blue Gem patt., transfer dec. w/ cut-sponge border, blue eagle transfer, mkd. "R. Hammersley, Gem", w/ British registry mark dated Apr. 23, 1868, 8¾" diam. $180.00

A-PA Apr. 1997   Horst Auction Center

Gaudy Dutch

Left to Right

Teapot, Dove patt., w/ lid, slight chip, 9¼" L, 6¼" H $5,000.00
Teapot, War Bonnet patt., w/ lid, slight nick, 11¼" L, 6¼" H . .$3,300.00
Teapot, Oyster patt., w/ lid, wear, 9¾" L, 5¾" H $3,000.00

A-PA Apr. 1997   Horst Auction Center

Spatterware

Left to Right

Plate, Columbine patt., w/ gr. no-center daisies border, minor glaze nicks, 6⅝" diam. $140.00
Cup & Saucer, Columbine patt., w/ gr. no-center daisies border, Eng., 1835-1853, saucer 5⅝" diam., cup w/ slight chip, 3¾" diam., 2⅜" H . .$170.00
Plate, Pansy patt., w/ blue bowknot border, unmkd., chip, 9⅞" diam. $180.00

A-PA Apr. 1997   Horst Auction Center

Spatterware

Left to Right

Coffee Pot, red Holly patt., matching lid, some glaze wear & slight chip, 8⅝" H, ...$400.00
Platter, red Holly patt., impr. "Elsmore & Forster, Tunstall" 1859-1867, 13½" x 10¼" $350.00
Cup & Saucer, child's mini. red & gr. , slight nicks, saucer 4⅜" diam., cup 2⁷⁄₁₆" diam., 1⅞" H $85.00

A-PA Apr. 1997   Horst Auction Center

Spatterware

Row 1, Left to Right

Soup & Plate, red, 12-sided, unmkd., 10½" diam. $450.00
Plate, red & blue, 12-sided, unmkd., slight nick on underside, approx. 10½" diam. $475.00

Row 2, Left to Right

Cup & Saucer, red Star patt., saucer 5¹³⁄₁₆" diam., cup w/ slight chip, 4⅛" diam., 2⁷⁄₁₆" H $725.00
Cup & Saucer, red Star patt., saucer w/ chip on base, 5¾" diam., cup w/ minor nicks & discoloring, 3⅞" diam., 2½" H $400.00

A-PA Apr. 1997   Horst Auction Center

Spatterware

Left to Right

Cup & Saucer, yel. Thistle patt., saucer 5⅞" diam., cup w/ minor flakes, 4⅛" diam., 2½" H $2,150.00
Plate, blue Thistle patt., 12-sided, unmkd., 8⅜" diam. $550.00
Cup & Saucer, purple Thistle patt., saucer 5¹³⁄₁₆" diam., cup w/ slight nick, 3⅞" diam., 2⁹⁄₁₆" H $600.00
Plate, red & gr. rainbow Thistle patt., 14-sided, impr. "B", slight chip, 7¼" diam. $2,250.00
Cup & Saucer, yel. Thistle patt., saucer w/ slight nick, 5⅞" diam., cup w/ slight chip, 3¹⁵⁄₁₆" diam., 2½" H $1,650.00

A-PA Apr. 1997   Horst Auction Center

Spatterware Tea Set, 10-pc. child's mini. blue Fort patt., teapot w/ lid, 6¾" L, 4¼" H, sugar bowl w/ lid, 3⅝" H, 4 cups & saucers, saucers 4½" diam., cups 2¹⁵⁄₁₆" diam., 1¾" H . . .$2,600.00

A-PA Apr. 1997   Horst Auction Center

Spatterware

Left to Right

Plate, Adams Rose-type flowers, 12-sided, unmkd., some discoloring, 9½" diam. $150.00
Cup & Saucer, blue Spray patt., impr. w/ crescent-shaped mark, saucer 6" diam., cup w/ minor glaze flakes & slight nick, 3¾" diam., 2⁹⁄₁₆" H . .$300.00

A-PA Apr. 1997   Horst Auction Center

Spatterware

Left to Right

Plate, blue Peafowl patt., impr. "Cotton & Barlow, 9¾" diam. $1,100.00
Cup & Saucer, red & blue varigated Peafowl patt., saucer 5¹³⁄₁₆" diam., cup w/ minor glaze nicks, 4" diam., 2¹¹⁄₁₆" H $1,500.00
Plate, blue Peafowl patt., impr. "Cotton & Barlow" 9¾" diam. $1,750.00

A-PA Apr. 1997   Horst Auction Center

Spatterware

Left to Right

Milk Pitcher, blue Fort patt., impr. w/ "7", minor glaze nicks, 8½" H $800.00
Creamer, blue Fort pattern, green spatter ground, 4⅜" H $900.00
Plate, blue Pomegranate patt., impr. mark, 6⅝" diam. $500.00
Sugar Bowl, w/ lid, br. Four Petal Blue Flower patt., minor glaze nicks, 5⅜" H $1,200.00

A-PA Apr. 1997   Horst Auction Center

Pearlware

Row 1, Left to Right

Plate, 5-color polychrome dec., featuring a peacock-like bird, minor glaze wear & flakes on rim, unmkd., 9¼" diam. $625.00

Pitcher, blue, featuring a band around sides w/ pineapple-like motif, impr. "36", minor glaze wear, 9½" H $375.00

Plate, 5-color polychrome dec., featuring basket of flowers in yel., blue, ora., gr. & br., few slight nicks, 9⅜" diam. $350.00

Row 2, Left to Right

Mug, 5-color polychrome dec., featuring beehive, in yellow & brown, repr. on rim, 3¼" diam., 4⅝" H . . .$325.00

Teapot w/ Lid, 3-color polychrome dec., slight glaze nicks, int. discoloring, 10¼" L, 7¼" H $225.00

Creamer, 4-color polychrome dec., featuring hand painted scenic view, unmkd., minor glaze flaking, 3¹³⁄₁₆" H $550.00

Mug, 4-color polychrome dec., dk. br. bands w/ yel. floral rosettes, 4⅝" diam., 5¹⁵⁄₁₆" H $100.00

Cup & Saucer, 5-color dk. blue & polychrome dec., impr. "E. Wood & Sons, Burslem, Warranted", saucer w/ minor glaze flake, 5⅞" diam., cup w/ some glaze wear, 3¹³⁄₁₆" diam., 2⁷⁄₁₆" H $550.00

A-PA Apr. 1997   Horst Auction Center

Redware

Row 1, Left to Right

Flower Pot, 19th C., slip-dec., PA, chips, 7" diam., 6¹⁵⁄₁₆" H $625.00

Vase, 19th C., PA, unsgn., minor glaze flake, 4¾" diam., 7¼" H $300.00

Jar, w/ lid, 19thC., PA, glaze wear, chips, 6¼" diam., 9⅞" H $675.00

Row 2, Left to Right

Fish Mold, 19th C., PA, impr. scale & fin designs, some glaze wear, chips, 14⅜" L, 7⅛" W, 2³⁄₁₆" H $400.00

Vegetable Dish, 19th C., PA, some glaze wear, 10¾" x 8⅛" x 2⅜" H . .$475.00

A-PA Apr. 1997   Horst Auction Center

Spatterware Cups & Saucers, set of six br. & blk. Rainbow Adams Rose patt., five of six saucers w/ impr. rosette-type mark, 5⅝" diam., cups w/ some chips & one has pc. broken out of rim, 3¹¹⁄₁₆" diam., 2½" H .$1,600.00

A-PA Apr. 1997   Horst Auction Center

Spatterware

Row 1, Left to Right

Plate, red w/ blue tansfer of peacock & fountain, 12-sided, unmkd., minor discoloring & age line, 8⅜" diam. $175.00

Cup & Saucer, red w/ a blk. Royal Standard transfer, saucer 5⅞" diam., cup w/ chip, 3¹³⁄₁₆" diam., 2¾" H $400.00

Plate, blue Schoolhouse patt., br. spatter ground, unmkd., 8³⁄₁₆" diam. . . .$3,600.00

Row 2, Left to Right

Plate, blue Schoolhouse patt., blk. spatter ground, 12-sided, unmkd., 7³⁄₁₆" diam. $2,600.00

Cup & Saucer, child's red & blue rainbow, saucer 4¹⁄₁₆" diam., cup w/ minor glaze nicks, 3" diam., 1⅞" H $425.00

Plate, blue Schoolhouse patt., br. spatter ground, unmkd., 6⁵⁄₁₆" diam. . . .$1,900.00

A-PA Apr. 1997   Horst Auction Center

Spatterware

Left to Right

Wash Bowl & Pitcher Set, purple & blue rainbow, unmkd. bowl, slight chip on base, 12½" diam., 4⅛" H, pitcher has line down side & 5" around base, 10½" H .$1,250.00

Platter, purple & blue rainbow, unmkd., minor glaze wear, 15¹³⁄₁₆" x 12⅛ $1,200.00

A-PA Apr. 1997   Horst Auction Center

Spatterware

Row 1, Left to Right

Cup & Saucer, red Deer patt., slight nick on saucer, 5⁹⁄₁₆" diam., cup 3¹¹⁄₁₆" diam., 2¼" H $1,275.00

Cup & Saucer, blue Rooster patt., cup impr. w/ "U" shaped mark, saucer 5¾" diam., cup 4" diam., 2⁵⁄₁₆" H $1,350.00

Creamer, blue Rooster patt., unmkd., slight chip on base, 3⁷⁄₁₆" H . .$900.00

Cup & Saucer, blue Deer patt., minor glaze nick on cup, saucer 5⅝" diam., cup 3⅞" diam., 2¼" H $1,500.00

Row 2, Left to Right

Cup & Saucer, blue Dove patt., saucer impr. w/ double line mark, cup impr. w/ "O", saucer 5¾" diam., 2⁵⁄₁₆" H .$1,500.00

Cup & Saucer, gr. Cluster of Buds patt., saucer w/ impr. single line mark, 5⅝" diam., cup 4" diam., 2½" H $300.00

Cup & Saucer, dk. blue Parrot patt., saucer 5¹⁵⁄₁₆" diam., cup w/ glaze wear, chips & nicks, 4¹⁄₁₆" diam., 2⅜" H $1,100.00

A-PA Apr. 1997   Horst Auction Center

Spatterware

Left to Right

Sugar Bowl, blue Fort patt., w/ lid, slight glaze chip, 7" H $600.00

Coffee Pot, blue Fort patt., w/ lid, minor glaze nicks, 8" H $1,900.00

Cup & Saucer, red Fort patt., saucer 5¹¹⁄₁₆" diam., cup 4¹⁄₁₆" diam., 2½" H . .$1,700.00

A-VT Apr. 1997   Am. Stoneware Auction

Churn, 6 gal., M. Woodruff, Cortland, nice floral $600.00

A-PA Apr. 1997   Horst Auction Center

Spatterware

Row 1, Left to Right

Plate, blue Profile Tulip patt., 12-sided, impr. "Stoneware, B&T", 9⁵/₁₆" diam. . $475.00

Plate, blue Profile Tulip patt., unmkd. slight glaze nick, 9¾" diam. . .$300.00

Row 2, Left to Right

Plate, blue Profile Tulip, 12-sided, impr. "14", 9¼" diam. $550.00

Cup & Saucer, yel. Profile Tulip, saucer w/ some discoloring, 6" diam., cup w/ minor glaze flakes, 3⅞" diam., 2½" H $2,400.00

Creamer, red Profile Tulip patt., octagonal-shape, scalloped rim, 5⅝" H $1,050.00

Plate, two-toned gr. & blue rainbow Profile Tulip patt., 12-sided, unmkd., 8⅜" diam. $1,500.00

A-PA Apr. 1997   Horst Auction Center

Spatterware

Row 1, Left to Right

Plate, red Open Tulip patt., 12-sided, unmkd., 10½" diam. $1,300.00

Bowl, red Open Tulip patt., slight chip & nicks, 6½" diam., 4³/₁₆" H . .$400.00

Plate, gr. and blue rainbow Open Tulip patt., 12-sided, unmkd., 8⅝" diam.$400.00

Row 2, Left to Right

Plate, purple Open Tulip patt., 12-sided, unmkd. sm. flaw, 8¼" diam. . . .$675.00

Plate, red & blue rainbow Open Tulip patt., 12-sided, glaze wear, unmkd. 8⅜" diam. $1,600.00

A-PA Apr. 1997   Horst Auction Center

Flask, 5-color polychrome dec., w/ parrot-like bird on front, initials "HL" on back in a foliated wreath, 5⅝" diam., 2¼" D, 7" H $1,150.00

A-PA Apr. 1997   Horst Auction Center

Pearlware

Row 1, Left to Right

Plate, overall dk. blue floral dec., unmkd., minor glaze flake, 10" diam. $500.00

Plate, 4-color polychrome dec., peafowl perched in a gr. spatter tree, minor glaze wear & slight chip, 9¾" diam. $475.00

Row 2, Left to Right

Bank, dk. blue onion-shaped, coin slot on top of bank, few age lines, approx. 3½" diam., 5¼" H $250.00

Cup & Saucer, 5-color polychrome dec. child's mini, peafowl in yel., ora., blue & dk. br., saucer w/ slight nick, 4⅛" diam., cup 2⁷/₁₆" diam., 1½" H . .$700.00

A-PA Apr. 1997   Horst Auction Center

Pearlware

Left to Right

Plate, 4-color polychrome dec., w/ Am. eagle in center, unmkd., minor glaze flakes, 7⁵/₁₆" diam. . . .$1,200.00

Charger, 5-color polychrome dec., w/ Peafowl in gr. spatter tree, minor glaze nick unmkd., 13⅛" diam. $1,300.00

Plate, 3-color polychrome, w/ pineapple design, unmkd. sgn. "Lizzie Forney", 7⁷/₁₆" diam. $1,200.00

A-PA Apr. 1997   Horst Auction Center

Pearlware Platter, dk. blue dec., emb. edge, impr. "15", 16⅛" x 13⅛" $750.00

A-PA Apr. 1997   Horst Auction Center

Gaudy Dutch

Left to Right

Soup Plate, Single Rose patt., minor wear, 10" diam. $1,300.00

Soup Plate, War Bonnet patt., mkd. "2/1037", minor wear to red polychrome, 9¾" diam. $1,600.00

A-PA Apr. 1997   Horst Auction Center

Adams Rose

Row 1, Left to Right

Pitcher, chip on base & handle, 8" H $1,000.00

Vegetable Dish, impr. "Adams", minor glaze nick & wear, 9⅞" x 8" x 1⁷/₁₆" H $300.00

Row 2, Left to Right

Platter, impr. "Adams", minor glaze wear, 12" x 10" $375.00

Cup & Saucer, impr. "Adams", saucer w/ minor early repr., 6¼" diam., cup w/ minor glaze nicks, 4" diam., 2⁵/₁₆" H $65.00

Bowl, unmkd., 5⅝" diam., 2⅞" H $325.00

Cup & Saucer, impr. "Adams", saucer w/ slight chip, 6¼" diam., cup w/ two slight nicks, 4" diam., 2¼" H $110.00

Platter, impr. "Adams", & "6", 11⅛" x 9¼" $250.00

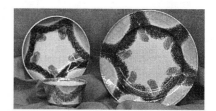

A-PA Apr. 1997   Horst Auction Center

Spatterware

Left to Right

Cup & Saucer, red & yel. & gr. Festoon patt., saucer 5¹⁵/₁₆" diam., cup w/ two minor glaze nicks, 3¾" diam., 2⅜" H $1,500.00

Plate, red, yel. & gr. Festoon patt., slight nick on rim, sm. flaws, 8⁷/₁₆" diam. $4,200.00

A-PA Apr. 1997 Horst Auction Center

Redware and Earthenware

Row 1, Left to Right

Tobacco Jar, 19th C., Am. w/ name "W. Scrafton" molded into side, overall gr. & br. mottling, glaze chip, 6½" diam., 9½" H $400.00
Pitcher, 19th C., Shenandoah Valley, PA, attrib. to John Bell, minor glaze flakes, 4⅞" diam., 8¾" H $400.00
Flower Pot, 19th C., w/ saucer attached, impr. "Solomon Bell, Strasburg, Va", crimping on pot's rim w/ chips, 7¼" diam., 6¾" H . . .$1,300.00

Row 2, Left to Right

Pitcher, late 19th or early 20th C., attrib. to Jacob Medinger, PA, unmkd., 8" H $450.00
Butter Tub, 19th C., overall mottled gr. & br. ground, glaze flakes & wear, 10⅝" diam., 6¼" H $1,900.00
Fish Mold, 19th C., PA, bright ora. ground w/dark br. splotches, minor glaze wear & nicks, 13½" L, 6⅝" W, 2¾" H $1,800.00

A-PA Apr. 1997 Horst Auction Center

Redware

Row 1

Sugar Bowl, w/ lid, 19th C., PA, mottled gr. & br. glaze, some glaze wear & slight chips on rim, 5" diam., 5¾" H $1,000.00

Row 2, Left to Right

Ring Safe, 19th C., attrib. to Hagerstown or Washington Co. areas, lead glaze w/ manganese specks, unmkd., 3¾" diam., 1 15/16" H $325.00
Spaniel, 19th C., attrib. to Shenandoah Valley Potters, lt. gr. w/ dk. br. splotches, 2½" W, 2" D, 1¾" H $350.00
Bowl, 19th C., PA, orange/brown ground w/ dk. br. mottling, 4⅜" diam., 2" H $500.00

A-PA Apr. 1997 Horst Auction Center

Redware Holy Water Font, 19th C., PA, orangish-brown color, nick on rim, glaze chip & wear, 3 7/16" W, 1 15/16" D, 9⅜" H $300.00

A-PA Apr. 1997 Horst Auction Center

Redware

Row 1, Left to Right

Crock, PA, w/ yel. slip, dk. br. ground, significant glaze wear, chips, unmkd., 4⅞" diam., 5 15/16" H $550.00
Creamer on Base, 19th C., Am. figural cow creamer, cow's mouth serves as spout, prof. repr., minor nicks on base, 9" L, 4¼" W, 7½" H $500.00
Vase, late 19th or early 20th C., by Jacob Medinger, Montgomery Co., PA., unmkd., slight chip on base, 6⅜" diam., 8" H $1,000.00

Row 2, Left to Right

Seated Spaniel, 19th C., PA, ora. ground w/ dk. br. dec., unmkd., chip & slight glaze chip, 5⅜" W, 2¾" D, 7¼" H $600.00
Creamer, 19th C., Am., overall gr. & dk. br. mottling, 3¼" H $225.00
Bank, 19th C., br. stripe design, onion-shaped, 4½" diam., 5½" H $350.00
Cup w/ Spout, 19th C., PA, ora. ground w/ gr. slip splotches, unmkd., minor glaze flakes & nicks, 3 11/16" diam., 3" H $700.00
Bank, PA, jug-shaped, attrib. to George Wagner, Carbon Co., br. & gr. mottled dec.,unsigned, approx. 3⅛" diam., 4½" H $1,200.00
Handled Mug, 19th C., PA, yellow/orange ground w/ br. sponge-like splotching, chips & glaze wear, 3⅝" diam., 4 7/16" H $600.00

A-PA Apr. 1997 Horst Auction Center

Spatterware

Row 1, Left to Right

Plate, yel. peafowl patt., overall yel. spatter ground, unmkd., 7½" diam. .$3,800.00
Pitcher, yel., blk., blue, gr. & red rainbow, unmkd., 8¾" H $4,100.00
Plate, gr. Peafowl patt., minor & slight glaze nick, unmkd., 12-sided, 8⅜" diam. $850.00

Row 2, Left to Right

Pitcher, red w/ gr. eagle & shield transfer, minor discoloring, unmkd., 7½" H $700.00
Cup & Saucer, yel. Profile Tulip patt., saucer 6" diam., cup 4" diam., 2 9/16" H $2,800.00
Cup & Saucer, yel. Peafowl patt., 5¾" diam. saucer, cup w/ slight glaze flake, 3¾" diam., 2 9/16" H $1,150.00
Cup & Saucer, Thistle patt., red & yel. rainbow, saucer 5⅞" diam., cup w/ two slight nicks, 4" diam., 2½" H $2,500.00
Pitcher, red Peafowl patt., overall red spatter, minor glaze wear & nicks, 6 7/16" H $2,500.00

A-PA Apr. 1997 Horst Auction Center

Mocha

Left to Right

Mug, yel. band w/cat's eye designs in lt. blue, br. & white, 4 9/16" diam., 5¾" H $1,950.00
Bowl, ora. band w/ earthworm design in blue, white, & dk. br., minor glaze wear & slight nick, 9⅛" diam., 4" H $1,650.00
Pitcher, earthworm designs in br., lt. blue & white, some glaze wear, 7⅜" H $725.00

A-PA Apr. 1997 Horst Auction Center

Left to Right

Mini. Empire Bureau, 19th C., paint dec., painted golden yel. w/ br. graining, $8\frac{3}{4}$" W, $5\frac{3}{4}$" D, $9\frac{3}{8}$" H . . .$950.00
Child's Mug, polychrome dec. canary yel., $2\frac{1}{4}$" diam., $2\frac{1}{4}$" H $725.00
Child's Mini. Wash Bowl & Pitcher Set, Adams Rose, pitcher $3\frac{1}{8}$" H, wash bowl w/ slight chip & two slight nicks, $3\frac{7}{8}$" diam., $1\frac{5}{8}$" H $900.00

A-PA Apr. 1997 Horst Auction Center

Cigar & Match Holder, late 19th C., Am. yel. ware, impr. "BB", $8\frac{1}{4}$" W, $5\frac{5}{8}$" D, $4\frac{3}{16}$" H $800.00

A-PA Apr. 1997 Horst Auction Center

Redware Figural Lion, cigar & match holder, 19th C., glaze wear, slight nicks & chips, 7" W, $6\frac{3}{4}$" D, $5\frac{1}{4}$" H $650.00

A-PA Apr. 1997 Horst Auction Center

Redware Urn, 19th C., 1-pc. pedestal base, attrib. to Bell Family, beautiful ora. ground w/ overall mottled dec., lrg. chips, $12\frac{1}{2}$" diam., $12\frac{1}{2}$" H $4,000.00

A-PA Apr. 1997 Horst Auction Center

Pearlware

Row 1, Left to Right

Plate, 4-color polychrome, sm. ora. Adams rose-type flower w/ dk. blue buds, unmkd., $7\frac{1}{4}$" diam. $275.00
Mug, 5-color polychrome, featuring songbird in yel., ora., br. & dk. blue, unmkd., $4\frac{1}{8}$" diam., $5\frac{13}{16}$" H $2,000.00
Pitcher, 5-color blue & polychrome dec., chip on inside rim of foot, slight chip on spout, $6\frac{3}{4}$" H $400.00
Bowl, 4-color polychrome dec., featuring basket of flowers, unmkd., slight chips on inside of foot, $6\frac{1}{4}$" diam., $2\frac{15}{16}$" H $450.00
Mug, 3-color polychrome dec., featuring an ora. strawberry-like design., some glaze wear, $4\frac{5}{16}$" diam., $5\frac{11}{16}$" H . .$500.00
Plate, 4-color polychrome dec. & emb. shell-edge, featuring a lrg. yel. & br. tulip, impr. w/ rosette-like mark on bottom, $6\frac{9}{16}$" diam. $600.00

Row 2, Left to Right

Creamer, 3-color dk. blue & polychrome dec., lrg. dk. blue flowers w/ gr. & dk. br. leaves, some glaze wear & slight chip, $6\frac{1}{8}$" L, $4\frac{1}{2}$" H . .$350.00
Cup & Saucer, 7-color polychrome dec., featuring a peafowl-type bird, saucer w/ slight chip on base, 5" diam., cup w/ minor flakes to blue polychrome on rim, 3" diam., $1\frac{15}{16}$" H $500.00
Pearlware Platter, 3-color blue & polychrome dec., ora. 6-petaled flower in center, unmkd., $5\frac{7}{8}$" x $4\frac{1}{2}$" $475.00
Cup & Saucer, 5-color polychrome dec., featuring a songbird in yel., ora., br. & dk. blue, saucer w/ slight chip on base, $5\frac{1}{2}$" diam., cup w/ slight chip & slight nicks on inside of rim of foot, $3\frac{5}{8}$" diam., $2\frac{5}{16}$" H $600.00

A-PA Apr. 1997 Horst Auction Center

Candlesticks, pr., scroddle dec., diamond in circle trademark, $3\frac{3}{8}$" diam., $4\frac{5}{8}$" H $350.00
Bowl, marbelized leaf cup-shaped, br. band w/ two marbelized leaf designs, minor glaze nicks, $3\frac{1}{2}$" diam., $2\frac{7}{8}$" H . .$1,200.00

A-PA Apr. 1997 Horst Auction Center

Spatterware

Left to Right

Plate, purple Tree pattern, impr. "Best Goods", $8\frac{1}{16}$" diam. $2,250.00
Cup & Saucer, blue Tree patt., saucer w/ slight nick, $5\frac{15}{16}$" diam., cup $3\frac{15}{16}$" diam., $2\frac{9}{16}$" H $1,100.00
Cup & Saucer, red Bird-on-Bar patt., saucer w/ underglaze blk. "x", $5\frac{13}{16}$" diam., cup w/ minor repr., $3\frac{7}{8}$" diam., $2\frac{3}{8}$" H $850.00
Plate, red Bird-on-Bar patt., underglaze blk. "x" mark, minor glaze nick, $7\frac{1}{16}$" diam. $1,800.00

A-PA Apr. 1997 Horst Auction Center

Mocha

Row 1, Left to Right

Sugar Bowl w/ Lid, speckled & checkered, bands of br. on bowl & lid, minor glaze wear & chip, $3\frac{7}{8}$" diam., $4\frac{1}{2}$" H $1,700.00

Row 2, Left to Right

Mush Cup, in shades of br., cocoa & blight blue band, slight chip on side of foot, minor glaze wear, $3\frac{15}{16}$" diam., $2\frac{7}{8}$" H $500.00
Pepper Pot, yel. band on side w/ earthworm & cat's eye designs in lt. blue, dk. br. & white, slight glaze chip, minor flakes, $4\frac{1}{4}$" H $1,750.00

A-PA Apr. 1997 Horst Auction Center

Wash Bowl, scroddle dec., marbelizing in shades of br., lt. blue, white & yel., chip on inside rim & rim of foot, $15\frac{3}{8}$" diam., $5\frac{3}{8}$" H $725.00

A-PA Apr. 1997   Horst Auction Center

Gaudy Dutch

Teapot, w/ lid, Dove patt., impr. w/ circle mark, slight chips, 9⅝" L, 5¾" H $8,000.00
Cup & Saucer, Dove patt., saucer 5½" diam., cup w/ slight chip & nick,3⅝" diam., 2½" H $1,250.00
Plate, Dove patt., impr. w/ asterisk-type mark, minor flakes, 7½" diam. . . .$850.00
Creamer, Grape patt., mkd. "2/1036", slight discoloring, 5⅞" L, 4¼" H .$1,150.00

A-PA Apr. 1997   Horst Auction Center

Pearlware

Pitcher, 4-color dk. blue polychrome dec., minor glaze wear, 7" H $1,000.00
Coffee Pot, 5-color polychrome dec., w/ peafowl in blue, ora., yel. & br., slight chip on inside rim, 9⅞" H $2,400.00
Pitcher, polychrome dec., two oval reserves w/ "Duke of York" on horseback, minor glaze wear, unmkd., 7½" H $850.00

A-PA Apr. 1997   Horst Auction Center

Figural Pearlware Pitcher, 4-color dk. blue polychrome dec., overall yel. & dk. blue floral dec. w/ gr. & br. leaves, minor glaze flake, unmkd., 9½" H $2,050.00

A-PA Apr. 1997   Horst Auction Center

Row 1, Left to Right

Whieldon Plate, 5-color w/ scalloped emb. feather edged rim, unmkd., slight chip & minor glaze wear 9¹¹⁄₁₆" diam., .$750.00
Pearlware Tray, Blue Willow patt., transfer dec., w/ lattice border, edged in blue, unmkd., very minor glaze wear, 9¼" x 7⁵⁄₁₆" $200.00
Whieldon Plate, 4-color w/ serpentine rim, unmkd., chips, 9¼" diam. . . .$700.00

Row 2, Left to Right

Mini. Empire Mocha Creamer, bands of ora. & gray, dk. br. stripe around base, minor glaze wear, 3⅞" H $800.00
Mocha Mug, ora. bans & blk. stripes, some glaze wear, 3⅜" diam., 4¾" H $900.00
Mocha Bowl, lt. yel. band w/ overall blue, white & br. cat's eye designs, rim has been repr., 4⅝" diam., 2¾" H $375.00
Mocha Pepper Pot, lt. blue wide bands & stripes, slight glaze nick, 4¾" H $150.00
Mocha Mug, wide ora. band w/ blk. seaweed design, lt. gr. accent, 3⅝" diam., 3¾" H $650

A-PA Apr. 1997   Horst Auction Center

Spatterware

Row 1, Left to Right

Plate, blue Acorn patt., 12-sided, unmkd., minor glaze flake, 9⅜" diam. . . .$1,150.00
Cup & Saucer, purple & blk. rainbow Memorial Tulip patt., saucer 5⅝" diam., cup w/ minor glaze flakes, 3⅞" diam., 2⅝" H $4,300.00
Cup & Saucer, red Acorn patt., impr. w/ "W", saucer 5¹⁵⁄₁₆" diam., cup w/ minor glaze nick, 4" diam., 2⅝" H . . .$3,200.00
Plate, purple Acorn patt., 12-sided, unmkd., minor glaze nick, 9⁵⁄₁₆" diam. $1,250.00

Row 2, Left to Right

Plate, red Memorial Tulip pattern, unmarked, 7⁷⁄₁₆" diam. $1,850.00
Plate, red Memorial Tulip pattern, unmarked 7⁷⁄₁₆" diam. $1,800.00

A-PA Apr. 1997   Horst Auction Center

Row 1, Left to Right

Redware Doorstop, lion shaped, 19th C., sgn. "AM", lrg. chips, 9¾" x 5⅛" x 8" H $525.00
Earthenware Pitcher, 19th C., attrib. to Bell family, yel. ground w/ overall br. & gr. mottling, 8¾" H $1,150.00
Yellow Ware Spaniel, 19th C., cobalt blue dec., chip on inside rim, 8⁷⁄₁₆" W, 6⅜" D, 10" H $1,700.00

Row 2, Left to Right

Redware Pitcher, 19th C., PA, ora. & gr. mottled ground w/ dk. br. splotches, slight chips & minor glaze nicks, 7¼" H $1,100.00
Redware Soap Dish, 19th C., Am., yel. ground w/ gr. splotches, seaweed designs, glaze chips on base, minor wear, 5¾" W, 5⅛" D, 3-4" H . .$750.00
Redware Figural Cigar Holder, 19th C., Am., mottled br. ground, damage to glaze & slight chip & flakes, 6⅛" W, 5⅛" D, 5" H $4,000.00
Redware Cream Jug, 19th C., PA, w/ side handle & lid, dk. ora. br. ground w/ overall mottling, few glaze flakes, 5⅜" diam., 5½" H $350.00
Earthenware Parrot, 19th C., gr., unmkd., 9¾" H $225.00

A-PA Apr. 1997   Horst Auction Center

Gaudy Dutch

Row 1, Left to Right

Plate, Double Rose patt., minor glaze flakes, 7¹¹⁄₁₆" diam. $800.00
Plate, Carnation patt., minor wear & flakes, 8⅜" diam. $1,050.00

Row 2, Left to Right

Soup Plate, Grape patt., mkd. , minor wear, 8¼" diam. $950.00
Cup & Saucer, Urn patt., saucer w/ slight chip, 5⁹⁄₁₆" diam., cup 3⅝" diam., 2⁵⁄₁₆" H $950.00
Plate, Dove patt., impr. w/ circle mark, minor flake & glaze wear, 6⁷⁄₁₆" diam. $900.00
Soup Plate, Grape patt., mkd. , minor wear, 3³⁄₁₆" diam. $950.00

A-PA Apr. 1997 Horst Auction Center

Spatterware

Row 1, Left to Right

Wash Bowl & Pitcher Set, blue, "Adams Rose" design on pitcher, unmkd., 9 5/8" H, wash bowl, 12 sided, unmkd., minor glaze nick, & tight 1/4" line on rim, 13 7/8" diam., 4 3/8" H $1,250.00

Bowl, blue Adams Rose patt., line extending down side from rim, 10 1/4" diam., 4 15/16" H $500.00

Row 2, Left to Right

Cup & Saucer, red & gr. rainbow Adams Rose patt., sgn. by William Adams & sons, saucer w/ slight chip on base, cup w/ two slight chips, saucer 6" diam., cup 4 1/16" diam., 2 5/8" H $400.00

Wash Bowl & Pitcher Set, blue , pitcher w/ "Adams Rose" design, unmkd., 9 5/8" H, wash bowl 12-sided, unmkd., minor glaze ick, tight line on rim, 13 7/8" diam., 4 3/8" H $1,250.00

Cup & Saucer, red Cluster of Buds patt., saucer 5 9/16" diam., cup 4" diam., 2 9/16" H $500.00

A-MA Dec. 1996 Skinner, Inc.

Oyster Plates, 12 limoges porcelain, Fr., enamel dec. shell & foliate design to yel., blue, gr., pink, white & peach ground colors, lt. surface & gilt rim wear, 7 3/4" W $1,150.00

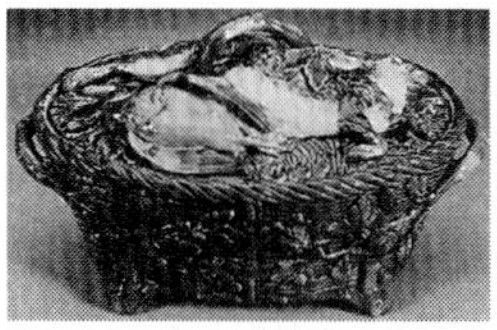

A-MA May 1997 Skinner

Game Pie Dish, Minton Majolica, Eng., ca. 1877, impr. marks, line in base, handle restored, 14" L $1,610.00

A-PA Apr. 1997 Horst Auction Center

Pearlware

Row 1, Left to Right

Soup Plate, blue emb. edge 3-color polychrome dec., w/ lrg. ora. petaled flower, impr. "S. Tams Warranted Staffordshire", minor glaze wear, 10 1/4" diam. .$1,000.00

Charger, blue shell edge 5-color polychrome dec., w/ lrg. yel. & br. urn w/ yel., ora., blue & gr. flowers, unmkd., minor glaze nicks, 14 1/4" diam. $2,000.00

Soup Plate, gr. shell edged 4-color polychrome dec., w/ Am. eagle, unmkd., slight nicks on underside, 8 1/4" diam. . . .$500.00

Row 2, Left to Right

Plate, blue emb. edge Kings Rose polychrome dec., unmkd., minor glaze flake, 7 1/16" diam. $800.00

Plate, blue shell edge 5-color polychrome & spatter dec., w/ peacock-type bird, unmkd., minor glaze flakes on rim, 6 3/16" diam. $2,050.00

Plate, blue shell edged 5-color polychrome spatter dec. w/ peafowl on gr. spatter tree, minor glaze flakes, 6 7/16" diam. $800.00

A-PA Apr. 1997 Horst Auction Center

Mocha

Row 1, Left to Right

Bowl, wide ora. band having earthworm design in ora., dk. br., lt. blue & white, chips, 8 11/16" diam., 4 1/8" H $700.00

Footed Bowl, bluish gray band w/ earthworm design in blue, dk. br. & white, minor glaze nicks, 8 7/8" diam., 4 1/2" H $675.00

Bowl, lt. br. band w/ earthworm in white & shades of br., minor glaze wear, chips, 6 1/2" diam., 3 5/16" H $750.00

Row 2, Left to Right

Mug, white ground w/ lt. br. band & blk. seaweed designs, minor glaze wear, 3 3/8" diam., 4 7/8" H $450.00

Pepper Pot, yel. ware, w/ two narrow cream band flanked by dk. br. stripes, slight glaze chips on base, 4 1/4" H $900.00

Bowl, lt. br. band w/ blk. seaweed designs, minor glaze nicks, 4 9/16" diam. 2 9/16" H $600.00

A-PA Apr. 1997 Horst Auction Center

Pearlware

Row 1, Left to Right

Shallow Plate, polychrome dec., yellow/orange w/ gr. & br. around border, impr. "B", 9 7/8" diam. $150.00

Pitcher, dk. blue dec., minor repr., 8 1/4" H $260.00

Creamer, dk. blue & polychomre, mkd. w/ incised "x" on bottom, 6" L, 5" H .$250.00

Teapot w/ Lid, dk. blue & polychrome, glaze flakes on tip of spout, 9 3/8" L, 5 1/4" H $200.00

Row 2, Left to Right

Plate, 5-color polychrome dec., w/ cock bird, chip on back, 10" diam. . . .$1,500.00

Mug, dk. br. polychrome dec., 4 1/16" diam., 5 5/8" H $110.00

Cup & Saucer, dk. blue & polychrome dec., border of yel., gr. & dk. blue, saucer w/ minor glaze flakes, 5 1/2" diam., cup w/ minor glaze nick, 3 3/4" diam., 2 3/8" H $650.00

A-PA Apr. 1997 Horst Auction Center

Pearlware

Row 1, Left to Right

Plate, blue shell-edged 5-color polychrome dec., 8 1/4" diam. $2,000.00

Charger, blue shell-edge, 4-color polychrome dec., 14 3/8" diam. $1,350.00

Pearlware Plate, br. shell edge, 2-color polychrome dec., 8 3/8" diam. $250.00

Row 2, Left to Right

Plate, blue emb. edge, 4-color polychrome dec., lrg. blue & ora. flower design, minor glaze flakes, 8 3/4" diam. $875.00

Flower Pot, blue feather edged 3-color polychrome dec., slight chip, 5" diam., 4 5/16" H $550.00

Toddy Plate, blue shell edge 5-color polychrome dec., w/ yel. & ora. flower design, unmkd., 4 7/16" diam. $1,750.00

Plate, gr. shell edge 5-color polychrome dec., w/ parrot-type bird on a gr. spatter tree, unmkd., 8 3/16" diam. $650.00

A-MA Dec. 1996   Skinner, Inc.

Left to Right

Ewer, Royal Worcester porcelain, Eng., 1896, raised leaf & floral designs in gilt & red enamel, lt. gilt wear, 15¾" H . .$1,495.00
Porcelain Items, two Royal Worcester, Eng., late 19th c., a two-handled vase w/ gilt & enameled leaf, berry & spider dec., 12¼" H; covered biscuit jar, enamel floral designs, 7¼" H $1,092.50
Vase, Royal Worcester porcelain, Eng., 1888, gilt dragon-form handles w/ enameled floral sprays, gilt rim wear, 15¾" H $747.50

A-MA Dec. 1996   Skinner, Inc.

Back Row

Nautilus Shell Vase, Royal Worcester porcelain, Eng., 19th c., staining, 8½" H $230.00

Front Row

Porcelain Items, three Royal Worcester, Eng., late 19th/early 20th c., including basket 3" H, leaf-form dish 7" L, & bamboo-form vase 8" L, lt. gilt wear throughout $230.00

A-MA Dec. 1996   Skinner, Inc.

Tea Set, Paris porcelain, Fr., 19th c., gilt trim & floral designs, enameled floral panels, incl. a teapot, 5¾" H; creamer; sugar, broken handle; wastebowl, 8" Diam.; eight cups & saucers; gilt wear throughout $632.50

A-PA Apr. 1997   Horst Auction Center

Spatterware

Left to Right

Plate, red Wigwam patt., unmkd., 8½" diam. $400.00
Plate, red Wigwam patt., unmkd., minor glaze nick, 8½" diam. .$450.00
Cup & Saucer, red Wigwam patt., saucer 5¹⁵⁄₁₆" diam., cup minor glaze wear, 3¹¹⁄₁₆" diam., 2¾" H $525.00
Plate, blue Wigwam patt., unmkd., some glaze wear, slight nick & chip, 8½" diam. $260.00
Plate, gr. Wigwam patt., glaze flakes, 8½" diam. $500.00

A-PA Apr. 1997   Horst Auction Center

Left to Right

Cups & Saucers, four sets of matching polychrome dec., Cabbage Rose pearlware, 2 saucers w/ minor glaze nick, 5⅞" diam., 1 cup w/ minor glaze wear, 3¾" diam., 2⅜" H $350.00
Adams Rose Charger, mkd. "Eng.", impr. w/ trademark of the G. Jones & Sons Factory, 12" diam. $500.00
Staffordshire Bull's Head, covered cheese dish, dk. blue, unmkd., 9⅞" W, 10¼" D, 7" H $1,600.00

A-MA May 1997   Skinner

Row 1, Left to Right

Wedgwood Jug, Queen's ware, Eng., ca. 1778, blk. transfer dec., impr. maker, spout restored, 8¾" H $3,737.50
Wedgwood Jug, Queen's ware "Irish Volunteers", Eng., ca. 1780, polychrome dec. blk. transfer, slight rim line, chip, 7½" H $4,600.00
Wedgwood Jug, Queen's ware, Eng., ca. 1780, blk. transfer, impr. lower case mark, chip, 8½" H $2,530.00

A-MA Sept. 1996   Skinner, Inc.

Dinner Service, Royal Worcester blue & white porcelain partial service for 12, 1889, dinner plates, rimmed bowls, luncheon, salad, & finger bowls, butter pats, demitasse & tea cups & saucers, five covered servers, tureen, five platters, & approx. ten misc. serving pcs. $3,335.00

A-MA Sept. 1996   Skinner, Inc.

Left to Right

Miniature Ewer, Coalport "jeweled" porcelain, ca. 1885 w/ ivory ground, painted w/ an oval reserve of a river landscape on a turq. jeweled ground, faory marks, 7¼" H $977.50
Dessert Plate, Royal Worcester painted porcelain, sgn. T. Lockyer, date code for 1923, guilded edge, factory marks, 8½" diam. $345.00

A-MA May 1997   Skinner

Row 1

Teapot, Cover & Stand, Neale & Co., solid blue jasper, Eng., ca. 1785, lrg. hairlines, 5" H, stand w/ scalloped rim, impr. marks, 7⅛" H $805.00

Row 2, Left to Right

Bough Pots & Covers, pr., Adams solid Jasper, Eng., late 18th C., impr. marks, sm. rim chips, 7" H .$1,725.00
Egg Cups, four, Adams solid blue Jasper, Eng., late 18th C., impr. marks, 2⅝" H $2,185.00

A-MA May 1997   Skinner

Row 1, Left to Right

Staffordshire Teapot, creamware, covered, Eng. ca. 1760, w/ Chinese figures, 4¼" H $2,185.00
Staffordshire Teapot, leaf-molded creamware, covered, Eng., ca. 1765, enamel dec., chips, restored, 4" H . . .$2,990.00
Staffordshire Teapot, lead glaze creamware, covered, Eng. ca. 1760, restor. sm. chip to spout, 5⅜" H $2,300.00
Staffordshire Teapot, commemorative creamware, covered, Eng., ca. 1763, figures of George II & Queen Charlotte, restor., sm. chips, 4½" H $9,775.00
Staffordshire Teapot, creamware, covered, Eng., ca. 1760, restor. chips, 5" H . . . . .N/S

Row 2, Left to Right

Staffordshire Teapot, enamel dec w/ cover, Eng., ca. 1755, restor., 4¼" H$2,185.00
Staffordshire Teapot, salt glaze, covered, Eng., ca. 1760, chips, body hairlines, 4¼" H $2,185.00
Staffordshire Teapot, enameled salt glaze, "Landskip", Eng., ca. 1765, chips restored, 4½" H . . . . .N/S
Salt Glaze Teapot, enamel dec., covered, Eng., ca. 1760, 4¾" H $2,530.00
Staffordshire Teapot, white salt glaze, covered, Eng., ca. 1760, fossil design in blk. to a blue field, chips & repairs, 4½" H N/S

A-MA May 1997   Skinner

Wedgwood Jelly Mold, Queen's ware w/ cover, Eng., late 18th C., polychrome enamel floral dec., chips, impr. mark, 10½" H $4,025.00

A-MA May 1997   Skinner

Wedgwood Bowl, Fairyland Lustre, Eng., ca. 1920, patt. Z4968, printed mark, 9" diam. $3737.50

A-VT Apr. 1997   Am. Stoneware Auction
Batter Jug, 1 gal., dotted flowers, base chip $400.00

A-VT Apr. 1997   Am. Stoneware Auction
Rockingham Spitoon, emb. panels, minor rim chip $30.00

A-VT Apr. 1997   Am. Stoneware Auction
Jar, 1½ gal., L. Lehman & Co, NY, double floral $175.00

A-VT Apr. 1997   Am. Stoneware Auction
Jar, 1 gal., Goodwin & Webster, rim chips $225.00

A-VT Apr. 1997   Am. Stoneware Auction
Pitcher, hound handled, emb. dec., Rockingham glaze, minor chips $140.00

A-VT Apr. 1997   Am. Stoneware Auction
Crock, 2 gal., Athens Pottery, NY, floral, dated 1898, tight line & chips $125.00

A-VT Apr. 1997   Am. Stoneware Auction
Jar, 3 gal., N. Clark & Co., Lyons, fancy floral, repr. $375.00

A-VT Apr. 1997   Am. Stoneware Auction
Churn, 4 gal., Whites, Utica, blue wavy lines $300.00

A-VT Apr. 1997   Am. Stoneware Auction
Jug, 3 gal., W. Whitman, Havana NY, double floral, minor fry $175.00

A-VT Apr. 1997   Am. Stoneware Auction
Crock, 2 gal., Haxstun & Co., Ft. Edward, NY, blue floral, repr. chip $225.00

Left to Right

Buffalo Pottery Deldare
Emerald Vase, stylized foliate motif in shades of gr. & white on an olive ground, stamp mark, 6½" diam., 8½" H $805.00
Pitcher, "The Great Controversy" sgn. W. Fozter, stamped mark, 7" W, 12" H $287.50
King Fisher Vase, Edowlman, olive ground, dec. in stands of gr. & white, stamped mark & artist signature, 6½" diam., 7¾" H $1,380.00
Luncheon Service, pitcher 5½" W, 5¾" H, creamer 4½" W, 2¾" H, sugar 5½" W, 4" H, six teacuts 4¼" W, 2" H, six saucers 6" diam., six luncheon plates 8½" diam., six dessert plates 6¼" diam., serving tray 7" diam., serving bowl 9" diam., mkd. w/ stamp $1,955.00

Row 1, Left to Right

Dedham Pottery
Wild Rose Plate, medium blue dec. on even crackle glaze, stamped in blue, w/ impr. rabbit, 8½" diam. $1,955.00
Wild Rose Plates, one of two, stamped in blue, peppering, 6" diam., also bear plate, 8¾" diam. .$1,035.00
Crab Plate, deep blue, dec. on crackle glaze, stamped in blue, one impr. rabbit, 10" diam. $546.25
Elephant Items, one of four, cup & saucer stamped in blue, 6" diam., 3" H, saucer stamped in blue, pitted, 6" diam., ashtray, stamped in blue, 4" diam., plate, stamped in blue, "Dedham Tercentenary 1636-1936", some staining, 8½" diam. $805.00

Row 2, Left to Right

Turtle Plate, deep blue dec. on fine crackle glaze, stamped in blue, one impr. rabbit, 10" diam. $1,610.00
Turkey Plate, dk. blue dec. on fine crackling glaze, stamped in blue, one impr. rabbit, minor repr., 10" diam. $230.00
Turkey Items, two, cup & saucer, stamped in blue, 6" diam., 3" H, plate stamped in blue, "Dedham Tercentenary 1636-1936", 6" diam. . . . . .N/S

C.U.P.S. Pottery, dolphin plate, dk. blue dec. on a five to ¼" crackle glaze, impr. C.U.P.S., hairlines, 6¼" diam.$402.50

Row 3, Left to Right

Polar Bear Cup & Saucer, deep blue dec. on crackle glaze, stamped blue, 6" diam., 3" H $345.00
Polar Bear Plate, lt. blue dec. on an uneven crackle glaze, stamped in blue, one impr. rabbit, rim nicks, 10" diam. $402.50
Seven Plates, one pictured, iris plate, stamped in blue, one impr. rabbit, 6" diam., iris plate stamped in blue, "H.F.G. Co., 11/13/15", one impr. rabbit, 6" diam., birds in potted ora. tree, stamped in blue, one impr. rabbit, 6" diam., grape plate stamped in blue, one impr. rabbit, repr., 6" diam., pond lily plate, stamped in blue, 6" diam., iris plate, chipped, 6" diam., butterfly plate, nicks, 6" diam. $488.75
Butterfly Plate, deep blue dec. on crackle glaze, stamped in blue, one impr. rabbit, 10" diam. $690.00
Owl Plate, cobalt blue dec. on a stark white crackle ground, stamped twice in blue, rim nicks, 8¼" diam. $1,380.00

Dedham Pottery
Scottie Dogs Plate, deep blue dec. on a crackle glaze, stamped in blue, two impr. rabbits, 8½" diam. $1,955.00
Scottie Dogs Plate, deep blue dec. on fine crackle glaze, stamped in blue, two impr. rabbits, 8½" diam. $1,495.00
Scottie Dog w/ Toad Plate, deep blue dec/ on stark white crackle glaze, stamped in blue, two impr. rabbits, 8½" diam. $1,495.00
Scottie Dogs Plate, deep blue dec. on a crackle glaze, stamped in blue, two impr. rabbits, 8½" diam. $1,610.00

A-MA June 1997   Skinner, Inc.
Haviland Limoges Set, porcelain, Fr., ca. 1880, raised gilt foliate dec. to central enameled pheasant designs, incl. shaped oval platter , 18″ L, 12 plates, 8¼″ diam., & shaped cream dish, 7½″ L $1,495.00

A-PA June 1997   Pook & Pook, Inc.
Clews Platter, historical blue transfer dec. "America & Independence", 19th C., 14¾″ L $1,600.00
Ridgway Platter, historical blue transfer dec. "Alms House, NY", 19th C., minor flake, 16⅝″ L $400.00
Wood & Sons Platter, historical blue, "Niagara from the American Side", 19th C., 14¾″ L $1,500.00
Chamberpot, historical blue transfer dec. "Washington Independence", chips, 19th C., 5½″ H, 9⅜″ diam. $1,600.00

A-VA May. 1997 Green Valley Auctions, Inc.
Cookie Jars
Regal China, Majorette $290.00
Regal China, Davy Crockett .$350.00
Shawnee, Winnie Bank $325.00

A-VA May. 1997 Green Valley Auctions, Inc.
Cookie Jars
Disney, Eyeore, int.white, crazing .$600.00
Twin Winton, Ole King Cole . . .N/S
Shawnee, Smiley $200.00

A-VA May. 1997 Green Valley Auctions, Inc.
Cookie Jars
Am. Bisque, Dog in Basket, flake on rim & base, partial paint $40.00
Am. Bisque, Milk Wagon, dk. horse $50.00
Brush McCoy, Lrg. Peter Pan, darkened crazing $700.00

A-VA May. 1997 Green Valley Auctions, Inc.
Cookie Jars
California Orig., Santa Claus .$200.00
Brush McCoy, Cow w/cat finial, factory gold cat, rope & bell, damage to lid $100.00
California Orig., Superman, worn spot on rear bottom edge . . .$250.00
McCoy, Chef, face is turquoise blue, chip under rim $230.00

A-VA May. 1997 Green Valley Auctions, Inc.
Cookie Jars
Brush McCoy, Elephant, crazing. $275.00
McCoy, Teepee, flakes under base$190.00
McCoy, Christmas Tree, separation on rim of base $350.00
Brush McCoy, Pumpkin w/ lock on door, darkened crazing $375.00

A-VA May. 1997 Green Valley Auctions, Inc.
Cookie Jars
McCoy, Jack-O-Lantern, repr. chip, darkened crazing $375.00
McCoy, World Globe, partial paint, sm. chip $100.00
Redwing, Jack Frost $500.00
McCoy, Barnum's Animals . .$225.00

A-VA May. 1997 Green Valley Auctions, Inc.
Cookie Jars
Am. Bisque, Wilma on Telephone $750.00
Brush McCoy, Hillbilly Frog, separation in brim, repair to base .$4,300.00
McCoy, Red Leprechaun, sm. flake, sm. chips repr. $1,250.00

A-VA May. 1997 Green Valley Auctions, Inc.
Cookie Jars
Abington, Pumpkin $550.00
Abington, Mother Goose, orig. label $550.00
Abington, Bo Peep $425.00
Abington, Pumpkin, orig. label . .$400.00

A-VA May. 1997 Green Valley Auctions, Inc.
Cookie Jars

Abington, Miss Muffet $350.00
Abington, Wigwam, minor flake .$450.00
Am. Bisque, Yogi Bear, perfect .$325.00
Abington, Jack in the Box . .$325.00

A-VA May. 1997 Green Valley Auctions, Inc.
Cookie Jars
Am. Bisque, Popeye, original pipe $525.00
Am. Bisque, Spaceship, darkened crazing $175.00
Am. Bisque, Olive Oyl, short hairlines, missing flower $1,550.00
Am. Bisque, Popeye, chip on hat, crazing, no pipe $450.00

A-NJ Jan. 1997   David Rago Auctions, Inc.

Roseville Pottery, Luffa Patt.

Row 1, Left to Right

Vase, br., two-handled conical, foil label, 12¼" x 7¼" . . . . .N/S
Vase, gr., two-handled stout, 9¼" x 7" $400.00
Vase, gr. barrel-shaped two-handled, tight hairlines, 9½" x 7" $150.00
Vase, br., tall two-handled, foil label, 12½" x 8" $450.00

Row 2, Left to Right

Vases, two br., two-handled pcs., one barrel-shaped & one tapering, sm. burst glaze bubble, one w/ foil label, both 6" $600.00
Wall Pocket, br., two sm. chips to back, 8¼" x 6" $700.00
Vase, br., two-handled tapering, minute glaze speck, 6¼" x 3¾" $125.00
Vase, gr., two-handled, strong mold & color, 6" x 4" $375.00
Wall Pocket, br., strong mold, foil label, 8½" x 5¾" $700.00
Candlesticks, 3 br., two-handled, bruise to rim of one, 5" x 3¼" $250.00

A-NJ Jan. 1997   David Rago Auctions, Inc.

Roseville Pottery, Wisteria Patt.

Row 1, Left to Right

Vase, two-handled conical, 8¼" x 4½" $375.00
Vase, br., fine two-handled, excellent mold, hairline & bruise, foil label, 15½" x 7" $700.00
Vessel, spherical two-handled, minor nick, foil label, 6" x 8½" $500.00
Vase, blue two-handled conical, 9¼" x 6½" $900.00
Vase, br., two-handled, minor roughness to rim, 5" x 6½" $225.00

Row 2, Left to Right

Vase, br. tapering, two-handled, sm. firing discoloration, 3⅞" x 6¼"$175.00
Vase, blue, two-handled, 5½" x 6¼" $400.00
Vase, br., pear-shaped two-handled vase, 6" x 4½" $350.00
Wall Pocket, blue, excellent mold & color, minor flaws, 8¼"x7" .$1,400.00
Squat Vessel, br., two-handled, burst glaze bubble, foil label, 4" x 6½" $250.00

A-NJ Jan. 1997   David Rago Auctions, Inc.

Roseville Pottery, Futura Patt.

Row 1, Left to Right

Vase, squat base in mottled blue-green glaze, foil label 10½" x 7¼" $1,000.00
Vase, "seagull", tight 2" line at rim, 10¼" x 4¼" $600.00
Vessel, two-handled, four-sided vessel in pink & gr., 8¼" x 6¼" $650.00
Vase, two-handled, flaring on a pedestal base, 12¼" x 4¾" .$1,500.00
Vase, w/ a stepped-in rim, gr. gloss finish, sm. drill hole, blk. label, 10¼" x 8" $500.00

Row 2, Left to Right

Vase, beehive-shaped two-handled, 7" x 5½" $1,100.00
Vase, pink two-handled, 4" x 6½" $300.00
Vase, pink & blue star-shaped, restoration to points & nick, blk. label, 8¼" x 3¾" . . . . .N/S
Window Box, w/ gr. buttresses on ora. & blue ground, restorations, short hairline, blk. label, 5" x 16" x 5" .N/S
Vase, flaring four-sided in matte pink & greyish-green, 7¼"x3½" sq. $550.00

A-PA April 1997   Pook & Pook Inc.

Row 1, Left to Right

Cup & Saucer Sets, two Gaudy Dutch & deep dish in the Urn patt., 6" diam. $500.00
Teapot, Gaudy Dutch in Grape patt., 11¼" L, 6" H, sm. crack, together w/ covered sugar in Oyster patt., 5½" H $900.00
Teapot, Gaudy Dutch in the Double Rose patt., 10½" L, 6¼" H . .$1,600.00

Cup & Saucer, Gaudy Dutch in the Sunflower patt., 4¼" H, w/ creamer . .$1,300.00

Row 2, Left to Right

Cup Plate, Gaudy Dutch in the Double Rose patt., 4⅜" diam., hairline, together w/ Gaudy Dutch plates in the War Bonnet patt., 6" diam., crack & Grape patt., 6¼" diam., ...$600.00
Cup & Saucer, Gaudy Dutch in the Dove patt., together w/ 2 cup & saucer sets in the Single Rose patt., minor loss to rim $1,700.00
Creamer & Sugar, Gaudy Dutch, in Single Rose patt., repr. to lid of sugar, 3¾" & 5½" H $1,100.00
Coffee Pot, dome lidded, Gaudy Dutch in the Single Rose patt., 11¾" H $8,500.00
Teapot, Gaudy Dutch in Grape patt., 11¼" L, 6" H, sm. crack, together w/ covered sugar in Oyster patt., 5½" H $900.00
Deep Dishes, two Gaudy Dutch in the War Bonnet patt., 8¼" diam. $1,300.00

Deep Dish & Bowl, Gaudy Dutch in the Carnation patt., 10" H, & 5⅝" diam., losses to rim dec. of bowl $1,300.00

Row 3, Left to Right

Cup & Saucer Sets, two Gaudy Dutch in the Butterfly patt. $1,000.00
Creamer & Sugar, Gaudy Dutch, in Single Rose patt., repr. to lid of sugar, 3¾" & 5½" H $1,100.00
Deep Dish & Bowl, Gaudy Dutch in the Carnation patt., 10" H, & 5⅝" diam., losses to rim dec. of bowl $1,300.00
Cup Plate, Gaudy Dutch in the Double Rose patt., 4⅜" diam., hairline, together w/ Gaudy Dutch plates in the War Bonnet patt., 6" diam., crack & Grape patt., 6¼" diam., ...$600.00
Cup & Saucer, Gaudy Dutch in the Sunflower patt., w/ creamer 4¼" H $1,300.00
Cup & Saucer Sets, two Gaudy Dutch & deep dish in the Urn patt., 6" diam. $500.00

A-VA May. 1997 Green Valley Auctions, Inc.

Cookie Jars

Blk. Americana, Mammy, mosaic tile, blue dress $450.00

Blk. Americana, Weller Mammy $1,900.00

Blk. Americana, Mammy, mosaic tile, yel. dress, repr. $450.00

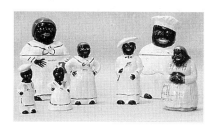

A-VA May. 1997 Green Valley Auctions, Inc.

Cookie Jars

Row 1, Left to Right

Blk. Americana, Mammy, Pearl China Co., repr. chip $550.00

Blk. Americana, Chef, Pearl China Co. $850.00

Row 2, Left to Right

Blk. Americana, Sm. Salty & Peppy, Pearl China Co., minor flakes .$40.00

Blk. Americana, Lg. Salty & Peppy, Pearl China Co. $200.00

Blk. Americana, Mammy String Holder, National Silver Co. $170.00

A-VA May. 1997 Green Valley Auctions, Inc.

Cookie Jars

Blk. Americana, Mammy, partial paint & crazing $225.00

Blk. Americana, Luzianne Mammy, touch up $650.00

Blk. Americana, Chef, sm. hairline, normal crazing $275.00

A-IA Mar. 1997   Jacksons

Pitcher, blue/grey stoneware, acanthus leaf mold, Schroeder Bros. $423.00

A-NJ Jan. 1997   David Rago Auctions, Inc.

Roseville Pottery

Row 1, Left to Right

Falline Vase, br. two-handled ribbed,¼" firing flaw, sm. bruise, 9½" x 8" . . . . .N/S

Falline Vase, br. two-handled ribbed, great mold, base chip re-glued, 9" x 7¾" $500.00

Ferrella Bowl & Vessel, br. oval footed bowl, 5½", & a two-handled squat vessel, 6¼" $550.00

Falline Urn, br., foil label, 8¼" x 6" $650.00

Falline Vase, blue footed w/ two lrg. handles, sm. chip repr., 6¼" x 6¼" . . . N/S

Ferrella Centerpiece Bowl, w/ attached frog, short hairline, 5" x 9½" $150.00

Row 2, Left to Right

Ferrella Bowl & Vessel, br. oval footed bowl, 5½", & a two-handled squat vessel, 6¼" $550.00

Ferrella Squat Vessel, w/ two upward handles, sm. firing chip, glazed over, 4¼" x 6" . . . . .N/S

Falline Ovoid Vase, br., two-handled, 6¼" x 5" $600.00

Falline Vase, br., two-handled, 7" x 5½" $500.00

Farrella Centerpiece Bowl, w/ attached flower frog, restoration to sm. chips, 4½" x 9½" $125.00

A-NJ Jan. 1997   David Rago Auctions, Inc.

Roseville Pottery, Sunflower Patt.

Row 1, Left to Right

Ovoid Vase, good mold & color, 8¼" x 6" $1,100.00

Vase, ¾" spider crack, 10" x 7½" $650.00

Jardiniere, excellent mold & color, 6" x 8¼" $800.00

Vase, crisp mold, repr. at rim, 8" x 6¾" $550.00

Row 2, Left to Right

Squat Vase, two-handled, 5" x 5" $450.00

Vase, two-handled tapering, 5" x 4¼" $425.00

Vase, two-handled, 5" x 4" . .$425.00

Vase, two-handled, 5" x 4" . .$425.00

Vase, flaring, good mold & color, blk. label, 7¼" x 5" $700.00

Vase, two-handled w/ flaring rim, strong mold & color, 4" x 5¾" $475.00

Vase, two-handled, burst bubble at base, short hairline, 4" x 5½" .$300.00

Vase, two-handled cylindrical, 6" x 5" $425.00

Vase, two-handled cylindrical, burst bubble to rim, 6" x 5" $325.00

A-NJ Jan. 1997   David Rago Auctions, Inc.

Roseville Pottery

Row 1, Left to Right

Jonquil Jardiniere, two handled, crisp mold, great color, nicks, blk. label 8¼" x 10¾" $450.00

Jonquil Jardiniere, two-handeled, good mold, nicks on high points, blk. label, 9" x 12" . . . . .N/S

Row 2, Left to Right

Jonquil Vase, two-handled flaring, strong mold, minute bruise, incised 4, 7¼" x 4¾" $150.00

Jonquil Vase, two-handled gourd-shaped, sm. nick, 7" x 8" $200.00

Jonquil Vase, two-handled vase, good mold, burst bubbles, blk. label, 9¼" x 6¼" $350.00

Dahrose Vase, two-handled, 6¾" x 7½" $350.00

A-IA Nov. 1996   Jackson's

A-MA Oct. 1996   Skinner, Inc.

Left to Right

Marblehead Pottery Vase, stylized lt. blue foliate design on a dk. matte blue ground, impr. mark, 5½" diam., 6½" H $8,050.00
Marblehead Pottery Vase, deep gr. w/ red highlights, speckled matte gr. ground, sgn. H.T., impr. M.P., 5¼" diam., 6" H $10,925.00

Nippon

118-Wall Plaque, h/p, white rose dec., gr. "M" in wreath mark, 10" diam. $82.50
119-Humidor, h/p, House in meadow, EE mark, 6½" H $192.50
120-Wall Plaque, h/p, Indian on horseback, gr. "M" in wreath mark, 10½" diam. $990.00
121-Wall Plaque, h/p, Moriage Florals, gr. maple leaf mark, 8" diam. $82.50
122-Wall Plaque, h/p, Fall scene, gr. "M" in wreath, 10" diam. $60.50
123-Pitcher, h/p, House in meadow scene, gr. "M" in wreath mark, 8" diam. $88.00

124-Table Lamp, h/p, two lt., cut glass finial carved walnut base, 22" H $220.00
125-Tankard, h/p, gr., gold, red florals on blk. ground, gr. "M" in wreath mark, 5½" H $110.00
126-Chamber Stick, h/p, Moriage & florals, no mark, 7" H $49.50
127-Bowl, h/p, Egyptian motif, gr. "M" in wreath mark, 7½" diam. $275.00
128-Condiment Set, h/p, four pc., House in Meadow, mustard, s&p, tray, gr. "M" in wreath mark $38.50
129-Bowl, h/p, Pickard Studio dec., Pickard gold leaf mark, 7½" diam. $165.00

A-PA Mar. 1997   Glass Works Auctions

Shaving Mug, Am., ca. 1885-1925, Order of Elks, "T & V Limoges Fr.", 3⅞" H $70.00
Shaving Mug, Am., ca. 1885-1925, emblem of American Order of Knights of Maltese Cross, 3½" H $250.00
Shaving Mug, Am., ca. 1885-1925, bust of an Indian, "T & V Limoges Fr.", 3⅝" H $160.00

A-PA Mar. 1997   Glass Works Auctions

Shaving Mug, Am., ca. 1885-1925, cabinet makers tools, 3⅜" H, worn gold trim $130.00
Shaving Mug, Am., ca. 1885-1925, baker putting bread into an oven, 3⅝" H $95.00

A-PA Mar. 1997   Glass Works Auctions

Shaving Mug, Am., ca. 1885-1925, farmer plowing his field,½" chip, "T & V Limoges Fr.", 3⅝" H $145.00
Shaving Mug, Am., ca. 1885-1925, blacksmith shoeing a horse, "T & V Limoges Fr.", 3⅝" H $300.00
Shaving Mug, Am., ca. 1890-1925, horse drawn "Ice" wagon, "T & V" 3½" H $425.00

A-PA Mar. 1997   Glass Works Auctions

Shaving Mug, Am., ca. 1885-1925, horse drawn blk. coach, "Germany", 3¾" H $375.00
Shaving Mug, Am., ca. 1885-1925, horse drawn delivery wagon, "T & V Limoges Fr.", 2"L chip, 3⅝"H .$180.00
Shaving Mug, Am., ca. 1885-1925, horse drawn high wheel buggy, "T & V" 4" H $210.00

A-IA Nov. 1996   Jackson's

Nippon

1-Handled Vase, h/p, coarse linen finish, gold dec., gr. maple leaf mark, 5½" H $687.50

2-Vase, h/p, fine linen finish, yel. & pink roses, blue maple leaf mark, 5" H $385.00

3-Vase, h/p, fine linen finish, gold art deco dec., blue maple leaf mark, 8" H $1,265.00

4-Charger, h/p, fine linen tapestry finish, raised gold edge, blue maple leaf mark, 12" diam. $2,640.00

5-Basket, h/p, linen tapestry finish, blue maple leaf mark, 9" H .$1,870.00

6-Vase, h/p, fine linen tapestry finish, blue maple leaf mark, 6" H . . .$990.00

7-Vase, h/p, coarse linen tapestry finish, w/ h/p birds & florals, blue maple leaf mark, 6" H $440.00

8-Whiskey Jug, h/p, Eng., Moriage dec. handle, gr. "M" in wreath mark, no stopper, 6" H $385.00

9-Vase, h/p, 2 handled, gold thistle dec., blue maple leaf mark, 7" H . . . .
. . . .$440.00

10-Lidded Urn, h/p, rose floral dec., raised gold dec., gr. maple leaf mark, 8" H $935.00

11-Whiskey Jug, h/p, w/ stopper, Egyptian motif, adv. E.M. Higgins Old Velvet, gr. "M" in wreath mark, 6½" H $825.00

12-Basket, h/p, handled, blue "M" in wreath mark, 10" H $880.00

13-Vase, h/p, 2 handled, raised gold dec., gr. maple leaf mark, 10" H $550.00

14-Vase, h/p, handled, blue maple leaf mark, 7½" H $440.00

15-Vase, h/p, floral dec. w/ gr. "M" in wreath mark, 12" H $522.50

16-Vase, h/p, cobalt blue, gold dec., blue maple leaf mark, 7" H . .$462.50

17-Vase, h/p, pretzel handles, gold floral dec. w/ raised enameling, blue wreath mark, 9½" H $192.50

18-Basket Vase, h/p, handled, raised gold dec. w/ colored enameling, blue maple leaf mark, 9" H $550.00

19-Jug, h/p, Griffins head on handle, art deco floral & gold dec., blue maple leaf mark, no stopper, 7" H . .$137.50

20-Vase, h/p, 2 handled, cartoon scene, gr. "M" in wreath mark, 5" H $275.00

21-Mug, h/p, Egyptian warship, gr. "M" in wreath mark, 6" H . . .$385.00

22-Tray, h/p, Arab by the Campfire, blue maple leaf mark, 11" x 7½" .$440.00

23-Hanging Basket, h/p, gr. "M" in wreath mark, hairline crack, 6" H $82.50

24-Vase, h/p, Moriage, gr. maple leaf mark, 5½" H $82.50

25-Vase, h/p, 3 handled, elephant head & tusk handles, gr. "M" in wreath mark, 7" H $467.50

26-Vase, h/p, 2 handled, gold dec., blue maple leaf mark, 5" H . .$357.50

27-Vase, h/p, winter scene, gr. TE-OH Nippon mark, 7" H $220.00

28-Jug, h/p, Moriage dec., mauve & chartreuse background, gold L&R crown Nippon mark & dec. touch marks, no stopper, 9" H $165.00

29-Bowl, h/p, Moriage dec., gr. "M" in wreath, 9" H $192.50

30-Vase, h/p, Moriage dec. gr. "M" in wreath mark, 9" H $275.00

31-Candlestick, h/p, cartoon scenic, gr. "M" in wreath mark, 8½" H $247.50

32-Ewer, h/p, yel. & red roses w/ gold dec. lattice, blue maple leaf mark, 7" H $82.50

33-Bowl, h/p, Jap. pagoda scene, raised enameling, gr. "M" in wreath mark, 6½" diam. $38.50

34-Vase, h/p, Moriage dec., gr. "M" in wreath mark, 8½" H $330.00

35-Floral Plaque, h/p, roses in Moriage basket, gr. "M" in wreath mark, 10" diam. $247.50

36-Vase, h/p, cartoon scene, blue maple leaf mark, 8½" diam. . . .$330.00

37-Bowl, h/p gold handled, gr. "M" in wreath mark, 7" diam. $44.00

A-MA Oct. 1996   Skinner, Inc.

Teco Pottery Buttress Vase, satin matte gr. glaze, impr. Teco three times, 5½" diam., 10¼" H $2,300.00
Teco Pottery Vase, bulbous-form w/ flaring rim under a satin matte gr. glaze, impr. Teco twice, 4¾" diam., 6" H $402.50

A-IA Nov. 1996   Jackson's

Nippon unless noted

38- Vase, h/p, Moriage gold dec., blue maple leaf mark, 9" H $99.00

39-Covered Urn, h/p, "Peace Bringing Back Abundance", on rev., floral on obverse, h/p Nippon in script, 11½" H . . .$2,200.00

40-Ewer, h/p, red & yel. roses on gold lattice, gr. luster dec., blue maple leaf mark, 12½" H $385.00

41-Tankard, h/p, Moriage dec. w/ yel. & red floral on gold background, unmkd., 16" H $715.00

42-Vase, h/p, Mt. Fuji in background, cobalt blue dec., red SNK mark, 12½" H $440.00

43-Vase, h/p, gold dec. w/ red & purple grapes, blue maple leaf mark, 11½" H $192.50

44-Vase, h/p, purple ground behind a gr. iron fence, blue imperial mark, 8½" H $110.00

45-Ginger Jar, h/p, unusual Moriage Bird of Paradise, raised enamel blk background, Nippon circle mark, 6½" H $110.00

46-Vase, h/p, Moriage dec., gr. "M" in wreath mar, 8" H $302.50

47- Spoon Holder, h/p, scenic dec., gr. "M" in wreath mark, 8" L .$110.00

48-Spoon Holder, h/p, gr. "M" in wreath mark, 8" L $55.00

49-Vase, h/p, w/ raised Moriage dec., gr. "M" in wreath mark, 9½" H $330.00

50-Vase, h/p, gr. "M" in wreath mark, 6½" H $82.50

51-Vase, h/p, azure blue background, blue maple leaf mark, 9" H . . .$330.00

52-Vase, h/p, Coralene, stylized yel. florals, azure blue background, burgandy kinran mark w/ pat. date, 9" H $907.50

53-Wall Plaque, h/p, Galle scene, Moriage dec., blue maple leaf mark, 10" diam. $247.50

54-Relief Plaque, h/p, molded in, lion & lioness, gr. "M" in wreath mark, 10½" diam. $440.00

55-Vase, h/p, blown out dec., raised gold enameling, blue maple leaf mark, 9" H $880.00

56-Vase, h/p, floral dec., gr. "M" in wreath mark, 8½" H $165.00

57-Ewer, h/p, Moriage dragon dec., w/ yel. glass eyes, Paulownia flower & leafs mark, 10½" H $495.00

58-Cracker Jar, h/p, footed, Moriage dragon dec., gr. "M" in wreath mark, 7" H $412.50

59-Candlestick, h/p, Moriage dragon dec., sq. base, gr. "M" in wreath mark, 11" H $110.00

60-Cracker Jar, h/p, covered, 3 footed, gold dec., blue "M" in wreath mark, 7½" H $55.00

61-Tankard, h/p, w/ flared base, raised gold enamel dec., blue maple leaf mark, 10" H $82.50

62-Vase, h/p, hidden image florals along collar, blue maple leaf mark, 9" H $330.00

No Longer Nippon

63-Wedgewood Creamer & Sugar, h/p, gr. "M" in wreath mark, 5" H $357.50

64-Wedgewood Bowl, h/p, 3 figural winged griffin base, rose floral int., gr. "M" in wreath mark, 8" diam. $605.00

65-Wedgewood Loving Cup, h/p, white on blue floral, gr. "M" in wreath mark, 5½" H $302.50

66-Wedgewood Basket, h/p, w/ enameled cherry blossom dec., gr. "M" in wreath mark, 5½" H $275.00

67-Wedgewood Bread Tray, h/p, rim w/ rose floral int., gr. "M" in wreath mark, 10½" L $137.50

Nippon

68-Humidor, h/p, sailboat scene, gr. "M" in wreath mark, 5½" H . .$742.50

69-Humidor, h/p, owl in pine tree, gr. "M" in wreath mark, 5½" H . .$82.50

70-Humidor, h/p, floral & fern dec., blue maple leaf mark, 6" H . .$220.00

71-Ashtray/Match Holder, h/p, art deco, rising sun mark, 3" H . . .$60.50

72-Humidor, h/p, sailboat scene, gr. "M" in wreath mark, 5½" H . .$522.50

73-Cigarette Box, h/p, covered, gr. "M" in wreath mark, 4½" x 3½" x 2½" $467.50

74-Humidor, h/p, w/ faux coralene enamel dec., gr. "M" in wreath mark, 7" H $880.00

75-Humidor, h/p, art deco design, rising sun mark, 5" H $82.50

76-Ashtry/Match Holder, h/p, gr. "M" in wreath mark, 3½" H . . .$93.50

77-Humidor, h/p, pictorial hunt scene, blue maple leaf mark, 6" H $275.00

78-Humidor, h/p, art deco, gr. "M" in wreath mark, 5" H $66.00

79-Humidor, h/p, covered, elk scene w/ Moriage oak leaves & acorns, gr. "M" in wreath mark, 5½" H . .$880.00

A-PA Mar. 1997   Glass Works Auctions

Shaving Mug, Am., ca. 1885-1925, steer's head & crossed butcher's tools, "J & C Bavaria", 3⅞" H $140.00

Shaving Mug, ca. 1885-1925, cabinet maker, 3⅝" H, ...$400.00

A-OH Dec. 1996   Garth's Auctions

Row 1, Left to Right

Rookwood Vase, matte blue glaze, dated 1928, sm. flake, 5" H . . .$82.50

Legras Cameo Toothpick, sgn., gr. foliage w/ frosted clear ground cased w/ ora. & gr. end of day color, 2⅞" H $60.50

Sabino Glass Owl Vase, opal. greyish pink, engr. "Sabino 1969", 4½" H . $412.50

Bowl, w/ loop of ora. & opal. white, engr. "Sabino 5-1973", 3⅝" H . .$550.00

Wine Glass, deep cranberry & gr., engr. "Sabino", 5⅜" H $220.00

Vase, deep red w/ gr. metallic highlights, engr. "Sabino 1969", 5⅜" H $522.50

Row 2, Left to Right

Porcelain Figurine, "Boehm Hummingbird, 8¼" H $220.00

Royal Worcester Birds, pr., "Audubon Warbler Dendrocca Audubon & Palo Verdi", 8" H $990.00

Porcelain Figurine, 2 birds, "Boehm, Snow Bunting", 12½" L $770.00

Boehm Porcelain Figurines, two, "Cane May Warbler", loose leaf, 9¼" H, & "Crocus", not pictured, 5" H $467.50

A-IA Nov. 1996   Jackson's

Nippon

130-Tea Set, h/p, 11 pc., geese in lake scene, Paulownia flowers mark, $192.50

131-Suger & Creamer, h/p, covered, deer in meadow scene, TN wreath mark, 4" H $165.00

132-Mug, h/p, deer in meadow, TN wreath mark, 5" H $110.00

133-Wall Plaque, h/p, owl on branch, gr. "M" in wreath mark, 8" diam. $220.00

134-Hanging Basket, h/p, floral dec., amber & lt. blue background, gr. "M" in wreath mark, 4" H . . .$506.00

135-Sugar & Creamer, h/p, covered, woodland scene, blue "M" in wreath mark, 4" H $275.00

136-Shaving Mug, h/p, cartoon scene of Indian in canoe, raised enameled dec., gr. "M" in wreath mark, 3½" H $275.00

137-Sugar & Creamer, h/p, covered, pinhead Moriage dec., floral medallions, sugar bowl w/ hidden blownout clamshell dec., no mark, 4½" H$49.50

138-Whiskey Jug, h/p, sailboat scenic, gr. "M" in wreath mark, 5½" H $660.00

139-Pintray, h/p, Galle scene, blue maple leaf mark, 6" L $110.00

140-Sugar & Creamer, h/p, covered, gold dec., gr. "M" in wreath mark, 5" H $110.00

141-Mug, h/p, Moriage dec. handle, gr. "M" in wreath mark, 5" H .$302.50

142-Vase, h/p, gold floral & cobalt, blue maple leaf mark, 5½" H .$357.50

143-Syrup, h/p, covered w/ underplate, gr. "M" in wreath mark, 5" H $192.50

144-Bread Plate, h/p, yel. & red floral w/ gold dec., blue maple leaf mark, 14" L $71.50

145-Cream Pitcher, h/p, cobalt & gold dec. w/ red & pink roses, blue maple leaf mark, 5" H $154.00

146-Nappy, h/p, hunt scene w/ Moriage dec., blue maple leaf mark, 6" diam. $110.00

A-MA June 1997   Skinner, Inc.

Eng. Vase, Moorcroft Flambe Wisteria design, ca. 1930, impr. marks, 16" H $977.50

A-PA Mar. 1997 Glass Works Auctions

Shaving Mug, Am., ca. 1885-1925, bluebird on a dogwood branch, "A. Kern Barber Supply Co. St. Louis", 3⅝" H $140.00
Shaving Mug, Am., ca. 1890-1925, pretty woman, "CFH", 3⅝" H .$210.00

A-PA Mar. 1997 Glass Works Auctions

Shaving Mug, Am., ca. 1885-1925, birds sitting on branch, "J & C Bavaria", 3¾" H $120.00
Shaving Mug, Am., ca. 1890-1925, two horses & two birds, "W.G. & Co. Limoges Fr.' & Koken St. Louis Trade Mark", 3 ⅞" H $120.00
Shaving Mug, Am., ca. 1885-1925, "Use Tonique De Luxe The Liquid Head Rest", 3⅞" H $75.00

A-PA Mar. 1997 Glass Works Auctions

Shaving Mug, Am., ca. 1885-1925, eagle & crossed Am. Flags, "T & V Limoges Fr.", 3⅝" H $120.00
Shaving Mug, Am., ca. 1953, lamp lighter, "Sportsman" in gold gilt, 3⅞" H $80.00

A-PA Mar. 1997 Glass Works Auctions

Shaving Mug, lot of 2, Am., ca. 1885-1925, Odd Fellow Encampment, purple tent, "W Austria", 3⅝" H, & farmer plowing a field, "T & V Limoges Fr." $100.00

A-PA Mar. 1997 Glass Works Auctions

Shaving Mug, Am., ca. 1885-1925, artists pallet, 3½" H $350.00
Shaving Mug, Am., ca. 1885-1925, mkd. "W.G. & Co. Limoges France", 3⅞" H $160.00

A-PA Mar. 1997 Glass Works Auctions

Shaving Mug, Am., ca. 1885-1925, detailed bar room scene, "P. Kawalkowski Made in Ger.", 4" H $200.00
Shaving Mug, Am., ca. 1885-1925, bar room scene, "T & V Limoges Fr." , 3⅝" H $325.00
Shaving Mug, Am., ca. 1885-1925, emblem for Benevolent Order of Railroad Trainmen, "P. German", 3¾" H . . .$170.00

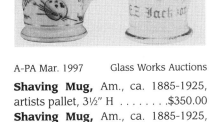

A-PA Mar. 1997 Glass Works Auctions

Shaving Mug, Am., ca. 1885-1925, telegraph key, 3½" H $240.00
Shaving Mug, Am., ca. 1885-1925, tinsmiths bucket & tools, 3½" H .N/S
Shaving Mug, Am., ca. 1885-1925, skull & crossed bones, "T & V Limonges Fr.", 3⅝" H $210.00

A-PA Mar. 1997 Glass Works Auctions

Shaving Mug, Am., ca. 1885-1925, artists pallet, "D. & Co.", 3⅞" H $350.00
Shaving Mug, Am., ca. 1885-1925, hunter & two rabbits, 3⅞" H .$350.00

A-PA Mar. 1997 Glass Works Auctions

Shaving Mug, Am., ca 1953. The Farmer, "John Hudson Moore Co.", 3⅞" H $160.00

A-PA Mar. 1997 Glass Works Auctions

Shaving Mug, lot of 5, Am., 1953, two "The Autoist", "The Horseman", "The Lamplighter", & "The Policeman", all 3¾" H $150.00

A-PA Mar. 1997 Glass Works Auctions

Row 1, Left to Right

Shaving Mug, Am., ca. 1885-1925, electric trolley, "T & V Limoges Fr.", 3⅝" H $425.00
Shaving Mug, Am., ca. 1885-1925, horse drawn open delivery wagon, "T & V Limoges Fr.", 3⅝" H $425.00
Shaving Mug, Am., ca. 1885-1925, emblem for "A.O.K. M.C.", full yel. wrap, "T & V Fr.", 3½" H $250.00

Row 2, Left to Right

Shaving Mug, Am., ca. 1885-1925, horse racing scene, "Koken Barbers' Supply Co. St. Louis U.S.A.", 4" H .$850.00
Shaving Mug, Am., ca. 1885-1925, red caboose w/ letters "P.R.R.", "Koken Barber's Supply Co. St. Louis U.S.A.", 4" H $250.00
Shaving Mug, Am., ca. 1885-1925, breeder standing next to a prized steer, 3⅞" H $400.00
Shaving Mug, Am., ca. 1890-1925, auctioneer in a top hat, "T & V Fr.", 3⅞" H $525.00

A-IA Nov. 1996   Jackson's

Nippon

147-Vase, h/p, art deco, TE-OH mark, 7½" H $71.50
148-Bowl, h/p, red floral dec., gr. "M" in wreath mark, 7½" diam. $110.00
149-Chocolate Pot, h/p, covered, gold, gr. & red dec., blue maple leaf mark, 11½" H $110.00
150-Tray, h/p, Nile scene w/ gold highlights, "M" in wreath mark, 12" diam. $220.00
151-Fernery, h/p, oval, pictorial lake scene, gr. "M" in wreath mark, 8" x 6" $220.00
152-Nut Set, h/p, 5 pc., w/ Moriage dec. of peanuts, gr. "M" in wreath mark, 8" diam. $82.50
153-Vase, h/p, cobalt & gold dec. w/ red roses, blue maple leaf mark, 6½" H
. . . .$38.50
154-Muffiniere, h/p, floral dec., blue maple leaf mark, 5½" H $126.50
155-Nappy, h/p, gold floral & grape dec., RC Noritake Nippon mark, 7" L $49.50
156-Bowl, h/p, floral dec. edge, gr. "M" in wreath mark, 7½" diam. $49.50
157-Bowl, h/p, blown out w/ hazelnut dec., gr. "M" in wreath mark, 8" L $55.00
158-Basket, h/p, blown out peanut design, gr. "M" in wreath mark, 6" L $99.00

159-Muffiniere, h/p, gold floral dec. on blue background, S & K mark, 5" H
. . . .$71.50
160-Tea Strainer, h/p, 2 pc., gold floral dec., blue maple leaf mark, 4" diam.
. . . .$88.00
161-Toothpick Holder, h/p, 3 handled Nile scene dec. w/ Moriage trees, gr. "M" in wreath mark, 2" H .$143.00
162-Toothpick Holder, h/p, 3 handled, sailboat scene, gr. "M" in wreath mark, 2" H $60.50
163-Toothpick Holder, h/p, 3 handled, roses floral dec., rising sun mark, 2" H $71.50
164-Toothpick Holder, h/p, 3 handled, elk in trees, red background, gr. "M" in wreath mark, 2" H $60.50
165-Teapot, h/p, figural elephant, multi-color floral, circular Nippon mark, 7" H $55.00
166-Incense Burner, h/p, raised enamel dec., blue circular Nippon mark, 6" H $77.00
167-Teapot, h/p, figural elephant, blue w/ multi-color floral, circular Nippon mark, 7" H $66.00
168-Toothpick Holder, h/p, 3 handled, sailboat scene, gr. "M" in wreath mark, 2" H $126.50
169-Toothpick Holder, h/p, 3 handled, sailboat scene, gr. "M" in wreath mark, 2" H $93.50

170-Egg Cup, h/p, pictorial scene, repr. stem, 2½" H $11.00
171-Egg Cup, h/p, sailboat scene, 2½" H $82.50
172-Tea Strainer, h/p, 2 pc., gold & burgundy dec., blue maple leaf mark, 4½" diam. $176.00
173-Syrup, h/p, covered & underplate, gold dec. & floral medallions w/ yel. band, gr. "M" in wreath mark, 4½" H $27.50
174-Ring Tree, h/p, blue florals, gold hand, gr. "M" in wreath mark, 3½" diam. $33.00
175-Syrup, h/p, covered & underplate, gold dec., blue maple leaf mark, 4½" H $143.00
176-Ring Tree, h/p, red & pink roses, gold hand, gr. maple leaf mark, 3½" Diam $33.00
177-Syrup, h/p, covered & underplate, gr. & gold dec., blue maple leaf mark, 6" H $60.50
178-Hat Pin Holder, h/p, hanging, purple violet florals, blue maple leaf mark, 7" L $324.50
179-Ring Tree, h/p, gr. maple leaf mark, 3½" H $44.00
180-Syrup, h/p, curved & underplate, repr., gold dec. w/ red & yel. roses, RC Noritake Nippon mark, 5" H $44.00
181-Ring Tree, h/p, w/ bluebirds, gr. crown mark, 4" H $27.50
182-Syrup, h/p, covered & underplate, gold floral dec., blue wheel mark, 4½" H $11.00
183-Trivet, h/p, cottage pictorial, gr. "M" in wreath mark, 6½" diam. . .
. . . .$137.50
184-Bowl, h/p, Egyptian princess portrait, gr. "M" in wreath mark, 7" diam. $275.00
185-Bread Tray, h/p, gold dec. w/ floral medallions, gr. RC Noritake Nippon mark, 13" L $110.00
186-Trivet, h/p, Egyptian princess portrait, gr. "M" in wreath mark, 7" diam. $275.00
187-Trivet, h/p, raised enamel dec., gr. "M" in wreath mark, 6" diam. . . . .
. . . .$192.50
188-Ashtray, h/p, Dutch windmill w/ raised enameling, blue maple leaf mark, 5½" diam. $38.50
189-Ashtray, h/p, playing cards, blue "M" in wreath mark, 5" diam. . . . . . .
. . . .$165.00
190-Match Holder, h/p, scenic medallion w/ raised enamel dec., blue maple leaf mark, 5" H $159.50
191-Soups, h/p, set of 4 covered & underplates, blk. & gold dec. w/ floral medallions, gr. "M" in wreath mark, 4" H $165.00
192-Pancake Server, h/p, covered, gold dec., gr. RC Nippon mark, 9" diam.
. . . .$71.50
193-Ashtray & match holder, h/p, cow in meadow scene, gr. "M" in wreath mark, 3" H $280.50
194-Ashtray & match holder, h/p, house on hill scene, gr. "M" in wreath mark, 6" x 4" $115.50
195-Ashtray, h/p, sailboat sunset scene, gr. "M" in wreath mark, 5" diam.
. . . .$192.50

A-IA Nov. 1996   Jackson's

Nippon

81- Fernery, h/p, Nile scene, orig. tin liner, gr. "M" in wreath mark, 3" H $385.00

82-Fernery, h/p, poinsettia dec., gr. "M" in wreath mark, 3½" H . . .$55.00

83-Fernery, h/p, 3 sided, Egyptian dec., gr. "M" in wreath mark, 4" H $357.50

84-Fernery, h/p, 3 footed, w/ raised enameling, gr. "M" in wreath mark, 8" diam. $110.00

85-Fernery, h/p, 3 sided, Moriage dec., gr. "M" in wreath mark, 4" H $385.00

86-Fernery, h/p, sq. footed, gold dec. w/ enameled jewels, tin liner, blue maple leaf mark, 6" sq. $137.50

87-Fernery, h/p, rose & gold dec., blue maple leaf mark, hairline, 7" diam. $165.00

88-Milk Server, h/p, covered w/ underplate, floral banded dec., gr. "M" in wreath mark, 6" H $110.00

89-Milk Server, h/p, covered, matching underplate, red & floral dec., gr. maple leaf mark, 6" H $165.00

90- Milk Server, h/p, covered w/ matching underplate, floral & gold band dec., blue "M" in wreath mark, 6" H $110.00

91-Cracker Bowl, h/p, art deco dec. w/ gold handles, gr. "M" in wreath mark, 5" H $137.50

92-Milk Server, h/p, covered w/ matching underplate, purple & red rose handled dec., blue maple leaf mark, 6" H $110.00

93-Milk Server, h/p, covered, gr. luster w/ gold dec., matching underplate, blue maple leaf mark, 6½" H . .$110.00

94-Milk Server, h/p, covered, w/ matching underplate, gr. "M" in wreath mark, 6" H $137.00

95-Fernery, h/p, hexagon footed, floral dec., gr. "M" in wreath mark, 4½" H $110.00

96-Cracker Jar, h/p, 3 handled footed, multi-colored dec., gr. "M" in wreath mark, 6½" H $110.00

97-Wall Plaque, h/p, white Moriage, gr. "M" in wreath mark, 9" diam . . .$330.00

98-Cracker Bowl, h/p, covered, gold dec. w/ florals, RC Nippon mark, 5½" H $55.00

99-Cracker Bowl, h/p, pictorial scene, gr. "M" in wreath mark, 5" H $71.50

100-Matching Vases, h/p, pr., pictorial scene, gr. "M" in wreath mark, 7" H $55.00

101-Cracker Jar, h/p, covered, floral & gold dec., crown Nippon mark, 7" H $137.50

102-Vase, h/p, 3 handled, EE mark, 10" H $165.00

103-Vase, h/p, Moriage scrolled dec., floral background, tree crest mark, 5½" H $137.50

104-Vase, h/p, red & white iris florals, EE mark, 9" H $302.50

105-Cracker Bowl, h/p, gold rococo dec., gr. background w/ h/p floral medallions each mkd. RC Noritake Nippon, 6½" H $55.00

106-Milk Server, h/p, underplate, RC Noritake mark $302.50

107-Wall Plaque, h/p, pictorial scene, gr. "M" in wreath mark, 8½" diam. $71.50

108-Vase, h/p, purple & gr. wisteria w/ gold dec., blue maple leaf mark, 9" H $192.50

109-Powder Jar, h/p, covered, cobalt & gold grape dec. w/ h/p center, apricot & floral dec., gr. "M" in wreath mark, 6½" diam. $203.50

110-Sq. Bowl, h/p, ext. dec. in br. & blk. mottled finish, int. of purple violets, gr. "M" in wreath mark, 8" sq. $60.50

111-Server, h/p, w/ matching trivet, pictorial scene, blue maple leaf mark, 6½" H $330.00

112-Souvenir Plate, h/p, Mt. Ranier & Lake Washington, violet floral on gr. border, SNB mark, 8½" diam. $247.50

113-Pancake Server, h/p, covered, scrolled gold dec., w/ molded rococo design, blue maple leaf mark, 10" diam. $82.50

114-Milk Pitcher, h/p, floral & gold dec., gr. "M" in wreath mark, 7" H $82.50

115-Vase, h/p, pictorial w/ trees in silhouette, gr. "M" in wreath mark, 9½" H $88.00

116-Chocolate Pot, h/p, gold grape dec., blue maple leaf mark, 10½" H $330.00

117-Plate, h/p, pink & yel. roses w/ gold dec. border, gr. maple leaf mark, 10" Diam $60.50

A-MA Oct. 1996   Skinner, Inc.

Left to Right

Weller Sicard Vase, irid. glaze, sgn. Weller Sicard, 4¼" diam., 9" H $1,035.00

Weller Sicard Vase, irid. glaze, sgn. Weller, Sicard, 3" W, 5" H . . .$488.75

Weller Sicard Vase, irid. glaze dec. w/ foliate design, impr. Weller, 557, 6" diam., 7" H $2,415.00

Weller Sicard Vase, ribbed sides, irid. glaze dec. w/ gr. clovers, mkd. "27", 5" W, 8" H $1,092.50

A-VT Apr. 1997   Am. Stoneware Auction

Jug, 2 gal., I. Nusbaum, Albany NY, base chip $75.00

A-VT Apr. 1997   Am. Stoneware Auction

Cooler, 2 gallon, blue sponged dec. $130.00

A-VT Apr. 1997   Am. Stoneware Auction

Crock, 4 gal., N. Rigeberg, NY $175.00

A-VT Apr. 1997   Am. Stoneware Auction

Bowl, nest of 3, emb. w/ blue .$90.00

A-VT Apr. 1997   Am. Stoneware Auction

Crock, 2 gal., Cowden & Wilcox, Harrisburg, drooping floral $250.00

A-VT Apr. 1997   Am. Stoneware Auction

Jar, Whites, Utica, blue emb. leaves $40.00

A-VT Apr. 1997   Am. Stoneware Auction

Jar, 2 gal., N. White, Utica, strong blue floral, minor chips $150.00

A-VT Apr. 1997   Am. Stoneware Auction

Jar, 1/2 gal., impr. F/H. Myers/F, blue floral $150.00

A-VT Apr. 1997   Am. Stoneware Auction

Jar, 1/2 gal., Jas. Hamilton & Co., Greensboro, PA $125.00

A-VT Apr. 1997   Am. Stoneware Auction

Jug, 1 gal., Whites, Utica, chipped in making $275.00

A-VT Apr. 1997   Am. Stoneware Auction

Early Crock, 3 gal., free standing, handles lightly incised on both sides $525.00

A-VT Apr. 1997   Am. Stoneware Auction

Jar, 2 gal., ...$225.00

A-VT Apr. 1997   Am. Stoneware Auction

Jug, 1 gallon, incised blue tulip $1,000.00

A-VT Apr. 1997   Am. Stoneware Auction

Pitcher, 1 gal., incised J.E. Daily w/ flowers, dated 1900 . . . .$525.00

A-VT Apr. 1997   Am. Stoneware Auction

Spittoon, sm., blue floral, minor hairlines $175.00

A-VT Apr. 1997   Am. Stoneware Auction

Crock, 2 gal., NY/Stoneware Co.,/Fort Edward, NY, blue ground, minor fry . . $550.00

A-VT Apr. 1997   Am. Stoneware Auction

Jug, 2 gal., Martin Crafts Boston, deep blue floral $200.00

A-VT Apr. 1997   Am. Stoneware Auction

Jar, 3 gal., Commreaws, impr. swags & tassels, spider line $475.00

A-VT Apr. 1997   Am. Stoneware Auction

Crock, 1½ gal., blue bugle . .$450.00

A-VT Apr. 1997   Am. Stoneware Auction

Jug, 2 gal., Lyman & Clark, Gardiner, ochre floral, minor chips $350.00

A-VT Apr. 1997   Am. Stoneware Auction

Crock, 4 gal., blue bird, repr. crack in back $300.00

A-VT Apr. 1997   Am. Stoneware Auction

Cooler, 2 gal., Harts, Fulton, NY, blue script $325.00

A-VT Apr. 1997   Am. Stoneware Auction

Jug, 2 gal., T Crafts, ochre floral, minor chips $225.00

A-VT Apr. 1997   Am. Stoneware Auction

Crock, 3 gal., Burger & Co., Rochester, NY, blue wreath, minor chips $225.00

A-VT Apr. 1997   Am. Stoneware Auction

Stein, Br. Sleepy Eye, western stoneware, minor line in rim . .$80.00

A-VT Apr. 1997   Am. Stoneware Auction

Churn, 5 gal., J. Burger, Rochester, NY, sunflower & leaves, hairlines $325.00

A-VT Apr. 1997   Am. Stoneware Auction

Crock, 1 gal., L. Lehman & Co., NY, nice floral $225.00

A-VT Apr. 1997   Am. Stoneware Auction

Spongeware Spitoon, dec. all around $70.00

A-VT Apr. 1997   Am. Stoneware Auction

Cake Crock, 1 gallon, strong floral $350.00

A-VT Apr. 1997   Am. Stoneware Auction

Batter Pail, 1 gal., bird on branch, rim chip $725.00

A-VT Apr. 1997   Am. Stoneware Auction
Jar, 3 gal., W. Hart, Ogdensburgh, floral, chip $125.00

A-VT Apr. 1997   Am. Stoneware Auction
Jug, 2 gal., Whites Binghamton, nice floral, ...$250.00

A-VT Apr. 1997   Am. Stoneware Auction
Crock, 4 gal., N. Clark & Co., Lyons, "4" in blue, tight line $80.00

A-VT Apr. 1997   Am. Stoneware Auction
Cooler, 1 gal., "Blind Pig", PA or OH, spout chip $250.00

A-VT Apr. 1997   Am. Stoneware Auction
Jug, 2 gal., Passaic, NJ, script $175.00

A-VT Apr. 1997   Am. Stoneware Auction
Crock, 1 gal., blue drum, minor chips $550.00

A-VT Apr. 1997   Am. Stoneware Auction
Jug, 4 gal., F.B. Norton & Co., MA, parrot on plumes, some fry $250.00

A-VT Apr. 1997   Am. Stoneware Auction
Jug, 1 quart, possibly southern, animal form $200.00

A-VT Apr. 1997   Am. Stoneware Auction
Bottle, 1 qt. spongeware, pour spout w/ loop handle $35.00

A-VT Apr. 1997   Am. Stoneware Auction
Jug, 2 gal., W. Roberts Binghamton, NY, bird on floral, minor fry $250.00

A-VT Apr. 1997   Am. Stoneware Auction
Jar, 2 gal., grocers mark Rochester, NY, rim chips & spider $90.00

A-VT Apr. 1997   Am. Stoneware Auction
Jug, 2 gal., D. Roberts & Co., Utica, NY, blue floral $30.00

A-VT Apr. 1997   Am. Stoneware Auction
Crock, 5 gal., Ottman Bros., Fort Edwards, NY, floral, tight lines & chips $135.00

A-VT Apr. 1997   Am. Stoneware Auction
Bank, figural, great face & form $350.00

A-VT Apr. 1997   Am. Stoneware Auction
Jug, 3 gal., Charlestown, grapes on vine, minor chips $300.00

A-VT Apr. 1997   Am. Stoneware Auction

Jar, 1½ gal., Julius Norton, VT, floral, tight lines & chip $150.00

A-VT Apr. 1997   Am. Stoneware Auction

Billhead, J & E Norton, dated July 1857, 11" x 16", creased $350.00

A-VT Apr. 1997   Am. Stoneware Auction

Cooler, 3 gal., flowers, leaves & dots, minor chips $300.00

A-VT Apr. 1997   Am. Stoneware Auction

Jar, 2 gal., Burger Bros. & Co., NY, floral, repr. chips $150.00

A-VT Apr. 1997   Am. Stoneware Auction

Jug, 2 gal., I. Seymour & Co., Troy, incised bird on leaf, repr. spots $275.00

A-VT Apr. 1997   Am. Stoneware Auction

Jar, 2 gal., strong blue front & back, mishaped $150.00

A-VT Apr. 1997   Am. Stoneware Auction

Crock, 1½ gal., blue floral dated 1876 . . . .$325.00

A-VT Apr. 1997   Am. Stoneware Auction

Whiskey Canteen, emb. Fleishmann Co., minor base chip $50.00

A-VT Apr. 1997   Am. Stoneware Auction

Jug, 3 gal., J & E Norton, Bennington VT, blue floral, base chip $250.00

A-VT Apr. 1997   Am. Stoneware Auction

Cooler, 6 quart, Gate City Water Cooler, floral, minor chip $450.00

A-VT Apr. 1997   Am. Stoneware Auction

Crock, 3 gal., blue floral, one handle replaced $85.00

A-VT Apr. 1997   Am. Stoneware Auction

Ovoid Jar, 2 gal., Clark & Co., Lyons, strong floral $225.00

A-VT Apr. 1997   Am. Stoneware Auction

Churn, 5 gal., C.E. Pharis & Co., Geddes, NY, blue floral, rim chips $425.00

A-VT Apr. 1997   Am. Stoneware Auction

Match Holder, 3", Am. Brew Co., Rochester, NY $130.00

A-VT Apr. 1997   Am. Stoneware Auction

Crock, 3 gal., J. Burger Jr., Rochester NY, double floral, rim chips . .$225.00

A-OH Aug. 1996   Garth Auctions

Hepplewhite Grandfather's Clock, walnut w/ figured walnut veneer & banded inlay, dovetailed bonnet, brass works w/ painted metal face, moon phases dial & calendar movement, w/ weights & pendulum, second hand is missing, veneer damage & repr. & feet replaced, bonnet has lost columns, corner moldings & top of goosenecks replaced, old brass finials have repr., 97¾" H $3,080.00

A-OH Aug. 1996   Garth Auctions

Tall Case Clock, ref. pine, wooden works w/ second hand & painted wooden face labeled "S. Hoadley Plymouth", pewter hands are soldered w/ weights & pendulum, brass finials & H block plinths are replaced, 80½" H $1,650.00

A-MA Mar. 1997   Eldred's

Long Case Clock, PA, walnut w/ turned finial, thirty-hour movement, painted dial sgn. "Daniel B. Garper, AT86, Allentown, Pa.", moon dial w/ revolving globe, works not orig., finial repl., 93" H $1,650.00

A-OH Nov. 1996   Garth's Auctions

Hepplewhite, Tall Case Clock, ref. mah. brass fittings, brass works & metal face not orig., second hand, w/ weights & pendulum, worn, minor veneer damage & sm. patch in door, 94½" H $7,150.00

A-MA June 1997   Skinner

Tall Case Clock, painted pine, Silas Hoadley, Plymouth, CT, ca. 1825, w/ brass urn finials, wooden dial & thirty-hour wooden movement, painted old blk., 91" H $2,530.00

A-MA June 1997   Skinner

Tall Case Clock, pine, Riley Whiting, Winchester, CT, early 19th C., w/ polychrome & gilt wooden dial & thirty-hour wooden weight driven movement, old ref., loss of height, 85" H $1,265.00

A-MA Jan. 1997　　　　　　Skinner

Fed. Tall Case Clock, prob. MA., ca. 1810, glazed tombstone door, white painted moon phase dial & polychrome & gilt Am. shield spandrels & eight-day weight driven movement, imper., 85" H $6,900.00

A-MA Jan. 1997　　　　　　Skinner

Chippendale Tall Case Clock, N.E., late 18th C., painted iron dial w/ dial flanked by free-standing base stop fluted columns, old finish, imper., 93" H $4,025.00

A-MA Jan. 1997　　　　　　Skinner

Fed. Tall Case Clock, cherry inlaid, VT, early 19th C., painted moonphase iron dial inscribed "Nichols Goddard Rutland No 138", old finish, imper., 89¼" H $5,175.00

A-MA Oct. 1996　　　　　Skinner, Inc.

Tall Case Clock, Fed. mahogany inlaid, attrib. to Edward Moulton, Rochester, N.H., 1807-25, w/ moon faced calendar dial & red, gold & gr. spandrels w/ urns & sim. quarter fan inlay, eight-day weight-driven movement, bonnet w/ quarter fan inlay, case w/ stringing & crossbanded mahogany veneer & rope inlay, old surface, two rear feet repl., & minor dial retouch, 91" H $10,350.00

A-MA Oct. 1996　　　　　Skinner, Inc.

Tall Case Clock, Fed. mahogany inlaid, Simon Willard, Roxbury, MA, c. 1800, the hood w/ pierced fretwork joining three reeded plinths above an arched cornice molding & glazed tombstone door w/ white painted dial w/ polychrome & gilt birds in the arch, inscribed "Simon Willard", w/ molded door inlaid w/ cross-banding & flanked by brass mounted stop fluted quarter columns on a base inlaid w/ crossbanding, old finish, imp., 89" H . .$20,700

A-MA June 1997　　　　　Skinner

Fed. Tall Case Clock, cherry inlaid, N.E., ca. 1810, w/ polychrome iron rocking ship dial & eight-day weight driven brass, crossbanded inlay & stringing, ref., restor., 90½" H . .$8,050.00

A-MA Mar. 1997   Skinner

Fed. Tall Case Clock, Boston, ca. 1800, mah. case w/ inlaid stringing, moon phase dial w/ second hand & calendar aperture inscribed "Aaron Willard Jr. Boston", gilt & polychrome Am. shields, old refinish, eight-day brass weight, restoration, 95½" H $19,550.00

A-MA Mar. 1997   Skinner

Fed. Tall Case Clock, mah. inlaid, Boston, ca. 1800, moon phase dial w/ floral painted spandrels, inscribed "warranted for Mr. Daniel Phillips Simon Willard, old ref., restor., 96½" H $40,250.00

A-OH Nov. 1996   Garth's Auctions

Tall Case Clock, ref. walnut case, brass fittings, old painted wooden face w/ new brass works, repl. door, crest & finials, 90½"H 1,760.00

A-MA Mar. 1997   Skinner

Fed. Tall Case Clock, mah. inlaid, MA, ca. 1810, dial w/ polychrome floral dec., second hand inscribed "Sam L Rogers", brass eight-day weight driven movement, old ref., restor., 89¼" H $10,350.00

A-MA Mar. 1997   Skinner

Fed. Tall Case Clock, birch inlaid, prob. MA, 1790-1810, case inlaid w/ stringing, dial w/ polychrome dec., ref., eight-day brass weight driven movement, restor., 86¾" H $6,325.00

A-OH Dec. 1996   Garth's Auctions

Tall Case Clock, Cherry w/ old dk. red opaque finish w/ gold painted trim, dovetailed bonnet, wear & touch up repr. w/ new screws, w/ weights & pendulum, age cracks, some restoration & replm., loose veneer 92" H $1,320.00

A-OH Aug. 1996   Garth Auctions

Ogee Shelf Clock, rosewood veneer facade, brass works w/ separate alarm movement, pendulum & key, "Waterbury", painted metal face & rev. painted glass w/ vintage in blue, yel. & gr., veneer is worn & has repr., 18⅝" H, 12⅛" W $165.00

"Regulator" Wall Clock, w/ oak case, brass works w/ pendulum & key, restored w/ replaced crest & bottom bracket, 37¾" H, 18½" W $192.50

Shelf Clock, Rosewood veneer facade, brass works w/ separate alarm movement, pendulum key, "Seth Thomas", metal face is worn, some veneer damage, rev. painted bird w/ dragonfly, 15¾" H, 10¼" W $192.50

Calendar Shelf Clock, ref. walnut case w/ two dials, double faces mkd. "ST" & "Patented Feb 15, 1876" w/ key, 20" H, 12¾" W $385.00

Ogee Shelf Clock, mag. veneer facade, brass works, pendulum, weights & key, "Chauncey Jerome", metal face is worn & bottom glass has crack, 25¾" H, 15¼" W $220.00

Ogee Shelf Clock, mag. veneer facade, brass works, pendulum, weights & key, "Joseph Ives", metal face is worn, top glass is cracked & bottom glass lost paint, veneer repr., 29½" H, 17" W $632.50

Ogee Shelf Clock, rosewood veneer facade, brass works, pendulum, weights & key, "Seth Thomas", replaced face & paper label is worn, rev. dec. glass has gold lattice & vase of flowers, 25" H, 15¼" W $165.00

Ogee Shelf Clock, w/ double doors, mag. veneer facade, brass works, pendulum, weights & key, "Wm. L. Gilbert", metal face is worn & rev. painted bottom glass is replaced, 30½" H, 16" W $192.50

A-OH Dec. 1996   Garth's Auctions

Tall Case Clock, ref. cherry, dovetailed bonnet, broken arch pediment, brass works w/ painted metal face, phases of moon dial, second hand & calendar movement, replacements, 91½" H $3,850.00

A-OH Aug. 1996   Garth Auctions

Scottish Tall Case Clock, ref. mag. w/ flame veneer, brass works w/ painted metal face, second hand & calendar movement, weights, key & pendulum, well executed repairs & backboards partially replaced, 85½" H $2,145.00

A-PA Nov. 1996   Pook & Pook Inc.

Chippendale Tall Case Clock, Am. gumwood, 8-day wooden faced works, no weights, 87½"H $1,500.00

A-MA June 1997   Skinner, Inc.

George III Tall Case Clock, late 18th C., works sgn. Matt. Worgan, Bristol, w/ wood chopper automation in arch, shaped door & paneled plinth, restoration, 93" H $6,612.00

A-MA June 1997   Skinner, Inc.

George III Tall Case Clock, mah., ca. 1780, works by Thomas Davies, Chester, losses, 95" H $4,140.00

A-OH May 1997   Garth's Auctions

Grandfather Clock, Hepplewhite, cherry w/ old alligatored varnish finish, brass works & painted metal face w/ calendar movement & second hand, w/ weights, pendulum & key, minor repairs to case & feet are repl., floral dec. on face is worn, 91" H $7,150.00

A-MA Oct. 1996   Skinner, Inc.

Blk. Banjo Player Timepiece, painted emb. white metal, Am. or Euro., late 19th c., w/ lever movement, the figure rolls his eyes while he holds a drink sitting on a keg, 9" H, 4" W, 2⅛"D $1,092.50

A-MA Mar. 1997   Skinner

Banjo Timepiece, mah., prob. MA, ca. 1820, carved giltwood case, Eglomise tablets depicting "The Constitution's Escape", restored, 35" H . .$920.00
Fed. Banjo Timepiece, mah., gilt & gesso, Boston, early 19th C., painted dial inscribed "Sawin", gilt framed eglomise tablets, "The Wasp & Reindeer", restored, 33½" H $1,265.00

A-MA Dec. 1996   Skinner, Inc.

Delft Clock, 19th C., blue dec. white, slight glaze wear, 17½" H . . .$316.25

A-OH Oct. 1996   Garth's Auctions

Shelf Clock, mah. veneer case, wooden works, paper label "Eli Terry Jr & Co.", rev. painting & finials repl., face, numbers repainted, w/ weights, pendulum & key, door mkd. "Edward Petz 1805", 31" h $880.00

A-NH Mar. 1997   Northeast Auctions

Shelf Clock, CT, mah. pillar & scroll by Eli & Samuel Terry, 32" H . . .$1,700.00

A-MA Mar. 1997   Skinner

Fed. Shelf Clock, pillar & scroll mah., attrib. to Eli Terry, CT, ca. 1818, wooden thirty-hour weight driven movement, w/ outside escapement, ref., restored, 28¾" H $2,070.00

A-MA Jan. 1997   Skinner

Clock, mah. pillar & scroll, Waterbury, CT, ca. 1825, thirty-hour wooden movement, imper., 16½" W, 4½" D, 29¾" H $920.00

A-MA Jan. 1997   Skinner

Pillar & Scroll Clock, mah., Ephraim Downes, CT, ca. 1825, w/ thirty-hour wooden weight driven movement, old finish, imper., 31" H $920.00
Shelf Clock, mah., E. & G.W. Bartholomew, CT, ca. 1830, flanking blk. painted & stenciled columns, eglomise tablet of landscape, painted wood dial & gilt spandrels, thirty-hour wooden weight driven movement, 16½" W, 29¾" H $690.00

A-MA Dec. 1996   Skinner, Inc.

Louis XVI Mantle Clock, gilt bronze & white marble figural, c. 1790, Cronier, Paris, giltwood oval base, minor losses, 14½" H $3,105.00

A-OH Jan. 1997   Garth's Auctions

Banjo Clock, mah. veneer case w/ inlay, walnut secondary wood, brass works, gilded cast iron eagle replm., repairs to case, faded numerals, 37½" H $1,320.00

A-OH Jan. 1997   Garth's Auctions

Banjo Clock, ref. mah. veneer, repl. eglomise glass & "H. Tifft Pat.", repl. eagle finial, face flaked & crazed, 31½" H $825.00
d
by pierced brass brackets, imper., 34¼" H $1,092.50

A-MA June 1997   Skinner, Inc.

Austrian Mantel Clock, part-gilded beechwood, gilt metal & alabaster mounted temple-form, ca. 1840 w/ mirrored back, restorations, 25"H $2,300.00

A-MA Mar. 1997   Eldred's

Banjo Clock, E. Howard No. 1, dial sgn., Am., 19th C., red, blk. & gilt glasses, walnut case, 50" H $2,750.00

A-MA Mar. 1997   Eldred's

Banjo Clock, E. Howard, dial sgn., Am., 19th C., maroon, blk. & red throat glasses, mah. case, 38" H . .$1,650.00

A-MA June 1997   Skinner, Inc.

Regency Mantel Clock, gilt bronze mounted mah., 19th C., sgn. T. Baldwin London, 19½" H $1,495.00

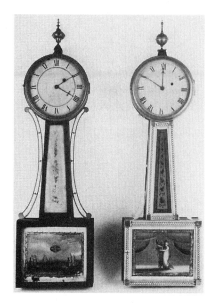

A-MA Jan. 1997   Skinner

Fed. Banjo Timepiece, mah., prob. NH, ca. 1820, molded brass bezel, white painted dial, eglomise tablet inscribed "Constitutions Escape", brass pierced brackets w/ eight-day weight driven movement, imper., 34" H $1,610.00
Fed. Banjo Timpiece, mah. & gilt gesso, MA or NH, ca. 1820, brass bezel, white painted metal dial, eglomise tablets, lower showing woman playing a harp, eight-day weight driven movement, restored, 33¼" H $1,150.00

A-OH Nov. 1996   Garth's Auctions

Banjo Clock, attrib. to Lemuel Curtis, mah. case w/ gilded facade & bracket & brass trim, replms., old regilding w/ repairs to facade, w/ weight, key & pendulum 41" H $3,300.00

A-MA June 1997   Skinner

Fed. Banjo Timepiece, gilt gesso & mah., prob. Concord, MA, ca. 1820, w/ eight-day weight driven brass movement, the lower showing landscape w/ cottage & figure flanked by pierced brass brackets, imper., 34¼" H $1,092.50

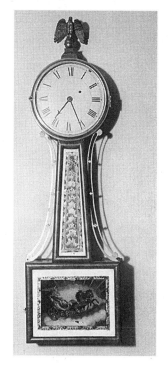

A-OH Nov. 1996   Garth's Auctions

Banjo Clock, mah. & mah. veneer w/ brass trim, flaking & old touch up repr. w/ repainted white borders, repl. finial & repainted face, w/ weight, key & pendulum, 32¾" H $1,265.00

A-MA Mar. 1997   Eldred's

Banjo Clock, E. Howard No. 1, dial sgn., Am., 19th C., red, blk. & gilt glasses, walnut case, 50" H $2,750.00

A-MA Mar. 1997   Eldred's

Banjo Clock, E. Howard, dial sgn., Am., 19th C., red, gr. & blk. glasses, mah. case, 32" H ....N/S

A-MA Mar. 1997   Eldred's

Banjo Clock, E. Howard, dial sgn., Am., 19th C., maroon, blk. & gilt throat glass, mah. case, 28½" H $1,540.00

A-MA Mar. 1997   Eldred's

Banjo Clock, E. Howard, dial sgn., Am., 19th C., maroon, blk. & red throat glasses, mah. case, 38" H . .$1,650.00

A-MA Mar. 1997   Eldred's

Banjo Clock, E. Howard, dial sgn., Am., 19th C., maroon, blk. & gilt throat glass, mah. case, 28½" H $1,100.00

A-MA Mar. 1997   Eldred's

Banjo Clock, E. Howard, dial sgn., Am., 19th C., mah. case, 34" H $1,870.00

A-MA Mar. 1997   Eldred's

Banjo Clock, Am., mah. w/ gilt & reverse-painted throat & lower tablet, brass side arms & presentation bracket, face repainted, finial & weights missing, 37" H $495.00

A-OH Jan. 1997   Garth's Auctions

Banjo Clock, mah. veneer case w/ brass trim, brass works w/ weight & pendulum, veneer damage, face worn, 40½" H $935.00

A-MA Oct. 1996   Skinner, Inc.

Banjo Timepiece, Fed. mahogany inlaid, inscribed "Willard's Patent," Boston, c. 1810, mahogany case w/ brass molded bezel, painted dial, throat eglomise tablets & patriotic tablet of flags & cannons framed by cross banding & stringing & flanked by pierced side arms, tablets appear to be orig. dial repl., 35½" H $6,900.00

A-PA Mar. 1997   Bill Bertoi Auctions

Doorstops
Rooster, 4½" x 3" $495.00
White Rooster, 4½" x 3" $330.00
Cardinal, 5" x 3" $248.00
Brown Owl, 4½" x 3" $468.00
Parrot, Hubley, 4¾" x 2¾" $143.00

A-PA Mar. 1997   Bill Bertoi Auctions

Mechanical Banks
Zoo Bank, iron bank, Kyser & Rex Co., ca. 1894 . .$990.00
Halls Liliput, J & E Stevens Co. $770.00
Halls Liliput, J & E Stevens Co. $1,485.00
Halls Liliput, J & E Stevens Co. $550.00
Afghanistan, Mechanical Novelty Works, ca. 1885, . . .$1,540.00
Bank of Edu. & Econ., Proctor-Raymond Co., nickeled cast
iron, ...$413.00

A-PA Mar. 1997   Bill Bertoi Auctions

Mechanical Banks
Dog on Turntable, Judd Mfg. Co., ca. 1870's, . . .$1,430.00
Dog on Turntable, copper bronze plated, Judd Mfg. Co., ca.
1870's, ...$935.00
Bird on Roof, J & E Stevens Co. $1,595.00
Fortune Teller, savings bank $143.00
Give Me a Penny, Friend W. Smith, Jr., Bridgeport,
CT $2,200.00
United States Safe, J & E Stevens Co., ca. 1880's, missing
paper picture $660.00

A-PA Mar. 1997   Bill Bertoi Auctions

Still Banks
Billy Goat, J & E Stevens Co., ...$2,860.00
Circus Ticket Collector, Judd Mfg. Co., multicolor . . .$2,420.00
Girl in Chair, W.S. Reed Toy Co., Edwin Mosler Collect-
ion $9,350.00
Peg-Leg Begger, Judd Mfg. Co., second casting . .$330.00
Pig in Highchair, J & E Stevens Co., pat. 8/24/1897 . . .$660.00

A-PA Mar. 1997   Bill Bertoi Auctions

Doorstops
Parrot on Stump, 10½" x 7" $83.00
Cocatoo, 8½" x 6½" $165.00
Swallows, Hubley, 8½" x 7½" $633.00
Parrot in Medallion, 9¼" x 5" $110.00

A-PA Mar. 1997   Bill Bertoi Auctions

Doorstops
Sleeping Cat, bronze tone, 3⅜" x 9⅝" $468.00
Hunchback Cat, 10⅝" x 7½" $248.00
Fireside Cat, Hubley, 5⅝" x 10¾" $187.00

A-PA Mar. 1997   Bill Bertoi Auctions

Doorstops
Whippet, 6¾" x 7½" $248.00
Pekingese, Hubley, 14½" x 9" $2,860.00
Puppies in Basket, mkd. "Wilton, Wrightsville, PA," 7" x 7⅜"
. . . .$248.00

A-PA Mar. 1997   Bill Bertoi Auctions

Door Knockers
Butterfly on Flowers, 4" x 2½" $633.00
Butterfly, Waverly Studios, 3½" x 2¾" $495.00
Lrg. Butterfly, Judd Co., 4½" x 4¼" $440.00
Butterfly, Hubley, 3½" x 2¾" $440.00
Woodpecker, Hubley, 3¾" x 2¾" $330.00

A-PA Mar. 1997   Bill Bertoi Auctions

Doorstops

Left to Right

Whimsical Clown, partial repaint, 6½" x 9½" . .$1,760.00
"Chicken Snatcher", 7½" x 8¾" $4,620.00

A-PA Mar. 1997 Bill Bertoi Auctions

Doorstops

Left to Right

The "Tiger", Hubley, sgn. by Fish, 9⅜" x 4¼" . . .$2,310.00
Sm. Footmen, Hubley, sgn. by Fish, 9⅛" x 6" $523.00
Parlor Maid, Hubley, sgn. by Fish, 9¼" x 3½" . . .$1,100.00
Charleston Dancers, Hubley, sgn. by Fish, 8⅞" x 5⅜" $825.00

A-PA Mar. 1997 Bill Bertoi Auctions

Doorstops

Row 1

Clown, two-sided, Judd Co., 8" x 3½" $908.00
Clown, two-sided, 10" x 4½" $2,750.00
Organ Grinder, 9⅞" x 5¾" $495.00
Colonial Lawyer, Waverly Studios, 9⅝" x 5¼" . . .$743.00

Row 2

Pilgrim Boy, Judd Co., 8¾" x 6" $330.00
Swinging Golfer, Hubley, 10" x 7" $743.00
Putting Golfer, Hubley, 8⅜" x 7" $358.00
Colonial Pilgrim, Bradley & Hubbard, sgn. "B&H" .$39.00

A-PA Mar. 1997 Bill Bertoi Auctions

Doorstops

Snooper, embossed "The Snooper", 13¼" x 4½" . .$825.00
Old Salt, full figured, 11" x 4⅛" $330.00
Girl Holding Dress, Bradley & Hubbard, 13" x 6¾" $4,950.00
Large Gnome, mkd. "Pocono Mts.", 13¼" x 6½" . .$358.00

A-PA Mar. 1997 Bill Bertoi Auctions

Doorstops

Jonquils, Hubley, 7½" x 8" $330.00
Zinnias, Hubley, "Made in USA", 9¾" x 8½" $385.00
Calla Lillies, Hubley, "Made in USA", 7¼" x 5⅛" . .$440.00
Narcissus, Hubley, 7¼" x 6¾" $385.00
Flower, 9¾" x 6¼" $413.00
Primrose, Hubley, 7⅜" x 6¼" $715.00

A-PA Mar. 1997 Bill Bertoi Auctions

Doorstops

Fr. Basket, Hubley, 11" x 6¾" $248.00
Tiger Lilies, Hubley, 10½" x 6" $440.00
Lillies of the Valley, Hubley, 10½" x 7½" $385.00
Iris, Hubley, 10⅝" x 6¾" $550.00
Rose Basket, Hubley, 11" x 8" $121.00

A-PA Mar. 1997 Bill Bertoi Auctions

Doorstops

Three Roses in Vase, National Foundry, 10½" x 7" $720.00
Tulips in Pot, blk. overpaint on pot, 10½" x 5⅞" .$633.00
Basket of Tulips, Hubley, 13" x 9" $1,260.00
Poppy Basket, mkd. C.H.F. Co. $2,200.00
Flower, wedged back, 9¼" x 6" $468.00

A-PA Mar. 1997 Bill Bertoi Auctions

Doorstops

Flower, 7½" x 6½" $385.00
Tulip Pot, 9" x 8" $743.00
Modernistic Flower, 10" x 9¾" $1,650.00
Poinsettia, 9¾" x 4⅞" $275.00
Poinsettia, 8½" x 4⅞" $358.00

A-PA Mar. 1997   Bill Bertoi Auctions

Doorstops

Whistling Boy, pot metal, cast iron base, 10″ x 5½″ $413.00
Boy w/ Hands in Pocket, Judd Co., 10½″ x 3⅝″ .$330.00
Major Domo, Judd Co., 8⅜″ x 5⅛″ $138.00
Bellhop, Judd Co., 8⅞″ x 4⅝″ $165.00

A-PA Mar. 1997   Bill Bertoi Auctions

Doorstops

Left to Right

Fawn, sgn. "Taylor Cook", 10″ x 6″ $468.00
Rabbit w/ Tophat, 9⅞″ x 4¾″ $798.00
Game Cock, Hubley, 6¾″ x 7″ $1,073.00

A-PA Mar. 1997   Bill Bertoi Auctions

Doorstops

Left to Right

Sleeping Cat, Hubley, 7½″ x 8″ $1,375.00
Sculptured Cat, mkd. "Sculptured Metal Studios" $880.00
Sitting Cat, 8½″ x 7½″ $413.00

A-PA Mar. 1997   Bill Bertoi Auctions
Beagle Pup Doorstop, 8″ x 7½″. $963.00

A-PA Mar. 1997   Bill Bertoi Auctions

Doorstops

Row 1

Old Woman, Bradley & Hubbard, 11″ x 7″ $1,265.00
Woman w/ Flowers, & shawl $176.00
Woman w/ Parasol, sgn. Sarah Symmons, 12″ x 6¼″ . .$495.00
Woman w/ Muff, 11½″ x 6½″ $209.00

Row 2

Colonial Women, two, 7″ x 3¾″ & 10½″ x 5½″ . . .$330.00
Woman Holding Hat, 8″ x 4½″ $413.00
Two Women, 6⅜″ x 4⅛″ & 6¾″ x 3¾″ $187.00
Three Women, Hubley Span. girl 9″ x 5″, Hubley Fr. girl, 9¼″ x 5½″ & Woman w/ hat Box 6¾″ x 5¼″ $220.00

A-PA Mar. 1997   Bill Bertoi Auctions

Doorstops

Row 1

Dutch Girl, Judd Co., 7⅛″ x 5¾″ $138.00
Boy in Tuxedo, Judd Co., 7¼″ x 4⅜″ $523.00
Lil Bo Peep, 6¾″ x 5″ $275.00
Pied Piper & Miss Muffett, 7¼″ x 5″ & 7¾″ $440.00

Row 2

Maiden, 8⅞″ x 3¾″ $198.00
Boy w/ Basket, fruit basket $330.00
Minuet Girl, Judd Co., 8½″ x 5″ $193.00
Woman w/ Curtsy, Judd Co. $121.00
Little Girl, Judd Co. $688.00

A-MA Oct. 1996 Skinner, Inc.

Turned Low Post Bed, painted & stencil dec., New. Eng., 1830-45, old red ground w/ blk. accents & gold stenciled dec., imp., 46" H, 51" W $920.00

A-NH Mar. 1997 Northeast Auctions

Bedstead, New Eng. Sheraton carved birch, serpentine folding tester, 55" W, 75" L, 66½" H $3,250.00

A-MA Oct. 1996 Skinner, Inc.

Classical Carved Bedstead, mahogany & mahogany veneer, Mid Atlantic states, 1825-35, w/ reeded raked crest above spiral carved columns, on turned feet ending in brass balls, old refinish, minor imp., 34½" H, 79" W, 29½" D $1,265.00

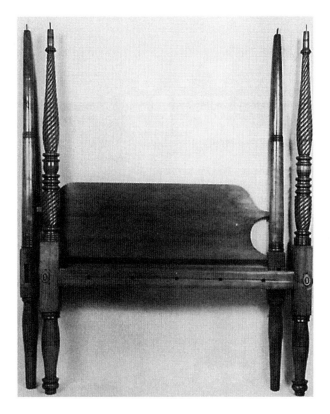

A-MA Mar. 1997 Eldred's

Field Bed, Am. Sheraton, maple w/ rope-turned foot posts, bowed tester, 70" H $1,650.00

A-NH Mar. 1997 Northeast Auctions

Bedstead, Sheraton, red-painted, w/ tester & rails, 57" W, 90" H $5,500.00

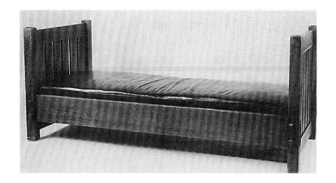

A-MA May 1997   Skinner

Gustav Stickley Day Bed, orig. pegs, med. br. finish, repl. br. leather, 83½" H, 36" D, 34" W $4,025.00

A-MA May 1997   Skinner

Stickley Day Bed, original finish & cushions, 72" W, 28" D, 22" H $1,150.00

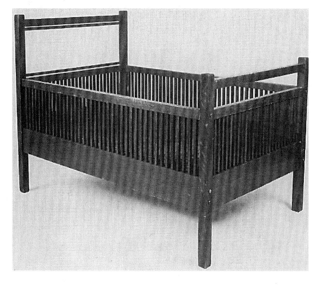

A-MA May 1997   Skinner

Gustav Stickley Child's Bed, orig. deep br. finish, Gustav red decal., nice repl. leather mattress on rope foundation, 35½" W, 56¾" D, 42¾" H $8,050.00

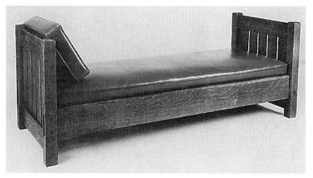

A-MA Oct. 1996   Skinner, Inc.

Stickley Day Bed, orig. finish, repl. br. leather w/ cushion, 80" W, 31" D, 29" H $4,025.00

A-MA June 1997   Skinner, Inc.

Beds, pr., aesthetic carved mah., ca. 1880, 35¾" W, 78" L, 60" H $690.00

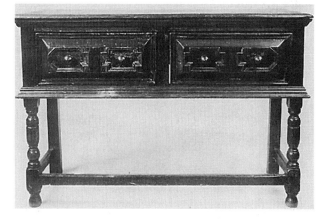

A-MA June 1997   Skinner, Inc.

Baroque Side Table, Italian, walnut, 18th C., top split, 47½" W, 19" D,   32" H $2,300.00

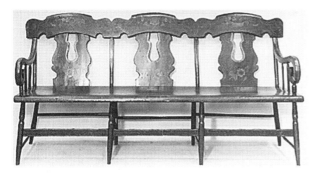

A-OH Aug. 1996 　　　　　　　　　　　Garth Auctions

Decorated Bench, orig. br. paint w/ gr., yel. & white striping & polychrome stenciled fruit & flowers, wear, old touchup repairs & revarnished, one arm has repr., labeled "J. Swint, Chair maker", 77¾" L $1,540.00

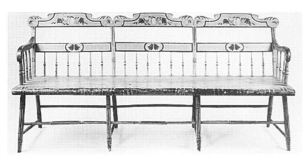

A-MA June 1997 　　　　　　　　　　　　　Skinner

Windsor Armchair, hickory ash & chestnut, PA, 1760-80, old refinish, imper., 38" H $5,462.50

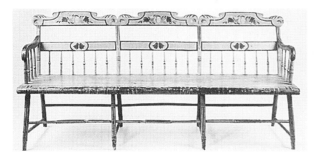

A-MA June 1997 　　　　　　　　　　　　　Skinner

Settee, 1830's, w/ old lt. gr. ground paint, accented by gold & gr. striping, fruit stencil dec., 72" W, 32¼" H　. .$1,955.00

A-PA June 1997 　　　　　　　　　　　Pook & Pook, Inc.

Windsor Bench, PA, ca. 1790, branded 3 times on the seat "D. Perkins", orig. painted surface, repr. to 1 arm, 74¼" W, 30½" H $18,000.00

A-MA June 1997 　　　　　　　　　　　　　Skinner

Settee, PA, early 19th C., yel. ground w/ gold & olive-green fruit & floral stencil dec., early surface, repairs, 32" H, ...$1,725.00

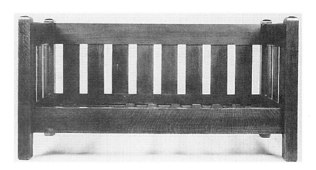

A-MA Oct. 1996 　　　　　　　　　　　Skinner, Inc.

Limbert Oak Settle, orig. medium br. finish, some wear, missing cushions, 74" W, 30" D, 36" H $2,990.00

A-OH May 1997 　　　　　　　　　　　Garth's Auctions

Settle Bench, child size, weathered, repairs & red repaint, 74" L $357.50

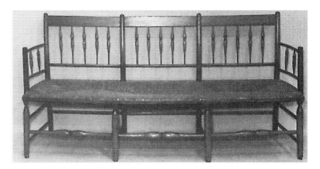

A-OH May 1997 　　　　　　　　　　　Garth's Auctions

Windsor Bench, Sheraton w/ bowed seat frame, ref. hardwood w/ turned spindles, posts & rungs, old rush seat, NY, break in one arm at back post, 73" L $770.00

A-MA June 1997   Skinner

Candlestand, tiger maple & cherry, N.E., early 19th C., old ref., imper., 16" W, 18" D, 27½" H $402.50

A-OH Nov. 1996   Garth's Auctions

Chippendale Candlestand, PA, tile top, ref. walnut, one board dish turned top, attrib. to Lancaster County, age cracks, 19" diam., 29" H . . .$2,310.00

A-OH Nov. 1996   Garth's Auctions

Hepplewhite Candlestand, tilt top, ref. birch base & curly maple top, one board top, traces of old red, latch repl., 16¼" x 22¼", 26¾" H $1,760.00

A-MA Jan. 1997   Skinner

Chippendale Candlestand, prob. Hartford, CT, late 18th C., old ref., imper., 25" H $920.00

A-MA Jan. 1997   Skinner

Fed. Candlestand, maple octagonal, N.E., early 19th C., old surface, minor imper., 16¾" x 19¼", 26¾" H .$517.50
Candlestand, cherry octagonal, prob. CT, early 19th C., old ref., minor imper., 16⅝" x 20⅞", 27⅞" H $690.00

A-MA June 1997   Skinner

Candlestand, tiger maple, N.E., 19th C., sq. molded top, old refinish, imper., 16¼" W, 16¾" D, 25½" H . . .$1,150.00

A-MA Jan. 1997   Skinner

Fed. Candlestand, mah., N.E., ca. 1790, old ref., 15½" W, 22½" D, 28" H $1,265.00

A-MA Jan. 1997   Skinner

Tip Table, mah. carved, N.E., old ref., patch to post, 18¼" diam., 27½" H $805.00

A-MA Mar. 1997   Skinner

Fed. Candlestand, mah. w/ drawer, CT, ca. 1790, old ref., 14¾" W, 14½" D, 29½" H $2,990.00

A-NH Mar. 1997   Northeast Auctions
Chippendale Dining Chairs, set of six, carved mah., prob. Portsmouth, NH $6,500.00

A-MA Jan. 1997   Skinner
Side Chairs, set of six, painted & dec., Mid Atlantic State, 1815-25, dk. gr. ground, w/ gold & yel. striping, cane seats, old surface, minor imper., 32" H $2,185.00

A-MA Jan. 1997   Skinner
Dining Chairs, set of eight, tiger maple, N.E., ca. 1835, ref., minor restoration, 33" H $3,335.00

A-MA June 1997   Skinner
Fed. Side Chairs, set of eight, mah. veneer, Boston, 1815-25, veneered panels, repairs, 32¾" H $4,312.50

A-MA June 1997   Skinner
Windsor Side Chairs, set of six maple & pine, early 19th C., ref., 34½" H $2,875.00

A-MA Oct. 1996   Skinner, Inc.
Masonic Windsor Armchairs, twelve, stamped "C. Robinson maker Rochester NY," 1830-40, rosewood grained w/ a gold Masonic compass & sq. symbol on crest, yel. painted accents, natural maple arms, old surface, minor repairs, 33¼" H ...$7,475.00

A-MA Oct. 1996   Skinner, Inc.
Chippendale Side Chairs, cherry, set of four, CT River Valley, 1760-80, w/ molded seat frames above cabriole legs, pad feet, old refinish, slip seats covered in muslin, imp., 38" H $8,050.00

A-MA Oct. 1996   Skinner, Inc.
Classical Carved Side Chairs, set of four, mahogany, possibly N.Y., ca. 1820, scroll carved crests inlaid w/ brass stringing above carved splats on slip seats & sabre legs joined by carved seat rails, old refinish, imp., 34" H $2,415.00

A-MA Oct. 1996   Skinner, Inc.

Windsor Side Chairs, set of six painted bow-back, w/ five matching & one very similar chair, New. Eng., early 19th c., old blk. paint, imp., 37½" H $8,050.00

A-MA Oct. 1996   Skinner, Inc.

Side Chairs, set of six grained painted, Portland, Maine, attrib. to the Walter Corey Chair Factory, c. 1850, w/ gold & br. graining, simulating rosewood, old dry surface, repl. caning, minor imp., 33½" H $920.00

A-MA Mar. 1997   Skinner

Windsor Side Chairs, set of six, polychome dec., impr. "T.H. Br. Warranted", late varnish, 33½" H, w/ a similar yel. child's chair $3,737.50

A-MA June 1997   Skinner, Inc.

George III Dining Chairs, set of ten, mah., late 19th C., w/ two arm & eight side chairs, upholstered w/ br. leather, arm chairs w/ casters $4,600.00

A-MA Mar. 1997   Skinner

Dining Chairs, set of six, mah. & mah. veneer, N.E., ca. 1820, old ref., 33" H $1,725.00

A-MA Sept. 1996   Skinner, Inc.

Dining Chairs, set of six mah., mid 19th c., comprising two armchairs & four side chairs, restorations, 36¼" H, 34¼" W .$2,070.00

A-MA June 1997   Skinner

Windsor Side Chairs, set of six, N.E., 1800-20, old blk. paint, minor imper. 32½" H $6,325.00

A-MA Oct. 1996   Skinner, Inc.

Left to Right

Stickley Armchairs, U-back, orig. med. br. finish, 27" W, 20¾" D, 36" H $920.00
Stickley Side Chairs, U-back, orig. overcoated med. br. finish, repl. br. vinyl cushions, 19¾" W, 17" D, 36" H $920.00

A-NH Mar. 1997   Northeast Auctions

Q.A. Side Chairs, two matching Philadelphia, walnut, attrib. to William Savery $9,250.00

A-MA Jan. 1997   Skinner

Roundabout Armchair, painted, N.E., mid 18th C., blk. over red paint, old surface, late 19thC. alts, height loss, surface imper., 29" H $1,035.00

A-MA Jan. 1997   Skinner

Side Chairs, two maple & ash banister-back, prob. CT, 1735-75, old rush seats, old ref., minor height loss, 43 - 43½" H $977.50

A-MA Jan. 1997   Skinner

Windsor Highchair, painted, rod-back, N.E., 19th C., "TH" carved under seat, old red paint, minor surface imperf., 32½" H $1,150.00

A-MA Jan. 1997   Skinner

Windsor Side Chairs, pr. of ash & pine, N.E., early 19th C., old ref., repr., 38¾" H $1,150.00

A-MA Jan. 1997   Skinner

Roundabout Chair, red stained maple & ash, N.E., 1780-1800, traces of red paint, minor height loss, surface imper., 29¼" H $747.50

A-MA Jan. 1997   Skinner

Windsor Side Chairs, pr., maple, pine & ash, N.E., ca. 1780, 36½" H $2,990.00

A-MA Jan. 1997   Skinner

Roundabout Chair, red stained maple, N.E., early 19th C., old surface, repairs, paint & height loss, 29" H $690.00

A-MA Jan. 1997   Skinner

Chippendale Side Chairs, pr., Boston-Salem area, 1755-85, upholstered seats, old ref., minor repr., 37½" H $6,900.00

A-MA Jan. 1997   Skinner

Side Chairs, two, Milford, CT, 1790-1800, ref., minor imper., 41¾" H & 42" H $632.50

A-MA Jan. 1997   Skinner

Side Chairs, two maple & ash, banister-back, prob. CT, 1735-75, rush & splint seats, old ref., very minor imper., 44¼" H, & 44½" H $977.50

A-MA Jan. 1997   Skinner

Windsor Chair, pine & ash, CT, 1790-1810, ref., pieced feet, 37⅛" H $920.00
Windsor Chair, ash pine & maple, N.E., ca. 1780, ref., repairs, 36½" H $632.50

A-MA June 1997   Skinner

Windsor Side Chair, CT, ca. 1780, old br. painted surface, 37¼" H $2,990.00

A-MA June 1997   Skinner

Windsor Armchair, maple & ash, CT, 1780-1800, old dk. surface, imper. including rear height loss, 36¼" H $1,610.00

A-MA June 1997   Skinner

Chippendale Side Chairs, pr., mah., PA, 1755-85, shaped crests w/ beaded edges, old surface, imper. 41" H $35,650.00

A-NH Mar. 1997   Northeast Auctions

Q.A. Chair, New Eng., maple in orig. red $5,750.00

A-NH Mar. 1997   Northeast Auctions

Wm. & Mary Chair, CT, red-painted Spanish foot, Southbury area . .$7,000.00

A-NH Mar. 1997   Northeast Auctions

Windsor Armchairs, pr., CT "State House", school of John & Horace Wadsworth, Hartford, ...$17,000.00

A-OH Nov. 1996 Garth's Auctions

Chippendale Side Chair, Newport, RI, walnut w/ old finish, slip seat frame reupholstered in gold velvet, age crack, 38" H $4,950.00

A-OH Nov. 1996 Garth's Auctions

Side Chair, early Boston, maple w/ mellow ref., mortised & pinned back, cracked blk. leather reupholstery, repairs & edge damage, 43⅛" H $6,710.00

A-OH Nov. 1996 Garth's Auctions

Q.A. to Chippendale Chair, transitional, ref. mah., crack in one post, foot partially restored, reupholstered seat in gold striped brocade, 37½" H . . .$715.00

A-OH Nov. 1996 Garth's Auctions

Ladderback Armchair, PA, maple & hardwood w/ old dk. finish, repl. rush seat, restorations, age cracks, 43" H $2,530.00

A-OH Nov. 1996 Garth's Auctions

Hepplewhite Side Chairs, pr., MA, attrib. to Salem, mah. w/ old finish, reupholstered seats worn, 37¾" H $2,420.00

A-OH Nov. 1996 Garth's Auctions

Q.A. to Chippendale Chair, transitional, walnut w/ old finish, repairs, glue blocks in seat frame repl., edge damage, reupholstered in gold stripe brocade, 37½" H $1,155.00

A-OH Nov. 1996 Garth's Auctions

Hepplewhite Side Chair, ref. mah., old seat frame reupholstered in salmon brocade, glue blocks added to seat frame, 37⅝" H $550.00

A-OH Nov. 1996 Garth's Auctions

Chippendale Chair, MA, ref. mah., base of feet worn & drilled out for casters, repairs, reupholstered in dk. red velvet, 37¾" H $1,925.00

A-MA Oct. 1996 Skinner, Inc.

Chippendale Corner Chair, cherry, prob. central MA c. 1780, old finish, 31" H $1,840.00

A-MA Oct. 1996   Skinner, Inc.

Side Chairs, pr., N.Y. City, 1805-15, w/ orig. faux tiger maple ground accented w/ dk. painted striping and stenciled grape clusters centered on the crest & compass seat, orig. surface incl. the seats scored to sim. fine rush, minor imp., 33½" H $1,725.00

A-MA Mar. 1997   Skinner

Windsor Highchair, painted, possible MA, ca. 1780, old worn red umber & blk. graining, freehand yel. dec., 35¾" H $28,750.00

A-MA Mar. 1997   Skinner

Left to Right

Side Chair, turned banister-back, N.E., 18th C., imperf., 42½" H $345.00
Side Chair, painted & turned banister-back, MA, 18th C., 46" H . . .$1,380.00

A-MA Oct. 1996   Skinner, Inc.

Windsor Knuckle Armchair, ash, pine & maple, New. Eng., c. 1780, old refinish, 37½" H $1,955.00
Sack-back Windsor Chair, attrib. to Samuel Wing, Sandwich, MA, 1800-08, old refinish, 36¾" H $920.00

A-MA Mar. 1997   Skinner

Q.A. Roundabout Chair, walnut, RI, late 18th C., orig. Spanish br. paint, minor imper., 30½" H $4,312.50

A-MA Mar. 1997   Skinner

Left to Right

Windsor Side Chair, ash, cherry & maple brace-back fan-back, N.E., ca. 1780, 36" H $1,150.00
Windsor Side Chair, ash & maple fan-back, N.E., ca. 1780, ref., 37½" H .$517.50

A-MA Oct. 1996   Skinner, Inc.

Windsor Continuous Armchair, ash, pine & maple, New. Eng., c. 1780, old refinish, minor imp., 38¼" H . . .$977.50

A-MA Oct. 1996   Skinner, Inc.

Arts & Crafts Morris Chair, adjustable pins, orig. finish, 31¼" W, 36" D, 40" H $1,495.00

A-MA Mar. 1997   Skinner

Shaker Side Chair, painted w/ tilters, N.E., early 19th C., orig. red-brown painted surface, stamped "1", repl. tape seat, surface abrasions, 41" H $4,312.50

A-MA Mar. 1997   Skinner

Left to Right

Shaker #7 Rocker, armed, production chair, attrib. to the Shakers of Mt. Lebanon, NY, late 19th/early 20th C., old fin., repl. red & blk. tape seat, 41½" H $747.50

Shaker #7 Rocker, armed, production chair, bears decal of Shakers of Mt. Lebanon, NY, late 19th/early 20th C., w/ shawl bar, old dk. varnish, repl. red & blk. tape seat, 41" H $1,380.00

A-MA May 1997   Skinner

Left to Right

Roycroft Chair, orig. dark finish, orb mark, 17" W, 16½" D, 43½" H $1,150.00

Roycroft Chair, orig. dk. finish, orb mark, 17" W, 16½" D, 43½" H $1,150.00

A-MA June 1997   Skinner, Inc.

Baroque Armchairs, pr., walnut & caned, 48" H $1,840.00

A-MA May 1997   Skinner

Gustav Stickley Morris Chair, orig. deep chocolate finish, orig. pegs & washers, seat cushion & rope seat foundation, repr. to arm, sgn. Gustav red decal, 30¼" W, 36¼" D, 37¼" H $16,100.00

A-MA Oct. 1996   Skinner, Inc.

Stickley Morris Chair, adjustable bar on pegs, orig. finish, repl. cushions, 32" W, 35" D, 41" H $1,495.00

A-OH May 1997   Garth's Auctions

Shaker Rocker, armchair, impr. "3" on top slat & orig. stenciled label "Shaker's Trade Mark, Mt. Lebanon, NY", worn old fin. w/ traces of orig. dk. fin., repl. woven reed seat damaged, glued split in one rocker, 34¾" H $330.00

A-OH May 1997   Garth's Auctions

Windsor Armchair, old mellow ref., underside of seat has traces of old paint & is stamped "P.S. Byrn 1708", one knuckle arm is an old repl., 43½" H $3,960.00

A-OH May 1997   Garth's Auctions

Windsor Chair, worn blk. repaint, branded "I. Sporson", repairs & replacements, incl. ended out side edge of seat, repairs to arm, one arm rebroken at bend, 38¾" H . . .$935.00

A-OH May 1997   Garth's Auctions

Armchair, dec. highback, orig. red & blk. graining w/ yel. striping & stylized floral dec. w/ cornucopias & foliage in yel., gr., blk. & br., seat orig. upholstered & only has red ground coat, also has plugged potty seat hole, minor wear & repr. break in lower slat of back, 47" H $385.00

A-OH Oct. 1996   Garth's Auctions

Blanket Chest, dec. pine w/ old repaint, br. graining w/ dovetailed case, refaced center drawer front, orig. lock & key, 49" W, 23¼" D, 29½" H $1,430.00

A-MA Jan. 1997   Skinner

Chest of Drawers, grain painted, prob. Maine, 1835-45 w/ochre & red graining simulating mah., old surface, orig. pulls, minor imper., 41⅝" W, 20" D, 42½" H $575.00

A-MA June 1997   Skinner

Painted Box, Am., dated 1811, grained w/ faux stringing & cross-banding, reserve below keyhole states "E. White 1811", paint wear, lacking lock, 25½" W, 12¼" D, 9" H ..$345.00

A-MA June 1997   Skinner

Pine Chest, grain painted drawers, N.E., 19th C., w/ molded lidded till, orig. burnt sienna & yel. graining, orig. pulls, minor imper. 36⅞" W, 18¼" D, 31¼" H ..$1,150.00

A-OH Nov. 1996   Garth's Auctions

PA Blanket Chest, dec., pine w/ orig. red paint, gr. & yel., dovetailed case, hinges repl., three feet ended out, age cracks, 41½" W, 20" D, 24¾" H $1,925.00
Platter, red spatterware, peafowl in gr., yel., blue & blk., stains, hairlines, filled chip, 15¾" L $962.50

A-MA Oct. 1996   Skinner, Inc.

Blanket Chest, tiger maple, N.Y. State, early 19th c., stamped "E. Swan" on backboard, top opens to storage space, early surface & dec., old repl. brasses, minor imp., 36" H, 37" W, 17¾" D $3,737.50

A-MA Mar. 1997   Skinner

Child's Chest, painted pine & poplar chest, over drawer, prob. N.E., ca. 1800, molded hinged top above a case of single drawer, old dk. gr. paint, imper., 26¾" W, 11½" D, 22" H ..$2,530.00

A-MA June 1997   Skinner

Six-Board Chest, grained pine, N.E., 19th C., w/ lidded till, w/ ora. & burnt sienna graining, imper., 37½" W, 17¼" D., 21⅛" H $1,495.00

A-MA May 1997   Skinner

Roycroft Chest, cast iron hardware, orb mark, orig. dk. finish, missing int. tray, minor seam splits, 39¼" W, 21¾" D, 19" H $17,250.00

A-MA June 1997   Skinner, Inc.

George III Writing Chest, mah., 45" W, 24" D, 33¼" H $3,450.00

A-MA Oct. 1996   Skinner, Inc.

Six-board Chest, New. Eng., painted, early 19th c., fancifully grained w/ gold & burnt sienna, molded top lifts w/ lidded till, orig. putty painted surface, imp., 18" H, 36¼" W, 15" D $2,990.00

A-MA Mar. 1997   Eldred's

Sheraton Sofa, mah., scrolled arms & turned legs, 72″ L $825.00

A-OH Aug. 1996   Garth Auctions

Chippendale Sofa, mah. base, reupholstered in gold & olive striped velvet, 81″ L $1,155.00

A-NH Mar. 1997   Northeast Auctions

Sofa, New Eng. Sheraton mah. inlay, stiles & rail w/ inlay geometric design, 69″ L $1,800.00

A-NH Mar. 1997   Northeast Auctions

Sofa, Am. Sheraton carved mah., flat crest above armrest, reed over urn turned support, 74″ L $1,600.00

A-OH Nov. 1996   Garth's Auctions

Fed. Sofa, mah. frame w/ carving by McIntire, MA, pale blue upholstery, minor sm. repairs, 76½″ L $9,350.00

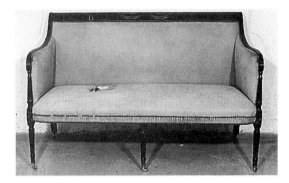

A-OH Nov. 1996   Garth's Auctions

Fed. Sofa, attrib. to Duncan Phyfe, mah. frame w/ old finish, some repairs & added braces to frame, old worn & faded salmon upholstery, 60¼″ L $12,650.00

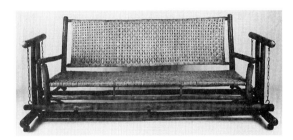

A-MA May 1997   Skinner

Swing Settee, hickory, orig. finish, webbing in excellent condition, unsigned, 90″ W, 33″ D, 30¼″ H $6,612.50

A-OH Nov. 1996   Garth's Auctions

Rococo Revival Sofa, Victorian, carved rosewood frame, reupholstered in gr. & red on an ivory ground, repairs, 64″ L $1,265.00

A-OH Nov. 1996   Garth's Auctions

Victorian Sofa, ref. finger carved walnut frame, repairs, reupholstered in pale blue brocade, 58½" L $275.00

A-OH Dec. 1996   Garth's Auctions

Victorian Sofa, walnut frame, ref. & reupholstered in burgundy red velvet, 56½" L $495.00

A-OH Aug. 1996   Garth Auctions

Baroque style sofa, w/ matching armchair, ornate walnut frame w/ burl veneer, reupholstered in pastel floral brocade on a white ground, early 20th c., 85" L $440.00

A-OH Aug. 1996   Garth Auctions

Empire sofa, ref. mag. frame w/ well detailed carving & flame grain veneer, reupholstered in pale gold damask w/ four throw pillows, 89" L $1,210.00

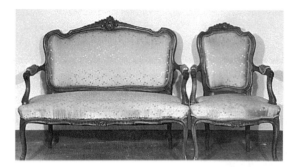

A-OH Aug. 1996   Garth Auctions

French Style Parlor Suite, five pc. w/ carved walnut frames, settee 48" L, pr. of armchairs & pr. of side chairs, upholstered in worn & stained gold fabric, edge braid is loose & incomplete, early 20th c. $880.00

A-OH Aug. 1996   Garth Auctions

Victorian finger carved settee, walnut frame w/ traces of rosewood graining, reupholstered in greenish yel. raw silk, 60¾" L $275.00

Parlor Suite, rosewood & marquetry, ca. 1865-75, comprising two settees, two pairs of armchairs, & two side chairs $7,475.00

A-OH Jan. 1997   Garth's Auctions

Corner Cupboard, two-piece, cherry w/ old finish, dovetailed drawer, hardware replaced, pine and poplar secondary woods, 42¼" W, 95 ½" H $4,400.00

A-OH Jan. 1997   Garth's Auctions

Hepplewhite Secretary, two part, ref. birch, dovetailed drawers, int. top w/ adjustable shelves, pull out candle shelves, repl. brasses, pine secondary wood, 39¾" W, 81¼" H $4,400.00
Q.A. Candlesticks, pr., brass, size varies slightly, 6⅞" H, & 6¾" H $797.50

A-OH Aug. 1996   Garth Auctions

Hepplewhite Secretary, cherry w/ inlay & old mellow ref., dovetailed drawers, both cases are dovetailed, edge damage, old repairs w/ some inlay missing, lid may be old replm., int. drawers have repairs & restoration, pine secondary wood, brasses are old replacements, 41" W, cornice is 11⅝" x 44½", 80½" H $4,510.00
Staffordshire Plate, dk. blue transfer "La Grange, the Residence of the Marquis Lafayette", impr. "E. Wood", wear, stains, minor crazing & roughness on table ring, 10¼" D $137.50
Staffordshire Milk Pitcher, blk. transfer "Lafayette, the Nation's Guest" & "Washington, His Country's Father", stains & hairlines, 5⅛" H $220.00
Staffordshire Tall Pot w/ Waste Bowl, pot has dk. blue transfer of Lafayette at the tomb of "Franklin", pinpoint flakes & tip of spout is damaged, mismatched lid damaged & glued, 10⅝" H, waste bowl w/ gaudy blue & white dec., edge damage & stains, 6" D $330.00

A-OH Oct. 1996   Garth's Auctions

Empire Corner Cupboard, one pc., ref. walnut, two nailed drawers, 56¼" W, 83¾" H $1,980.00

A-MA Mar. 1997   Eldred's

Corner Cupboard, Am., late 18th/early 19th C., yel. pine, cut in half between upper & lower door & re-attached, once painted med. brown, prob. Mid-Atlantic states, 87" H . .$880.00

A-MA Oct. 1996   Skinner, Inc.

Chippendale Corner Cupboard, New. Eng., pine paneled, 18th c., old refinish, minor imp., 88" H, 45" W, 20" D $4,600.00

A-OH Oct. 1996   Garth's Auctions

Empire Cupboard two pc., ref. cherry & walnut, feet missing & castors added, 44" W, 81¾" H $1,815.00

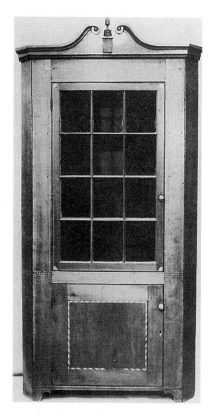

A-OH July 1997   Garth's Auctions

Corner Cupboard, one-pc., cherry w/ old mellow ref., old glass, one cracked, some inlay damage & age cracks, cornice is an old addition, poplar secondary wood, incl. cornice 92½" H, 48" W $4,950.00

A-OH Oct. 1996   Garth's Auctions

Country Wall Cupboard, PA, two pc., cherry & poplar w/ red repaint, dovetailed drawers in base, edge damage & repl. hardware, 53¾" W, 80¼" H $3,190.00
Ovoid Jug, stoneware, w/ applied handle, impr. "T.S_afts & Co. Whately", chips on lip, 12" H $93.50
Ovoid Jar, stoneware w/ applied handles, misshapen w/ firing chip, hairline in base, 9½" H $110.00
Ovoid Jug, stoneware w/ applied handle, impr. "Boston", grey salt glaze w/ tan highlights, flake on lip, 12" H $247.50
Ovoid Jar, stoneware w/ applied handles, impr. "4", wear, 15" H . .$275.00

A-OH Oct. 1996   Garth's Auctions

Corner Cupboard, grain painted, two pc., poplar w/ old br. graining over lt. colored repaint, blk. stain, 40½" W, 80¾" H $2,145.00
Stoneware Jug, w/ applied handles, cobalt blue dec., inscription on bottom "Zoar Pottery. Zoar, Ohio", chips on lip, 15" H $104.50

A-OH Oct. 1996   Garth's Auctions

Wall Cupboard, MD, two pc., ref. pine & poplar, dovetailed drawers, mismatched pcs., molding, feet & cornice repl., 50¾" W, 80⅜" H $880.00
Pitcher, blue & white sponge ware, circle design, hairline, 8⅞" H $330.00
Pitcher, blue & white stoneware w/ molded fruit, crow's foot & rim chip, 8¼" H $110.00
Pitcher, blue & white spone spatter, hairline, 8⅞" H $192.50
Pitcher, blue & white sponge ware pitcher w/ molded band, flakes, 11½" H $385.00

A-OH Oct. 1996   Garth's Auctions

Wall Cupboard, two pc., poplar w/ old br. graining over red, dovetailed drawers, replacements, edge damage, one foot repl., 46¼" W, 83½" H $1,540.00
Vase, blue & white sponge ware, red clay, 4¼" H $22.00
Pitcher, blue & white sponge ware, no lid, minor edge chips, 5½" H $412.50
Pitcher, blue & white sponge ware, chips, stains & crazing, hairline, 7" H $55.00
Pitcher, blue & white sponge ware, chips & hairline, 9" H $220.00

A-MA Jan. 1997   Skinner
Corner Cabinet, cherry glazed, NY, 1830's, upper case w/ three-shelf int., lower case doors conceal one-shelf int., old repl. pulls, ref., minor imper., 43" W, 21¼" D, 88" H $4,600.00

A-MA June 1997   Skinner
Fed. Desk Bookcase, mah. veneer carved & glazed, N.E., ca. 1815-1825, old ref., restor. $1,495.00

A-OH Nov. 1996   Garth's Auctions
Jelly Cupboard, pine w/ old red, rat-tail hinges, 41½" W, 68¾" H $4,730.00

A-MA June 1997   Skinner
Corner Cupboard, glazed pine paneled, 19th C., glazed doors open to three-shelved int., cockbeaded drawer, refin., restor., 48½" W, 21½" D, 87" H . .$2,415.00

A-NH Mar. 1997   Northeast Auctions
Chippendale Chest, New Eng., maple bonnet-top chest on chest, 39" W, 84" H $7,500.00

A-OH Nov. 1996   Garth's Auctions
Q.A. Corner Cupboard, CT, cherry w/ mellow ref., pine backboards, cornice replm., repairs & doors reworked, 42¾" W, 79½" H $4,180.00
Windmill Weight, cast iron horse, made by Dempster Mill Mfg. Co., NE, old blk. paint, 17" L, 16½" H .$385.00

A-MA Jan. 1997   Skinner

Fed. Desk Bookcase, mah. inlaid glazed, prob. MA, ca. 1790, fold-out writing surface, three cockbeaded drawers, imper., 40" W, 19¼" D, 76" H . . .$2,990.00

A-MA Jan. 1997   Skinner

Corner Cupboard, pine glazed, prob. N.E., late 18th C., recessed paneled doors enclosing one shelf, old ref., minor imper., 45" W, 26" D, 91" H $2,415.00

A-MA Jan. 1997   Skinner

Step-Back Cupboard, painted pine paneled, N.E., early 19th C., three-shelved int., & one shelf int., painted red, hardware repl., imper., 36" W, 15½" D, 80½" H $2,415.00

A-MA Mar. 1997   Skinner

Fed. Desk & Bookcase, mah. veneer glazed, MA, ca. 1820, baize lined writing surface & cockbeaded drawers, old ref., old pulls, imper., 36¼" W, 18" D, 65½" H $1,610.00

A-MA May 1997   Skinner

Limbert Bookcase, tapered paneled sides, three adjusting shelves, orig. br. finish, unsgn., 36" W, 14" D, 58¼"H . . .$3,105.00

A-MA Jan. 1997   Skinner

Corner Cabinet, cherry painted glazed, N.E., upper case has two-shelf int., lower case has two recessed paneled doors opening to a one-shelf int., old red paint w/ recent varnish, pulls not orig., imper., 40" W, 20" D, 82" H $5,750.00

A-MA Mar. 1997   Skinner

Chippendale Desk & Bookcase, mah. carved, Boston area, 1770-1800, cock-beaded drawers, repl. brasses, restor., 40⅜" W, 22⅜" D, 95½" H $14,950.00

A-OH Nov. 1996   Garth's Auctions

Corner Cupboard, one pc., cherry w/ mellow ref., dovetailed drawer, 46" W, 78" H $4,675.00

A-OH Nov. 1996   Garth's Auctions

Corner Cupboard, two pc., ref. poplar w/ dk. stain, top w/ butterfly shelves, int. pale gr. repaint, pieced repairs, feet & cornice repl., 44¾" W, 83" H $2,970.00

A-OH May 1997   Garth's Auctions

Chippendale Secretary, two-pc., cherry w/ old mellow finish, four dove-tailed drawers, fitted int. w/ pigeon holes, pine & poplar secondary wood, orig. brasses, escuts. repl., minor repairs, cornice 11½" x 41¾", base 18¾" x 40", 83" H $8,800.00

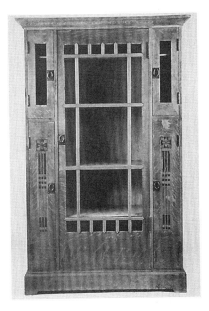

A-MA May 1997   Skinner

China Cabinet, Shop of the Crafters, inlaid wood, some overcoat to orig. color, 42" W, 15¾" D, 63¼" H $3,450.00

A-OH Nov. 1996   Garth's Auctions

Plantation Desk, two pc., walnut w/ old ref., dovetailed drawers, poplar secondary wood, label "Johnston, Meader & Co. Mfg. ...", OH, minor repairs & replm.,   34½"   W,   72½" H $1,430.00

A-OH Nov. 1996   Garth's Auctions

Wm. & Mary Highboy, Am. walnut & pine w/ burl veneer facade, dovetailed drawers, replacements, repairs, pine secondary wood, 34½" W, 61½" H . .$9,350.00

A-MA Mar. 1997   Eldred's

Sheraton Secretary, Am. Empire, mah. & mah. veneers, brass urn finials, upper secion w/ two drawers, lower section w/ fold-down writing surface & three crotch-veneer drawers w/ beaded edges & stamped brass pulls, 37½" W, 18½" D, 64½" H $1,320.00

A-MA Oct. 1996   Skinner, Inc.

Chippendale Desk Bookcase, cherry, prob. central MA, late 18th c., flat carved cornice, thumb-molded doors w/ recessed panels opening to shelves, dovetailed bracket feet, repl. brasses, old refinish, imp., 81½" H, 40½" W, 20" D $5,750.00

A-PA June 1997   Pook & Pook, Inc.

William & Mary Desk, Chester County, walnut secretary, 2 faux drawers above 3 long drawers, restorations, 35" W, 79½" H $7,500.00

A-MA Oct. 1996   Skinner, Inc.

Chippendale Desk & Bookcase, cherry paneled & carved, New London County, CT, ca. 1780, raised panel doors w/ open valanced compartments, above end-blocked serpentine drawers, some brass orig., old refinish, top may be of different origin, 79" H, 41¾" W, 19½" D $9,200.00

A-MA Oct. 1996   Skinner, Inc.

Chippendale Style High Chest, carved cherry, CT River Valley, 82" H, 39" W, 19" D $11,500.00

A-OH Nov. 1996   Garth's Auctions

Empire Secretary, two pc., mah. flame grain veneer, dovetailed drawers, repairs, edge & veneer damage, pine secondary wood, 38" W, 72½" H $990.00
Satsuma Charger, woman & children playing w/ cat, polychrome & gilt w/ dk. red center, some wear, 19" diam. .$495.00

A-OH Nov. 1996   Garth's Auctions

Victorian Secretary, two pc., walnut w/ rose wood graining, one drawer & cylinder top w/ fitted int. w/ two drawers & pigeon holes, labeled "Wms. & Co. Elyria, Ohio", 39¼" W, 88" H $1,760.00

A-OH Dec. 1996   Garth's Auctions

Victorian Wardrobe, ref. walnut w/ burl veneer panels, two dovetailed drawers, shelves on one side, poplar secondary wood, orig. hardware, 54" W, cornice is 25¼" x 59", 98¾" H $1,815.00

A-OH Nov. 1996   Garth's Auctions

Corner Cupboard, pine & poplar w/ old ref., repl. hinges & wooden knobs, pieced repairs, 43½" W, 75¾" H $880.00

A-OH Dec. 1996   Garth's Auctions

Wall Cupboard, one-piece stepback, ref. cherry, two dovetailed drawers, pieced repairs, cornice replaced, 50½" W, 20" D, 82½" H $1,622.50

A-OH Dec. 1996   Garth's Auctions

Q.A. Highboy, cherry w/ old mellow ref., eleven overlapping dovetailed drawers, top & bottom close mismatch, replaced brasses, restored bonnet top, base 17¾" x 35¼", 78" H $5,500.00

A-OH Aug. 1996   Garth Auctions

Kitchen Wall Cupboard, two pc., ref. ash & poplar, ends of base have diamond shaped cutouts w/ screen, left drawer is replaced, cornice replaced, mismatched hardware, 50" W, Cornice is 13¼" x 43¼", base shelf is 19" x 51½", 90" H $605.00

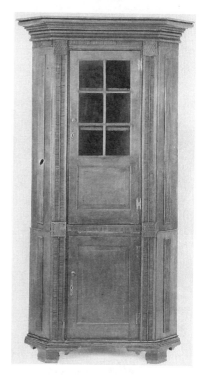

A-PA June 1997   Pook & Pook, Inc.

Chippendale Corner Cupboard, NJ two pc., ca. 1770, retains old red surface, brass H-hinges, restoration to feet & mullions, 31" W, 94" H $3,500.00

A-PA Nov. 1996   Pook & Pook Inc.

Chippendale Secretary Bookcase, PA, mah., ca. 1780, upper section w/ broken pediment top centering on peanut-form cartouche, fall front concealing amphitheatered & shell carved int. w/ reeded & flame finialed document drawers, brass side handles & rococo brasses appear orig., restoration to int., 91½"H, 41¾"W $13,000.00

A-MA Sept. 1996   Skinner, Inc.

Louise IV Armoire, provincial oak, late 18th/early 19th c., 83" H, 56" W, 26" D $3,737.50

A-MA Dec. 1996   Skinner, Inc.

Louis XV Provincial Oak Armoire, 19th c., 84" H, 51½" W $3,105.00

A-MA Dec. 1996   Skinner, Inc.

Louis XV Armoire, Provincial fruitwood, late 18th/early 19th c., rest., 93" H, 56" W, 23¾" D $3,737.50

A-MA Dec. 1996   Skinner, Inc.

Breakfront Bookcase, Victorian gilt metal mounted walnut, late 19th c., several panes broken, 87¼" H, 73" W, 16¾" D $6,900.00

A-PA June 1997   Pook & Pook, Inc.

Chippendale Highboy, ca. 1770, 5 long drawers w/ polychromed rose & leaf carved stiles, base w/ one long drawer over 3 short drawers, restorations to pediment & mid molding, 86½" H . . . . .N/S
Canton Platter, Chinese export blue & white, 17¼" L $425.00
Canton Charger, Chinese export blue & white, 14½" diam. $750.00

A-MD Mar. 1997 DeCaro Auction Sales, Inc.

Q.A. Secretary Desk, CT, ca. 1760, cherry, 2 parts, 37½" W, 20" D, 75" H $21,000.00

A-VA Apr. 1997   Ken Farmer Auction

Oak China Cabinet, curved glass, ca. 1890, foliate & egg carved molding, paw feet, oak shelves, 71" x 49" x 14" $3,410.00

A-NH Mar. 1997   Northeast Auctions

Secretaire Abattant, PA, ormolu-mounted mah., 34½" W, 66" H $40,000.00

A-MA Jan. 1997   Skinner

Cupboard, painted paneled & carved pine, NJ, early 19th C., three-shelved int., old red wash, repl. hardware, imper., 40½" W, 17¼" D, 48" H $3,450.00

A-PA April 1997   Pook & Pook Inc.

Hepplewhite Linen Press, PA, cherry, ca. 1810, retains orig. oval brasses, 40" W, 83½" H $5,500.00

A-PA April 1997   Pook & Pook Inc.

Corner Cupboard, PA, 2-pc. pine, ca. 1800, upper section w/ arched doors, lower section w/ 2 paneled doors & bracket feet, 44" W, 91" H . .$3,200.00

A-PA June 1997   Pook & Pook, Inc.

Shrank, PA, walnut three part, ca. 1770, w/ brass H-hinges, 5 drawer base, feet & cornice restored, 70" W, 94¼" H $5,750.00

A-MA Oct. 1996   Skinner, Inc.

Desk Bookcase, Fed. mahogany & mahogany veneer, MA., c. 1820, glazed doors enclose compartments & drawers w/ fold-out writing surface, old finish, repl. brasses, minor imp., 54½" H, 39" W, 20" D $2,070.00

A-OH May 1997   Garth's Auctions

Chippendale Chest, CT, ref. cherry, dovetailed cases, minor repairs to feet & drawer edges, minor age cracks, repl. brasses, cornice is 19" x 38½", 35½" W, 73½" H $7,700.00

A-PA June 1997   Pook & Pook, Inc.

Chippendale Secretary, PA, walnut, ca. 1800, 2 notched corner panel doors, fully fitted butler's desk int. over 3 long drawers, 42" W, 103" H $7,500.00

A-OH Aug. 1996   Garth Auctions

Country Hoosier Cupboard, old dk. worn finish, two drawers, two pull out bins & pull out breadboard, top surface has remains of old covering, 42" W, 25" D, 64" H $110.00

A-MA June 1997   Skinner

Dresser, painted pewter, NY or NJ, 19th C., old red paint, restor. 72½" W, 20" D, 87½" W $5,175.00

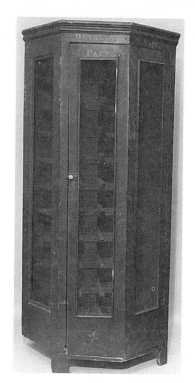

A-OH Oct. 1996   Garth's Auctions

Octagonal Pie Safe, poplar w/ orig. red & blk. graining w/ gold stenciling, mkd. "Octagon Safe Pat'd 1870", 36" across, 67½" H $1,650.00

A-MA Jan. 1997 — Skinner

Fed. Chest of Drawers, cherry bird's-eye maple & mah., prob. NH, 1820-30, cockbeaded drawers, ref., repl. brasses, 38⅝" W, 18" D, 40¾" H . . .$4,025.00

A-MA Jan. 1997 — Skinner

Tiger Maple Bureau, prob. N.E., ca. 1825, incised beaded drawers, old emb. brass pulls, old ref., minor imper., 47" W, 22½" D, 49¾" H $2,415.00

A-MA Jan. 1997 — Skinner

Chippendale Desk, tiger maple slant lid, northern N.E., late 18th C., scratch beaded graduated drawer on molded base, orig. brass, surface imper., 40" W, 19¼" D, 41½" H $5,175.00

A-MA Jan. 1997 — Skinner

Chippendale Desk, maple slant lid, N.E., 1780-1800, sm. valanced open compartments & drawers above four grad. drawers, bracket base, ref., old repl. brasses, restoration, 37¾" W, 18¾" D, 42½" H $2,070.00

A-MA Jan. 1997 — Skinner

Tall Chest of Drawers, painted pine, CT River Valley, mid 18th C., repl. brasses, old red paint, restored, 38¼" W, 18⅛" D, 48¾" H $3,220.00

A-MA Jan. 1997 — Skinner

Fed. Bureau, cherry, prob. N.E., ca. 1810, old ref., orig. brasses, imper., 44" W, 19¼" D, 42½" H $862.50

A-MA Jan. 1997 — Skinner

Chippendale Tall Chest, prob. MA, late 18th C., five graduated thumb molded drawers, old ref., imper., 36" W, 19" D, 48¾" H $2,760.00

A-MA June 1997 — Skinner

Chippendale Chest of Drawers, mah. carved veneer, Boston or Salam MA, 18th C., w/ cockbeaded venerred drawers, shell-carved central drop, orig. brass, old surface, imper., overall 41½" W, 24½" D, 35½" H . .$74,000.00

A-MA June 1997 — Skinner

Fed. Lady's Desk, mah. veneer, N.E., early 19th C., doors open to int. of sm. drawers & compartments, fold-out lined writing surface, old surface, repl. brass, imper., 39¼" W, 17" D, 51" H . . .$1,725.00

A-OH Aug. 1996 Garth Auctions

New Eng. Q.A. Highboy, cherry w/ old finish, nine dovetailed overlapping drawers, top has dovetailed case, minor edge damage, knee returns & brasses replaced, poplar & chestnut secondary wood, 34" W, cornice is 20" x 38", 76¼" H $14,850

A-OH Aug. 1996 Garth Auctions

Sheraton High Chest, cherry w/ old mellow ref., paneled ends, nine dovetailed overlapping drawers, feet are ended out, drawer overlap has repr. & one section of overlap is damaged, cornice has pieced repairs, poplar secondary wood, old brasses in orig. holes, 46" W, cornice is 23" x 48", 70¼" H $2,200.00

A-OH Aug. 1996 Garth Auctions

Empire Chest, ref. cherry, four dovetailed drawers w/ applied edge beading, poplar secondary wood, repl. feet, 41" W, top is 20½" x 42½", 41¼" H $550.00

A-MA June 1997 Skinner

Chippendale Chest of Drawers, cherry, PA, 18th C., thumb-molded graduated drawers, repl. brasses, old ref., repairs, 38" W, 19¼" D, 34⅛" H $4,312.50

A-OH Jan. 1997 Garth's Auctions

Chippendale Chest, walnut w/ old mellow finish, dovetailed drawers, foot facing repl., poplar secondary wood & old brasses, top stained, 39" W, 36¼" H . .$5,500.00
Canton Candlesticks, two blue & white, not a pr., one has hairlines, 7⅞" H $440.00
Canton Bowl, blue & white, 10¼" diam., 4½" H $907.50

A-OH Jan. 1997 Garth's Auctions

Chippendale Chest of Drawers, mah. w/ old ref., dovetailed drawers, pine secondary wood, repl. brasses, restoration, 30¼" W, 33 ¼" H .$3,300.00
Q.A. Candlesticks, pr., brass, scalloped base w/ floral detail, 9⅛" H $660.00
Canton Dish, blue and white, w/ end handles, hairline, 10¾" L $825.00
Canton Pitcher, blue and white, handle and lid, foo dog finial, minor chips, lid is mismatched $550.00

A-OH Aug. 1996 Garth Auctions

Chippendale High Chest, curly walnut w/ old finish, dovetailed case, dovetailed drawers, repairs to feet, replaced brasses & ends of cornice moldings are replaced, poplar secondary wood, 37¾" W, cornice is 23" x 42¼", 61" H $9,350.00
OH Ovoid Jug, stoneware w/ applied handle, impr. "I.M. Mead & Co. 3", cobalt blue at handle & label, hairline cracks & minor flakes on lip, 16" H $220.00

A-MA June 1997   Skinner

Chippendale Drawers, cherry, chest, CT, 18th C., old ref., repl. brass, restored, 37½" W, 20¼" D, 37¼" H $3,335.00

A-MA June 1997   Skinner

Chippendale Desk, wavy birch oxbow slant lid, NH, late 18th C., w/ int. of sm. drawers & valanced compartments, orig. brass, old ref., repairs, 41" W, 19½" D, 43⅝" H $5,175.00

A-MA June 1997   Skinner

Fed. Chest of Drawers, cherry inlaid bowfront, MA, early 19th C., stringing above a conforming case of cockbeaded drawers, veneered skirt, repl. brass, imper., 38" W, 21⅝" D, 36½" H $2,300.00

A-MA June 1997   Skinner

Chippendale Drawers, cherry carved, CT, mid-late 18th C., w/ dentil molding on cornice, bracket base, old ref., repl. brass, repairs, 38" W, 19¼" D, 43½" H $2,070.00

A-MA June 1997   Skinner

Chippendale Slant Lid Desk, tiger maple, N.E., late 18th C., int. opens to valanced compartments & sm. drawers, repl. brass, ref., rest., 40" W, 19½" D, 41" H $2,760.00

A-MA June 1997   Skinner

Chest, grained & veneered, N.E., 1835-45, w/ orig. ora. & yel. tiger maple simulation, mah. veneer on drawer fronts & scrolled columns, orig. turned pulls, minor surface imper., 41" W, 17" D, 47" H $287.50

A-MA June 1997   Skinner

Chippendale Tall Chest, maple, RI, late 18th C., old brass, ref., imper., 36" W, 16¾" D, 59" H $8,337.50

A-MA June 1997   Skinner

Chippendale Tall Chest, tiger maple, RI, 18th C., old repl. brass, ref., imper., 37" W, 18" D, 56⅝" H $10,350.00

A-MA Mar. 1997   Skinner

Chippendale Desk, mah. carved, fall front, MA, last quarter 18th C., cockbeaded drawers, old ref., repl. brasses, minor imper., 41¾" W, 22" D, 44¼" H . .$25,300.00

A-OH Oct. 1996   Garth's Auctions

Chippendale Chest, ref. cherry, dovetailed case & drawers, feet have some repr., repairs to drawer overlaps, replaced brasses, 36" W, 50¼" $2,640.00

A-NH Mar. 1997   Northeast Auctions

Chippendale Desk, Newport block-and-shell carved mah., Goddard-Townsend School, thumbmolded drawers on base, 36½" W, 21½" D, 42" H $32,500.00

A-NH Mar. 1997   Northeast Auctions

Q.A. Highboy, MA, maple, in two parts, 39¼" W, 20" D, 64½" H $14,500.00

A-MA Oct. 1996   Skinner, Inc.

Classical Bowfront Bureau, mahogany veneer, No. Shore, MA, w/ concentric circles outlining ovolo corners, cockbeaded drawers, old varnished surface, orig. turned pulls, minor imp., 43½" H, 38 W, 18" D $862.50

A-NH Mar. 1997   Northeast Auctions

Chippendale Dressing Table, Boston, carved mah. blockfront kneehole, centered recessed door, 30" W, 30" H .$105,000.00

A-MA Jan. 1997   Skinner

Chippendale Chest on Chest, maple, MA or NH, 18th C., dovetailed case, graduated thumb-molded drawers, orig. brass, old ref., 38½" W, 18½" D, 76½" H $11,500.00

A-MA Mar. 1997   Skinner

Chippendale Desk, cherry & tiger maple, slant lid, possible MA, late 18th C., old ref., old repl. brasses, minor imper., 35⅝" W, 18¾" D, 41⅝" H $4,312.50

A-MA Jan. 1997   Skinner

Chippendale Desk, cherry slant lid, prob. RI, ca. 1780, thumb-molded graduated drawers, old refinish, replaced brasses, imperfections., 28" W, 20" D, 42½" H $3,737.50

A-MA Mar. 1997   Skinner

Chippendale Drawers, walnut chest, PA, late 18th C., cock beaded drawers, old oval brasses, old ref., minor repairs, 41½" W, 20½" D, 44" H $4,025.00

A-OH Nov. 1996   Garth's Auctions

Q.A. Chest on Chest, PA, walnut w/ worn orig. finish, dovetailed cases & drawers, pine & oak secondary woods, brasses repl., mkd. "1738 + 3 mo.", some edge damage, 37¾" W, 69¼" H $41,800.00

A-MA Jan. 1997   Skinner

Six-Board Chest, painted & dec. pine, N.E., early 19th C., top lifts to a molded & lidded till on a molded base, early sponge paint on red ground, blk. painted feet, early paint, imper., 50" W, 22" D, 23" H $460.00

A-OH Nov. 1996   Garth's Auctions

Chippendale to Hepplewhite, transitional serpentine chest, ref. mah., dovetailed drawers, repl. brasses, age cracks, pine secondary wood, 42¼" W, 39¾" H $5,775.00

Coffee Pot, oriental export, berry lid finial, round medallions , red, blue & gilt, wear & roughness, 9⅛" H $1,100.00

Oval Bowl, w/ undertray, salt glaze, edge wear & hairlines, 11⅛" L $1,320.00

Coffee Pot, oriental export, berry lid finial, Armorial design in red, blue & gilt, spout reglued, 9¾" H . . .$880.00

A-OH Nov. 1996   Garth's Auctions

Hepplewhite Chest, bowfront, mah. veneer, dovetailed drawers, brasses repl., pine & mah. secondary woods, damage & replacements, 34½" W, 37" H . .$1,650.00

Q.A. Candlesticks, two similar, octagonal bases & stems, one has old repr., 7" H & 7⅛" H $962.50

Hepplewhite Mirror, serpentine, mah. veneer w/ inlay, dovetailed drawers & beaded edge standards, pine & mah. secondary woods, edge & veneer damage, repl. knobs, 17¾" W, 8" D, 22½" H $495.00

A-OH Nov. 1996   Garth's Auctions

Chippendale Desk, MA, mah. w/ old finish, dovetailed drawers in beaded frame, minor edge damage & pieced repairs, two feet ended out, replms., pull out center w/ several hidden drawers, pine secondary wood, 41" W, 22" D., 44" H $8,800.00

Brass Candlesticks, two, similar, domes bases, one stem soldered, 8½" H & 9" H $1,072.50

Delft Bowl, blue & white, broken & repr., 12½" diam., 6½" H . . .$1,155.00

A-MA Mar. 1997   Skinner

Chippendale Drawers, cherry chest, CT, ca. 1780, four cockbeaded drawers, old ref., restor., 39¼" W, 19" D, 33½" H $2,645.00

A-OH Nov. 1996   Garth's Auctions

Hepplewhite Desk, two pc., Salem, MA, ref. mah. w/ figured veneer & inlays, dovetailed drawers, top w/ fitted int. of drawers & pigeon holes, pine secondary wood, minor age cracks & damage, brasses & hinges repl., 42"W, 20¼"D, 53¼"H $2,420.00

A-MA Oct. 1996   Skinner, Inc.

Pine Chest, painted, w/ orig. ball feet, orig. cleats & early blk. paint over red ground, repl. brasses, old surface, 41¼" H, 36" W, 17¼" D $4,025.00

A-MA Oct. 1996   Skinner, Inc.

Blanket Chest, red painted pine, New. Eng., early 19th c., old red paint, repl. pulls, minor imp., 45" H, 42" W, 18¾" D $1,955.00

A-MA Mar. 1997   Skinner

Fed. Bureau, carved mah. veneer, MA, ca. 1815, beaded edge & drawers, old ref., orig. brasses, imper., 41¾" W, 22⅝" D, 41¾" H $1,380.00

A-MA Oct. 1996   Skinner, Inc.

Bureau, Fed. cherry & bird's-eye veneer, N.H. or MA, c. 1820, top w/ reeded edge & ovoid corners, cockbeaded drawers w/ bird's eye maple panels, cross-banding the stringing w/ flanking quarter engaged reeded posts, swelled turned legs, old repl. brasses & old finish, imp., 37½" H, 40" W, 19½" D $1,725.00

A-NH Mar. 1997   Northeast Auctions

Q.A. Highboy, New Eng., mah. bonnet-top in two parts, 41" W, 84" H $20,000.00

A-MA Mar. 1997   Skinner

Fed. Chest, mah. carved & veneer drawers, MA, ca. 1820, old repl. pulls, old finish, imper., 40¾" W, 19½" D, 41" H $1,150.00

A-MA Oct. 1996   Skinner, Inc.

Chippendale Slant Lid Desk, painted maple, prob. MA, c. 1780, cockbeaded case of four graduated drawers on ogee bracket feet, repl. brasses, old red stained finish, restoration, 43" H, 40½" W, 19" D $2,760.00

A-MA Mar. 1997   Skinner

Chippendale Chest of Drawers, mah. veneer, MA, ca. 1780, four graduated cockbeaded drawers, old ref., some old brasses, restoration, 40" W, 19⅛" D, 35¾" H $2,875.00

A-MA Mar. 1997   Skinner

Store Keeper's Desk, grain painted, N.E. or NY, early 19th C., top lifts, valanced compartments, late 19th C. br. & gold graining, 33" W, 20" D, 48" H $1,840.00

Chest of Drawers, maple, cherry & tiger maple, VT, 42½" W, 19⅜" D, 45" H $6,325.00

Chippendale Drawers, mah., serpentine front chest, Boston, 1760-80, cockbeaded drawers, old color & old ref., orig. brass, shrinkage cracks, 33¼" W, 17¾" D, 32" H $178,500.00

George III Partners Desk, mah., ca. 1800, w/ leather inlay top, ornate rococo brasses, 30" H, 57" W, 35½" D $8,500.00

Table Cabinet, rosewood, marquetry & parcel-gilt, NY, 19th C., minor damages, 26" W, 15" D, 14½" H . .$546.25

Chippendale Drawers, maple carved tall chest, N.E., last quarter 18th C., six thumb molded graduated drawers, old ref., repl. brasses, restor., 36" W, 18" D, 56¾" H $5,060.00

Chippendale Desk, maple slant lid, MA, late 18th C., int. of document drawers & sm. drawers, ref., repl. brasses, repairs, 34⅝" W, 17⅝" D, 43⅜" H $4,600.00

Am. Empire Bureau, mah. & mah. veneer, early 19th C., mkd. "Walter Corey, Furniture Warehouse...Portland, ME." 43½" W, 20¼" D, 51½" H $1,495.00

Fed. Bureau, cherry, MA, ca. 1800, cockbeaded drawers, old ref., repl. brasses, minor imperf., 37½" W, 19½" D, 37¼" H . . $2,070.00

Map Case, pine w/ old br. repaint w/ red & yel. striping & dec., eight dovetailed drawers, top w/ "VR" crest, & "For Q.A. & Country", sides have "... Admiralty House, Bermuda", feet repl., age cracks, 46½" W, 32¼" D, 45" H $3,410.00

George III Slant Lid Desk, mah. and marquetry, 19th C., 33" W, 18" D, 38½" H $1,840.00

A-MA June 1997   Skinner, Inc.
George III Chest, mah., 18th C., 43½"
W, 21¼" D, 38" H $1,495.00

A-MA June 1997   Skinner, Inc.
George III Chest of Drawers,
bowfront, mah., restorations, 36¼" W,
18½" D, 35" H $1,380.00

A-PA June 1997   Pook & Pook, Inc.
Chippendale Chest, PA, walnut,
ca. 1790, feet restored, 38" W, 65¼"
H $3,400.00
Stoneware Crock, ten-gallon, blue
dec. by "William Mfg., New Geneva,
PA", 21½" H $800.00

A-MA June 1997   Skinner, Inc.
William & Mary Chest of Drawers,
oak & burlwood, restorations, 37½" W,
21¾" D, 36" H $2,760.00

A-PA June 1997   Pook & Pook, Inc.
Cherry Desk, CT, ca. 1760, slant lid
enclosing a fitted int. over 4 long drawers,
minor repr. to lid, 44½" H, 37" W$5,500.00

A-VA Apr. 1997   Ken Farmer Auction
Chest of Drawers, NC, early 19th C.,
old varnish on cherry, yel. pine secondary, dovetailed, one board top w/
molding below, solid ends, turned feet,
51" x 42½" x 19" $770.00

A-PA June 1997   Pook & Pook, Inc.
Hepplewhite Chest, PA, cherry, ca. 1819,
inscribed on bottom "John Histand, May 14,
1819", 38¾" W, 71½" H $6,500.00

A-MA Apr. 1997   Skinner, Inc.
Chest of Drawers, George III style,
brass inlaid mah., late 19th C., four
graduated drawers $1,150.00

A-MA June 1997   Skinner, Inc.
William & Mary Chest of Drawers,
walnut & burl walnut, restorations, 38"
W, 22½" D, 35" H $2,185.00

A-NH Mar. 1997   Northeast Auctions

Q.A. Table, MA, mah., oblong top, 30"
L, 28" H $85,000.00

A-NH Mar. 1997   Northeast Auctions

Chippendale Table, Newport, carved
mah. slab-top, attrib. to John Townsend, oblong top above a frieze w/
cross-hatch scribing on bottom edge.
top 48" x 23½", 33" H $35,000.00

A-NH Mar. 1997   Northeast Auctions

Card Table, New Eng. Hepplewhite,
Eagle, inlay dec., top 36" x 17½", 28¾"
H $15,000.00

A-NH Mar. 1997   Northeast Auctions

Q.A. Table, RI, maple black-painted porringer, top 34" x 24½", 26½" H .$47,500.00

A-NH Mar. 1997   Northeast Auctions

Wm. & Mary Table, NH, maple w/
shoe-foot hutch table, top 43" x 44",
28" H $12,000.00

A-NH Mar. 1997   Northeast Auctions

Chippendale Table, MA, carved
mah., 33" L $7,500.00

A-OH Jan. 1997   Garth's Auctions

Q.A. Table
walnut w/ some curl & old ref., pine &
chestnut secondary woods, return
on leg repl., restoration, age cracks,
15¼" x 41¼" w/ 15⅞" leaves, 28¼"
H $1,375.00

A-OH Aug. 1996   Garth Auctions

PA Chippendale Table, tilt top, ref.
walnut, birdcage w/ turned posts &
dish turned top, one foot replaced, top
is a replm. made w/ old wood & repr.,
36" D, 29" H $825.00

A-NH Mar. 1997   Northeast Auctions

Chippendale Table, PA, mah. tilt top,
ring turned pedestal w/ compressed
ball, 35" diam., 29" H $4,000.00

A-MA Oct. 1996   Skinner, Inc.

Classical Table, mahogany veneer,
prob. Baltimore, MD. area, 1815-20, w/
reeded top, brass paw feet, two cockbeaded end drawers, one working, one
sim., repl. brass, old refinish, very
minor imp., 29" H, 24" W, extended
42¾" D $977.50

A-NH Mar. 1997   Northeast Auctions

Dressing Table, New Eng. Sheraton, white painted & dec., grapevine & floral motifs, gilding, 34½" L, 44½" H . .$5,500.00

A-NH Mar. 1997   Northeast Auctions

Sofa Table, rosewood inlay, two frieze drawers w/ opposing sham drawers, brass toes on rollers, label of "J. Taylor, cabinetmaker...Boston.", top 27" x 37", 28½" H $6,500.00

A-NH Mar. 1997   Northeast Auctions

Regency Table, rosewood, red inset leather top over drawer . .$11,000.00

A-MA Jan. 1997   Skinner

Fed. Card Table, mah. & bird's eye maple inlaid, Boston, ca. 1815, old ref., minor imper., 36¼" W, 17½" D, 29¾" H . .$3,737.00

A-MA Jan. 1997   Skinner

Tavern Table, painted pine & maple, northern N.E., mid 18th C., scrubbed top w/ breadboard ends, old red paint, 37¾" W, 23⅝" D, 23½" H . . .$1,840.00

A-MA Jan. 1997   Skinner

Chippendale Tea Table, mah. tilt top, possibly N.E., late 18th C., repairs, 33" diam., 27" H $977.50

A-MA Mar. 1997   Skinner

Fed. Card Table, mah. veneer carved, MA, leaf carving, colonettes & reeding, orig. surface, minor surface imper., 36" W, 17¾" D, 28½" H $5,462.50

A-MA Jan. 1997   Skinner

Work Table, mah. carved & veneer, Boston, ca. 1830, top drawer fitted w/ adjustable work easel, lower drawer w/ faux two drawer facade, old ref., minor imper., 22½" W, 19" D, 30" H . . .$1,840.00

A-MA Jan. 1997   Skinner

Federal Table, New Eng., 1810-20, cockbeaded veneered sides, brass feet on castors, old ref., imper., 19¾" W extended, 39" D, 28" H $1,092.50

A-MA Jan. 1997   Skinner

Chippendale Tea Table, mah. carved, prob. N.E., ca. 1780, old ref., 30½" diam., 28" H $1,725.00

A-MA Jan. 1997   Skinner

Q.A. Tea Table, maple, N.E., mid 18th C., old ref., minor imper., 28" W, 21¾" D, 26" H $2,875.00

A-MA Jan. 1997   Skinner

William & Mary Tavern Table, maple, N.E., mid 18th C., old ref., restored, 34" W, 22¾" D, 23" H $1,150.00

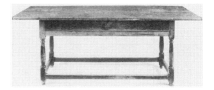

A-MA June 1997   Skinner

Stretcher Base Table, pine & maple, N.E., 18th C., top w/ bread board ends, single drawer, old painted surface w/ traces of red & blk., 69¼" W, 32¾" D, 27⅞" H . $10,925.00

A-MA Oct. 1996   Skinner, Inc.

Q.A. Table, drop leaf, York, Maine area, attrib. to Samuel Sewall, late 18th c., old surface, missing applied skirt shaping, 25⅝" H, 31⅛" W, 9½" D $9,200.00

A-MA Jan. 1997   Skinner

Maple Chair Table, prob. N.E., late 18th C., old ref., minor imper., 41¾" diam., 28" H $3737.50

A-MA Jan. 1997   Skinner

Drop Leaf Table, bird's-eye & tiger maple, NY or OH, ca. 1840, ref., 20" W, 42" D, 30" H $3,450.00

A-MA Jan. 1997   Skinner

Fed. Pembroke Table, mah. & mah. veneer, possibly NY, ca. 1810, old finish, 23" W, 36" D, 28¾" H $862.50

A-MA Mar. 1997   Skinner

Fed. Card Table, mah. inlaid, MA, ca. 1815, satinwood panels, old ref., 35½" W, 17¼" D, 29½" H $8,625.00

A-MA Jan. 1997   Skinner

Fed. Card Table, mah. inlaid, prob. Providence, RI, ca. 1790, old finish, 36" W, 18" D, 28½" H $2,875.00

A-MA Jan. 1997   Skinner

Stand w/ Drawer, bird's eye maple & cherry, N.E., early 19th C., applied beaded edge, old finish, imper., 20" W, 19" D, 26¼" H $862.50

Skinner Sale #1766³¹
A-MA Mar. 1997   Skinner

Fed. Candlestand, MA, ca. 1790, old finish, minor imper., 27" H . $5,175.00

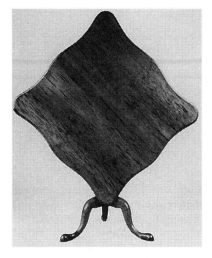

A-MA Jan. 1997   Skinner

Chippendale Tea Table, cherry, prob. MA, ca. 1780, ref., imper., top 33" x 31½", 28¾" H $920.00

A-MA June 1997   Skinner

Q.A. Dining Table, maple, MA, mid 18th C., ref., repairs, 47½" W, 14½" D, 29¼" H $2,530.00

A-MA June 1997   Skinner

Fed. Card Table, mah. inlaid, prob. MD, ca. 1800, skirt divided into three panels, contrasting veneer, old ref., imper., 36" W, 17¾" D, 29½" H $1,380.00

A-MA June 1997   Skinner

Fed. Card Table, mah. & flame birch veneer, MA, ca. 1800, w/ inlaid edge & ovolo corners, old ref., minor imper., 36" W, 17¾" D, 30" H $1,955.00

A-MA June 1997   Skinner

Fed. Card Table, mah. & flame birch veneer, MA., ca. 1800, edge of top outlined in patterned inlay, old ref., 35¾" W, 16½" D, 29½" H $8,050.00

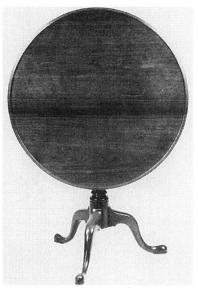

A-MA June 1997   Skinner

Chippendale Tea Table, walnut dish-top, PA, 18th C., top tilts, birdcage & pedestal on cabriole leg base, restor., 33½" diam., 29" H $862.50

A-MA June 1997   Skinner

Fed. Card Table, mah. veneer, MA, early 19th C., w/ beaded edges on table top, old ref., imper., 36" W, 17¾" D, 28⅜" H $977.50

A-MA June 1997   Skinner

Fed. Breakfast Table, mah., prob., NY, ca. 1815, w/ applied brass ball feet, old surface, repl. pulls, imper., 34" W

A-MA June 1997   Skinner

Fed. Drop Leaf Table, mah., N.E., early 19th C., w/ old refinish, minor imper., 41¾" W, 18⅞" D, 28¾" H$460.0022" D, 29" H $1,610.00

A-MA Sept. 1996   Skinner, Inc.

George III Style Hunt Table, mah., 19th c., restoration, 29¼" H, 83½" W, extended 54¾" D $2,990.00

A-MA Oct. 1996   Skinner, Inc.
Chippendale Slab Table, carved mahogany, North Shore MA, 1760-80, thumb molded marble top w/ shaped corners above a conforming mahogany apron w/ carved scroll double cock-beading, the beading on the front cabriole legs diverges at the knee to join the apron & also follows the arris knees, terminating in floral devices, the legs continuing to webbed claw & ball feet, old finish, minor imp., 28" H, 26" W, 22" D $222,500.00

A-MA June 1997   Skinner
Fed. Two-Part Dining Table, mah. veneer, early 19th C., N.E., w/ reeded top edge above venerred skirt, old ref., minor imper., 45¾" W, 30½" H, 89¼" extended D $4,025.00

A-MA June 1997   Skinner
Fed. Dining Table, cherry & walnut veneer, NY or N.E., ca. 1825, w/ old ref., restor., 44" W, 84¼" extended D., 29⅝" H . . .$1,380.00

A-MA Oct. 1996   Skinner, Inc.
Shaker Trestle Table, cherry, Harvard, MA community, ref., restored, 28¼" H, 72" W, 30½" D $6,325.00

A-MA Dec. 1996   Skinner, Inc.
Louis XIII Oak Side Table, 18th c., restorations, worm holes, 28" H, 36" W, 23¾" D $1,955.00

A-MA Dec. 1996   Skinner, Inc.
George III Style Dining Table, mahogany & yewwood, 19th c., 30" H, 85" W, 39" D $2,415.00

A-MA Dec. 1996   Skinner, Inc.
George III Style Dining Table, mahogany & satinwood cross-banded, late 19th/20th c., 29" H, 51" L, 70" W $6,900.00

A-MA June 1997   Skinner
Chair Table, N.E., early 19th C., red & blk. graining simulating rosewood, 42¼" W, 42½" D, 28½" H $4,887.50

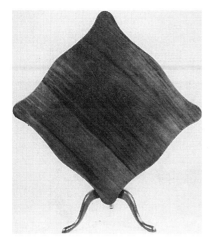

A-MA June 1997   Skinner

Chipendale Tea Table, prob. RI, late 18th C., old ref., imper. 35" W, 36" D, 27¾" H $862.50

A-OH Nov. 1996   Garth's Auctions

Hepplewhite Table, ref. cherry w/ inlay, pine & maple secondary woods, 16¾" x 35⅝", w/ 8¾" leaves, 28" H $6,050.00

A-OH Nov. 1996   Garth's Auctions

Q.A. Table, hardwood w/ old red, dovetailed apron, swing legs & top w/ wrt. iron butterfly hinges, pine secondary wood, 15" x 41½" w/ 14¾" leaves, 28¼" H $28,600.00

A-MA Oct. 1996   Skinner, Inc.

Stretcher Base Table, pine, 18th c., New. Eng., w/ two-board top, old ref. surface, orig. turned pull, two rear feet pieced, 27¼" H, 39⅛" W, 27" D .$3,737.50

A-MA June 1997   Skinner

Q.A. Dining Table, maple, N.E., late 18th C., old varnish stain, imper., 38¾" W, 37" D, 27" H $2,760.00

A-MA Oct. 1996   Skinner, Inc.

Table w/ Drawer, Fed. cherry inlaid, CT River Valley, c. 1800, legs inlaid w/ ovals & banding of contrasting woods continuing under the drawer, old refinish, 28½" H, 27¾" W, 18½" D $9,775.00

A-MA Mar. 1997   Skinner

Stretcher Base Table, pine & maple, MA, 18th C., ref., a patch in top, 35" W, 25½" D, 25½" H $1,495.00

A-MA Oct. 1996   Skinner, Inc.

Q.A. Dining Table, cherry, CT River Valley, first-half 18th c., top w/ molded edge above four cabriole legs joined by shaped valanced apron, old repr. to leg, 27½" H, 47" W, 48" D $3,737.50

A-MA Oct. 1996   Skinner, Inc.

Chippendale Birdcage Tea Table, walnut, New. Eng., late 18th c., vase & ring form post on a tripod cabriole base, pad feet, old finish, minor imp., 29" H, 33¼" Diam. $2,300.00

A-MA Oct. 1996   Skinner, Inc.

Chippendale Tea Table, mahogany, MA, late 18th c., serpentine top w/ molded edge on a vase & ring turned post on a cabriole tripod base w/ pad feet on platforms, refinish, minor imp., 28" H, 33" x 31¾" Top $2,300.00

A-MA Oct. 1996   Skinner, Inc.

Pembroke Table, Fed. mahogany inlaid, attrib. to William Whitehead, N.Y., 1790-1810, line inlaid oval top above bowed drawers at either end, one working, one sim., flanked by bookend inlay, orig. brass, old refinish, imp., 27¾" H, 30¾" W, 19½" D, 39⅛" Ext. $8,050.00

A-MA Mar. 1997   Skinner

Fed. Pembroke Table, cherry inlaid, MA or CT, ca. 1800, ref., 20" W, 39½" D, 28¾" H $2,645.00

A-MA Mar. 1997   Skinner

Q.A. Table, maple drop leaf, N.E., 18th C., ref., restored, 51¼" W extended, 17⅜" D, 27" H $1,955.00

A-MA Oct. 1996   Skinner, Inc.

Card Table, mahogany carved & mahogany veneer, MA, ca. 1815, shaped molded top on a conforming beaded skirt w/ beaded canted corners, stamped "J, Deblois" on back, old refinish, imp., 30½" H, 35½" W, 18" D $977.50

A-MA Oct. 1996   Skinner, Inc.

Classical Breakfast Table, mahogany carved, prob. N.Y., c. 1825, cockbeaded inlaid apron w/ working & faux drawers on a turned acanthus carved post & four acanthus carved legs ending in hairy paw feet, ref., 29" H, 40" W, 48½" D $1,150.00

A-MA Mar. 1997   Skinner

Fed. Card Table, mah. inlaid, prob. Boston, ca. 1790, old ref., minor imper., 43⅝" W, 18" D, 30" H $2,990.00

A-MA Oct. 1996   Skinner, Inc.

Card Table, Fed. mahogany inlaid & mahogany veneer, N.Y., c. 1790, demilune folding top w/ inlaid stringing, on a conforming skirt of three panels of inlaid stringing, front legs w/ bookend inlay, old refinish, repairs & imp., 29" H, 35¾" W, 17¾" D $1,495.00

A-MA June 1997   Skinner

Stretcher Base Table, pine & maple, N.E., 18th C., old red paint on base, top has gr. & red paint, imper., 43⅜" W, 30⅛" D, 27" H $3,737.50

A-MA Oct. 1996   Skinner, Inc.

Tea Table, Fed. cherry inlaid, MA or CT, late 18th c., compass inlay of contrasting woods, bordered by stringing on a vase & ring turned post & tripod cabriole leg base & ending in pad feet on platforms, ref., 29½" H, 31¾" sq. top $4,312.50

A-MA June 1997 Skinner, Inc.

Library Table, gothic revival mah., ca. 1840-50, sienna marble top over two drawers, trestle base w/ curved Gothic finial, 50¼" W, 29" D, 30¼" H $5,175.00

A-MA June 1997 Skinner, Inc.

Georgian Style Dining Table, mah. & beechwood, late 19th C., w/ two additional leaves, 24 x 48", table 72" W, 47" D, 29½" H $5,175.00

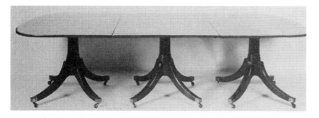

A-MA Apr. 1997 Skinner, Inc.

George III Dining Table, mah., late 18th C., w/ two leaves, restorations, 109" L, 49" D, 28" H $23,000.00

A-MA Mar. 1997 Skinner

Dining Table, mah. carved, possibly N.E., ca. 1825, cast brass feet, w/ additional leaf, old ref., alterations, 47" W, 74½" D w/ leaf, 27¾" H $4,600.00

A-PA Jan. 1997 Pook & Pook Inc.

Tavern Table, oak, ca. 1740, notched corner top, 29¼" W, 94" L, 38" H $9,000.00

A-MD Mar. 1997 DeCaro Auction Sales, Inc.

Sheraton Drop Leaf Table, bold tiger maple, NH, ca. 1810, base retains orig. red wash $4,000.00

A-MD Mar. 1997 DeCaro Auction Sales, Inc.

Chippendale Dining Table, North Shore, MA, ca. 1770, mah., 48" L, 28" H $7,000.00

A-MA Mar. 1997   Skinner

Fed. Card Table, mah., MA, ca. 1790, old ref., restor., 35½" W, 16¾" D, 28¾" H $1,840.00

A-MD Mar. 1997 DeCaro Auction Sales, Inc.

Chippendale Candlestand, Charleston, SC, Ca. 1770, mah. . . .$3,000.00

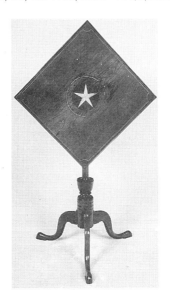

A-MD Mar. 1997 DeCaro Auction Sales, Inc.

Fed. Candlestand, CT, ca. 1790, w/ tilting top, inlaid star & string inlay running perimeter of top, cherry $1,600.00

A-MA Oct. 1996   Skinner, Inc.

Gustav Stickley Table, single drawer, orig. worn finish, 48" W, 30¼" D, 29" H $1,380.00

A-MA June 1997   Skinner, Inc.

Dining Table, mah., late 18th/early 19th C., restorations, open, 86" W, 46¼" D, 29½" H $4,600.00

A-MA June 1997   Skinner, Inc.

George III Writing Table, mah., 19th C., w/ inset gr. tooled leather, 52¼" W, 28" D, 30½" H $3,450.00

A-MA June 1997   Skinner, Inc.

George III Pembroke Table, mah. & bird's-eye maple, 18th C., 37" W, 32½" D, 29" H $2,530.00

A-MA June 1997   Skinner

Work Table, tiger maple, mid Atlantic states, ca. 1825, ref., minor imper., 21" W, 17¾" D, 29" H $1,092.50

A-MA June 1997   Skinner

Q.A. Dining Table, prob. MA., ca. 1770, demi-lune cutout apron, old refinish, imper., 36" W, 35¾" D, 26¾" H $1,495.00

A-MA June 1997   Skinner

Chair Table, pine & maple, northern Euro., ref., restored, 46½" W, 36¾" D, 26½" H $2,990.00

A-MA May 1997   Skinner

Roycroft Library Table, carved orb mark on leg, ref., 72" W, 41¾" D, 30" H . . . . .N/S

A-MA Jan. 1997   Skinner

Fed. Tiered Sideboard, mah. & maple veneer, MA, early 19th C., cockbeaded drawers, rosewood veneer & stringing w/ end cabinets on mah. legs, repl. brass, imper., 69⅝" W, 26½" D, 43¾" H $4,600.00

A-MA Jan. 1997   Skinner

Fed. Sideboard, mah. inlaid, Hartford, CT, ca. 1790, old repl. brasses, Am. shield & anchor, old finish, minor imper., 77" W, 28½" D, 42" H $33,350.00

A-MA Oct. 1996   Skinner, Inc.

Sideboard, Fed. mahogany inlaid, MA, 1790-1800, projecting center & geometric inlaid edge above a conforming case of projecting drawer & two cupboard doors w/ borders of geometric stringing inlay & cockbeading flanked by short drawers & cupboard doors, legs w/ string & bellflower inlay joined by straight skirt w/ geometric inlaid legs, old brasses, old finish, minor imp., 41" H, 67½" W, 20¼" D $11,500.00

A-MA May 1997   Skinner
Row 1, Left to Right

Lifetime Dining Chairs, set of four, quarter-sawn oak w/ orig. seats, orig. finish & paper labels, 17" W, 16½" D, 37½" H . . .$690.00
Limbert Sideboard, paneled sides, through tenons, hardware w/ deep patina, arched apron, orig. finish, brand mark, 45" W, 19¼" D, 51¾" H $2,530.00
Lifetime Dining Chairs, set of four, quarter-sawn oak w/ orig. seats, orig. finish & paper labels, 17" W, 16½" D, 37½" H $690.00

A-MA May 1997   Skinner

Limbert "Ebon-Oak" Server, orig. finish & patina to metal fittings, two branded marks, orig. key, inlaid ebony, paneled sides w/ through tenons, 38" W, 17¼" D, 41¼" H . . .$2,587.50

A-MA May 1997   Skinner

120-Weller Knifewood Vases, pr., florals dec. in matte cream & gr. colors, impr. mark, 2½" diam., 7" H $172.50
Limbert Sideboard, orig. lt. oak finish & hardware, brand mark 48" W, 20½" D, 44¾" H $2,185.00

A-MA Jan. 1997   Skinner

Vitrine Cabinet, mah. & mah. veneer, mid Atlantic states, 1815-25, cockbeaded pedimented backboard, glazed doors, ref., 28¾" W, 12½" D, 33" H $1,840.00

A-MA Jan. 1997   Skinner

Left to Right

Stand, red stained birch, MA or NH, early 19th C., old surface, minor imper., 14¾" x 15¼", 26¾" H $977.50
Fed. Stand w/ Drawer, wavy birch, N.E., ca. 1810, ref., restorations, 19¼" x 20", 27¾" H $517.50

A-MA May 1997   Skinner

Left to Right

Stickley Rocking Morris Chair, orig. finish w/ minor overcoat to arms, one peg repl., 25¾" W, 40" H . . .$2,875.00
Stickley Tabouret, orig. finish, 16¾" W, 17" D, 19¼" H $690.00
Pottery Vase, dec. w/ three Aztec faces, deep matte gr. glaze, sgn. Potnique, 8" W, 5½" H $115.00
J.M. Young Morris Chair, orig. finish, paper label, 29½" W, 37" D, 35" H $1,955.00

A-MA Mar. 1997   Skinner

Dressing Mirror, mah. inlaid, prob. Eng., ca. 1800, reeded support w/ turned bone finials, sq. corners w/ diamond stringing on four turned bone feet, 21" W, 8¾" D, 23½" H . .$920.00

A-MA Mar. 1997   Skinner

Cherry Kas, 18th C., paneled doors open to a two-shelved int., repl. pulls, ref., restored, 62" W, 21" D, 69¾" H . .$2,415.00

A-MA May 1997   Skinner

Left to Right

Stickley Rocker, v-sided arms, drop in spring cushion, orig. finish, Flint retail tag, 28" W, 25¼" D, 39" H $977.50
Arts & Crafts German Bowl, dec. w/ yel. flowers w/ gr. foliate designs in blue ground, 8" diam., 3" H . . .N/S
Tobey Chalet Magazine Stand, dk. br. finish, orig. tacks, missing leather, 12¾" W, 12¾" D, 43" H $1,265.00
Stickley Rocker, orig. finish, branded mark, 26" W, 20" D, 34" H . . .$460.00

A-MA Jan. 1997   Skinner

Sideboard, walnut inlaid, prob. N. or S. Carolina, 1850-75, old ref., imper., 44" W, 19¾" D, 37" H $3,737.50

A-MA Jan. 1997   Skinner

Lady's Desk, stained pine, carved fall front, prob. N.E., ca. 1900, 24" W, 12½" D, 52½" H $862.50

A-MA May 1997   Skinner

Stickley Server, ref., sgn. "The work of...", missing two bail handles, 44" W, 18" D, 39½" H $2,070.00

A-MA May 1997   Skinner

Left to Right

Limbert Rocking Morris Chair, orig. lt. br. finish w/ overcoat, orig. pegs, orig. leatherette cushions, brand mark, 31" W, 39½" D, 36" H $4,025.00
Roseville Pottery, futura jardiniere & pedestal, molded leaves in colors of yel., gr. & lavender on an orange-brown ground, 14½" W, 28½" H $1,840.00
Limbert Rocking Morris Chair, orig. med. br. finish w/ slight overcoat, plaid fabric cushions, brand mark, 31" W, 39½" D, 36" H $2,530.00

A-MA May 1997   Skinner

Left to Right

Lifetime Morris Chair, pegged const., through tenons on arms, quartersawn oak, repl. leather cushions, 32½" W, 36" D, 41½" H $2,875.00
313-Pottery Vase, dec. w/ three Aztec faces under a deep matte gr. glaze, sgn. Potnique, 8" W, 5½" H $115.00
L.& J.G. Stickley Tabouret, arched stretcher, clip corner top, orig. finish, 16¾" W, 17" D, 19¼" H $690.00
Harden Morris Chair, paddle arm, unsgn., arched apron, orig. dk. br. finish, 31½" W, 35" D, 38" H . . . . .N/S

A-MA May 1997   Skinner

Left to Right

Gustav Stickley Table, unsgn., deep reddish br. orig. finish, minor separations to top, 40" W, 42" D, 30" H $5,462.50
Arts & Crafts Armchair, orig. dk. finish, 27¾" W, 21½" D, 39½" H . . . . .N/S

A-MA May 1997   Skinner

Harden Sideboard, attrib., orig. med. br. finish, quartersawn oak, felt line center drawer, int. shelf, 52⅛" W, 20⅞" D, 51¼" H $805.00

A-MA Oct. 1996   Skinner, Inc.

Stickley Book Rack, paper label, orig. finish, 42¼" W, 12" D, 36" H $1,955.00
Arts & Crafts Bookcase, revolving, three int. shelves, dk. finish, 20¾" sq., 44" H $575.00

A-MA Oct. 1996   Skinner, Inc.

Stickley Bookcase, single-door, three shelves, orig. finish, through tenons & arched toe board, repair to back leg, 22" W, 11" D, 50" H $1,840.00
Arts & Crafts Sewing Rocker, orig. finish, 17" W, 15¼" D, 32¼" H $460.00

A-MA Oct. 1996   Skinner, Inc.

Stickley Morris Chair, attributed adjustable pegs, orig. finish, repl. cushions, 31½" W, 35" D, 46" H $2,760.00
Stickley Tabouret, arched cross stretcher base, cleaned finish, stain to top, unsgn., 18" diam., 20" H .$577.50

A-MA Oct. 1996   Skinner, Inc.

Gustav Stickley Morris Chair, paddle arms, orig. worn finish, sgn. Gustav, red mark, repl. br. leather upholstery, missing corbel, 29" W, 32" D, 43" H $1,955.00
Limbert Oval Table, oak, sq. cut outs & arched apron, orig. finish w/ some color added, 45" W, 30" D, 29" H $2,990.00

A-MA Apr. 1997   Skinner, Inc.

Lady's Desk & Chair, Victorian Bird's-eye Maple Faux Bamboo, 19th C., 32" W, 22½" D, 55" H . . .$3,737.50

A-MA June 1997   Skinner, Inc.

Collector's Cabinet, gothic revival walnut, 19th C., molded top w/ a glazed velvet lined compartment, 26½" W, 18¾" D, 33" H $2,530.00
George III Armchair, mah. & caned, early 19th C., w/ loose leather cusions, caning distressed, 40" H . . .$3,105.00

A-PA Jan. 1997   Pook & Pook Inc.

Bookcase, Scottish Georgian, ca. 1770, in 3 sections, top w/ broken arch pediment w/ carved rosettes & pierced fretwork, 2 glass doors, base w/ single drawer, 46" W, 12" D, 84" H $4,000.00
Tall Case Clock, Irish oak, mid 18th C., 8-day brass face works, engr. "John Reilly, Dublin", restoration to base, 94" H $1,900.00

A-MD Mar. 1997 DeCaro Auction Sales, Inc.

Sheraton Cylinder Roll Desk, MA, ca. 1790-1800, mah. w/ satinwood veneers & checkerboard inlay on all drawers & cylinder roll, fitted int. w/ writing slide, 39" W, 22" D, 46½" H $7,250.00

A-MA Apr. 1997   Skinner, Inc.

Swiss Music Box, 13-inch cylinder on stand, ca. 1900, w/ three additional cylinders, on a burl walnut & ebonized stand w/ turned legs, 43" W, 22" D, 34" H $6,612.50

A-MA Apr. 1997   Skinner, Inc.

George III Sideboard, mah. & ebony inlay, restorations, 56½" L, 24" D, 36" H $2,760.00

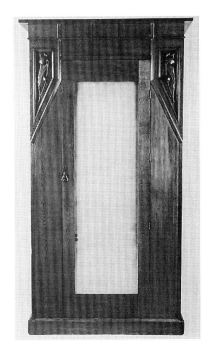

A-MA May 1997   Skinner

Arts & Crafts Armoire, Eng., sgn. Abbot & Co. Art Furnishers Ripon, hammered copper panels, w/ repousse floral panels, 46" W, 20½" D, 8' 2½" H $1,495.00

AGATA GLASS was patented by Joseph Locke of the New England Glass Company of Cambridge, Massachusetts, in 1877. The application of a metallic stain left a mottled design characteristic of agata, hence the name.

AMBER GLASS is the name of any glassware having a yellowish-brown color. It became popular during the last quarter of the 19th century.

AMBERINA GLASS was patented by the New England Glass Company in 1833. It is generally recognized as a clear yellow glass shading to a deep red or fushcia at the top. When the colors are opposite, it is known as reverse amberina. It was machine-pressed into molds, free blown, cut and pattern molded. Almost every glass factory here and in Europe produced this ware; however, few pieces were ever marked.

AMETHYST GLASS — The term identifies any glassware made in the proper dark purple shade. It became popular after the Civil War.

ART GLASS is a general term given to various types of ornamental glass made to be decorative rather than functional. It dates primarily from the late Victorian period to the present day and, during the span of time, glassmakers have achieved fantastic effects of shape, color, pattern, texture and decoration.

AVENTURINE GLASS — The Venetians are credited with the discovery of aventurine during the 1860s. It was produced by various mixes of copper in yellow glass. When the finished pieces were broken, ground or crushed, they were used as decorative material by glassblowers. Therefore, a piece of aventurine glass consists of many tiny glittering particles on the body of the object, suggestive of sprinkled gold crumbs or dust. Other colors in aventurine are known to exist.

BACCARAT GLASS was first made in France in 1756 by La Compagnie des Cristelleries de Baccarat—until the firm went bankrupt. Production began for the second time during the 1820s and the firm is still in operation, producing fine glassware and paperweights. Baccarat is famous for its earlier paperweights made during the last half of the 19th century.

BOHEMIAN GLASS is named for its country of origin. It is ornate, overlay, or flashed glassware, popular during the Victorian era.

BRISTOL GLASS is a lightweight opaque glass, often having a light bluish tint, and decorated with enamels. The ware is a product of Bristol, England—a glass center since the 1700s.

BURMESE — Frederick Shirley developed this shaded art glass at the now-famous old Mt. Washington Glass Company in New Bedford, Massachusetts, and patented his discovery under the name of "Burmese" on December 15, 1885. The ware was also made in England by Thomas Webb & Sons.

Burmese is a hand-blown glass with the exception of a few pieces that were pattern molded. The latter are either ribbed, hobnail or diamond quilted in design. This ware is found in two textures or finishes: the original glazed or shiny finish, and the dull, velvety, satin finish. It is a homogeneous glass (singlelayered) that was never lined, cased or plated. Although its color varies slightly, it always shades from a delicate yellow at the base to a lovely salmon-pink at the top. The blending of colors is so gradual that it is difficult to determine where one color ends and the other begins.

CAMBRIDGE glasswares were produced by the Cambridge Glass Company in Ohio from 1901 until the firm closed in 1954.

CAMEO GLASS can be defined as any glass in which the surface has been cut away to leave a design in relief. Cutting is accomplished by the use of hand-cutting tools, wheel cutting and hydrofluoric acid. This ware can be clear or colored glass of a single layer, or glass with multiple layers of clear or colored glass.

Although cameo glass has been produced for centuries, the majority available today dates from the late 1800s. It has been produced in England, France and other parts of Europe, as well as the United States. The most famous of the French masters of cameo wares was Emile Gallé.

CANDY CONTAINTERS were used for holding tiny candy pellets. These were produced in a variety of shapes—locomotives, cars, boats, guns, and such, for children.

CARNIVAL GLASS was an inexpensive, pressed iridescent glassware made from about 1900 through the 1920s. It was made in quantitites by Northwood Glass Company, Fenton Art Glass Company and others, to compete with the expensive art glass of the period. Originally called "taffeta" glass, the ware became known as "carnival" glass during the 1920s when carnivals gave examples as premiums or prizes.

CORALENE — The term coralene denotes a type of decoration rather than a kind of glass—consisting of many tiny beads, either of colored or transparent glass—decorating the surface. The most popular design used resembled coral or seaweed, hence the name.

CRACKLE GLASS — This type of art glass was an invention of the Venetians that spread rapidly to other countries. It is made by plunging red-hot glass into cold water, then reheating and reblowing it, thus producing an unusual outer surface which appears to be covered with a multitiude of tiny fractures, but is perfectly smooth to the touch.

CRANBERRY GLASS — The term "cranberrry glass" refers to color only, not to a particular type of glass. It is undoubtedly the most familiar colored glass known to collectors. This ware was blown or molded, and often decorated with enamels.

CROWN MILANO glass was made by Frederick Shirley at the Mt. Washington Glass Company, New Bedford, Massachusetts, from 1886-1888. It is ivory in color with a satin finish, and was embellished with floral sprays, scrolls and gold enamel.

CROWN TUSCAN glass has a pink-opaque body. It was originally produced in 1936 by A.J. Bennett, president of the Cambridge Glass Company of Cambridge, Ohio. The line was discontinued in 1954. Occasionally referred to as Royal Crown Tuscan, this ware was named for a scenic area in Italy, and it has been said that its color was taken from the fresh-colored sky at sunrise. When trans-illuminated, examples do have all of the blaze of a sunrise—a characteristic that is even applied to new examples of the ware reproduced by Mrs. Elizabeth Degenhart of Crystal Art Glass, and Harold D. Bennett, Guernsey Glass Company of Cambridge, Ohio.

CUSTARD GLASS was manufactured in the United States for a period of about 30 years (1885-1915). Although Harry Northwood was the first and largest manufacturer of custard glass, it was also produced by the Heisey Glass Company, Diamond Glass Company, Fenton Art Glass Company and a number of others.

The name custard glass is derived from its "custard yellow" color which may shade light yellow to ivory to light green—glass that is opaque to opalescent. Most pieces have fiery opalescence when held to the light. Both the color and glow of this ware came from the use of uranium salts in the glass. It is generally a heavy type pressed glass made in a variety of different patterns.

CUT OVERLAY — The term identifies pieces of glassware usually having a milk-white exterior that have been cased with cranberry, blue or amber glass. Other type examples are deep blue, amber or cranberry on crystal glass, and the majority of pieces has been decorated with dainty flowers. Although Bohemian glass manufacturers produced some very choice pieces during the 19th century, fine examples were also made in America, as well as in France and England.

DAUM NANCY is the mark found on pieces of French cameo glass made by August and Antonin Daum after 1875.

DURAND ART GLASS was made by Victor Durand from 1879 to 1935 at the Durand Art Glass Works in Vineland, New Jersey. The glass resembles Tiffany in quality. Drawn white feather designs and thinly drawn glass threading (quite brittle) applied around the main body of the ware, are striking examples of Durand creations on an iridescent surface.

FLASHED WARES were popular during the late 19th century. They were made by partially coating the inner surface of an object with a thin plating of glass or another, more dominant color—usually red. These pieces can readily be identified by holding the object to the light and examining the rim, as it will show more than one layer of glass. Many pieces of "rubina crystal" (cranberry to clear), "blue amberina" (blue to amber), and "rubina verde" (cranberry to green), were manufactured in this way.

FINDLAY or ONYX art glass was manufactured about 1890 for only a short time by the Dalzell Gilmore Leighton Company of Findlay, Ohio.

FRANCISWARE is a hobnail glassware with frosted or clear glass hobs and stained amber rims and tops. It was produced during the late 1880s by Hobbs, Brockunier and Company.

FRY GLASS was made by the H.C. Fry Company, Rochester, Pennsylvania, from 1901, when the firm was organized, until 1934 when operations ceased. The firm specialized in the manufacturing of cut glassware. The production of their famous "foval" glass did not begin until the 1920s. The firm also produced a variety of glass specialties, oven wares and etched glass.

GALLÉ glass was made in Nancy, France, by Emile Gallé at the Gallé Factory founded in 1874. The firm produced both enameled and cameo glass, pottery, furniture and other art nouveau items. After Gallé 's death in 1904, the factory continued operating until 1935.

GREENTOWN glass was made in Greentown, Indiana, by the Indiana Tumbler and Goblet Company from 1894 until 1903. The firm produced a variety of pressed glasswares in addition to milk and chocolate glass.

GUNDERSON peachblow is a more recent type art glass produced in 1952 by the Gunderson-Pairpoint Glass Works of New Bedford, Massachusetts, successors to the Mt. Washington Glass Company. Gunderson pieces have a soft satin finish shading from white at the base to a deep rose at the top.

HOBNAIL — The term hobnail identifies any glassware having "bumps"—flattened, rounded or pointed—over the outer surface of the glass. A variety of patterns exists. Many of the fine early examples were produced by Hobbs, Brockunier and Company, Wheeling, West Virginia, and the New England Glass Company.

HOLLY AMBER, originally known as "golden agate," is a pressed glass pattern which features holly berries and leaves over its glossy surface. Its color shades from golden brown tones to opalescent streaks. This ware was produced by the Indiana Tumbler and Goblet Company for only 6 months, from January 1 to June 13, 1903. Examples are rare and expensive.

IMPERIAL GLASS — The Imperial Glass Company of Bellaire, Ohio, was organized in 1901 by a group of prominent citizens of Wheeling, West Virginia. A variety of fine art glass, in addition to carnival glass, was produced by the firm. The two trademarks which identified the ware were issued in June 1914. One consisted of the firm's name, "Imperial," and the other included a cross formed by double-pointed arrows.

The latter ll of their present production—including reproduced carnival glass.

LATTICINO is the name given to articles of glass in which a network of tiny milk-white lines appear, crisscrossing between two walls of glass. It is a type of filigree glassware developed during the 16th century by the Venetians.

LEGRAS GLASS, cameo, acid cut and enameled glasswares were made by August J.F. Legras at Saint-Denis, France, from 1864-1914.

LOETZ GLASS was made in Austria just before the turn of the century. As Loetz worked in the Tiffany factory before returning to Austria, much of his glass is similar in appearance to Tiffany wares. Loetz glass is often marked "Loetz" or "Loetz-Austria."

LUTZ GLASS was made by Nicholas Lutz, a Frenchman, who worked at the Boston and Sandwich Glass Company from 1870 to 1888 when it closed. He also produced fine glass at the Mt. Washington Glass Company. Lutz is noted for two different types of glass—striped and threaded wares. Other glass houses also produced similar glass and these wares were known as Lutz-type.

MARY GREGORY was an artist for the Boston and Sandwich Glass Company during the last quarter of the 19th century. She decorated glassware with white enamel figures of young children engaged in playing, collecting butterflies, etc., in white on transparent glass, both clear and colored. Today the term "Mary Gregory" glass applies to any glassware that remotely resembles her work.

MERCURY GLASS is a double-walled glass that dates from the 1850s to about 1910. It was made in England as well as the United States during this period. Its interior, usually in the form of vases, is lined with flashing mercury, giving the items an all over silvery appearance. The entrance hole in the base of each piece was sealed over. Many pieces were decorated.

MILK GLASS is an opaque pressed glassware, usually of milk-white color, although green, amethyst, black, and shades of blue were made. Milk glass was produced in quantity in the United States during the 1880s, in a variety of patterns.

MILLEFIORI — This decorative glassware is considered to be a specialty of the Venetians. It is sometimes called "glass of a thousand flowers," and has been made for centuries. Very thin colored glass rods are arranged in bundles, then fused together with heat. When the piece of glass is sliced across, it has a design like that of many small flowers. These tiny wafer-thin slices are then embedded in larger masses of glass, enlarged and shaped.

MOSER GLASS was made by Kolomon Moser at Carlsbad. The ware is considered to be another type of art nouveau glass as it was produced during its heyday during the early 1900s. Principal colors included amethyst, cranberry, green and blue, with fancy enameled decoration.

MOTHER-OF-PEARL, often abbreviated in descriptions as M.O.P., is glass composed of two or more layers, with a pattern showing through to the other surface. The pattern, caused by internal air traps, is created by expanding the inside layer of molten glass into molds with varying design. When another layer of glass is applied, this brings out the design. The final layer of glass is then acid dipped, and the result is mother-of-pearl satinware. Patterns are numerous. The most frequently found are the diamond quilted, raindrop and herringbone. This ware can be one solid color, a single color shading light to dark, two colors blended or a variety of colors which include the rainbow effect. In addition, many pieces are decorated with colorful enamels, coralene beading, and other applied glass decorations.

NAILSEA GLASS was first produced in England from 1788 to 1873. The character-istics that identify this ware are the "pulled" loopings and swirls of colored glass over the body of the object.

NEW ENGLAND PEACHBLOW was patented in 1886 by the New England Glass Company. It is a single-layered glass shading from opaque white at the base to deep rose-red or raspberry at the top. Some pieces have a glossy surface, but most were given an acid bath to produce a soft, matte finish.

NEW MARTINSVILLE PEACHBLOW GLASS was produced from 1901-1907 at New Martinsville, Pennsylvania.

OPALESCENT GLASS — The term refers to glasswares which have a milky white effect in the glass, usually on a colored ground. There are three basic types of this ware. Presently, the most popular includes pressed glass patterns found in table settings. Here the opalescence appears at the top rim, the base, or a combination of both. On blown or mold-blown glass, the pattern itself consists of this milky effect—such as Spanish lace. Another example is the opalescent points on some pieces of hobnail glass. These wares are lighter weight. The third group includes opalescent novelties, primarily of the pressed variety.

PEKING GLASS is a type of Chinese cameo glass produced from the 1700s, well into the 19th century.

PHOENIX GLASS — The firm was established in Beaver County, Pennsylvania, during the late 1800s, and produced a variety of commercial glasswares. During the 1930s the factory made a desirable sculptured gift-type glassware which has become very collectible in recent years. Vases, lamps, bowls, ginger jars, candlesticks, etc., were made until the 1950s in various colors with a satin finish.

PIGEON BLOOD is a bright reddish-orange glassware dating from the early 1900s.

POMONA GLASS was invented in 1884 by Joseph Locke at the New England Glass Company.

PRESSED GLASS was the inexpensive glassware produced in quantity to fill the increasing demand for tablewares when Americans moved away from the simple table utensils of pioneer times. During the 1820s, ingenious Yankees invented and perfected machinery for successfullly pressing glass. About 1865, manufacturers began to color their products. Literally hundreds of different patterns were produced.

QUEZAL is a very fine quality blown iridescent glassware produced by Martin Bach, in his factory in Brooklyn, New York, from 1901-1920. Named after the Central American bird, quezal glassware has an iridescent finish featuring contrasting colored glass threads. Green, white and gold colors are most often found.

ROSALINE GLASS is a product of the Steuben Glass Works of Corning, New York. The firm was founded by Frederick Carter and T.C. Hawkes, Sr. Rosaline is a rose-colored jade glass or colored alabaster. The firm is now owned by the Corning Glass Company, which is presently producing fine glass of exceptional quality.

ROYAL FLEMISH ART GLASS was made by the Mt. Washington Glass Works during the 1880s. It has an acid finish which may consist of one or more colors, decorated with raised gold enameled lines separating into sections. Fanciful painted enamel designs also decorate this ware. Royal Flemish glass is marked "RF," with the letter "R" reversed and backed to the letter "F," within a four-sided orange-red diamond mark.

RUBINA GLASS is a transparent blown glassware that shades from clear to red. One of the first to produce this crystal during the late 1800s was Hobbs, Brocunier and Company of Wheeling, West Virginia.

RUBINA VERDE is a blown art glass made by Hobbs, Brocunier and Company, during the late 1800s. It is a transparent glassware that shades from red to yellow-green.

SABINO GLASS originated in Paris, France, in the 1920s. The company was founded by Marius-Ernest Sabine, and was noted for art deco figures, vases, animals, nudes and animals in clear, opalescent and colored glass.

SANDWICH GLASS — One of the most interesting and enduring pages from America's past is Sandwich glass produced by the famous Boston and Sandwich Glass Company at Sandwich, Massachusetts. The firm began operations in 1825, and the glass flour-ished until 1888 when the factory closed. Despite the popularity of Sandwich Glass, little is known about its founder, Deming Jarvis.

The Sandwich Glass house turned out hundreds of designs in both plain and figured patterns, in colors and crystal, so that no one type could be considered entirely typical—but the best known is the "lacy" glass produced there. The variety and multitude of designs and patterns produced by the company over the years is a tribute to its greatness.

SILVER DEPOSIT GLASS was made during the late 19th and early 20th centuries. Silver was deposited on the glass surface by a chemical process so that a pattern appeared against a clear or colored ground. This ware is sometimes referred to as "silver overlay."

SLAG GLASS was originally known as "mosaic" and "marble glass" because of its streaked appearance. Production in the United States began about 1880. The largest producer of this ware was Challinor, Taylor and Company. The various slag mixtures are: purple, butterscotch, blue, orange, green and chocolate. A small quantity of pink slag was also produced in the inverted fan and feather pattern. Examples are rare and expensive.

SPANISH LACE is a Victorian glass pattern that is easily identified by its distinct opalescent flower and leaf pattern. It belongs to the shaded opalescent glass family.

STEUBEN — The Steuben Glass Works was founded in 1904 by Frederick Carter, an Englishman, and T.G. Hawkes, Sr., at Corning, New York. In 1918 the firm was purchased by the Corning Glass Company. However, Steuben remained with the firm, designing a bounty of fine art glass of exceptional quality.

STIEGEL-TYPE GLASS — Henry William Stiegel founded America's first flint glass factory during the 1760s at Manheim, Pennsylvania. Stiegel glass is flint or crystal glass; it is thin and clear, and has a bell-like ring when tapped. The ware is quite brittle and fragile. Designs were painted freehand on the glass—birds, animals and architectural motifs, surrounded by leaves and flowers. The engraved glass resulted from craftsmen etching the glass surface with a copper wheel, then cutting the desired patterns.

It is extremely difficult to identify, with certainty, a piece of original Stiegel glass. Part of the problem resulted from the lack of an identifying mark on the products. Additionally, many of the craftsmen moved to other areas after the Stiegel plant closed—producing a similar glass product. Therefore, when one is uncertain about the origin of this type ware, it is referred to as "Stiegel-type" glass.

TIFFANY GLASS was made by Louis Comfort Tiffany, one of America's outstanding glass designers of the art nouveau period, from about 1870 to the 1930s. Tiffany's designs included a variety of lamps, bronze work, silver, pottery and stained glass windows. Practically all items made were marked "L.C. Tiffany" or "L.C.T." in addition to the word Favrile".

TORTOISESHELL GLASS — As its name indicates, this type glassware resembles the color of tortoiseshell and has deep rich brown tones combined with amber and cream-colored shades. Tortoiseshell glass was originally produced in 1880 by Francis Pohl, a German chemist. It was also made in the United States by the Sandwich Glass Works and other glass houses during the late 1800s.

VAL ST. LAMBERT Cristalleries, located in Belgium, was founded in 1825 and the firm is still in operation.

VASA MURRHINA glassware was produced in quantity at the Vasa Murrhina Art Glass Company of Sandwich, Massachusetts, during the late 1900s. John C. DeVoy, assignor to the firm, registered a patent on July 1, 1884, for the process of decorating glassware with particles of mica flakes (coated with copper, gold, nickel or silver) sandwiched between an inner layer of clear or transparent colored glass. The ware was also produced by other American glass firms and in England.

VASELINE GLASS — The term "vaseline" refers to color only, as it resembles the greenish-yellow color typical of the oily petroleum jelly known as Vaseline. This ware has been produced in a variety of patterns both here and in Europe—from the late 1800s. It has been made in both clear and opaque yellow, vaseline combined with clear glass, and occasionally the two colors are combined in one piece.

VERLYS GLASS is a type of art glass produced in France after 1931. The Heisey Glass Company, Newark, Ohio, produced identical glass for a short time, after having obtained the rights and formula from the French factory. French-produced ware can be identified from the American product by the signature, the French is mold marked, whereas the American glass is etched script signed.

WAVECREST GLASS is an opaque white glassware made from the late 1890s by French factories and the Pairpoint Manufacturing Company at New Bedford, Massachusetts. Items were decorated by the C.F. Monroe Company of Meriden, Connecticut, with painted pastel enamels. The name wavecrest was used after 1898 with the initials for the company "C.F.M. Co." Operations ceased during World War II.

WEBB GLASS was made by Thomas Webb & Sons of Stourbridge, England, during the late Victorian period. The firm produced a variety of different types of art and cameo glass.

WHEELING PEACHBLOW — With its simple lines and delicate shadings, Wheeling Peachblow was produced soon after 1883 by J.H. Hobbs, Brockunier and Company at Wheeling, West Virginia. It is a two-layered glass lined or cased inside with an opaque, milk-white type of plated glassware. The outer layer shades from a bright yellow at the base to a mahogany red at the top. The majority of pieces produced are in the glossy finish.

Early Auction Co.

A-OH Apr. 1997

Row 1, Left to Right

566-Tiffany Lamp, leaded shade mkd. Tiffany Studios, NY, golden leaves, gr. slag ground, bronze verdigris urn base, impr. Tiffany Studios, NY, w/ firm's circular logo, 18" diam. $8,350.00

601-Fr. Cameo Vase, blk. purple vine, lavender blue flowers, frosty & yel. ground, sgn. Gallé, 10" W, 8" H $5,000.00

546-Royal Flemish Vase, silver gray geese, sun outlined in raised gold, multi-color segments, gilt floral branch on rev., 14¼" H $5,750.00

480-Tiffany Vase, red footed, inverted trumpet form, sgn. L.C. Tiffany, Favrile, 5¾" H $2,600.00

543-Lamp, "puffy", ruby red rose tree, colorful butterfly, mkd. Pairpoint, 6" diam., tree trunk base, 11" H overall . $8,000.00

Row 2, Left to Right

507-Fr. Cameo Vase, "snowy woodland" sgn. Daum Nancy, dk. barren forest w/ marmalade sky, 11¾" H . . .$6,000.00

529-Steuben Vase, irid. blue, gold opal vines, sgn. F. Carder, Aurene, 8¼" H $4,250.00

524-Fr. Cameo Vase, dk. forest, mottle pink, pale yel. & clear sky, raindrop surface, sgn. Daum Nancy, 8¾" H $7,050.00

555-Steuben Tyrian Vase, irid. gray gr. body & red purple bluish body w/ golden hues, irid. blue ring, 7¾" H $8000.00

465-Fr. Cameo Creamer, blk. enamel scene on textured opal. ground, 4¼" H $2,250.00

547-Crown Milano Vase, pastel thistles outlined in raised gold, pale yel. ground, firm's paper label, 14" H $3,000.00

475-Eng. Cameo Vase, 3 color, white over red & leaves on frosty yel. ground, stmpd. Thomas Webb & Sons, 5" H $1,600.00

Row 3, Left to Right

469-Fr. Cameo Vase, ebony evergreens, golden ora. mountains, sgn. Mueller Fres, Luneville, 4¼" H .$1,500.00

520-Tiffany Cypriote Vase, irid. olive gr. body, textured w/ encrusted ruptured bubbles, sgn. L.C.T., 8" H . . . . .N/S

471-Fr. Pate-de-Verre Tray, yel. br. goldfish, yel. tray, sgn. A. Walter, Nancy, 5" diam., 2½" H $3,500.00

425-Burmese Fairy Lamp, dec. acid double dome shade, 3½" H, bases mkd. S. Clarke Fairy, dec. cone form holders, 2-3½" H & 1-5" H w/ lavender flowers & fall color leaves decor on all pieces., 9½" W, 10½" H overall .$3,800.00

474-Vase, golden almond ground, dec. w/ irid. gold pulled leaf design, sgn. L.C.T., 6¾" H $2,700.00

476-Eng. Cameo Vase, ivory base w/ bowl rim, stamped Thomas Webb & Sons Limited, 3¾" H $900.00

A-OH Apr. 1997   Early Auction Co.

Row 1, Left to Right

289-Compote, w/ 1892 U.S. half dollars, covered, 8″ diam., chip on finial, 12″ H $250.00

90B-Tankard Pitcher, cut glass, intaglio carved fuchsias, triple notch handle, 11½″ H $275.00

73-Cruet, cut glass, sgn. Hawkes, tri-con rim, hobstars, 5½″ H $160.00

89-Tankard Pitcher, cut glass, 20 pt. hobstar base, 11″ H $290.00

435-Steuben Luminary, relief portrait of Thomas Edison by Frederic Carder, 6½″ x 8½″ x¾″, clear glass block stamped 1929 C.G.W., lighted metal stand w/ column sides, 8¼″ W, 10¾″ H, overall base mkd. Edison,... 1885 . . . .$950.00

76-Global Cologne, cut glass, hobstars & fains, fluted neck, 5½″ H $150.00

63-Ice Cream Tray, cut glass, sgn. Hawkes, irises, buds & ferns, 9″ x 12″ L $300.00

287-Compote, w/ 1892 U.S. quarter frosted coins, covered, 6″ diam., 9″ H $350.00

Row 2, Left to Right

87-Stemware, 16 pcs., cut glass, 8 wines, 4½″ H, & 8 cordials, 4¼″ H $150.00

78-Dresser Box, cut glass, flashed stars, mkd. Sterling cover . . .$135.00

69-Cylindrical Vase, cut glass, monumental, hobstars, bars of cane, 24 pt. hobstar base, 24″ H $2,700.00

68-Squared Bowl, cut glass, Kimberly variant, 24 pt. hobstar center, 10½″ diam., 3½″ H $425.00

85-Vase, cut glass, 24 pt. hobstar bottom, tooth chip, 16½″ H $200.00

286-Compote, w/ 1892 U.S. quarter frosted coins, 7″ diam., 7″ H .$195.00

72-Bowl, cut glass, sgn. Libbey w/ sabre, 5 pt. hobstar center, prism border $500.00

Row 3, Left to Right

75-Cruet, cut glass, hobstars & fans, tri-con spout, 6″ H $95.00

74-Cruet, cut glass, button hobnail, tri-con rim, 6¾″ H $125.00

82-Whiskey Tumblers, three, cut glass, hobstars & fan, minute rim chip, 2¼″ H $75.00

65-Global Milk Pitcher, cut glass, strawberry diamond & fan, 7″ H $325.00

61-Global Decanter, cut glass, hobstars & fans, faceted stopper, repr. stem, 7″ H $150.00

88-Punch Bowl, two part, cut glass, 24 pt. hobstar base, prism cuttings, tooth missing, 12¼″ diam., 6¼″ H, base w/ step-cut shoulder, 12½″ H overall, includes 14″ diam. beveled mirror . . . $1,000.00

60-Decanter, cut glass, ships, 24 pt hobstar base, 8″ H $375.00

90-Compote, cut glass, pinwheels, fans, hobstars & bars, 8″ diam., 6¾″ H $150.00

77-Dresser Box, cut glass, flashed stars, rayed cross-hatched diamonds, mkd. Sterling cover, 4½″ diam., 2½″ H $145.00

Row 4, Left to Right

64-Global Cream Pitcher, cut glass, relief diamond patt., 4¾″ H . . .$75.00

80-Stemware, cut glass, 11 pcs., 5 goblets, 6½″ H, 4 wines, 4½″ H, sgn. J. Hoare & pr. cordials, 4¼″ H . .$300.00

86-Punch Bowl, cut glass, 16 pt. hobstar, disc base, 12″ diam., 12″ H $600.00

71-Compote, cut glass, intaglio grape pods & leaves, 5″ diam., 8″ H $225.00

90C-Basket, cut glass, paneled body, wheel carved daisies, 12½″ H $125.00

81-Creamer & Open Sugar, cut glass, hobstars, fans & thumbprints, loop handles, 2½″ H $75.00

Row 5, Left to Right

59-Bowl, cut glass, diamond vesicas w/ cane centers, 8″ diam. . . .$175.00

67-Book Paperweight, cut glass, pale gr., inscribed on rev. . . .$350.00

278-Hood Embellishment, frosted Lalique-style, woman's head profile, 6½″ L, 3½″ H $150.00

279-Hood Embellishment, frosted Lalique-style, woman's head profile, 4¾″ L, 3″ H $200.00

62-Tray, cut glass, rectangular, sgn. Hawkes, hobstars & dec. relief diamond, 3½″ x 7¼″ $175.00

66-Jelly Compote, cut glass, sgn. Hawkes, hobstars, faceted knob, 4″ diam., 4¼″ H $225.00

70- Hinged Box, cut glass, 23 pt. hobstar base $1,100.00

83-Repousse Pocket Flask, cut glass, acanthus leaf shoulders, mkd. Sterling, w/ maker's mark, 4½″ H $350.00

84-Silver Case, Fr. enamel, mkd. 900, scattered flowers in royal blue ground, hinged back, 1¾″ x 3″ L $425.00

79-Tumblers, three, cut glass, pinwheels & fans, one w/ chip, 4″ H $100.00

A-MA Oct. 1996   Skinner, Inc.

Row 1, Left to Right

Pressed Glass Spoon Holder, sandwich canary, star & punty footed, Sandwich, MA, 1840-65, cracks, chips, 4¾″ H $345.00

Pressed Glass, three pcs., amethyst, Am., 19th c., including a petal & loop candlestick, a pressed loop oil lamp & a dish, chips, minor cracks, lamp 9 ⅝″ H, dish 6″ Diam. $1,380.00

Blown, Molded & Pressed Glass, seven pcs. cobalt, Am., 19th c., including a vase, cologne, spoon holder, pr. of beakers, footed salt & spherical lamp, minor chips, mismatched stopper, vase 9 ⅜″ H $1,092.50

Colognes, ten freeblown & blown molded, 19th c., including one clear, four colored, four overlay & one w/ applied serpent, damage, minor chips, gilt wear, 3¼″- 11½″ H $1,725.00

Decanter, blown glass overlay, Am. 19th c., cut blue to white to clear, lacking stopper, minor chips, sick, 11⅜″ H $230.00

Row 2, Left to Right

Hexagonal Candlesticks, pr., cobalt blue pressed glass, Am., 1840-60, minor chips, minor cracks, 9¼″ H $862./50

Blown, Blown Molded & Pressed Glass, nine pcs., including a flip glass, a mercury tieback, an overlay mug, a beaker w/ millefiori base, a bear-form pomade jar, a pr. of amber dishes & two others, imp. $230.00

Cologne, sandwich blown molded glass overlay, 1850-70, cut blue to clear, minor chips, bubble burst, 11½″ H $977.50

Oil Lamp, Am., 19th c., freeblown ruby font above an opaque white pressed baroque base, gilt highlights, gilt wear, cracks, 12″ H . . . . . . .N/S

Hexagonal Candlesticks, two canary pressed glass, Am. mid 19th c., minor chips & cracks, 9″ H $460.00

A-OH Apr. 1997   Early Auction Co.

Row 1, Left to Right

293-Satin Vases, pr., blue hobnail, aqua elongated melon bodies shading to spring gr., 11" H $300.00

187-Lamp, rev. painted shade, blk. foliaged & evergreen trees, blue waterway & intense reddish ora. sky, blk. base w/ etched petal design, mkd. Moe Bridges, 15" diam., 21" H overall $1,200.00

516-Steuben Vase, gr. jade w/ alabaster foot, firm's acid block mark, 12½" H $375.00

199-Salt & Pepper, pr. shakers, Mt. Washington, "tomato", w/ pink & blue flowers on almond satin grounds, 1½" H $175.00

226-Ruby Lustres, pr., enamel dec., gold gilt design, 14" H $650.00

291-Vase, irid. reddish gold, sgn. Quezal 9" H $550.00

149-Lamp, Pittsburg, rev. painted shade, dk. gr., subdued color meadowland, dk. slender base, hammered ground, 14" diam. $1,100.00

290-Burmese Vase, Mt. Washington acid, 12" H $450.00

Row 2, Left to Right

237-Vase, sgn. Mt. Joye, irid. textured dec. w/ gilt, partial Cameo gilt background, 11½" H $850.00

170-Vase, glossy Wheeling Peachblow, 18½" H $3,000.00

259-Vase, irid. reddish gold, sgn. L.C. Tiffany, Favrile 4" H $525.00

245-Chandelier, sgn. Quezal, irid. gold w/ opal leaves w/ gr. tips, 5¾" H, ornate 4-arm brass fixture, 19" H w/ 24" chain $1,200.00

225-Peachblow Bowl, Mt. Washington, broken and reglued, 5½" diam., 2¾" H $275.00

264-Compote, irid. gold w/ lavender highlights, sgn. L.C.T. Favrile, 6" diam. $550.00

258-Moser Sherbet, 3" H, & matching underplate, 4¼" diam. . . .$225.00

270-Fr. Cameo Vase, sgn. Gallé w/ star, gr. & chartreuse against apricot & frosty ground, 12" H $1,200.00

198-Salt & Pepper, pr. shakers, Mt. Washington, "egg", enamel flowers, 2½" H $150.00

197-Royal Worcester Ewer, raised gold highlights, tan body, neck & base, mkd. Rudolstadt, Ger., R.W., 16½" H $350.00

54-Vase, glossy peachblow, amber handle, opal. flower, 5½" H . .$125.00

36-Steuben Goblet, irid. gold, sgn. Aurene, 6" H $250.00

Row 3, Left to Right

244-Quezal Gas Shades, pr., sgn., irid. opal body, dec. w/ gold & gr. leaves, 2" diam., 5" H $400.00

129-Fairy Lamp, 3½" H dome shade, clear Clarkes insert, cut glass stick base, 15" H overall $550.00

142-Vase, mkd. Pairpoint France, hand dec., colorful ducks, golden sun, yel. & tan ground, 15" H $750.00

261-Trumpet Vase, Fr. Cameo, sgn. Gallé, lavender & gray, w/ star, 5½" H $675.00

235-Collars & Cuffs Box, mkd. Wavecrest, mauve flowers w/ molded leafy vine dec. $350.00

251-Covered Tomato, blue, mkd. Royal Bayreuth, 4" diam., 3" H, circular leaf undertray, 5½" diam. . .$95.00

250-Tomato Pitcher, blue, mkd. Royal Bayreuth, gr. vine handle, 6" H $275.00

242-English Epergne, Victorian, beveled mirror, 11" diam., w/ yel. flowers, 2 cased conical overlay vases w/ applied yel. ferns, 5" H& clear trumpet form vase, 12" H overall . . . . .N/S

275- Vases, pr., mkd. Wavecrest, pink rosebuds, raised scrolls, blue ground, 7½" H $500.00

Row 4, Left to Right

243-Vases, pr., enameled, harbor scene, pale peachblow color sky, ornate metal bases, mkd. Deposé, attrib. to Legras, 11½" H $500.00

193-Porcelain Plaque, sgn. Wagner, monk w/ basket of falling wine bottles, gold velvet matte & frame, 7½" x 9½" H $1,400.00

46-Music Box, etched brass, multicolored bird springs up to sing from under a hinged enamel cover, 18th C. garden setting, enamel inserts on each side w/ dk. gr. accents, 3½" x 4" L, 1¾" H $3,400.00

266-Finger Bowl, Steuben, reddish gold calcite, 4½" diam., 2½" H, underplate 6¼" diam. $200.00

165-Cologne Bottles, Steuben, three matching, cardinal red swirled ribs, stopper w/ 4 clear tooled leaves, 3¾" diam., 6½" H, & matching pr., clear cane stoppers w/ cardinal red swirls, 3" diam., 8" H $900.00

292-Steuben Salt Dip, irid. blue, silver stamped Aurene, Haviland, 1½" diam., 1" H $500.00

274-Amberina Cruet, inverted thumbprint, clear reeded handle, 6¾" H $175.00

227-Coffee Pot, Fry Foval, opal w/ blue knob & handle, 11" H . .$200.00

172-Tobacco Humidor, covered, mkd. Handel, br. & white dog, gr. foliage ground w/ red br. & gr. body, sgn. Kelsey $1,100.00

246-Fr. Mantle Clock, ornate case w/ dolphin side ornaments, porcelain insert w/ garden scene, dec. porcelain urn finial, 18" H $1,000.00

Row 5, Left to Right

265-Steuben Sherbet, gold calcite, firm's paper label, 4" H & underplate 6" diam. $250.00

268-Salt & Pepper, pr. Amberina, 3¾" H $350.00

260-Bowl, yel. pastel, sgn. L.C.T. Favrile, 7½" diam., 1½" H . . .$300.00

200-Salt & Pepper, pr. shakers, Mt. Washington, "egg", enamel flowers, 2½" H $175.00

218-Burmese Vase, mkd. Queen's Burmese, Thomas Webb & Sons, 3" diam., 2¼" H $225.00

201-Peachblow Pear, New Eng., w/ long stem, 5½" H $125.00

222-Toothpick Holder, irid. bluish gold, sgn. L.C.T., 2" H $225.00

223-Toothpick Holder, irid. bluish gold, sgn. L.C.T., 2" H $225.00

37-Finger Bowl, irid. gold, sgn. Quezal, reddish blue cast, 5" diam., 2½" H .$250.00

267-Tiffany Vase, opal. golden graygreen, script etched L.C.T., 3¾" H $550.00

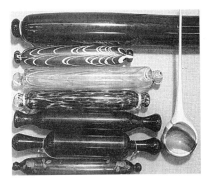

A-OH Aug. 1996   Garth Auctions

Top to bottom:

Blown Rolling Pin, cobalt blue, worn painted & transfer designs w/ flowers, ships & "Think On Me When Far At Sea", 29" L $110.00

Blown Rolling Pin, gr. w/ white looping, 14" L $192.50

Blown Rolling Pin, clear w/ white & pink looping, 17½" L $82.50

Blown Rolling Pin, clear w/ end of day colors in red & blue, 16" L $192.50

Blown Rolling Pin, heavy blk. glass, wear, 17" L $104.50

Blown Rolling Pin, deep amber, wear, chip on end & sm. broken blister, 17½" L $82.50

Blown Rolling Pin, amethyst, worn painted floral dec., 15" L $104.50

On right:

Blown Dipper, clear w/ red looping, white int. coating, 17¾" L $115.50

A-OH Apr. 1997   Early Auction Co.

Row 1, Left to Right

159-Amberina Tumblers, four D.Q. fuchsia, 3¾" H $320.00

156-Amberina Vase, Jack-in-Pulpit, inverted thumbprint body, amber ruffled edge, 13½" H $275.00

330-Burmese Vase, Mt. Washington acid, 4¾" H $225.00

355-Quezal Vase, irid. gold, 8" H $625.00

284-Lamp, rev. painted shade, rainbow color sky, bronze color textured base, 16" diam., 25" H overall $850.00

339-Vase, amber w/ gr. infused patt., attrib. to Nash, 6" H, 7" diam. $200.00

323-Perfume Bottle, irid. blue, sgn. Steuben Aurene, 4½" H $1,600.00

324-Steuben Cologne, irid. gold, sgn. Aurene, 4¼" H $1,100.00

357-Loetz Vase, trumpet-form, irid. "oil spots" mingled upon royal blue, 9" H $900.00

280-Sevres Charger, porcelain, gold scroll & floral border, sgn. E. Furloud, 17" diam. $850.00

340-Durand Vase, irid. royal blue w/ lavender cast, 9½" H $900.00

296-Vase, cased glossy Northwood "pull-up", yel. w/ ruby red & opal stripes, pink int., 5½" H $650.00

10-Tankard Pitcher, mkd. Willets Belleek, 17th C., colorfully dec., raised gold floral, 14" H $1,100.00

326-Steuben Lamp, red Aurene, decorated w/ irid. golden blue, 9" H $2,500.00

295-Bowl, cased glossy Northwood "pull-up", yel. w/ ruby red stripes, crystal trim, pink int., 12½" L, 7½" H $700.00

221-Vase, rainbow satin w/ ruffled rim, 5½" H $190.00

Row 2, Left to Right

318-Rookwood Ewer, standard glaze, 1899, initials Caroline Steinle, yel. flowers w/ foliage, 8¾" H $750.00

322-Covered Box, cobalt blue, red & yel. flowers on almond blue ground, sgn. Moorcroft w/ paper label, 4½" diam., 2¾" H $300.00

336-Nash Chintz Vase, silvery-blue textured veins on deep red ground, 8½" H $600.00

220-Vase, rainbow satin, swirl patt., 7¾" H $150.00

133-English Vase, rubina crystal w/ yel. enamel scrolls & floral sprays, gilt leaf rim & highlights, 9¼" H . .$95.00

307-Vase, Webb pink cased satin, shaded amethyst, dec. w/ raised gold branches, satin mauve int., 5" H $475.00

328-Steuben Vase, gr. jade, 8" H $350.00

152-Steuben Vase, pomona gr. ribbed, 10½" H $275.00

316-Vase, iridesent gray gr. on bluish maroon ground, sgn. Weller Sicard, 9" H $550.00

144-Porcelain Portrait, oval, lady wearing pearl necklace & pink gown, sgn. Wagner, 2½" x 3¼" H, dk. wooden frame $550.00

102-Vase, rose pink D.Q. M.O.P. w/ pear form body, 7¾" H $300.00

327-Vase, irid. gold, sgn. L.C. Tiffany, Favrile, 8" H $300.00

351-Steuben Vase, Ivory, 5" H .N/S

Row 3, Left to Right

354-Ramikin, Steven's & Williams, golden red jewel patt., 2" H, & underplate, 4¾" diam. $175.00

4-Vase, mkd. Lenox, Belleek, lavender & white lilac, 7" H $200.00

334-Durand Table Setting, 50 pcs., yel. lustre w/ emerald gr. edged rims .N/S

352-Rose Bowl, Pomona D.Q., pink stain wild rose & gr. foliage, frosty ground, 4" diam., 2" H $275.00

9-Vase, gr. & red, mkd. C.A.C. Belleek, 18½" H $400.00

312-Punch Cup, Fuchsia Amberina D.Q. w/ amber reeded handle . .$120.00

356-Nash Chintz Vase, emerald gr. w/ mottled br. & mustard stripes, opal & blue swirls, 7¼" H $1,000.00

363-Ewer, mottled pink spangled, clear branch handle, 9" H . . .$125.00

319-Mug, red & blk. raspberry w/ fall color foliage, initials Hattie M. Ross, sgn. Louwelsa Weller, 5¾" H . .$300.00

341-Vase, irid. reddish gold, sgn. Quezal, 9½" H $600.00

Row 4, Left to Right

368-Amberina Vase, rev. D.Q., 2 reeded amber handles, minute rim chip, 6¼" H $160.00

48- Bowl, Steuben Rosaline w/ rolled rim, signed F. Carder, 2½" H .$300.00

145-Fr. Enamel Portrait, woman wearing dec. gold accessories, purple & white cap, red ground, emerald gr. enamel, floral w/ brass trim, 4¾" diam., blk. wooden frame . . .$400.00

304- Photo Receiver, mkd. Nakara, portrait of Indian Chief, mustard yel. & olive gr. ground, 4" L, 2½" H .$400.00

337-Nash Chintz Vase, silvery-blue textured veins on deep red ground, 7½" H $1,050.00

338-Nash Chintz Parfaits, pr., 6½" H, blue & gr. pulled & ribbon design, pale aqua knob bases, sgn. Nash, 6½" H $275.00

8-Stein, mkd. C.A.C. Belleek, red currents & colorful leaves, sgn. T. Arten, 5½" H $150.00

335-Durand Center Bowl, yel. w/ opal Venetian swirl, royal blue pulled design & edge, 14" diam., 5" H . .N/S

321-Earthenware Vase, silver overlay, repeated silver plums, leafy branches across maroon body, 7¾" H $350.00

332-Burmese Bowl, glossy Mt. Washington, 2¼" H $375.00

Row 5, Left to Right

53-Gas Shade, Irid. bluish gold, sgn. RGF, Aurene, 2⅛" fitter, 5" H .$150.00

52-Gas Shade, sgn. Quezal, opal dec. w/ gr. & gold leaves, 2¼" fitter, 5¼" H $225.00

47-Finger Bowl, Steuben Rosaline, 6¼" diam., 2¼" H $175.00

333-Silver Tray, w/ pen, mkd. Tiffany & Co., sterling, 3" diam. $175.00

298-M.O.P. Pitcher, yel. satin D.Q., camphor reeded handle, 5" H $300.00

310-Steuben Darner, irid. blue w/ opal & royal blue vines, 5¾" H $1,000.00

305-Honeycomb Vase, pink cut velvet, camphor trim, 5½" H . . .$200.00

297-Finger Bowl, irid. gold, 4¼" diam., 2½" H, pod form tray, 5¾" diam., each sgn. Quezal $425.00

317-Vase, irid. bluish gr. w/ bluish purple ground, sgn. Weller Sicard, 5½" H $550.00

311-Vase, rainbow D.Q. M.O.P. w/ crystal base, mkd. pat., 10" H $450.00

303-Wavecrest Vases, pr., dec. w/ pale pink & foliage accented w/ enamel, ormolu feet, 6¼" H $300.00

151-Finger Bowl, aqua pastel, 5" diam., 2" H, ribbed gr. pastel underplate w/ aqua hue, 7" diam., both sgn. L.C. Tiffany Favrile $350.00

359-Cream Pitcher, Eng. egg-form, almond shading to pink then apricot, 7" H $90.00

A-MA Mar. 1997   Eldred's

Left to Right

Sandwich Glass, Christmas salt, in cranberry w/ pewter top, 19th C., ...$462.00

Blown Glass, two pcs., amethyst, Am., 19th C., tumbler & handled mug, 3¾" H . . . . .N/S

Sandwich Glass, ten, Christmas salts & peppers, 19th C., cobalt, amber, blue, blue-green, medium blue, aqua, amethyst, lt. amber, dk. amethyst, & painted milk glass $495.00

Blown Glass, two pcs., amethyst, Am., 19th C., tumbler & handled mug, 3¾" H . . . . .N/S

A-OH Apr. 1997   Early Auction Co.

Row 1, Left to Right

241-Vase, irid. blue, sgn. Durand, 9¼" H $800.00

240-Lamp, rev. painted shade, sgn. Jefferson, artist initials W.J.S., partial cloth label, dk. foliaged trees on chocolate br. coastline, swirl body w/ floral clusters, 24" H overall $2,200.00

182-Crown Milano Vase, raised gold leaf & berry wreath, floral sprigs on white opal glass, mkd. w/ red crown & leaf wreath $900.00

216-Burmese Bowl, dec. in red pods & colorful leaves, mkd. Queen's Burmese, Thomas Webb & Sons, 2¼" H $325.00

208-Pickle Castor, Mt. Washington Crown Milano insert, raised gold dec., yel. red & gray flowers w/ white D.Q. body, silver frame, silver fork & cover, 10" H $900.00

238-Vase, Fr. Cameo, med. gr. thistles, mottled gr. frost apricot blush ground, sgn. Gallé, 13¾" H . .$1,000.00

206-Pickle Castor, ruby Amberina hobnail insert, 4½" H, silver quadruple plated frame w/ 2 figural cherry & leaf branch base, 11" H . .$750.00

186-Covered Box, Fr. Cameo, fire polished, magenta, golden amber, Cameo sgn. Gallé & firm's paper label, 4" diam., 2¼" H . . .$1,750.00

239-Vase, trumpet form, sgn. L.C.T., dec. w/ gr. pulled leaves w/ irid. gold tips, opal ground, irid. gold int., Doré base, mkd. Tiffany Studios, NY, 14" H overall $1,400.00

501-Lamp, Fr. Cameo dome shade, sgn. Richard, burgundy bown trees, castle scene, tangerine ground, mkd. Ger., 16" H overall $2,500.00

43-Cameo Vase, Fr., sgn. Legras, blue mountains & peachblow color sky, 6" H $475.00

188-Vase, irid. bluish gold, sgn. Steuben Aurene, 12" H $750.00

Row 2, Left to Right

211-Pickle Castor, double, ea. insert has 3 acid etched herons, ornate Pairpoint silver frame, 14½" H . . .$550.00

173-Vase, pink M.O.P. herringbone, dec. w/ yel. overlapped coralene leaves $400.00

39-Durand Vase, irid. gold, dec. w/ opal leaves w/ royal blue, golden threads, 10" H $900.00

183-Cracker Barrel, Royal Flemish, bubble design in pastel hues, raised gold on maroon ground, floral emb. cover, 6" H . . . . .N/S

231-Vase, Fr. Cameo, pink body dec. w/ maroon flowers, sgn. A. DeLatte; Nancy, 7½" top diam., 6½" H $700.00

230- Vase, sgn. Quezal, reddish gold dec., opal body, 11¼" H$950.00

236-Bowl, Fr. Cameo, mottled chartreuse & chocolate br. ground, sgn. Legras, 6½" diam., 4½" H . .$450.00

58-Muffineer, Mt. Washington, mauve & pink floral, white ground, floral emb. cover, 2½" H . . .$400.00

41-Vase, Mt. Washington acid Burmese, 10½" H $300.00

40-Vase, irid. bluish gold, silver sgn. V. Durand, 6¼" H $600.00

155-Fr. Cameo Vase, mulberry pods, leafy vine textured frosty & apricot ground, sgn. Legras, 8" H $550.00

Row 3, Left to Right

160-Vase, satin Webb Peachblow, 12½" H $450.00

233-Loetz Bowl, irid. blue "oil spot", dec. w/ golden webbed design, stamped Loetz-Austria, 6¼" diam., 3½" H $650.00

131-Burmese Vase, mkd. Queen's Burmese Thomas Webb & Sons, 3" H $325.00

232-Vase, Fr. Cameo, sgn. Charder, purple floral w/ opal & lilac pale blue ground, LaVerre Francais .$1,200.00

234-Steuben Vase, irid. gold, sgn., 8½" H $1,000.00

202-Tankard Creamer, Fr. Cameo, sgn. Daum Nancy, chocolate br. foliaged trees, marmalade sky, ground down polished spout, 4¼" H $450.00

128-Fairy Lamp, acid Burmese, bowl 5" diam., 2¼" H, Clarkes clear pressed insert & Burmese shade, 3½" H $700.00

217-Burmese Vase, Webb acid petal top vase, 4" diam., 2¼" H $175.00

189-Vase, Steuben ivory ruffle top, 7¾" H $500.00

252-Punch Cup, Fr. enameled, 1¾" H, sgn. Daum Nancy, detailed blk. harbor scene, textured opal. ground $750.00

209-Pickle Castor, Rubina crystal w/ gr. coralene wreath w/ yel. red buds, silver triple plated ornate frame, cover & hand tongs, 12" H $800.00

Row 4, Left to Right

205-Pickle Castor, rubina frosted opal. hobnail insert, 4" H, silver plated frame, ornate tongs & cover, 12" H $450.00

190-Imperial Vase, "free hand", irid. bluish olive gr. body, dec. w/ bluish opal pulled swags, 11½" H $800.00

210-Pickle Castor, Vaseline Daisy & Button canoe insert, silver plated carriage, silver fork, 10" L, 8½" H $1,300.00

228-Steuben Bowl, gold calcite center, 11¾" diam., 3¼" H .$500.00

229-Burmese Vase, dec. w/ yellow red berries & multi-colored leaves $350.00

207-Pickle Castor, yel. satin D.Q. M.O.P., 4½" H, silver plated frame & dome cover, fork mkd. Reed & Barton, 11½" H $600.00

174-Crown Milano Sweetmeat, custard color molded w/ stars, gold starfish w/ jeweled tentacles, floral emb. cover $900.00

194-Steuben Vase, irid. blue, sgn. Steuben Aurene, 5½" H . . .$650.00

213- Toothpick Holder, irid. bluish gold, sgn. L.C.T., 2" H $200.00

212-Toothpick Holder, irid. bluish gold, sgn. L.C.T., 2" H $225.00

184-Morgan Vase, acid Wheeling Peachblow, slight purple blush, fitted within amber griffin holder, 7½" H $800.00

Row 5, Left to Right

192-Loetz Bowl, irid. opal w/ ext. purple threading, brass acanthus leaf base, 7" diam., 3¼" H $650.00

215-Nut Bowl, irid. bluish gold, sgn. L.C.T. Favrile, 2¾" diam., 1¼" H $250.00

38-Cordial, irid. gold, sgn. L.C.T., 5½" H $275.00

45-Sherbet, Steuben gold calcite, 6" diam., 3¾" H $225.00

125-Burmese Lamp, Mt. Washington acid, clear pressed Clarkes insert w/ clear ribbed candle holder, 7½" diam., 5½" H $750.00

219-Salt & Pepper, pr., Mt. Washington "egg" shaped, yel. or tan w/ pink, 2" H $125.00

180-Tumbler, New Eng. agata, 3¾" H $350.00

44-Finger Bowl, Steuben irid. gold, stamped Aurene, Haviland & Co., 6½" diam., 2½" H $500.00

176-Amberina Syrup, metal reeded collar, hinged cover, beautiful coloring, extensive damage $800.00

185-Rainbow Cruet, M.O.P. herringbone, vivid coloring, camphor handle & cut panel stopper, 8" H . .$1,500.00

42-Cameo Vase, honey amber dragonfly, aqua water & frosty sky, sgn. Gallé, 7¼" H $2,200.00

214-Nut Bowl, irid. bluish gold, sgn. L.C.T., 2¾" diam, 1" H $225.00

224-Nut Bowl, irid. bluish gold, 3" diam., 1" H $175.00

Right Center

A-OH Apr. 1997   Early Auction Co.

Row 1, Left to Right

496-Steuben Vase, irid. blue, sgn. F. Carder, Aurene, 5" H $750.00

580-Desk Lamp, shade sgn. L.C.T. Favrile, 7" diam., irid. gold "Murano" design, attached to gold Doré harp, molded petal-like base, impr. Tiffany Studios, N.Y., 13¾" H $3,550.00

494-Fr. Cameo Vase, shorelined blue blk. foliaged trees, yel. sky, sgn. deVez, 6¼" H $625.00

514-Steuben Vase, gr. jade w/ alabaster "M" handles, firm's fleur-de-lis acid mark, 12¼" H $1,250.00

489-Acid Burmese Vase, ruffle footed base, 4" H $325.00

612-Fr. Cameo Vase, lavender enamel flowers, mottled opal ground w/ pink tint shading to golden yel., sgn. Daum Nancy, 4¾" H $1,300.00

526-Trumpet Vase, Fr. Cameo, chartreuse & medium gr. branches, frosty & apricot ground, sgn. Gallé, 17¾" H $1,300.00

604-Fr. Cameo Box, maroon raspberries & vine, flowers on dusty pink ground, sgn. Muller Fres, Luneville, 2¾" H $550.00

567-Eng. Bride's Bowl, red Cameo, wreath of white morning glories, acid stamped Webb w/ sunbursts, ornate silver standard, 13" H $1,950.00

517-Steuben Vase, irid. blue, sgn. Aurene, 6" H $575.00

518-Steuben Vase, A.C.B. footed, gr. jade "Alicia" patt., textured alabaster ground, 6" H $500.00

510-Lamp, shade sgn. Handel, rev. peachblow color sky, gr. foliage woodland, serene waterway, bronze verdigris base, Handel cloth label, 17¾" diam., 24" H $8,000.00

467-Fr. Cameo Vase, ora. floral upon frosty & ora. ground, sgn. Gallé, 11" H $950.00

568-Pickle Castor, cranberry inverted coin spot, dec. w/ yel. enamel floral, ornate silver handled frame w/ tongs & cover, 14" H $650.00

Row 2, Left to Right

562-Cracker Barrel, opal Pairpoint, dec. w/ colorful floral sprays, highlighted w/ gold, silver rim, bail & floral cover mkd. Pairpoint, ...$550.00

623-Peachblow Vase, glossy Webb, dec. w/ raised gold floral, 9" H . . .$700.00

527-Fr. Cameo Vase, lavender & gr. blossoms, frost & apricot ground, sgn. Gallé w/ star, 17¾" H $1,500.00

499-Fr. Cameo Bowl, fire polished plum, almond ground, sgn. A. Delatte, Nancy, 5" diam., 2¾" H $725.00

605-Fr. Cameo Bowl, chocolate br. trees, golden ora. ground, sgn. Muller Fres, Luneville, 10¼" L, 3¾" H . .$1,200.00

513-Steuben Topaz Compote, covered w/ pear finial, 9½" H $525.00

585-Amberina Tumbler, red coloring shades into pale yel., dk. ruby to honey amber ribbing, 3¾" H $1,750.00

515-Steuben Vase, pink Cluthra, firm's fleur-de-lis mark, 10¼" H $1,850.00

619-Shaker, Mt. Washington "chick", pink & burgundy floral, metal chick head, 2¼" H $650.00

577-Cracker Barrel, Wavecrest Helmschmied Swirl, dec. w/ enamel blue & white flowers $650.00

603-Fr. Cameo Box, covered, burgundy vines & flowers on frosty ground, gr. tinted cover, ea. Cameo sgn. Gallé, 4" diam., 2½" H $900.00

608-Fr. Cameo Vase, olive gr. aquatic vegetation, yel. gold ground, aqua base, sgn. Gallé, 8" H $1,500.00

Row 3, Left to Right

445-Vase, sgn. V. Durand, irid. gold & royal blue, almond body wrapped in golden threads, 8" H $550.00

571-Biscuit Barrel, Mt. Washington Crown Milano, gilt wild roses, outlined w/ raised gold, pale yel. flowers, emb. cover & finial $950.00

554-Steuben Vase, irid. blue, firm's silver paper label, sgn. Steuben by Carder, 8" H $1,700.00

559-Muffineer, Findlay Onyx, 5" H $275.00

574-Vase, pulled gr. veined leaves, opal rim, golden int., pale gr. stem, emerald gr. petals on golden ground, sgn. L.C.T., 10½" H $3,750.00

615-Bowl, Steven's & Williams, yel. satin, w/ camphor matsu-no-ke design, 6" diam. 3" H $700.00

572-Rose Bowl, satin rainbow, w/ M.O.P. vines, 3 camphor branch feet & raspberry pontil, acid stamped Webb, 7" diam., 6" H $1,450.00

618-Salt & Pepper, pr., Mt. Washington, ea. have different yel. enamel flowers & painted foliage, 2½" H . . .$400.00

570-Fr. Cameo Bowl, aged dk. olive gr. foliaged tree, against peach & frosty sky, sgn. Gallé, 9½" diam., 5½" H .$2,600.00

558-Vase, sgn. Napoli, int. dimple body dec. w/ two chickens, gilt raindrops, gold scrolls, 8½" H $1,400.00

Row 4, Left to Right

563-Cracker Barrel, opal, fall color leafy branch, lavender blue, raspberries & white enamel flowers, pale pink ground, bail & cover mkd. M.W. $600.00

486-Nut Bowl, irid. bluish gold, sgn. L.C.T. Favrile, 2½" diam.,¾" H . .$170.00

485-Nut Bowl, irid. gold, sgn. L.C.T., 2½" diam., 1" H $180.00

493-Fr. Cameo Vase, yel. waterway, russet woodland, sgn. deVez, 8¼" H . .$900.00

488-Burmese Vase, glossy, tri-con crimped rim, 3½" H $280.00

521-Cordial, irid. gold, dimpled sides, sgn. L.C.T., 2¼" H $270.00

569-Pickle Castor, cranberry inverted thumbprint insert, enamel dec. blue & white flowers, inside rim chip, ornate silver frame w/ tongs & dec. cover $500.00

470-Fr. Cameo Vase, lavender-blue floral, aquatic plants against pale blue water, frosty gr. neck, sgn. Gallé, 12" H $2,000.00

579-Herringbone Vases, pr., apricot M.O.P., blue enamel on gilt leafy branches $400.00

468-Fr. Cameo Bowl, purple vine w/ floral pods, pink frost & golden ora. ground, sgn. Gallé, 5¼" diam., 4¼" H . . .$1,100.00

578-Cracker Barrel, Burmese color Mt. Washington, raised gold acorns & leaves tinted w/ pale gr. & dull red, Crown Milano mark, dec. rim, cover & bail, 6" H .$900.00

464-Fr. Cameo Vase, ora. & opal bulb on gr. stem, gilt highlights, sgn. Daum Nancy, 9½" H $2,700.00

624-Durand Vase, irid. blue "King Tut", bluish opal swirled veins, 6¾" H $900.00

611-Fr. Cameo Vase, golden br. trees, reflective lake, lilac pink ground, 7" L, 5" H $1,000.00

Row 5, Left to Right

421-Vase, irid. gold, sgn. L.C. Tiffany, Favrile $600.00

426-Fr. Cameo Vase, lilac & gray gr. phlox, ora. & frosty ground, sgn. Gallé, 4¾" H $650.00

448-Dresser Box, Wavecrest Helmschmied, dec. w/ white enamel flowers, blue ground, 4" diam., 2¾" H . .$250.00

617-Muffineer, Mt. Washington "ostrich egg", pastel pink on blue to yel. ground, 4¼" H $225.00

500-Fr. Cameo Bowl, frosty textured ground, dec. w/ gr. & gold leaves, gilted red berries, sgn. J. Mabut, A La Paix, Paris, 4" H $500.00

439-Toothpick Holder, irid. gold dimpled, sgn. L.C.T. Favrile, 2" H . .$275.00

607-Fr. Champagne, enamel, crystal bowl, 3 colorful cabochons, int. w/ yel. sun & dk. br. rays, etched Emile Gallé, intricately acid cut, gold gilt scrolls, gilt etched bottom, translated "Order of Russian family", St. Petersburg, 4¼" H $3,800.00

484-Toothpick Holder, Alexandrite form w/ peacock feather motif, 2" H .$1,400.00

586-Fr. Cameo Vase, lilac hydrangea w/ gr. & lilac leaves, frost, pink & lilac ground, sgn. Gallé, 3" H $500.00

576-Baroque Dresser Box, Wavecrest, daisy outlined w/ purple-brown, highlighted in pink enamel, w/ white enamel upon pale blue ground, white base & sides of cover, 7" diam., 3½" H $950.00

490-Trumpet Vase, irid. reddish gold, leaf motif, signed Nash, 5" H . .$425.00

519-Steuben Salt Cellar, Rosaline w/ alabaster foot, firm's fleur-de-lis mark, 1½" H $450.00

491-Fr. Cameo Box, covered, foliaged trees, mottled blue ground, sgn. Daum Nancy, 5½" diam., 2¾" H $2,200.00

A-OH Apr. 1997   Early Auction Co.

Row 1, Left to Right

575-Candlestick Vases, irid. gold shading to bluish purple, dec. faintly w/ blue pulled veins, sgn. L.C. Tiffany, Favrile, 9¼" H $1,000.00

552-Peachblow Cruet, New Eng., tri-con spout, almond handle, 5½" H $800.00

583-Lamp, Carlisle shade, "Garden of Allak" design, urn form base w/ Greek Key handles, mkd. Pairpoint, 23½" H overall $3,450.00

548-Oval Porcelain, portrait of woman, mkd. K.P.M., mounted in gilt oval frame, 14½" x 18" L overall $1,750.00

441-Steuben Finger Bowls, four, blue tipped rims, sgn. Aurene, 1¾" H, underplates 5¾" diam. $900.00

593-Eng. Cameo Vase, white bamboo stalks, citron yel. ground, 5½" H $1,250.00

437-Fr. Cameo Vase, irid. purple br. aquatic scene, yel. sky, sgn. Gallé, 5" H $900.00

588-Boudoir Lamp, frosty shade, rev. painted at rim w/ pink & white roses w/ gr. foliage, tan tree trunk base, 6" diam., 13" H overall $175.00

625-Vase, acid Burmese gray gr. ivy, br. vine, mkd. Thomas Webb & Sons, Queen's Burmese, 3¼" H $475.00

621-Trumpet Vase, irid. gold, silver sgn. Durand, 12" H $950.00

587-Pairpoint Lamp, "Hummingbird & Roses", Devonshire shade, multi-color flowers, bronze color paneled stem, mkd. Pairpoint Mfg. Co., 24" H . . . . .N/S

613-Moser Vases, pr., amethyst to clear, dec. w/ enamel yel. & purple pansies, gilt fernery, 12" H . . .$800.00

553-Amberina Cruet, fuchsia w/ inverted coin spots, tri-con rim, amber handle, 6" H $300.00

Row 2, Left to Right

418-Steuben Marmalade Pot, Verre-de-soie, w/ pink pear finial, minor chip on leaf, 4" H $175.00

626-Burmese Bowl, global acid w/ inverted thumbprint & rigaree collar, 2¾" H $300.00

460-Northwood Vase, lustreless white, pink & ora. w/ dk. veins, 9" H $500.00

589-Hanging Fixture, Fr. Cameo conical shade, burgundy stylized flowers, mottled pink, frost & ora. ground, gilt 3 arm frame, chain link ceiling mount, sgn. Charder, 11½" H, 48" L, overall $1,000.00

498-Vase, irid. blue w/ golden highlights, silver sgn. V. Durand . .$650.00

620-Console Set, Steuben Ivrene, oblong footed bowl, 6" H, 13" L, 4 matching candleholders, 3" .$1,500.00

406-Salt & Pepper, pr. Wavecrest, yel. flowers, 2½" H $225.00

483-Steuben Lamp, moss agate w/ textured body, pale amber ground, gold oriental style metal base, minor chips, 16" H, overall $1,600.00

573-Steuben Vase, pink Cluthra, fleur-de-lis mark, 8" H $1,500.00

457-Candleholder, irid. gold, hollow twist stem, sgn. L.C.T., 7" H . .$750.00

428-Burmese Fairy Lamp, Webb acid, dome shade rests on holder mkd. S. Clarke Fairy, 5" H overall . .$850.00

Row 3, Left to Right

411-Amberina Cruet, rev. swirl, tri-con rim, amber handle & faceted cut stopper, 6½" H $200.00

459-Vase, irid. bluish gold w/ cobalt blue vines, sgn. Loetz Austria, 9½" H $1,000.00

549-Porcelain Plaque, artist sgn. Nach Paul Thumann, E. Feith in gilt frame, late 18th C., 13" x 16" H overall $6,750.00

430-Fr. Cameo Vase, golden br. foliaged trees, frosty amber sky, sgn. D'Argental, 8" H $850.00

635-Global Vase, gr. pulled leaves w/ golden tips, opal ground, attrib. to Union Glass Co., 4½" H $650.00

592-Tankard Pitcher, Holly Amber, minor chips, 9" H $700.00

590-Lighting Fixture, Fr. Cameo shade, ebony trees, Prussian blue sky, gr. waterway, table mount gold pierced frame, sgn. Daum Nancy, 12" diam., 8" H $3,100.00

454-Moser Vase, two applied fish, colorful equatic plants, electric blue, 9½" H $450.00

622-Loetz Vase, emerald gr. silver overlay, 3 pulled silver raindrops, 5" H $550.00

Row 4, Left to Right

616-Center Bowl, irid. gold w/ emerald gr. leaves, hollow center core, sgn. L.C. Tiffany, Favrile, 10" diam., 2½" H .$800.00

581-Box, mkd. Tiffany Studios, NY, bronze verdigris filigree, carmel slag glass, 6½" L, 4" W, 2" H $300.00

582-Loetz Vase, irid. red "oil spot" w/ pulled gold & silvery trilings, dimpled body, 8" H $550.00

414-Bride's Basket, lilac satin, melon ribbed body, yel. floral vine, ornate silver holder, 13" H . . .$550.00

637-Jack-in-Pulpit Vase, Sandwich, tomato & yel. body, 4¼" H . . .$125.00

432-Durand Vase, "King Tut", royal blue & irid. gold design, drilled for lamp, 12" H $650.00

591-Fr. Cameo Vase, enameled dk. gr. trees & hillside, frosty & pink sky, sgn. Legras, 12"H $650.00

557-Loetz Vase, emerald gr., crinkled body overlaid from base w/ erupted design, rainbow essence, 7" H $375.00

643-Tankard Pitcher, New Eng. Peachblow, almond reeded handle, 8½" H $375.00

440-Vase, irid. gold, sgn. L.C. Tiffany Favrile, 4" H $525.00

627-Fr. Cameo Vase, mah. flowers & leaves, red & yel. mottled ground, sgn. D.'Aurys, 4½" H $350.00

Row 5, Left to Right

628-Fr. Cameo Vase, pinky olive nasturtiums & pod leaves, frosty gr. ground, sgn. P. Rigot, 3" H . . .$250.00

404-Mustard Pots, two, both Mt. Washington, pink floral vine, hinged cap & bail, 3" H, & one violet bouquet thumblift cap, scroll handle 3" H $350.00

638-Amberina Tumbler, swirl, 3¾" H $100.00

415-Hinged Box, oval white satin, lavender Victorian ladies & gent, brass scroll & ball feet, 5" L, 4¼" H $225.00

409-Peachblow Pear, New Eng., 4" H $125.00

629-Fr. Cameo Vase, blue blk. orchids & tangerine ground, sgn. Richard, 7¾" H $600.00

642-Burmese Vase, blue & gold enamel floral branches, golden moon & bird, 4½" H $575.00

639-Pomona Toothpick, Midwest, enamel meadow flowers & ferns, frosty inverted thumbprint body, 2½" H .$100.00

453-Liquor Set, stemware sgn. Moser, 12" diam. tray, decanter 11" H, stemmed glasses, 5¼" H, tumber 3¼" H, dec. w/ white lily & fernery, gr. elongated leaves $500.00

641-Salt Dips, pr., melon ribbed, blue w/ lilac & yel. flowers, blue ground, attrib. to Smith Bros., gold beaded tops, some beads missing, 1" H . . .$200.00

492-Fr. Cameo Bowl, blue textured, smokey colored poppy blossoms, gilt highlighted sgn. Daum Nancy, 5¾" diam., 3½" H $1,450.00

438-Mustard Pot, Wheeling Peachblow, metal rim, handle & thumblift cover, 2½" H $450.00

410-Compote, mkd. Libbey Amberina, coin spot, 6¼" diam., 4" H $1,150.00

A-OH Apr. 1997   Early Auction Co.

Row 1, Left to Right

313-Fr. Cameo Vase, emerald gr., gilt highlighted, ebony birds, 8¼" H . .$350.00
346-Vase, frosted female nudes w/ draped cloth, mkd. R. Lalique, 5½" H $700.00
434-Phoenix Lamp, "lovebird", floral base w/ mammal feet, silk shade, 9½" H, 32" H overall $220.00
645-Lalique Tray, frosty, unsgn., molded w/ seven dancing nudes w/ veils, 18" diam., 2¼" H . . . . .N/S
405-Lamp, leaded shade, chartreuse gr., emerald gr. faceted jewels dec. on blk. base, gilt acanthus leaves & leafy scrolls, 18" diam. $1,250.00
92-Lamp Base, mkd. Pairpoint, textured gr. body dec. w/ dk. gr. hearts & diamond motifs, red ora. flowers, brass color base, 21" H $350.00
254-Barrel Tumblers, four, Findlay Onyx, 3½" H $740.00

Row 2, Left to Right

253-Water Pitcher, Findlay Onyx, 8" H $850.00
196-English Epergne, cased, 9" diam., beveled mirror, 4 ruffle-top vases, pink interiors, white exteriors, red roses & gr. foliage, yel. rigaree collars, 14" overall $625.00
420-Lamp, cranberry font dec. w/ yel. vine, brass base, glass chimney .$250.00

191-Brass Triptych, ornate, rose garlands, framed ivories of youths, artist sgn. Reitz, hinged doors w/ colorful paper inserts, 3 beveled mirrors, 10" W, 17" H $1,400.00
348-Amberina-Verde Vase, Bohemian w/ inverted thumbprint, 9" H $400.00
203-GWTW Lamp, mini., white swirled global shade & body w/ ruby roses & gr. foliage, 10" H $175.00
132-Burmese Tumblers, three, Mt. Washington acid $33.00

Row 3, Left to Right

20-Tankard Pitcher, mkd. J.P.L. France, black brown ground, 13¼" H $175.00
248-Fr. Clock, entitled "Retour des Hirondelles", Par Rousseau, ornate figures atop onyx block case, porcelain dial w/ assorted flowers, 28" H . .$1,200.00
614-Banquet Lamp, frosted global shade, painted boquet of yel. & wine flowers, onyx stem base w/ silvercast global oil font, brass insert & base, 11" diam., 33" H overall $525.00
273-Sinclaire Nubian Vase, acid cut w/ oriental design, 8½" H . . .$850.00

Row 4, Left to Right

302-Cracker Barrel, frosted & textured, dec. in purple, golden leaves, silver rim w/ maker's marks, attrib. to Mt. Joye, 7" H $450.00
342-Vase, frosted, faintly mold mkd. Muller Fres, Luneville, 11¾" H .$400.00

255-Celery Holder, Findlay Onyx, 6¼" H $450.00
6-Vase, mkd. Lenox Belleek, white gown, pink flowering tree, 11½" H $400.00
195-Epergne, cranberry, 10" diam., 3 cranberry trumpet form vases, 21½" H overall $500.00
14-Vase, mkd. B & Co. France, ruby, blue, white & yellow, 15" H, 5" diam. $250.00
26-Vase, mkd. D & Co. France, purple & blue ground, gold leaf, 11" H $150.00

Row 5, Left to Right

124-Masonic Nappie, tri-angular, 5" diam. $200.00
124B-Covered Dolphin, beaded rim, minute chip, 4" H $175.00
127-Burmese Bride's Bowl, Mt. Washington acid, 9" diam., 4¾" H, silver plated holder mkd. JW-Tufts, 12" H . . .$500.00
370-Loetz Vase, emerald gr. w/ applied raindrops, 3½" H $225.00
19-Decanter, D & C Limoges, sgn. A. Heidride, 9½" H $400.00
374-Czech Perfume, canary yel. rev. swirl w/ patt. stopper, 5½" H $180.00
369-Phoenix Vase, blue grasshoppers on blades of grass, 7" H . .$150.00
130-Burmese Tumblers, pr., Mt. Washington, 3¾" H $220.00
120-Cactus Syrup, w/ metal thumblift cover, 6" H $120.00

A-OH Nov. 1996   Garth's Auctions

Row 1, Left to Right

Pitcher, blown glass, NY, amber w/ applied handle, broken blister, 4⅝" H $2,255.00
Stiegel Flask, amethyst diamond, 4¾" H $495.00
Pitcher, blown glass, NY, olive gr., Mt. Vernon Glass Works, 4⅜" H 1,760.00
Tumbler, blown glass, olive gr., labeled "Midwestern", broken blisters, 4" H $715.00

Row 2, Left to Right

Toilet Water Bottle, cobalt blue, blown 3-mold, plus tam-o-shanter cap, 5¾" H $302.50
Bowl, amber blown w/ rim, midwestern, 6½" diam., 4⅝" H $715.00
Gaffing Tool Holder, peacock blue, blown glass, applied base & segmented stem 4¾" H $577.50

Row 3, Left to Right

Flask & Bottle, olive amber pint flask, check in base & roughness, 7½" H; olive blown Ludlow bottle w/ applied lip, wear, bruise, 5⅝" H $192.50
Globular Bottle, amber blown, Zanesville, applied lip, minor wear, scratches, broken blister, stain, 7⅝" H $330.00
Three Pcs., olive blown bottle w/ flared lip, 7⅛" H; olive amber water bottle, 6½" H; olive amber blown saddle flask (not pict.), 6⅛"H . . .$220.00

A-OH Apr. 1997 — Early Auction Co.

Row 1, Left to Right

449-Pin Tray, mkd. Kelva, ormolu handles, 1¾" H $220.00

522-Lamp, Tiffany Cypriote heart form body w/ rainbow hues, burst bubble surface, sgn. Louis C. Tiffany, Favrile, ivory ball stem on gold Doré base, 26" H, cloth shade . . .$1,300.00

594-Lamp, leaded shade, plate mkd. Handel, dk. gr., scattered pink slag flowers & gr. leaves & border, bronze verdigris body, Crosier base, 18" diam., 24" H $2,800.00

565-Tiffany Place Setting, 5 pc., aqua pastel, 9" diam. plate, 2¼" H footed sherbet, stemware sgn. L.C.T. Favrile, 8½" H, 7½" H & 7¼" H $1,500.00

550-Grandeur Lamp, Tiffany's famous 12 branch lily lamp, irid. reddish gold w/ blue hues, sgn. L.C.T. Favrile, bronze base, mkd. Tiffany Studios, New York, 1 shade repr., 21" H . $18,500.00

Row 2, Left to Right

436-Finger Bowl, irid. gold, sgn. Ateuben Aurene, 2½" H, 6¼" diam. $300.00

632-Oriental Goblet, poppy, mkd. Steuben, pomona gr. stem & base, 8" H $750.00

442-Steuben Bowl, gold calcite, 8" diam., 3¼" H $350.00

541-Vase, pr. cut velvet "basketweave", blue to white, 6¼" H $850.00

532-Royal Vienna Plate, sgn. Wagner, mult-color border w/ raised gold leaves, 10" diam. $1,350.00

450-Moser Vase, amber, w/ applied sapphire blue salamanders, metal lion masked footed base, 12½" H .$325.00

Row 3, Left to Right

631-Durand Goblet, royal blue w/ opal pulled feathers, amber stem & base, 7" H $375.00

462-Desk Lamp, attached oval shade, etched dec., soft pink ground, int. w/ gr. leaves, blue stems, red berries on tan ground, silver stamped Bellova, Czech, 10" H overall $1,350.00

525-Fr. Cameo Vase, black-purple grape pods shading to lt. gray on base, marmalade & amethyst ground, sgn. Daum Nancy, 23½" H $9,000.00

256-Vases, pr. Steven's & Williams, 10¼" H, pink int. w/ ambertrim $300.00

609-Eng. Vase, cased silver overlay, glossy magenta surface, white int., 12" H . . . .N/S

600-Lamp, Pappillon "puffy" shade, pink & yel. roses, colorful butterflies on mottled lilac & frost background, multicolor accents, gilt baluster form base, mkd. Pairpoint, 9" diam. $4,600.00

416-M.O.P. Preserves Pot, amber satin, brass rim, handle & floral cover, 4" H $175.00

531-Peachblow Peach, shiny, amber stem 3" H $500.00

Row 4, Left to Right

537-Cracker Barrel, opal, stamped Pairpoint, floral assortment, silver rim, bail & cover, mkd. Mt. Washington, 7" H $500.00

598-Floriform Compote, irid. reddish gold, sgn. L.C.T. $650.00

630-Goblet, aqua pastel, sgn. L.C.T. Favrile. 8½" H $325.00

538-Cased Bowl, red int., white ext., 9" diam. 3½" H $325.00

596-Steuben Sherbets, four, inserts mkd. Windsor, sterling stemmed holders w/ emb. rims, 4" diam., 3½" H overall $600.00

610-Fr. Cameo Vase, chartreuse iris, lt. & dk. gr. leaves, white frosty ground, sgn. Gallé, 13¼" H .$1,600.00

401-Vases, pr. blue satin, melon body dec. w/ country scene, 8¼" H $250.00

Row 5, Left to Right

599-Jack-in-Pulpit Vase, irid. gold, sgn. L.C.T., firm's partial paper label, 8" H $2,000.00

597-Nash Bowl, sgn., irid. bluish gold w/ molded veins, 7¼" diam., 3¾" H . $950.00

533-Amberina Perfume, stopper w/ full length dauber, mkd. Libbey, 7" H . $1,900.00

528-Steuben Wall Plaque, yel. w/ stylized morning glories, leaves & flowers, Art Deco metal wall mount, chips in drilled holes, 10" diam.. 15" H overall $750.00

595-Steuben Nappie, irid. gold, sgn. Aurene, 4" diam. $650.00

596-Steuben Sherbets, four, inserts mkd. Windsor, sterling stemmed holders w/ emb. rims, 4" diam., 3½" H overall $600.00

A-MA May 1997 — Skinner

Rene Lalique Ceylan Vase, opal., stylized leafy branches retaining blue patine, nicks on rim edges, 9" H $4,205.00

A-OH Nov. 1996 — Garth's Auctions

Row 1, Left to Right

Flint Lamp, clear, four printie font w/ pewter collar, 12¼" H $137.50

Flint Lamps, two, one w/ pewter collar, sm. flakes, 10¼" H, other w/ brass collar, 7¼" H $165.00

Flint Candlesticks, pr., clear w/ dolphin bases, sm. edge flakes & one glued socket, 9⅛" H $110.00

Row 2, Left to Right

Eng. Sweetmeats, pr., clear blown w/ domed covers, 9⅝" H $715.00

Pitcher, bluish gray tint, clear blown, midwestern, check in base, 7" H $220.00

Sugar Bowl, clear blown, domed lid w/ applied finial, wear, chips & lrg. check, 9" H $110.00

A-MA May 1997 — Skinner

Paperweights

Left to Right

Baccarat, three 1970's series animal, hunter, swan & squirrel, complex millefiore & animal canes, 3-3¼" diam., ...$902.00

New Eng. Scrambled, three, two end-of-day multicolored cane weights, 2" & 2½" diam., & one swirled red, blue, gr. on white ball core, scratched, 2¾" diam. . . . . .N/S

St. Louis Garlanded, cane at side of high red cushion w/ six millefiore garlands & center star cane, 3¼" diam. . . . . .N/S

Charles Kaziun Pedestal, four, gold flecked white, pink & two gr. background for millefiore spider lilies, gold K on each, approx. 2" H, 1-1¼" diam. $1,265.00

A-OH Apr. 1997   Early Auction Co.

Row 1, Left to Right

584-Marquetry Table, Gallé, dk. thorny bough w/ blonde color flowers & buds, finely detailed wood grain surface, oriental inlay signature, 18" x 22" x 15" H $1,400.00

711-Vases, pr., blue satin, dec. w/ colorful enamel, dotted bird, one has paper label mkd. G. Boutigny Pilais Royal Paris, 10" H $500.00

672-Sevres Urn, porcelain matte dec. in pinks & lavenders, ornate gold ormolu trim, pineapple finial, 18" H $700.00

30-Vase, mkd. M.Z. Austria, sgn. Ella Simon, white & mauve, lilac gray body, 15" H $225.00

707-Steuben Urn Vase, ivory color, 7" H $85.00

670-Epergne, cranberry, 3 trumpet form vases, clear spiral rigaree trim, ruffled bowl 11" diam., 24" H overall $500.00

646-Fr. Cameo Vase, lavender pods, olive gr. leafy vines, frosty ground & lavender base, 17¼" H $1,500.00

Row 2, Left to Right

34-Urn Vase, irid. blue, raised gilt, prob. Czech, 10" H $195.00

16-Tankard Pitcher, bluish purple & red grape pods, 12¼" H $150.00

22-Vase, mkd. H. & Co. Bavaria, sgn. Carrie Yark, yel. br. berried branches, amethyst & yel. ground, 15" H . . .$200.00

669-Epergne, beveled circular mirror, 8" diam., spiral chartreuse rigaree trim, 17" H overall $600.00

29-Vase, mkd. Royal Bonn, Ger., pink & ruby w/ blue, raised gold floral, 6½" H $325.00

12-Tankard Pitcher, mkd. Willets Belleek, ruby, pink & yel., multi ground, 11½" H $150.00

21-Vase, mkd. W.G. & Co. France, gold scrolls, pink & purple flowers, dated Mar. 2,'92, 8" H $350.00

Row 3, Left to Right

709-M.O.P. Vase, pink satin "swag", w/ camphor twig handles, 5¼" H . .$375.00

281-Charger, mkd. Limoges France., natural tones, lotus blossoms, gold border, 13½" diam. $325.00

437B-Muffineer, Findlay Onyx, w/ gilt cap, 5½" H $225.00

13-Tankard Pitcher, mkd. J.P. France, sgn. F. Wirkner, 15" H $400.00

353-Perfume Lamp, Baccarat Amberina, wick inserts, 5" H $145.00

651-G.W.T.W. Pairpoint Lamp, dec. w/ pink lilies & dk. gr. foliage, med. gr. ground, glass chimney, 10½" H overall $475.00

649-Burmese Vase, Mt. Washington, glossy bag-form, dec. w/ applied floral & plume fern on rev., flower restored, 7" L, 7" H 625.00

17-Vase, mkd. Limoges, France, pink & gr., gold scrolled handles, 12" H $250.00

661-Wavecrest Dresser Box, blue daisies on pale pink molded cover, 2¼" H $275.00

650-Jack-in-Pulpit Vase, Mt. Washington acid Burmese, 15" H . .$550.00

463B-Muffineer, Findlay Onyx, line under frozen top, 5¼" H . . .$1,300.00

Row 4, Left to Right

28-Footed Bowl, mkd. T & V France, ora. & yel. w/ blue gr. & chartreuse leaves, 9" diam., 4½" H 150.00

658-Wavecrest "Cigarettes" Holder, pale gr. w/ yel. flowers, shield mkd., 2¾" H $450.00

662-Wavecrest Dresser Box, blow-out shell, blue bell flowers, pale pink shell base, 2¾" H $300.00

665-Fr. Vase, irid. textured cut panels, enamel dec., opal. yel. swirl body w/ leafy vine w/ pink roses, 6¼" H $500.00

27-Vase, multi-colors, unmkd. Old Paris, 13" H $425.00

656-Wavecrest Pin Tray, ormolu trim, pink daisies & yel. blow-out shell sides, shield mkd., 1½" H $100.00

732-Loetz Vase, irid. blue w/ twig patt., 5" H $250.00

648-Fr. Cameo Vase, purple floral clusters, pale frosty blue ground, sgn. Gallé, 5¾" H $400.00

647-Fr. Cameo Vase, barrel form, golden br. orchid on frosty ground, sgn. Gallé w/ star, 6" H $750.00

285-Chest Music Box, colorful multi-floral inlay, 8" cylinders, mkd. Made in Switzerland, 8½" x 17½" x 5½" H $1,000.00

Row 5, Left to Right

666-Covered Box, porcelain, gr. mkd. Pairpoint Limoges w/ crown, base w/ scattered pink rose sprays, 8" L, 3½" H $475.00

663-Finger Bowl, Vasa Murrhina, 4¾" diam., 2½" H, matching undertray, 6½" diam. $250.00

716-Shades, pr. A.C.B., gr. & apricot floral wreaths w/ netted design on white, 3⅛" fitters, 6" H $300.00

671-Peachblow Tumbler, glossy New Eng., 3¾" H $300.00

655-Wavecrest Dresser Box, pink asters w/ enamel highlights, pale yel. raised scroll edge, 5" L, 2¾" H . . .$300.00

272-Amberina Daisy & Button, 11 pcs., 9" diam. berry bowl & 10 - 4¾" diam., sq. individual bowls . . . .$60.00 ea.

653-Wavecrest Jewel Tray, pink & plum flowers, ormolu rim, 3¼" H $195.00

652-Wavecrest Box, mkd., blow-out shell covered, blue daisies & foliage, enamel highlights, yel. ground, 3" H . . .$400.00

664-Pairpoint Cracker Barrel, pink floral garlands, tan ground w/ gilt flowers, russet color base, mkd. Pairpoint, metal cover, 6" H $475.00

708-Florentine Cameo Bowl, rose pink, white enamel violets & leaves, 3¼" H $90.00

660-Wavecrest Vase, ornamental, blue flower boquets, egg-form body, ormolu handles, 7¼" H $275.00

657-Wavecrest Dresser Tray, "egg-crate", blue forget-me-nots, ormolu rim $145.00

A-MA May 1997   Skinner

Paperweights

Left to Right

Paul J. Stankard, double Showy Lady's Slipper, '81 inscribed, 3¼" diam. $1,495.00

Baccarat , scattered gridel silhouette, millefiore canes on upset muslin, 2¼" diam. $1,380.00

Baccarat Series, three, rooster, deer, partridges, w/ millefiore & animal canes, 1970's, 3¼" diam. $862.50

St. Louis Rose Spray, cane, six side facets, 3" diam. $172.50

A-MA May 1997   Skinner

Paperweights

Left to Right

New Eng. Glass Co., concentric rings of millefiore canes, base bruises, 2¾" diam. . . . . .N/S

D'Albret Sulphide Series, three, Columbus, Franklin Roosevelt, Jack & Jackie Kennedy, on blue amethyst & gr., 2¾" diam. $115.00

Paul J. Stankard, stylized flower, five petal red centered purple blossom & bud on twisted stems, white background, inscribed, '71, 2⅛" diam. $1,035.00

Fench Clichy, two, rose w/ millefiore rings, top bruise, 2½" diam., Baccarat red & white primrose on leafy stem, 2½" diam. $862.50

A-OH Apr. 1997   Early Auction Co.

Row 1, Left to Right

455-M.O.P. Vase, pink D.Q., yel. coralene dec., 8″ H $325.00

473-Lamp, rev. painted shade, dec. w/ summer foliaged trees, frosty yel. sky, lt. br. baluster base, mkd. Moe-Bridges, 8″ diam. $1,000.00

542-Pelaton Vase, white, applied clear, tooled base, 4″ H $200.00

602-Fr. Cameo Vase, honey amber floral, deep golden br. leaves, apricot & frosty ground, sgn. Gallé, 13½″ . . . . .N/S

556-Fr. Cameo Vase, engr. Daum Nancy, magenta, pale red & textured amethyst tulips, pink & lt. gr. ground, 9½″ H $7,500.00

511-Trumpet Vase, irid. bluish gold, 10¼″ H, sgn. L.C.T. Favrile, Doré pod base mkd. Louis C. Tiffany Furnaces, Inc. $1,100.00

535-Durand Vase, irid. blue, same color threading, yel. reeded florette, 9½″ H $1,900.00

544-Peachblow Vase, acid Wheeling, deep rich coloring, 9″ H $1,100.00

512-Tumbler, gr. opaque, blue gray mottled rim border, gilt trim, 3½″ H $425.00

564-Lamp, frosty dome shade, gilt stamped Pairpoint Corp., dec. w/ enamel goldenrods, internal w/ sponged yel. patt., 5″ diam., 11″ H overall $1,150.00

506-Fr. Cameo Vase, sgn. Lamartine, groves of autumn & olive evergreens against a pink & opal mottled sky, 12½″ H $3,300.00

Row 2, Left to Right

606-Fr. Cameo Vase, burgundy leafy branches, mottled frosty yel. & wine color ground, sgn. Daum Nancy, 8″ H . . . . .N/S

481-Webb Burmese Vase, glossy w/ petal top rim, 8″ H $1,600.00

419-Eng, Cameo Vase, white floral vine across textured confetti ground, stamped Thomas Webb & Sons, 3¼″ H . . .$550.00

504-Steuben Bowl, plum jade, Canton patt., 8″ diam., 4″ H . . .$2,000.00

456-M.O.P. Vase, Steven's & Williams Verde Rubina, 9¾″ H $600.00

551-Peachblow Cruet, shiney Wheeling, tri-con spout, amber handle, 5″ H $1,300.00

429-Vase, irid. gold, base sgn. Nash, stretch scalloped rim, textured leaves, 5½″ H $1,550.00

530-Peachblow Vase, New Eng., glossy, 15″ H $1,100.00

466-Fr. Cameo Vase, mottled pale yel. & opal ground, gilt sgn. Daum Nancy, 5″ H $3,750.00

433-Vase, irid. royal blue, gold int., faintly silver script mkd. Durand, 9½″ H $1,050.00

431-Vase, frosty, attrib. to Handel, sandy textured, water scene, blue gray windmills, 7″ diam., 4″ H $450.00

Row 3, Left to Right

479-Jack-in-Pulpit Vase, irid. gold, sgn. L.C.T., 8¾″ H $2,000.00

447-Fr. Cameo Vase, red floral & gr. foliage, yel. on neck, rusty red & gr. on lower body, sgn. Daum Nancy, 11½″ H $3,200.00

508-Vase, irid. gold, silver sgn. Durand, rosette on cover, 7″ H $1,050.00

497-Durand Vase, irid. blue, opal vines & leaves, gold foot, 8¼″ H $1,200.00

424-Burmese Vase, glossy, fall color vine w/ red berries stamped Queen's Burmese, Thomas Webb & Sons, 3″ H $550.00

495-Steuben Bowl, gr. jade, matzu patt. over alabaster, 7″ H . .$1,050.00

561-Burmese Vase, Webb trumpet form, acid finish dec. w/ gr. ivy & shadow leaves, hammered base mkd. BM Co., 7¾″ H overall $500.00

444-Steuben Candleholders, pr., gold calcite mushroom, 6″ H $1,250.00

458-Vase, emerald gr. w/ irid. blue "King Tut" design, silver sgn. V. Durand, 5½″ H $900.00

478-Royal Flemish Ewer, mkd., shadow gold outlined blossoms, overlaid w/ pale dull red medallions w/ raised gold rays, 10″ H $3,200.00

560-Muffineer, Wavecrest Helmschmied, burgundy & pink daisies, raised gold outlines, gilt highlights on creamy ground, 2¾″ H $450.00

Row 4, Left to Right

540-Burmese Vase, Mt. Washington, multi-shades of gr. ivy, firm's yel. paper label & a Cincinnati Harms Palais Royal label, 9½″ H $750.00

505-Fr. Cameo Vase, fall color ground, royal blue trailings throughout, brick red leaves, pedestal base, sgn. Gallé, 9″ H $2,750.00

502-Burmese Condiment Set, Mt. Washington, cruet dec. w/ white & yel. enamel, stopper highlighted w/ yel. red, 6¼″ H, Burmese color shaker w/ blue & white enamel, pink tinted w/ white flowers, each 3¾″ H, Pairpoint plated holder 10″ H $2,550.00

534-Dresser Box, Wavecrest Cameo, multi-color textured surface, 6″ diam., 3″ H $2,600.00

422-Trumpet Vase, pink pastel, clear foot w/ etched wreath, sgn. L.C.T. Favrile, 9¼″ H $850.00

477-Royal Flemish Vase, raised gold leaves, scattered oval jewels, russet br. patches, frost & pale yel. outlined w/ dec. raised gold scrolls, neck w/ gilt design, 7½″ H $2,500.00

423-Webb Burmese Sweetmeat, red flowers on gilt branches, silver rim, bail & disc cover, 4½″ diam. , 2½″ H . .$800.00

472-Vase, acid Wheeling Peachblow Morgan, fitted into amber Griffin holder, 7½″ H $1,050.00

536-Cameo Rose Bowl, red D.Q. M.O.P., white wild rose blossoms, 4″ H $700.00

461-Vase, glossy cased, stamped Steven's & Williams, "pull-up" in pink, cobalt & white, yel. int., 8″ H $725.00

Row 5, Left to Right

523-M.O.P. Vase, rainbow coin spot vase, tri-con rim, 4″ H $1,250.00

509-Vase, irid. gold, silver sgn. Durand, 7½″ H $700.00

413-Peachblow Cruet, shiny Wheeling, amber reeded handle & faceted cut stopper, 6½″ H $950.00

482-New Eng. Agata Tumbler, strong mottling & blue stains, 3¾″ H $800.00

503-Fr. Cameo Vase, mocha br. w/ golden ora. ground, sgn. Gallé, 5½″ H $700.00

539-Vase, amber, w/ pulled irid. bluish gold design, sgn. Loetz Austria, 4″ H $1,200.00

412-Cruet, glossy New Eng., tri-con spout, white agata stopper, 6½″ H $700.00

487-Match Holder, Holly Amber, 2½″ H $1,100.00

427-Fr. Cameo Vase, yel. br. floral on pink & frosty ground, sgn. Gallé, 4¾″ H $600.00

A-MA May 1997   Skinner

Paperweights

Left to Right

Baccarat, scattered millefiore, canes w/ Gridel animals incl. dancing devil, goose, deer, goat, kangaroo, cut down, 2″ diam. $862.50

Paul J. Stankard, spring beauty, three striped pink on white blossoms, inscribed '79, 3″ diam. $1,840.00

Baccarat Animal Series, three, 1970's, pelican, horse, elephant, central silhouettes w/ animal & millefiore cane, 3 - 3¼″ diam. $920.00

Paul J. Stankard, wildflower, yel. blossoms & buds w/ seed pod, inscribed, 3″ diam. $1,265.00

A-MA June 1997   Skinner

Row 1, Left to Right

Glass Pitchers, two, aqua threaded blown glass, minor chips & cracks, 8⅞" H, & 9" H $460.00
Sandwich Block Vases, pr. canary pressed glass four-printie, 1840-60, Barlow #3037, base chips, 11½" H $920.00
Looped Vase, blown glass, prob. Pittsburgh, 1820-40, clear w/ white looping, cased, open pontil, 11⅝" H $1,265.00
Sandwich Block Vases, pr. canary pressed glass four-printie, 1840-60, Barlow #3037, base chips, 11½" H $920.00
Glass Pitchers, two, aqua threaded blown glass, minor chips & cracks, 8⅞" H, & 9" H $460.00

Center, Left to Right

Sugar Bowl, cobalt blown molded, covered, prob. Steigel, 18th C., eleven diamond patt. lid & bowl, minor chips, 6½" H $2,415.00

Medicine Bottle, olive gr. blown molded, Am., 1830-45, "Dr. Phelps - Arcanum - Genuine", chips, roughness, 8¼" H .N/S
Medicine Bottle, olive amber blown molded, Am., 1830-45. "Phelp's Arcanum Worcester Mass.," minute chips, 8¾" H $920.00
Sandwich Bottle, cobalt blown molded, MA, 1825-40, w/ swirled body, 5¾" H $172.50

Row 3, Left to Right

Celery Vases, pr., fiery opal. & clear, Pittsburgh, 1820-40, flaring scalloped rims to fiery paneled bowls w/ clear stems & feet, 8¼" H $3,737.50
Glassware, 13 pcs., 19th C., incl. amber blown molded Griffith Hyatt & Co. bottle, two olive gr. bottles, Sandwich pressed diamond salt, two clear & one blown molded decanters, a clear blown peg lamp, a clear blown pitcher, three clear blown tumblers w/ rolled rims & a pressed clear wine, imper. . . .$920.00

Glassware, 10 pcs., 19th C., five cobalt pressed plates, a cobalt pressed polyhedron-form lamp, a cobalt blown covered sugar bowl w/ galleried rim, & three clear blown wines w/ folded feet, minor chips $977.50
Whimsey Mug, gr. glass blown molded, Am., 19th C. "Menouch Wiln", 4½" H $1,610.00
Glassware, 13 pcs., 19th C., incl. amber blown molded Griffith Hyatt & Co. bottle, two olive gr. bottles, Sandwich pressed diamond salt, two clear & one blown molded decanters, a clear blown peg lamp, a clear blown pitcher, three clear blown tumblers w/ rolled rims & a pressed clear wine, imper. . . .$920.00
Sugar Bowl, cobalt freeblown covered, Am., late 18th C., plain finial above flange lid, applied foot, 5¾" H $517.50
Celery Vases, pr., fiery opal. & clear, Pittsburgh, 1820-40, flaring scalloped rims to fiery paneled bowls w/ clear stems & feet, 8¼" H $3,737.50

A-OH Nov. 1996   Garth's Auctions

Compote, electric blue tree of life, w/ hand stem, sm. flakes & bruise in bowl, 9" diam., 9" H $148.50

A-MA May 1997   Skinner

Paperweights

Left to Right

Clichy Star Center, purple & gr. canes around pink circlet w/ central cane, base scratches, 2" diam. . . .$201.25
Charles Kaziun, four, blue, maroon & two gr. background w/ gold aventurine under spider lily blossoms, gold K at rev., approx. 1 - 1¼" diam., 2" H $1,150.00
St. Louis, hand cooler egg, cane on oval w/ white latticinio alternating pink to blue twists, 2⅞" H . . .$230.00
Paul J. Stankard, early spring, six petal white blossom on curved gr. stem w/ roots, inscribed "PJS '72", 2" diam. . . .$1,035.00

A-MA May 1997   Skinner

Paperweights

Left to Right

Paul J. Stankard, stylized flower, blk. ground, inscribed "PJS '71", 2⅛" diam. $977.50
Clichy Millefiore, multicolored canes on upset muslin, one bruise at side, 2⅛" diam. $488.75
Somerville Union, two, oversize bird weight w/ pr. of egrets & egg-filled nest, 3¾" diam., red poinsettia w/ petals, scratched, 3⅛" diam. .$345.00
Charles Kaziun, four, pink & white spider lilies on gold speckled blue ground, ea. w/ gold K, approx. 1 - 1¼" diam., 2" H$1,265.00

A-MA May 1997   Skinner

Paperweights

Left to Right

Baccarat, three, double overlay sulphide series, Mount Rushmore oval red, white & blue weight, 4" L, gr. on white Mozart, yel. on white Bonaparte, 3" diam. $402.50
Paul J. Stankard, dogwood, cobalt blue background w/ white blossom, PS cane within, inscribed '73, 2¼" diam. . .$977.50
St. Louis Blue Clematis, center SL 1972 cane w/ blue ribbed petals on white latticinio bed, six outer facets, 3" diam. $258.75
St. Louis, double overlay sulphide, Bicentennial Am. Eagle, w/ red cut to white five facet sides, 3" diam. . .N/S

A-OH Nov. 1996   Garth's Auctions

Purple Slag

Row 1, Left to Right

Two Mugs, molded flowers, bird & nest, 3⅜" H $38.50
Four Pcs., boot w/ spur toothpick, 3¼" H; sq. toothpick, 3¾" H; bowl 5" diam., 3⅜" H, & milk pitcher, 5" H $60.50

Row 2, Left to Right

Bowls, pr., covered, fluted patt., sm. chips, 8⅛" diam., 8½" H $110.00
Goblets, six, molded leaf design, 5⅝" H $93.50
Three Pcs., covered butter, repr., chips; creamer & sugar, hairline & chip, 5¾" H, 8⅜" H $165.00

Row 3, Left to Right

Plates, pr., 10⅜" diam. $82.50
Compote, figural stem, bust of Jenny Lind, broken blister, 8½" diam., 7⅜" H $88.00
Two Pcs., fluted celery vase, 8⅛" H; fluted elongated relish, pinpoint flakes, 10⅜" L $104.50

A-MA Oct. 1996   James D. Julia Inc.

Quezal Vase, gr. feathers on a white ground, base w/ gr. feathers w/ gold irid. feathers on white ground, int. strong textured gold irid. surface, base sgn. "Quezal", 7½" H $1,600.00
Thomas Webb Cameo Vase, sgn., ivory ground, verigated gilt mottling, gilt trim 8¼" H ....N/S
Thomas Webb Vase, sgn., scroll dec. on shaded ivory ground, sides of vase dimpled, neck hexagonal, 5¼" H $1,025.00
Crown Milano Vase, sgn., shaded white ground & scene in lavender, rev. also dec. w/ lavender flowers, top lavender trimmed in gold enamel & base retains orig. signature, 9¼" H $1,350.00
Agata Creamer, N.E. glass, w/ reeded handle, white bottom shaded to deep pink on top, 4¼" H $800.00

A-OH Nov. 1996   Garth's Auctions

Three Face Glass

Row 1, Left to Right

Compotes, two, covered, check in stem & sm. bruise, 9¼" diam., 14½" H; hole in bowl, 8½" diam., 13"H .$93.50
Two Pcs., sherbet, 4½" diam., 3⅛" H, salt w/ pewter lid, 3" H $126.50

Row 2, Left to Right

Compote, 9½" diam., 9½" H $115.50
Celery Vase, 9¼" H $126.50
Sugar & Creamer, sugar 9¾" H, creamer, 6⅞" H $159.50

Row 3, Left to Right

Goblets, four, 6⅜" H $302.50
Butter w/ Lid, footed, 8⅛" L .$82.50

Row 4, Left to Right

Cake Stand, 8½" diam., 6½" H ...$93.50
Cake Stand, 9¼" diam., 7¼" H ..$93.50
Cake Stand, chips, 10½" diam., 8¼" H $115.50

A-MA Oct. 1996   James D. Julia Inc.

Mt. Washington Crown Milano Vase, lt. beige & white ground, w/ dec. of pansies & stems, applied leaf handles, 5½" W, 8" H $1,000.00
Mt. Washington Gourd Vase, peach, acid finish w/ painted & enameled floral dec., beaded enameled top, deep color on glass, 4" W, 7" H $2,650.00

A-OH Nov. 1996   Garth's Auctions

Glass, Row 1-3 frosted Westward Ho by Gillinder & Sons

Row 1, Left to Right

Compote, covered, 8⅛" diam., 14½" H $242.00
Compote, covered, sm. flakes & chip, 7" diam., 12¾" H $126.50
Compote, covered, 8" diam., 11¾" H $165.00

Row 2, Left to Right

Footed Butter, covered, sm. edge flakes, 7" diam., 8¾" H $192.50
Spooner, 6½" H $93.50
Goblet, 6½" H $93.50
Wine, rare size, 4⅜" H $423.50
Sherbet, 4" diam., 2⅞" H $27.50

Row 3, Left to Right

Sugar Bowl, 9¾" H $192.50
Creamer, pinpoint flakes, 7"H $82.50
Water Pitcher, flakes, 9⅜"H $330.00

Row 4, Left to Right

Cake Stand, amber, cottage patt., 10" diam. 7¼" H $104.50
Cake Stand, amber, wear & scratches, pinpoints & broken blister, 10¼" diam., 8" H $93.50

A-MA Oct. 1996   James D. Julia Inc.

Cordial Set, 6-pc., (5 shown), including decanter & five cordials, colbalt cut to clear, cordial 5" H, decanter 8" H $105.00

A-MA May 1997   Skinner

Paperweights

Left to Right

Baccarat Animal Series, 1970's, dancing devil, monkey, grouse w/ millefiore & animal surrounding canes, 3 - 3¼" diam. $920.00

Paul J. Stankard, poinsettia, red blossom on leafy stem, inscribed, "Paul J. Stankard '71", 2¼" diam. $920.00

St. Louis Fuschia, cane below blossom w/ two buds & leafy stems on white latticinio bed, six side facets, 3" diam. $373.75

Charles Kaziun, four, gold aventurine on amethyst, yel. & two blue cushions w/ spider lily blossoms, each w/ gold K, approx. 2" H, 1 - 1¼" diam. $1,150.00

A-MA May 1997   Skinner

Left to Right

Cactus Rose Decanter, cut overlay, attrib. to Stevens & Williams, sapphire blue over citron yel. & colorless glass wheel-cut & engr. as blossoms, 15½" H $1,265.00

Crystal Decanters, two faceted, late 19th C., Euro. design, one teal gr., one colorless, 16" & 19" H . . . . .N/S

A-PA Mar. 1997   Glass Works Auctions

Barber Bottles, lot of 2, Am., ca. 1885-1925, deep ruby red & clear glass w/ ruby red flashing, 7½" H & 6½" H $120.00

A-MA May 1997   Skinner

Row 1, Left to Right

Vase, silver overlay, butterfly & iris, cased turquoise blue glass cylinder layered in sterling dec., 10" H . .$172.50

Rockwell Vase, silver overlay, int. in amber, amethyst, pink & frost, base stamped "Rockwell", shield, some paint loss, wear & stain, 14¼" H . .$690.00

Blk. Glass Compotes, two silver overlaid, graceful tazzas dec. w/ art deco and foliate motifs, minor silver loss, 6½" diam., 6" H $201.25

Row 2, Left to Right

Crystal Decanter, silver overlay, star-cut base, colorless glass stoppered pitcher, mono. FGS in reserve, stamped 9-/1000 fine & numbered, 7½" H . . . $546.25

Gorham Box, silver & enamel, hinged cover on wood lined box dec. w/ lakeside scene & two enameled mallard ducks in flight, some enamel damage, base stamped "Gorham Sterling 173", w/ hallmarks, 6" x 4" x 2" . . .$230.00 lights, 13½" W, 6½" H $2,350.00

A-MA Sept. 1996   Skinner, Inc.

Left to Right

Glass Decanters, matched pr. of Bohemian ruby overlay cut & frosted, 8¼" H $460.00

Glass Vases, pr. of Bohemian ruby overlay cut & frosted, late 19th c., each cut w/ deer in a forest landscape, 14½" H $1,035.00

A-PA Mar. 1997   Glass Works Auctions

Mineral Water Bottle, Am., ca. 1840-1855, bluish aqua, 8-sided, 7½" H $125.00

A-MA Oct. 1996   James D. Julia Inc.

Row 1, Left to Right

Nakara Covered Box, sgn., blue ground w/ pink flowers, beaded scrolls, 6" W x 3½" H $450.00

Wavecrest Box, egg crate design, pale green/blue mottled ground w/ pink rose dec., purple enamel branches w/ painted robin, brass & metal ring & ornaments, 5"W, 5"H $850.00

Mt. Washington Crown Milano Jewel Box, hinged w/ gold lily dec., pale beige ground, raised gold floral dec., orig. silver plated hardware w/ gold wash, "P.M.C." sig., 3" x 5" x 6" $700.00

Smith Bros. Sugar Bowl, sgn., covered, pale beige ground w/ lt. blue pansy dec., silver plated cover sgn. "S.B.", 4" W, 3¾" H $100.00

Row 2, Left to Right

Smith Bros. Sugar & Creamer, dec. opal ware, lt. beige & shaded blue ground w/ purple & lavender violet dec., silver plated, 3½" W, 3½" H $350.00

Mt. Washington/Smith Bros. Glass Vases, two, dec. opal, one w/ shaded yel. to white ground w/ rose dec., one is pale pink to white dec. w/ berry design, gold beaded tops, 4" W, 6¾" H $500.00

Mt. Washington Toothpick Holder, Burmese glass, yel. & white enamel, 1¾" W, 3" H $400.00

Wavecrest Sugar & Creamer, pr., transfer dec., shaded ground, 4½" W, 3" H $250.00

A-MA Oct. 1996   James D. Julia Inc.

Abino Vase, buffalo pottery, artist sgn. "C. Harris", dated "1912", superb glaze, w/ old restoration, 5½" W, 13" H $300.00

A-MA Oct. 1996   James D. Julia Inc.

Row 1, Left to Right

Legras Rose Bowl, sgn. enameled, clear glass w/ yel., ora., blk. & blue dec., stamped "Made in Fr.", 4" W, 3¾" H $170.00

Le Verre Fr. Cameo Vase, glass, olive gr. & br. mottled ground, w/ pink apples, leaves & stems, cane signature, 3" W, 5½" H $500.00

Daum Nancy Cameo Vase, glass, sgn., olive gr. w/ textured ground, leaf & fine dec. in gold, carved "Je mours ou je n attache", 3" W, 3½" H $700.00

Row 2, Left to Right

Fr. Cameo Vase, glass sgn. "Charver", frosted mottled ground w/ clear apricot & white mottling, shades of lavender blue & br., 4½" W, 3½" H $500.00

Cameo Vase, textured, ground in pale gr. to clear w/ cameo carved design in brick red & gold, fine detail, 6" W, 4¼" H $650.00

Fr. Art Vase, glass, w/ painted & enameled dec., yel. & gr. on shaded yel. & pink ground, 4" W, 7" H . . .N/S

A-PA Mar. 1997   Glass Works Auctions

Barber Bottle, Am., ca. 1885-1925, purple amethyst, white enamel "Mary Gregory", 8⅛" H $300.00

Barber Bottle, Am., ca. 1885-1925, purple amethyst w/ white enamel Mary Gregory dec., 8" H $175.00

Barber Bottle, Am., ca. 1885-1925, yel. gr. w/ white Mary Gregory dec., 7⅞" H $275.00

A-MA Oct. 1996   James D. Julia Inc.

Row 1, Left to Right

Steuben Fan Vase, jade gr. & alabaster, 9" W, 11" H $300.00

Art Glass Tazza, sgn. "Schneider", lemon yel. & opal. top w/ ora. mottled base, 12½" W, 3½" H $375.00

Loetz Art Glass Bowl, irid. gr. glass w/ applied dec., w/ white striping, 8" W, 4½" H $500.00

Row 2, Left to Right

Loetz Art Glass Vase, irid. pale lavender ground w/ all over gold raindrop design, gr. pulled trailings, 5½" W, 12½" H .N/S

Loetz Bowl, salmon colored iridescence w/ blue highlights, 8½" W, 5¾" H . . . . .N/S

Durand Vase, sgn., gold w/ random threading, irid. surface w/ blue highlights, 9" W, 8½" H $650.00

Euro. Art Glass Vase, clear surface w/ applied gr. glass rigaree on sides & rim, 5" W, 6½" H $250.00

Loetz Art Glass Shell, highly irid. blue shell atop a gr. base, purple highlights, 13½" W, 6½" H $2,350.00

A-PA Mar. 1997   Glass Works Auctions

Ink Bottles, lot of 2, lt. blue gr., 3⅛" H, & Mucilage Bottle, med. pink amethyst, 2¾" H $45.00

A-PA Mar. 1997   Glass Works Auctions

Paper Shaving Vase, Am., ca. 1890-1925, purple amethyst w/ white Mary Gregory dec., 8" H $725.00

A-PA Mar. 1997   Glass Works Auctions

Barber Bottles, lot of 2, Am., ca. 1885-1925, cobalt blue, w/ white, ora., & blue enamel dec., 6⅜" H & 7" H $160.00

A-PA Mar. 1997   Glass Works Auctions

Soda Bottle, Am., ca. 1820-1830, med. yel. olive amber egg shaped, 5⅞" H $475.00

Soda Bottle, "J.M. Flurshut - Cumberland", Am., ca. 1850-1860, chip, lt. bluish gr. torpedo, 8⅜" H . .$1,400.00

Soda Bottle, Am., ca. 1855-1865, bluish aqua ten-pin, 8¼" H . .$160.00

A-PA Mar. 1997   Glass Works Auctions

Soda Bottle, "Keach-Balt", Am., ca. 1850-1860, deep gr. torpedo, 8½" H . . .$775.00

A-PA Mar. 1997   Glass Works Auctions

Soda Bottle, "S. Smith - Auburn N.Y. - 1857", Am., ca. 1840-1855, 10-sided, 7¾" H $475.00

A-PA Mar. 1997   Glass Works Auctions

Grenade, Fr., ca. 1880-1900, med. ora. amber, 5¾" H $300.00

A-PA Mar. 1997   Glass Works Auctions

Fire Grenades, lot of 2, turquoise blue pint, 6⅛" H, aqua pint, 5⅞" H, chip . . $140.00

A-PA Mar. 1997   Glass Works Auctions

Fire Grenades, lot of 2, Am., ca. 1875-1885, yel. olive & med. apple gr., both 6¼" H $210.00

A-PA Mar. 1997   Glass Works Auctions

Fire Grenades, lot of 2, Am., ca. 1875-1885, one w/ chip at base, both are turquoise blue w/ orig. contents, 6¼" H $140.00

A-PA Mar. 1997   Glass Works Auctions

Labeled Master Inks, lot of 4, from "Standard Ink" & "Carter" companies, smooth bases, tooled mouths, some w/ pour spouts, 7½" to 9⅜" H $170.00

A-PA Mar. 1997   Glass Works Auctions

Pickle Jar, Am., ca. 1850-1860, emerald gr., iron pontil, rolled lip, 11½" H $2,300.00
Pickle Jar, Am., ca. 1855-1865, apple gr., smooth base, applied mouth, embossing, 10⅞" H $400.00

A-PA Mar. 1997   Glass Works Auctions

Ink Bottle, "E. Waters Troy. NY", Am., ca. 1845-1855, aqua, good whittle to glass, 5¼" H $550.00
Ink Bottle, "E. Waters Troy NY", Am., ca. 1845-1855, aqua, shallow open bubble, 6¾" H 400.00

A-PA Mar. 1997   Glass Works Auctions

Fire Grenade, Am., ca. 1880-1895, "P.R.R.", clear glass, 7¼" H . . .$750.00
Fire Grenade, Am., ca 1880-1895, "P.R.R.", lt. aqua glass, 7" H . .$775.00

A-PA Mar. 1997   Glass Works Auctions

Fire Grenades, lot of 2, Am., ca. 1875-1885, both turquoise blue pints, 6⅛" H & 6⅝" H $85.00

A-PA Mar. 1997   Glass Works Auctions

Pickle Jar, Am., ca. 1860-1870, emerald gr., hole w/ sizable cracks repr., 13¾" H $130.00
Pickle Jar, Am., ca. 1850-1865, emerald gr., smooth base, 11⅞" H .$775.00
Pickle Jar, Am., ca. 1855-1865, blue gr., iron pontil, rolled lip, 11¾" H $1,150.00

A-PA Mar. 1997   Glass Works Auctions

Pickle Jar, Am., ca. 1855-1865, grass gr. w/ hint of olive, iron pontil, applied mouth, 8½" H $2,150.00
Pickle Jar, Am., ca. 1850-1860, pale blue gr., open pontil, rolled lip, 7½" H $150.00
Pickle Jar, Am., ca. 1850-1860, "T. Smith & Co", aqua, 6-sided, open pontil, rolled lip, 9½" H $625.00

A-PA Mar. 1997   Glass Works Auctions

Ink Bottle, "Harrison's Columbian Ink", Am., ca. 1845-1855, deep cobalt blue, deep vivid color, 7" H . .$550.00
Ink Bottle, "E. Waters Troy. NY", Am., ca. 1845-1855, aqua, 5¼" H . .$325.00

A-IA Nov. 1996   Gene Harris Antique
                     Auction Center, Inc.
Goblet, polar bear patt. $100.00
Jumbo Goblet, Iowa City Glass .$700.00

A-IA Nov. 1996   Gene Harris Antique
                     Auction Center, Inc.
Figurine, Gillinder & Sons, boy w/
dog, 1876 Expo, 5⅜" L $625.00

A-IA Nov. 1996   Gene Harris Antique
                     Auction Center, Inc.
Plate, Atterbury fish plate w/ clear
border, pat. 1875, 12⅞" L x 9"
W $1,700.00

A-IA Nov. 1996   Gene Harris Antique
                     Auction Center, Inc.
Water Pitcher, bringing home the
cows patt. $600.00
Water Pitcher, bicycle girl . .$550.00

A-IA Nov. 1996   Gene Harris Antique
                     Auction Center, Inc.
Dish, terrestrial globe, by O'Hara Glass
Co., Chicago, IL, 9½" T . . .$1,900.00

A-IA Nov. 1996   Gene Harris Antique
                     Auction Center, Inc.
Epergne, Statue of Liberty, two-piece,
19¾" T $1,750.00

A-IA Nov. 1996   Gene Harris Antique
                     Auction Center, Inc.
Compote, dragon patt., 8¼" W, 8"
T $825.00

A-IA Nov. 1996   Gene Harris Antique
                     Auction Center, Inc.
Water Pitcher, heron and
cattail patt. $170.00
Water Pitcher, dolphin patt., frosted
base $550.00

A-IA Nov. 1996   Gene Harris Antique
                     Auction Center, Inc.
Wine Goblets, set of four, two shown,
horse shoe, prayer rug patt., 4" T. $625.00

A-IA Nov. 1996   Gene Harris Antique
                     Auction Center, Inc.
Goblet, ostrich patt. $50.00
Goblet, pig in corn patt. $575.00

A-IA Nov. 1996   Gene Harris Antique
                     Auction Center, Inc.
Compote, cabbage leaf patt., frosted,
9¼" T $425.00

A-PA Mar. 1997   Glass Works Auctions

Barber Bottle, Am., ca. 1885-1925, root beer amber, coinspot patt. w/ yel., ora. & white enamel dec., 7⅞" H $100.00

A-PA Mar. 1997   Glass Works Auctions

Barber Bottle, Am., ca. 1885-1925, opal. cranberry, white swirl patt., 6⅞" H $190.00

A-PA Mar. 1997   Glass Works Auctions

Barber Bottles, lot of 2, Am., ca. 1885-1925, purple amethyst & grass gr., both rib-pattern w/ red & white enamel dec., 6¾" H & 7¼" H . .$55.00

A-PA Mar. 1997   Glass Works Auctions

Barber Bottles, set of two, Am., ca. 1885-1925, D grass gr. w/ white, maroon & gold enamel dec., both approx. 7⅞" H $140.00

A-PA Mar. 1997   Glass Works Auctions

Fire Grenades, lot of 2, Am., ca. 1880-1890, turquoise blue pints, orig. contents, both 6¾" H $150.00

A-PA Mar. 1997   Glass Works Auctions

Barber Bottles, lot of 2, Am., olive yel. w/ ora. & white floral dec., 6⅞" H, & 8" H $120.00

A-PA Mar. 1997   Glass Works Auctions

Barber Bottles, lot of 2, Am., ca. 1885-1925, turquoise blue w/ red, yel. & white enamel floral dec., 7" H & 7⅞" H $170.00

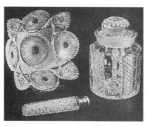

A-MA Oct. 1996   Skinner, Inc.

Cut Glass Bowl, Am. Brilliant, deep crimped edge w/ repeating faceted medallions, tiny point chips, 11½" diam., 3¼" H . . . . .N/S
Tiffany & Co. Scent Bottle, silver mounted cut glass, Am., Brilliant period, cane patt. tapered bottle w/ hinged cover & rim, impr., glass stopper missing, 6¼" L $172.50
Tobacco Jar, Am. Brilliant cut glass, matching cut glass top w/ star cutting repeated on base, 6" diam., 9" H $1,150.00

A-PA Mar. 1997   Glass Works Auctions

Cathedral Master Inks, lot of 2, Am., ca. 1920-1930, cobalt blue, "Carter's", orig. label & stopper, 9¾" H .$130.00
Cathedral Master Ink, Am., ca. 1920-1930, cobalt blue, "Carter's", tiny flake, 7⅞" H $140.00

A-PA Mar. 1997   Glass Works Auctions

Cathedral Master Ink, Am., ca. 1920-1930, cobalt blue, "Carter's", 6¼" H . . $160.00
Ink Bottle, "Kosmian Safety Ink", Am., ca. 1880-1895, medium smoky emerald gr., 7⅛" H $130.00

A-PA Mar. 1997   Glass Works Auctions

Grenade, Fr., ca. 1880-1900, yel. amber shading to ora. amber neck, 5½" H $275.00
Fire Grenade, Am., ca. 1875-1885, lt. electric cobalt blue quart, chip, 7⅞" H $95.00
Fire Grenade, Am., ca. 1883-1895, turquoise blue pint, 90% orig. label & contents, 6⅜" H $50.00
Fire Grenade, Am., ca. 1875-1885, cobalt blue, 6" H $200.00

A-PA Mar. 1997   Glass Works Auctions

Barber Bottle, Am., ca. 1885-1925, opal. clear glass, stars & stripes patt., 7⅛" H $160.00

A-MA Oct. 1996   James D. Julia Inc.

Row 1, Left to Right

Mt. Washington Crown Milano Jeweled Vase, gold & jeweled dec., pale peach & beige ground w/ gold scrolling around top, 7" W, 8¾" H $1,400.00

Mt. Washington Crown Milano Vase, pale beige & lime gr. ground w/ gold, berry pontil, sgn. w/ monogram & "01021", 5" W, 12½" H $900.00

Mt. Washington Burmese Glass Vase, deep salmon pink shading to yel., matte finish, 3¾" W, 10¼" H .N/S

Row 2, Left to Right

Mt. Washington Crown Milano Vase, w/ orchid dec. & painted Burmese ground, floral dec. in shades of maroon, white, gr., yel. & br. w/ much detailing, gold trim, 6" W, 14½" H $1,400.00

Mt. Washington Crown Milano Vase, dec. w/ multi-colored irises, top w/ scroll enamel & br. coloration, 11¾" H $600.00

Wavecrest Cracker Jar, w/ non-matching Pairpoint lid, dec. in pink & blue, 6" W, 8" H $150.00

Mt. Washington Covered Box, dec. opalware, "Collar & Cuffs", salmon poppy dec. w/ bright blue & white polka dot bow tie, white ground, sgn. "Pat'd Apr 10th, 1894" & numbered, 7" W, 3" H $700.00

A-PA Mar. 1997   Glass Works Auctions

Barber Bottle, Am., ca. 1885-1925, turquoise blue, w/ white & ora. enamel dec., 8⅜" H $120.00

Barber Bottle, Am., ca. 1885-1925, deep emerald gr.,w/ ora., blue, white & gold dec., 7" H $210.00

Barber Bottle, Am., ca. 1885-1925, pale apple gr., melon sided w/ coin spot patt. & white & ora. dec., 8⅛" H $80.00

A-MA Oct. 1996   James D. Julia Inc.

Row 1, Left to Right

Fr. Galle Cameo Wall Sconce, glass, orig. hammered brass & mah. holder, yel. ground w/ cranberry & purple leaves, glass is 9½" W, 10" H $3,000.00

Daum Nancy Cameo Vase, sgn. glass, frosted ground w/ pale pink & yel. internal dec., br./beige color flower, three spouted top, 5" W, 11" H . . . . .N/S

Fr. Galle Cameo Vase, glass, pale blue frosted ground w/ br. dec., excellent cameo carving, 3½" W, 8" H $900.00

Fr. Galle Cameo Vase, glass, glossy bleeding heart dec. w/ yel. ground, purple foot, all over cameo glass design, 4½" W, 8" H . . . . .N/S

Row 2, Left to Right

Daum Nancy Cameo Bowl, glass, internal dec. of yel. & ora. mottled colors w/ floral & leaf dec. in browns, 7¾" W, 3¼" H $2,250.00

Fr. Galle Cameo Vase, ora. ground, w/ glossy purple flowers, 3" W, 7¼" H $600.00

Daum Nancy Cameo Vase, sgn., glass & enameled, yel. opal. ground w/ br. mottling, textured & sculptured ground w/ floral leaf design in gr., br. & red, 2¾" W, 6¾" H $1,600.00

A-MA Oct. 1996   Skinner, Inc.

A-MA Oct. 1996   James D. Julia Inc.

Row 1, Left to Right

Daum Nancy Cameo Vase, sgn. mottled yel. & clear ground w/ amethyst bottom, gr. leaves & purple & red flowers, 2½" W, 1½" H $1,250.00

Fr. Cameo Pin Tray, glass, gr./br. color on frosted pale yel. ground, 3¾" W, 1" H $200.00

Daum Nancy Cameo Vase, glass & enameled, ground of pale apricot, peach, pink & opal. gr., cameo floral design w/ gold highlights, 1½" W, 2" H $1,150.00

Daum Nancy Cameo Vase, sgn., glass & enameled, yel./gr. mottled ground, trees & snow design, 1¾" W, 2" H $1,200.00

Row 2, Left to Right

Fr. De Vez Cameo Vase, glass, sgn., design in cobalt blue over yel. w/ a pink lining, 2" W, 5½" H $700.00

Fr. Daum Nancy Cameo Vase, ground in lime gr., apricot & clear, single carved layer design w/ gold trim, 2¼" W, 4" H . . . . .N/S

Fr. Galle Cameo Vase, glass, three color cameo design in shades of gr., white & pale pink, 3¾" W, 2¼" H . . . .N/S

Daum Nancy Cameo Perfume Bottle, sgn., yel. & pale cranberry stripes against opal. ground, highly carved floral design, enameled band on neck, amber stopper, 4" W, 4¾" H $1,800.00

Galle Cameo Liquor Flask, glass, lime gr. translucent ground, w/ white & pink enamel dec., silver screw cap w/ shot glass on bottom, 1¼" W, 5½" H $1,600.00

Left to Right

Galle Vase, glass black-eyed susan, frosted colorless oval layered w/ cornflower blue, emerald gr. & aubergine blk., cameo etched & cut as gr. centered blue blossoms, "Galle" in design at rev., 9¾" H . . . . .N/S

Galle Vase, cameo glass hydrangea, frosted pale blue & colorless glass layered in amethyst & mauve-green, cameo etched as blossom clusters, "Galle" in design at rev., 16" H . .$2,645.00

Galle Vase, cameo glass cabinet, early fiery opal. oval vessel, motif w/ "Galle" above lower border, 5¼" H . . . . .N/S

Galle Vase, cameo glass bleeding heart, oval colorless shaded to blue body layered in bright pink & olive gr., cameo etched & cut overall, "Galle" in design at side, 13" H $5,175.00

A-PA Mar. 1997   Glass Works Auctions

Barber Bottle, Am., ca. 1885-1925, purple amethyst, 7⅞" H $220.00
Barber Bottle, Am., ca. 1890-1925, clear glass encased in bark w/ multi-color label showing pretty girl, "Cologne", 7¾" H $205.00

A-PA Mar. 1997   Glass Works Auctions

Barber Bottle, Am., ca. 1885-1925, milk glass w/ multicolored dec. words "Bay Rum", 9⅜" H $150.00

A-PA Mar. 1997   Glass Works Auctions

Barber Bottle, Am., ca. 1885-1925, clear glass w/ yel. topaz flashing, Art Nouveau Cameo dec., 8⅛" H .$125.00

A-PA Mar. 1997   Glass Works Auctions

Barber Bottle, Am., ca. 1890-1910, yel. gr., w/ red white & gold enamel dec. 7¾" H $110.00

A-PA Mar. 1997   Glass Works Auctions

Barber Bottle, Am., ca. 1885-1925, deep purple amethyst, w/ white, red & gold enamel dec., 7½" H $70.00

A-PA Mar. 1997   Glass Works Auctions

Barber Bottle, Am., ca. 1885-1925, pale gr. thumbprint, Art Nouveau Cameo dec., 7⅞" H $300.00

A-PA Mar. 1997   Glass Works Auctions

Barber Bottle, Am., ca. 1885-1925, yel. gr., w/ white & red dec., some stain, 7¾" H $65.00
Barber Bottle, Am., ca. 1885-1925, deep yellowish gr. mallet form w/ white, yel. & ora. dec., 7¾" H $160.00

A-PA Mar. 1997   Glass Works Auctions

Barber Bottle, Am., ca. 1885-1925, purple amethyst, w/ red & yel. enamel dec., 7¾" H $95.00

A-PA Mar. 1997   Glass Works Auctions

Barber Bottle, Am., ca. 1885-1925, opal. cranberry hobnail patt., 7⅝" H $130.00

A-MA Oct. 1996   Skinner, Inc.

Steuben Aurene Vase, gold & gr. w/ platinum gold irid. surface dec. by sub-tle gr. swirls on ext., base inscribed "Aurene 131B", 4½" H $1,265.00

A-PA Mar. 1997   Glass Works Auctions

Barber Bottle, Am., ca. 1885-1925, cobalt blue bell form w/ red, white & gold enamel dec., 7⅞" H $190.00

A-PA Mar. 1997   Glass Works Auctions

Barber Bottle, Am., ca. 1885-1925, opal. cranberry, melon sided form w/ white stripe patt., 7¼" H $130.00

A-PA Mar. 1997   Glass Works Auctions

Row 1, Left to Right

Barber Bottle, Am., ca. 1885-1925, cobalt blue, multicolored enamel dec., 7⅝" H $180.00
Barber Bottles, set of two, Am., ca. 1885-1925, fiery opal. milk glass w/ colorful multicolored enamel Cherub" dec., 7½" H $850.00
Barber Bottle, Am., ca. 1885-1925, yel. topaz, w/ red, white, gr. & gold enamel floral dec., words "Bay Rum", 8¾" H $375.00
Barber Bottle, Am., ca. 1885-1925, milk glass w/ pink, br. & gold enamel dec., lt. blue ground, 7¾" H $275.00
Barber Bottle, Am., ca. 1885-1925, yellowish topaz, w/ white, gr. & ora. floral dec., 7" H $300.00

Row 2, Left to Right

Barber Bottle, Am., ca. 1885-1925, multicolored purple & silver art glass, 7⅜" H $400.00
Barber Bottle, Am., ca. 1885-1925, cranberry red w/ broken rib-pattern swirl, 6¾" H $65.00
Figural Whisk Broom, Am., ca. 1890-1920, bisque ceramic w/ red, blue & silver paint, 6⅞" H $275.00
Barber Bottle, Am., ca. 1885-1925, purple amethyst, white enamel dec. of a grist mill, words "Bay Rum", 7¾" H $240.00

A-PA Mar. 1997   Glass Works Auctions

Row 1, Left to Right

Barber Bottle, Am., ca. 1885-1925, fiery opal. milk glass w/ multicolored dec., words "Bay Rum", 9" H $375.00
Barber Bottle, Am., ca. 1885-1920, milk glass w/ multicolor dec. "Jas. Wolfinger Tonic", "W.T. & Co.", 9½" H ...$425.00
Barber Bottle, clear glass w/ multicolor label, Am., ca. 1885-1925, "E.S.N." mono., "W.T. & Co", 9⅝" H $275.00
Barber Bottle, Am., ca. 1885-1820, milk glass w/ multicolor decor "J.N. Hogarth Bay Rum", 9½" H $425.00
Barber Bottle, Am., ca. 1885-1925, opal. milk glass w/ multicolored enamel floral dec., 8⅞" H $350.00
Barber Bottle, Am., ca. 1890-1910, opal. turquoise blue stars & stripes patt., 7⅛" H $400
Barber Bottle, Am., ca. 1885-1925, frosted purple amethyst, w/ yel. & gold Art Nouveau floral dec., 7⅞" H $450.00
Barber Bottle, Am., ca. deep purple amethyst, white enamel dec. of a Sailing Vessel, 6⅝" H $275.00
Barber Bottle, Am., ca. 1885-1925, pink amethyst w/ white enamel Mary Gregory dec., "Vegederma", 8⅛" H $400.00

A-PA June 1997   Pook & Pook, Inc.

Decanters, three sm. lidded, ca. 1810, 2 w/ ribbed bodies & 1 w/ swirl ribbed body, 6½" to 7" H $800.00
Sugar Bowl, amethyst blown glass lidded, ca. 1800, w/ swirled finial lid, 7" H $2,000.00
Cobalt Sugar, Stiegel type, lidded quilted diamond patt., ca. 1800, minor chip to finial, 6½" H $2,800.00
Cobalt Glass Pitcher, 3-mold blown, ca. 1800, 4½" H, w/ a cobalt glass pitcher, ca. 1810, w/ globular body, flaring rim & swirl patt., 5¼" H $2,900.00
Cobalt Salts, three Stiegel type, ca. 1800, quilted diamond patt., together w/ 2 gr. Stiegel type salts $1,600.00
Cobalt Salts, five Stiegel type, ca. 1800, including 2 double ogee patt., 2 vertical ribbed patt. $900.00

Left

A-MA Oct. 1996   Skinner, Inc.

Steuben Peacock Vase, white, gold & gr. aurene on alabaster, smooth oval opaque white body w/ four gr. eye peacock feathers in gold Aurene dec., inscribed "Aurene 273" on base, 12½" H $4,600.00

Right

A-MA Apr. 1997   Skinner, Inc.

Am. Glass Vase, emerald gr. w/ silver overlay, ca. 1900, w/ scrolling foliage, chip to pontil, 16" H $1,092.50

A-IA Nov. 1996   Jackson's

A-MA Oct. 1996   James D. Julia Inc.

A-IA Nov. 1996   Jackson's

196-Fenton Vase, ground rim w/ minor flakes, 6½" $275.00

197-Fenton Vase, etched Fenton 1976, 8" H $192.50

198-Fenton Vase, experimental satin finish, 8" H $330.00

199-Fenton Vase, turq., molded Fenton mark, 7½" H $55.00

200-Fenton Vase, pink on custard, molded Fenton mark, 7½" H .$126.50

201-Fenton Vase, hanging heart patt., etched Fenton 1976, 4" H $49.50

202-Cambridge Bowl, oval footed shell in emerald, 8" L $22.00

203-Fenton Vase, turq. iris vase, hanging heart patt., etched Fenton, 11" H .$181.50

204-Fenton Vase, white on blk. amethyst, etched Don Fenton 8-7-81, 7½" H ...$93.50

205-Fenton Vase, rare satin finish, 10" H $165.00

206-Fenton Lemonade Set, rare custard hanging heart, 7 pc. .$302.50

207-Fenton Vases, pr. of blk. rose, Jack in the Pulpit, 8" H $77.00

208-US Glass Co. Fruit Bowl, in blk. amethyst, 8½" diam. $137.50

209-Cambridge Jug, crystal ball in emerald w/ clear handle, 9" H $49.50

210-Fenton, Sophisticated Lady, amethyst, mkd., sign Richard Delaney, 1-12-82, 11" H $220.00

211-Imperial Vase, crystal, ruby red, inverted baby thumbprint, silver floral overlay, 8" H $104.50

212-Fenton Vase, Burmese style, broken bottle mark, 5½" H ..$165.00

213-Hutchenreuther, Bavaria dinner plates, gold floral decor, w/ cobalt rim, John Wanamaker Studios, 11" diam. . $55.00

214-Bohemian, glass decanter set, red overlay w/ cut designs, decanter 14½" H, stemware 4" H $88.00

215-Limoge, h/p, tankard & 6 mugs, gold grapes & leaves, blue background, gold handles, mkd. JPL Fr., 13½" H $330.00

Row 1, Left to Right

Steuben Aurene Vase, sgn. "Aurene", gold color w/ purple highlights, 4½" W, 10¾" H $175.00

Steuben Basket, sgn. "Aurene", irid. gold color w/ purple/bronze highlights, 6¼" W, 7½" H $750.00

Tiffany Glass Vase, dec. olive gr. glass w/ brick red pulled feathering, irid. surface, 4" W, 6" H ....N/S

Steuben Aurene Atomizer, irid. & cut floral engraving, cobalt blue jeweled top w/ orig. metalware, base 3½" x 9¾" H $1,200.00

Row 2, Left to Right

Am. Art Glass Vase, irid. oyster white ground w/ heart shaped dec. in gold & gr., gold lining, 5½"W, 11½"H .$300.00

Tiffany Box, gold, covered, w/ much blue & purple, edge flakes, 5¼" x 2¾" H $300.00

Loetz Art Glass Vase, gold ground w/ purple & blue highlights, dec. in clear, 9¼" W, 7½" H $500.00

Durand Ginger Jar, sgn. art glass, covered, jade gr. ground w/ purple & blue King Tut design, amber finial, cover lighter, 5" W, 7" H $900.00

Tiffany Glass Vase, sgn. "L.C.T." opaque glass w/ highly irid. surface, 5½" W, 9" H ....N/S

A-MA Oct. 1996   James D. Julia Inc.

A-MA Oct. 1996   Skinner, Inc.

Left to Right

Tiffany Vase, blue irid., purple glass dec. by blue irid. luster, inscribed "L.C. Tiffany Favrile", 8" H $920.00

Tiffany Cased Vase, blue irid., teal blue oval body lined in opal white glass w/ smooth matte lustrous surface overall, inscribed "L.C. Tiffany Favrile 1735E", 5¾" H $747.50

Tiffany Vase, blue irid. leaf & fine, broad shouldered oval vessel of blue favrile glass cased to gold & opal int. & dec. w/ silvery heart & vine border, inscribed "L.C.T. 288B", 4½"H $862.50

Left to Right

Galle Cameo Banjo Vase, glass, frosted white & pale peach ground w/ purple & gr. design, star signature, 3½" W, 6¾" H $900.00

Fr. De Vez Cameo Vase, sgn. glass, pink ground w/ cobalt blue overlay, 3" W, 7" H $700.00

Galle Cameo Vase, glass, frosted & white ground w/ purple violet & leaf dec. 3" W, 3½" H ....N/S

Galle Covered Jar, pale blue & opal. ground w/ purple highlights, floral designed in lavender & gr., star signature, 4" W, 4¾" H $1,050.00

A-OH Dec. 1996   Garth's Auctions

Navaho Rug, aniline reds ora., yel., blk. & dk. blue w/ natural & dk. br., selvage worn, repairs, ca. 1885-1900, 4'2" x 5'9" $440.00

A-OH Dec. 1996   Garth's Auctions

Navaho Rug, serrate diamond cross in blk. & white w/ hook design in tan & red, slight pink tinge, 3' x 5'8" $165.00

A-OH Dec. 1996   Garth's Auctions

Navaho Rug, red serrate diamond center w/ carded gray ground, black & white border w/ fringe, 3'3" x 4'5" $330.00

A-OH Aug. 1996   Garth Auctions

Row 1, left to right:

Navaho Rug, prob. Klagetoh area, modified storm patt. w/ Tees-Nos-Pas type border, double dye red, blk. & natural on carded grey ground, central panel has mounted crosses & motifs for four sacred mountains, ca. 1935-40, lt. stains & red has bled some, 3'5" x 4'8" $715.00
Navaho Rug, transitional, alternating carded grey & red bands containing early directional terrace motifs in gold & dk. grey, some stains, sm. holes & warp breaks, 4'6" x 5'10" $330.00
Navaho Rug, transitional, interlocking banded feather patt. of finely hand carded natural, blue-purple, faded red & dk. br., late 1800's, stains, warp break & edge damage, 4'1" x 5'4" $715.00

Row 2, left to right:

Transitional Rug, Ganado double dye red, dk. br., natural & yel., warp breaks & some damage, red has bled slightly & one end turned over, 4'3" x 6'8" . . $770.00
Transitional Rug, Ganado w/ double dye red, ora., grey, natural & blk. colors, border design w/ double blk. banded edge, some staining, color bleeding & warp break w/ hole, 4'4" x 5'6" $231.00
Transitional Rug, Ganado area, border in double dye red, analine br., blk., carded grey & white, stains & slight color bleeding, 3'4" x 4'9" $220.00

Row 3, left to right:

Transitional Rug, lrg., whirling logs in dk. br. & red on a carded grey ground, central diamond bordered w/ white & blk. & white stepped terrace border, early 20th C. soft wool, red has bled, 4'7" x 7'8" $770.00
Transitional Rug, Gallup/Four Corners area, design in red, dk. br., & carded tan on natural open ground, tan linked hourglass tracing & red & blk. border, ca. 1925-40, minor stains, 3'8" x 6'8" $797.50
Transitional Rug, finely woven, design in red, ora. & dk. br. on carded tan/brown & natural ground w/ dk. br. border, ca. 1925-40, staining, warp break & ora. has bled, 3'3" x 6' $275.00

A-OH Dec. 1996   Garth's Auctions

Navaho Rug, serrate diamonds in red, dk. br., natural & tan, wear & some staining, 3'8" x 5'9" $880.00

A-MA Mar. 1997   Eldred's

Brass Double Lamp, w/ two cased gr. shades, pat. date 1881, 20½" H $357.50

A-MA Mar. 1997   Eldred's

Fluid Lamps, pr., overlay glass, white-cut-to-clear w/ brass collar & milk glass base, 19th C., 10" H $440.00

A-MA May 1997   Skinner

Handel Scenic Lamp, rev. painted, textured glass dome shade, hand-painted riverscape w/ tall gr. trees under sunset ora. skies, signed on edge "Handel 7124", three socket bronzed turned baluster base, shade 18" diam., 22" H $4,025.00

A-MA Oct. 1996   Skinner, Inc.

Wedding Lamps, pr. of blue & white pressed glass, D.C. Ripley & Co., pat. dated Feb. 1, 1870 & Sept. 20, 1870, minor chips, 13¼" H $2,645

A-MA Mar. 1997   Skinner

Hall Candle Light, clear blown glass, 19th C., in pressed brass mounts, 23" H $2,415.00

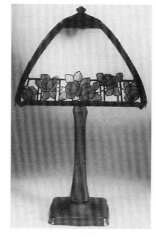

A-MA May 1997   Skinner

Handel Lamp, w/ rose panels, white slag glass w/ painted red & gr. florals, base w/ good patina, sgn. Handel, two panels repl., shade 11½" sq., 19" H$373.75

A-MA May 1997   Skinner

Handel Lamp, rev. painted butterflies & roses, textured domed glass hand-painted, sgn. "Handel 7032", mounted on dk. gold metal three-socket base, shade 18" diam., 23½" H . .$10,350.00

A-MA May 1997   Skinner

Handel Lamp, obverse painted daffodil, conical glass shade handpainted, mkd. "Handel 5648", mounted on three socket gilt metal triparte base w/ Handel label, old repaint on metal base, shade 18" diam., 23½" H $5,750.00

A-MA May 1997   Skinner

Tiffany Acorn Ceiling Lamp, leaded yel. amber & opal white rippled glass domed shade, beaded rim w/ four integrated hanging hooks, unsgn., central medallion repl., 20½" diam. . .$6,325.00

A-MA May 1997　　　　　　　　Skinner

Pittsburgh Lamp, rev. painted, labeled conical glass shade painted ora. amber & pink inside w/ blk. Arts & Crafts motif painted on ext. surface, two-socket base, paint worn, shade 14" diam., 18" H $1,265.00

A-MA May 1997　　　　　　　　Skinner

Wilkinson Waterlily Lamp, leaded glass, dome shade w/ pink & white blossoms, amber granite glass background, locked upon three-socket cast bronze base, 18" diam., 24½" H $3,450.00

A-MA May 1997　　　　　　　　Skinner

Table Lamp, leaded glass, scalloped border w/ pink & gr. blossom & leaf design, amber caramel slag brickwork, three socket brass hexagonal base, 19½" diam., 22" H $747.50

A-MA May 1997　　　　　　　　Skinner

Table Lamp, leaded bent panel, domed shade of caramel & gr. slag sections w/ rippled red accent glass, three-socket gilt metal cast foliate base, wear, restorations, 16" diam., 21" H $632.50

A-MA May 1997　　　　　　　　Skinner

Muller Fres Chandelier, art glass & wrt. iron, mottled ora., yel., blue glass, each mkd. "Muller Fres Luneville", blk. ceiling mount, minor chip on shade rims, 23" diam., 42" H $1,495.00

A-MA Oct. 1996　　　　　James D. Julia Inc.

Hanging Lamp, sapphire blue hobnail shade w/ blue hobnail font mounted in yel. brass frame, shade 7" H . $600.00

A-MA May 1997　　　　　　　　Skinner

Tiffany Table Lamp, "Blue" daffodil, yel. daffodil blossoms w/ sky-blue background, shade rim & base impr. "Tiffany Studios NY", shade 1497, base 360, 20" diam., 24½" H . . .$26,450.00

A-MA May 1997　　　　　　　　Skinner

Row 1, Left to Right

Tiffany Acorn Desk Lamp, leaded gr. & white glass segments w/ green-amber acorn-shaped leaf & vine border, some cracks, tag on edge "Tiffany Studios NY", 12" diam., 17" H $4,600.00

A-MA Oct. 1996　　　　　　　Skinner, Inc.

Table Lamp, Handel bent panel, amber slag glass panels overlaid w/ oak leaf metal framework w/ conforming applied color, two socket baluster base w/ orig. bronzed finish, worn, finial missing, rim repr., 16" diam., 21" H $920.00

A-MA Oct. 1996   James D. Julia Inc.

Hanging Lamp, cranberry shade mounted in yel. brass frame, shade patt. three rows of vertically expanded bull's eyes, shade 7" H $700.00

A-MA Oct. 1996   James D. Julia Inc.

Hanging Lamp, sapphire blue shade w/ opal. hobnails mounted in red brass frame, shade 6½" H $900.00

A-MA Oct. 1996   James D. Julia Inc.

Hanging Lamp, lavendar milk glass shade mounted in yel. brass frame, shade 5½" H $200.00

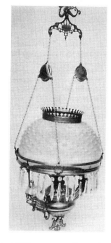

A-MA Oct. 1996   James D. Julia Inc.

Hanging Lamp, pink slag hobnail shade mounted in red brass frame, shade 7" H $1,400.00

A-MA Oct. 1996   James D. Julia Inc.

Hanging Lamp, pink & white satin MOP shade mounted in red brass frame, shade white outside & pink inside, shade 6½" H $1,600.00

A-MA Oct. 1996   James D. Julia Inc.

Hanging Lamp, amber expanded bull's eye patt. shade mounted in red brass frame, shade 6" H $550.00

A-MA Oct. 1996   James D. Julia Inc.

Hanging Lamp, cranberry shade mounted in yel. brass frame, top half of shade strong cranberry, bottom half is med. cranberry, shade 7"H . .$700.00

A-MA Oct. 1996   James D. Julia Inc.

Hanging Lamp, Francesware hobnail shade, amber & frosted crystal glass mounted in red brass frame, shade 6½" H $650.00

A-MA Oct. 1996   James D. Julia Inc.

Hanging Lamp, pink opal. hobnail shade mounted in a yel. brass frame, shade 7" H $1,100.00

A-MA Oct. 1996   James D. Julia Inc.

Hanging Lamp, dk. pink shading to light, etched shade mounted in red brass frame, 8″ W, 8″ H $500.00

A-MA Oct. 1996   James D. Julia Inc.

Hanging Lamp, dk. pink shading to lt. opal. hobnail shade in yel. brass frame, approx. 8½″ W, 9½″ H $300.00

A-MA Oct. 1996   James D. Julia Inc.

Sinumbra Lamp, electrified, painted blk. w/ dec. 7″ prisms, cut & frosted old shade dec. in peacock-like feather patt., 25½″ $1,700.00

Astral Lamp, electrified lamp w/ brass font, gold dec. white milk glass stem & cast brass foot, dec. frosted shade, doubled jeweled flat 7½″ prisms, overall 29″ H $700.00

A-MA Oct. 1996   James D. Julia Inc.

Hanging Lamp, pink satin etched shade mounted in red brass frame, shade, 8½″ W, 9¼″ H $575.00

A-MA Oct. 1996   James D. Julia Inc.

Hanging Lamp, pink opal. shade in red brass frame, shade approx. 8½″ W, 8½″ H $300.00

A-MA Oct. 1996   James D. Julia Inc.

Astral Lamp, electrified brass font w/ dec. heavy cast stem & double step blk. onyx foot, prism band mounts alt. 7″ spear cut & 6″ flat prisms, frosted cut shade dec., overall 28″ H $700.00

Astral Lamp, brass font w/ heavy cast brass stem on onyx foot, cut & frosted shade, P&A Argand burner, lamp includes complete set of 5½″ flat prisms, overall 24″ H $1,300.00

Sheffield Hurricane Lamps, pr., silver w/ frosted & cut inverted shades, 17¾″ H $85.00

A-MA Oct. 1996   James D. Julia Inc.

Hanging Lamp, pink opal. ribbed shade in yel. brass frame, approx. 7″ W, 8″ H $300.00

A-MA Oct. 1996   James D. Julia Inc.

Argand Lamp, electrified double lamp w/ crystal cut glass font, heavy frosted & cut matching shades, 24½″ H $1,100.00

A-MA Oct. 1996   James D. Julia Inc.

Owl Lamp, white milk glass w/ fired on paint in blk. & grays, nutmeg burner, 7¾" H $1,050.00
Owl Lamp, white milk glass w/ fired on paint in shades of gr., br. & blk., nutmeg burner, 7¾" H $900.00
Skeleton Lamp, white bisque w/ lavender & blue trim, gr. glass eyes, foreign burner, 5½" H . . . . .N/S
Lamp, end of day glass in shades of burgundy, blue, gr., yel. & white, hornet burner, 8½" H $50.00

A-MA Oct. 1996   James D. Julia Inc.

Slag Panel Chandelier brass frame have applied clusters of grapes, electrified, approx. 22" H $550.00

A-MA Oct. 1996   James D. Julia Inc.

Pairpoint Lamp, sgn. multi-hued scenic ground, brilliant deep gr. & blue, verde finish base, overall 22¾" $5,000.00

A-MA Oct. 1996   James D. Julia Inc.

Lamp, brilliant deep purple & gr. shade, base & shade sgn., shade diam. 5½" H, overall 12½" H $2,350.00

A-MA Oct. 1996   James D. Julia Inc.

Handel Lamp, sgn., soft blue/green ground w/ nine seagulls, sgn., bronze base, replaced sockets, shade diam. 18", overall 24½" H $6,800.00

A-MA Oct. 1996   James D. Julia Inc.

Handel Lamp, sgn., yel. ground w/ blk. & br. stripes & border w/ colorful birds amidst roses in shaded pink w/ green & brown foliage on blk. ground, shade diam., 18" $3,500.00
Table Lamp, electric, base sgn. "Pairpoint", shade transluscent w/ mottled orange/brown surface & green highlights, shade diam. 14¼", overall 21" H .$600.00

A-MA Oct. 1996   Skinner, Inc.

Galle Plaffonier, cameo glass, frosted shades of gr. & gray layered in burgundy red-maroon over gr., cameo cut & etched floral design, "Galle" at side in motif, mounted w/ three gilt metal chins & ceiling mount for lighting, shade 11½" diam., 6½" D . .$3,220.00

A-MA Oct. 1996   Skinner, Inc.

Handel Piano Lamp, leaded glass, gr. slag & granite glass segments, adjustable socket on curved "dog's leg" shaft, impr. "Handel", 7" diam., 22" L, 9" H $1,265.00

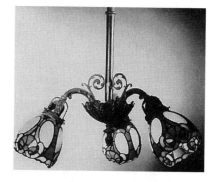

A-MA Oct. 1996   Skinner, Inc.

Ceiling Lamp, R. Williamson & Co. Chicago, leaded glass shades w/ opal. white granite ovals w/ amber-tan glass segments centering gr. slag shell-form devices at border, three-socket bronzed metal fittings w/ cast foliate elements, adjustable shades, 5" D, 5" diam. $2,875.00

A-OH Nov. 1996   Garth's Auctions

Silver Spoon, w/ cast bird on back & four sets of engr. initials, from 1756-1876, mkd. "J. Myers Phila", dents in bowl, 9¼" L $220.00
Silver Spoons, six, w/ tooled handle edge, London hallmarks for 1778-79, Hester Bateman, 8¼" L $715.00
Silver Spoons, nine w/ engr. crest, London hallmarks for 1806-7, Eley & Fearn, 6¾" L $165.00
Silver Spoons, two w/ engr. griffin handles, mkd. "D. Van Voorhis", w/ eagle, NY 1751-1824, 8¾" L $110.00
Silver Stuffing Spoon, London hallmarks for 1818-19, "T.B.", 12" L $55.00
Silver Server, w/ reticulated blade & engr. birds & flowers, Dublin hallmarks for 1778, "LH" $715.00
Silver Spoons, three w/ London hallmarks, tea caddy 1809-1810, "J.S." 3⅛" L,; dipper shaped sugar sifter, 1813-14, Eley, Fearn & Chawner, 4⅞" L; & stuffing spoon, 1811-12, Eley, Fearn & Chawner, engr. handle, 12" L $247.50
Silver Brandy Warmer, London hallmarks for E. Morley, ca. 1798, engr. bowl, 15¾" L $27.50
Silver Spoons, three, shell bowl salt mkd. "Owen"; demi-tasse w/ engr. handle, NY 1779-99, 5½" L; & demi-tasse, New Haven 1751-1827, 4" L $82.50
Silver Spoons, three by William Homes, bright cut engraving w/ "C", & two spoons w/ presentation engravings, Homes Sr. was nephew of Benjamin Franklin $522.50

A-MA Apr. 1997   Skinner, Inc.

Whiting Service, sterling flatware, Lily patt., thirty teaspoons, twenty-two luncheon forks, eighteen seafood forks, asst. serving pcs., seventeen bouillon spoons, sixteen sm. teaspoons, fifteen butter spreaders, thirteen: dinner forks, soupspoons, twelve: salad forks, dinner knives, eleven: ice cream spoons, grapefruit spoons, demitasse spoons, luncheon knives, most engr., Old English, approx. 243 troy oz. in a fitted mah. chest $9,775.00

A-MA Oct. 1996   Skinner, Inc.

Left to Right

Coin Silver Tea Set, John Moulton, Otto & Falk, PA, c. 1797, teapot & covered sugar, neoclassical urn-form w/ galleried top, & creamer, engr. w/ ribbon & foliate reserve, dents, repairs to creamer, teapot 11" H, approx. 40 troy oz. $2,415
Coin Silver, two pcs., Am., 19th c., including a footed teapot stand, Pear & Bacall Co., Boston, 1850-57, monogrammed, & a repousse dec. mug, Bailey & Co., Phil., 1848-65, minor dents, stand 8" L, 14 troy oz. $575.00
Coin Silver Tea Set, three-piece, Shreve, Brown. & Co., Boston, c. 1857, barrel-form teapot, creamer & open sugar, mkd. on base, minor dents, teapot 5" H, approx. 16 troy oz. $920.00
Coin Silver Covered Pitcher, Jesse Churchill & Treadwell, Boston, 1805-13, mkd. on base, engr. "Benjamin and Judith Bufsey," minor dents & scratches, 9½" H, approx. 25 troy oz. $2,645.00
Coin Silver Covered Sugar, Whartenby & Bumm, Phil., 1816-18, monogrammed, mkd. on base, minor dents, 9" H, approx. 25 troy oz. $431.25

A-MA Apr. 1997   Skinner, Inc.

Tiffany Sterling Compotes, 1875-91, chased floral rim & base, 10" diam., 4" H, approx. 50 troy oz. $3,450.00
Tiffany Sterling Centerbowl, 1875-91, oval form raised on four paw feet, chased floral rim & base, 17" L, 12½" W, 4½" H, approx. 61 troy oz. $5,750.00

A-MA Apr. 1997   Skinner, Inc.

Reed & Barton Service, sterling flatware, Francis I patt., twelve: luncheon forks, dessert spoons, soupspoons, bouillon spoons, dinner forks, butter spreaders, demitasse spoons, luncheon knives, seafood forks, salad forks, ice cream forks, dinner knives, twenty-four teaspoons, six tablespoons, eight serving pcs., three pc. & two pc. carving sets, script mono., approx. 234 troy oz. $4,025.00

A-OH Jan. 1997   Garth's Auctions

Silver

Tablespoons, two by Edward Lownes, PA, 1817, cast shell handle & engr. name w/ mono., 8¾" L $302.50

Forks, five silver luncheon w/ shell handle by Conrad Bard, PA, 1825, minor damage, mono., 7⅛" L $137.50

Forks, six w/ rattail handles by Ball, Blk. & Co., NY, 1850, 7⅝" L . .$203.50

Salad Forks, eleven w/ cast shell handles by Bailey & Co., PA, 1850, mono., 7¼" L $286.00

Tablespoons & Ladle, by Frederick Marquand, NY, 1823, pr. tbs. w/ shell handles, w/ mono., 8½" L, ladle w/ flower on handle w/ mono., 5½" L $220.00

Spoons, three pcs. by John B. Jones, Boston, 1782-1854, pr. of tbs., shell hendles 8¼" L, sugar spoon w/ flower on handle w/ mono. 5½" L . .$330.00

Ladle, w/ shell handle, monogram, John B. Jones, Boston, 12¾" L $330.00

Tablespoons, six w/ shell handles, mkd. "Winge", 8¾" L $110.00

Forks, two w/ shell handles, one by N. Harding & Co., MA, 1830, 7" L, one by A.E. Warner, MD, 1805, mono.,7¼" L, . .$93.50

Spoons, two w/ shell handles, one by Taylor & Hinsdale, NY, 1801, 7" L, one by Ward & Barhtolomew, Hartford, 1804, 6"L $27.50

A-MA Sept. 1996   Skinner, Inc.

Left to Right

Serving Pieces, five silver flatware, 19th c., Gorham soup ladle, Bigelow Bros. & Kennard engr. stuffing spoons, J.E. Caldwell ice cream slicer & spoon, Am. coin Olive patt. fish knife; approx. 25 troy oz. $862.50

Serving Pieces, two sterling flatware, Gorham pierced bowl cracker scoop, Durgin Dauphin pierced bowl croquette server, gold washed bowls, approx. 5½ troy oz. $920.00

A-OH Jan. 1997   Garth's Auctions

Row 1, Left to Right

Silver Julep, engr. "J.L. Wallace", mkd. "F. Spiegelhalder, Louisville", 3¾" H .$550.00

Silver Julep, engr. "S.C.M.", mkd. "T.W. Radcliffe", 3½" H $605.00

Silver Julep, engr. "R", mkd. "G & W, Tiffany & Co.", dents, 3¾" H .$192.50

Silver Julep, mkd. "Jaccard & Co. St. Louis" 1850, 3⅝" H $385.00

Silver Julep, engr. "A.M.C.", mkd. "T. Ayers", 3⅜" H $770.00

Row 2, Left to Right

Silver Julep, mkd. "W. Kendrick Louisville", dents, 3⅞" H $495.00

Silver Julep, engr. mono., mkd. "Gregg Hayden & Co.", 3½" H $440.00

Silver Julep, engr. presentation mono., mkd. "Gregg Hayden & Co", 3½" H $440.00

Silver Julep, engr. "Henderson Union & Hopkins Agl Asso.", mkd. "H. Hudson", dents, 3⅞" H $550.00

Silver Julep, mkd. "Hudson & Dolfinger, Louisville", dents, 3¾" H .$550.00

A-MA June 1997   Skinner

Silver Tea & Coffee Set, four pc., William B. North & Co., NY, 1822-29, w/ sheath of wheat finial, serpent-form spout, minor dents, repairs, 86 troy oz. $3,220.00

A-MA Sept. 1996   Skinner, Inc.

Tea Set, Reed & Barton, silver plated, six-pc., ca. 1885, acid-etched & engr. Elizabethan figural dec., teapot, creamer, open sugar, covered sugar, waste bowl, covered butter dish, butter knife missing, teapot 6⅞" H $258.75

A-OH Jan. 1997   Garth's Auctions

Silver

Fish Server, mkd. "I.W. Forbes", ca. 1805, NY, engr. monogram, 11⅝" L $440.00

Porringer, w/ handle, unmkd. engr. "M.S. Bishop", dents, 5½" diam. $275.00

Servers, two w/ engr. blades, "Sharrard", ca. 1850, KY, 8⅝" L; "Palmer & Bachelders, Pure Coin", ca, 1715, MA, 9⅝" L $412.50

Punch Ladle, w/ rattail handle, engr. "C.A.B.S.", mkd. "Merriman", 13" L $385.00

Punch Ladle, w/ shell bowl, London hallmarks for 1774-75, Bateman, engr. "J.C.", 12½" L $577.50

Ladle, shell bowl & rattail handle, engr. "Lizzie", PA, 8¾" L $110.00

Server & Fork, server engr. & mono., mkd. "Smith & Chamberlain...", MA, 8⅝" L; three tine fork, ivory insert, cracked mkd. "Daniel & Arter", 5¾" L $192.50

Carving Set, three pc., repl. stainless blades etc., mkd. "Made in Eng.", handles earlier w/ faint hallmarks, 12¼" L $159.50

Sauce Ladles, two similar w/ shell bowls, London Hallmark 1772-73, Tookey, 6¼" L; one mkd. "R.R.", 7⅛" L $192.50

A-MA May 1997   Skinner

Peterson Candlesticks, hand wrt., hammered finish, impr. Peterson logo, sterling, 4" diam., 10" H . . .$1,265.00

A-OH Aug. 1996   Garth Auctions

Silver Boxes, two, lined w/ wood, mkd. "950 silver", 6" L $187.00
Silver Souvenir Spoons, ten, nine "sterling" one plated, 6.5 troy oz. for nine $110.00
Dip Chamberstick, Wedgwood gr. jasper w/ white figures, impr. "Wedgwood", cone for snuffer but no snuffer, 6½" D .$110.00
California Gold, two half dollars: Washington head "1858" & octagonal Liberty head "1857" $82.50
Brooch & Earrings, gr. jasper w/ white figures, mkd. "Wedgwood Made in Eng.", silver colored mounts are mkd. "Silver FAW" $44.00
"Sterling" Silver Flatware, seventy-six pc. set, twelve pc. service plus extras, Baroque crest handles are monogrammed, 86 troy ox. modern wooden case $660.00
"Sterling" Silver Flatware, forty-seven pc. assembled set w/ similar design, some mkd. "Tress & Harrington", some monogrammed, wooden case $357.50
"Sterling" Silver Flatware, fifty pc. set, service for twelve plus three serving pcs., only eleven teaspoons, 39 troy oz.$522.50

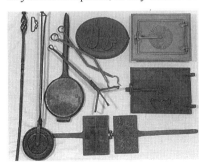

A-OH Nov. 1996   Garth's Auctions

Two Pcs., wrt. iron, poker w/ open spiral cage finial, 40" L, & striker from a flint & steel set $181.50
Waffle Irons, two, one all cast iron, other cast w/ wrt. iron handles, 23", 29½" L $187.00
Tools, two wrt. iron, ember tongs, 18¼" L, & pot lifter $214.50
Oval Firemark, cast iron "U.F" w/ pumper, 11½" L $104.50
Fire Box Doors, two cast iron w/ sunburst & fan detail, crack, 9¾" x 12½" & 9½" x 12½" $132.00
Wafer Iron, cast iron w/ dec., 5" x 7¼" w/ 12¼" handles $176.00

A-OH Nov. 1996   Garth's Auctions

Sawtooth Trammel, wrt. iron w/ simple tooling, pitted, 39" L ..$330.00
Chestnut Roaster, wrt. iron, hinged lid, locking device on handle, 32" L ..$357.50
Utensil Rack, wrt. iron w/ scrolled crest, 14" L $187.00
Utensils, four, wrt. iron, three skimmers & heart shaped utensil w/ handle $148.50
Toaster & Pan, wrt. iron toaster w/ wooden handle, 24" L, & cast iron tombstone shaped baking pan, "Lorfield 1", 6½" x 12" $159.50
Roasting Rack, wrt. iron w/ drip pan, 12⅜" L $302.50
Cast Steel Panel, scene of donkey cart & man, etc., inscribed "An Example of US Steel..." 25" W, 13" H $385.00
Two Pieces, wrt. iron kettle stand w/ three legs, pitted, 9" H, & cast iron tea kettle, mkd. "Eng., First Quality", holes, mismatched lid & handle reattached, 13" H $115.50
Posney Kettles, two, cast iron, w/ handles, 6" & 6½" diam. $115.50

A-MA Mar. 1997   Skinner

Left to Right

Brass Belted Andirons, pr., ball top, attrib. to R. Wittingham, NY, early 19th C., matching tongs & shovel, 20¼" H $1,610.00
Brass Belted Andirons, pr., double lemon top, prob. NY, early 19th C., beaded edge, 17½" H $747.50
Brass Belted Andirons, pr., urn-top, Am., early 19th C., 19" H $373.75
Brass Belted Andirons, pr., urn-top, prob. NY, ca. 1800, repl. log stops, 20¼" H $373.75

A-OH Nov. 1996   Garth's Auctions

Candle Holders, three wrt. iron sticking tommy, 12" L $357.50
Food Mold, copper oval melon rib, w/ wrt. iron handle, 17" L $220.00
Wrt. Iron Pcs., two, knife w/ brass trim, sm. nick, 13" L, & skewer stamped "E.R. Becker", 9½" L $143.00
Ash Shovel, wrt. iron, handle stamped "G. McRoberts", 18" $330.00
Drying Rack, wrt. iron, for clay pipes, penny feet, 12" L $357.50
Roasting Rack, adjustable wrt. iron, hanging hook, 25" H $522.50
Candle Lantern, tin w/ worn mustard gray repaint, mica insert in one window, 18" H $440.00
Roasting Rack, wrt. iron w/ spit, twisted detail, 13" L, w/ tin & iron coffee roaster, 22" L $357.50
Roasting Fork, wrt. iron, penny feet, 24" L $412.50

A-OH Nov. 1996   Garth's Auctions

Pewter Porringer, cast crown handle, mkd. "I.G.", pitting & pinpoint hole, 4¾" diam. $137.50
Pewter Porringer, w/ cast handle, mkd. "TD & SB", 3⅞" diam. ..$220.00
Pewter Porringer, w/ cast Boardman type handle, 3¼" diam. $27.50
Pewter Porringer, cast crown handle, mkd. "I.G.", battered & old repr., 4⅜" diam. $82.50
Flintlock Pistol, w/ curly maple stock, rod missing, 5" barrel, 9½" L $1,100.00
Barometer, "The Hughes - Owens Co. LTD, Montreal", w/ leather case, 3½" diam. $165.00
Portrait, mini on ivory, blk. lacquer frame w/ gilded cast brass trim, mkd. "Portrait of Captain Church...", frame 5⅞" W, 6⅜" H $1,320.00
Boxes, three, match box w/ cigar cutter, tin & nickel plated brass w/ bust of Admiral Dewey, 2⅝" L; pewter snuff box w/ cast design, battering, 3" L, white metal snuff box from Harrison campaign, splits in edge, 3¼" L ..$302.50

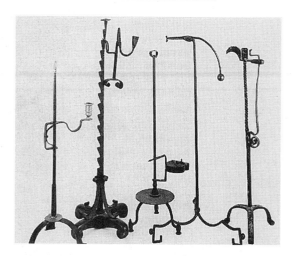

A-PA Jan. 1997   Pook & Pook Inc.

Left to Right

Candleholder, wrt. iron & brass table-top adjustable, 18th C., w/ brass finial, socket & plate, 25¼″ H $32,500
Candleholder, standing wrt. iron rush light, 18th C., w/ sawtooth shaft & wooden stretcher base, 30″ H . . .$950.00
Fat Lamp, table-top adjustable, 18th C., w/ turned shaft, circular pan & tripod base, 25¾″ H $850.00
Rush Light, table-top wrt. iron, 18th C., w/ ball handle, turned shaft & ornately scalloped tripod base, 28″ H $750.00
Candleholder, table-top wrt. iron rush light, early 18th C., w/ bird's head finial, twisted shaft & tripod base, 26″ H $800.00

A-PA Jan. 1997   Pook & Pook Inc.

Row 1, Left to Right

Candlestick, Eng. brass, 15th C., w/ circular top, knopped shaft & low circular base $2,000.00
Candlesticks, pr. Dutch copper, early 19th C., w/ octagonal mid drip, spiral shaft & domed octagonal repousse leaf & fruit dec. base, drilled, 10″ H $225.00
Candlestick, brass animalier socket, 19th C., in form of deer, 4½″ H $350.00

Row 2, Left to Right

Candlestick, pink brass low bell form, ca. 1600, together w/ rare pr. of low bell brass taper sticks, 17th C., 4″ H $2,750.00
Candle Snuffer, Eng. wrt. iron & wood, early 18th C., w/ engr., spring loaded mech., carved wooden handle, 8¼″ L . . .$3,000.00
Candle Snuffer, brass & iron, 17th C., w/ extensive repousse dec., together w/ dec. iron snuffer, 17th C., 8″ L $2,300.00
Taper Sticks, pr. brass, early 18th C., w/ baluster turned shafts on triangular bases, 3¹∕3″ H 2,400.00
Candlestick, Dutch heemskerk brass, ca. 1650, 7¼″ H, together w/ brass mid drip candlestick, 16th C., 5½″ H $1,800.00

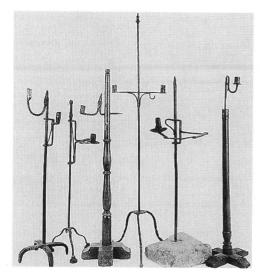

A-PA Jan. 1997   Pook & Pook Inc.

Left to Right

Candleholder, wrt. iron standing rush, late 17th/ early 18th C., 31½″ H $900.00
Candleholder, wrt. iron adjustable w/ accordian arm & penny feet, 18th C., 29½″ H $800.00
Standing Rush Light, wrt. iron, early 18th C., w/ wooden shoe foot base, 35″ H $950.00
Candleholder, standing adjustable double-arm, 18th C., w/ finialed top & tripod base w/ snake feet, 45½″ H $1,100.00
Candleholder, standing wrt. iron, 18th C., w/ adjustable folding arm socket & stone base, 33″ H $700.00
Candleholder, wrt. iron, standing rush light, early 18th C., w/ X-base, 32½″ H $950.00

A-MA June 1997   Skinner

Row 1, Left to Right

Pewter Fluid Lamps, pr., Am., 19th C., dents to burners, 9⅜″ H $431.25
Silver Plated Lamp, double magnifying, prob. Eng., 19th C., minor dents, surface wear, 10⅞″ H $201.25
Pewter Fluid Lamps, pr., Am., 19th C., dents to burners, 9⅜″ H $431.25

Row 2, Left to Right

Pewter Plates, one of two, Am., incl. PA, 1777-1818 & RI, 1817-56, 8⅜″ diam., & 8⅞″ diam. $172.50
Pewter Porringers, one of four, Hartford, CT, 1810-30, dents, minor cracks, minor pitting, 5″ diam. $977.50
Pewter Porringers, one of three, Am., incl. RI, 1817-56, Hartford, CT, 1810-30, Hartford, CT, 1805-20, repr., cracks, minor dents, 5-5⅜″ diam. $805.00
Pewter Plates, one of six, Middletown, CT, 1792-1820, pitting, 8¾″ diam. $1,035.00

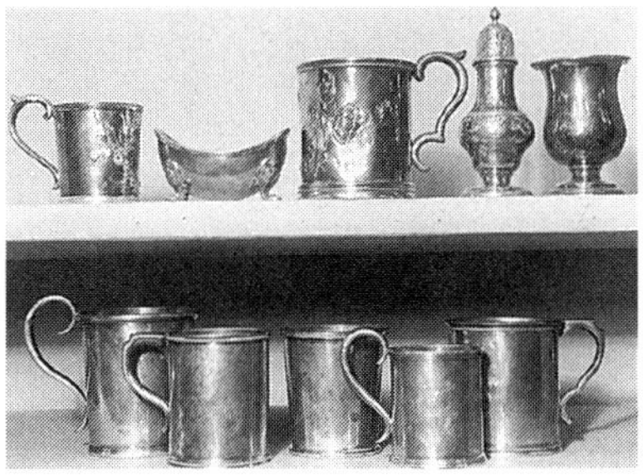

A-OH Jan. 1997 Garth's Auctions

Silver *Row 1, Left to Right*

Child's Cup, w/ chased flowers , engr. "Charlie" mkd. "Pure silver coin", 2⅝" H $247.50

Boat Shaped Salt, w/ hoof feet, indistinct hallmarks w/ "New York", feet a bit bent, 3⅜" L $165.00

Cup, w/ chased floral cartouche & engr. "Adele", battered & repr., 3½" H $82.50

Two Pcs., shaker w/ engr. floral designs, mkd. "W.G. & S.", dents & foot crooked, 4½" H, & urn shaped toothpick, dents 3⅛" H $71.50

Row 2, Left to Right

Julep Cup, engr. "... 1891", mkd. "Lincoln & Reed, Boston, Pure coin", dents, 3⅞" H $275.00

Child's Cup, engr. "To... Wm. John Louis, Montedonico", dented, 3" H $165.00

Julep, mkd. "Cook & Chatterton, Springfield, IL", 3" H $385.00

Child's Cup, engr. "... Feb. 28th '56 from L. Penkham", mkd. "Jones Ball & Co., ...",1850-52, dents, 3⅛"H $165.00

Cup, w/ repoussé floral medallion w/ engr. "... Dec. 25/'72", mkd. "Pure Coin", dents, 3⅛" H $220.00

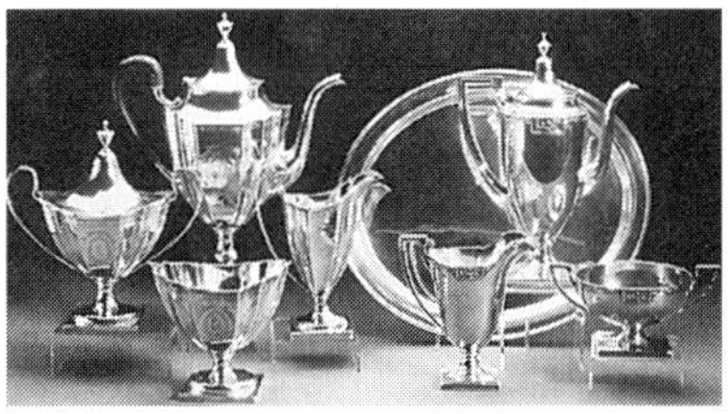

A-MA Sept. 1996 Skinner, Inc.

Left to Right

Coffee Set, Goodnow Sterling, ca. 1905, Fed. style, engr. monogram & date, coffee pot w/ wooden handle, creamer, covered sugar,waste bowl, pot 10⅝" H, approx. 46 troy. oz. $805.00

Coffee Set & Tray, Gorham Sterling Demitasse, urn & swag & Greek key details, coffee pot 9½" H, creamer, open sugar; Wilcox & Wagner oval tray 13$1/16$" L, approx. 46 troy oz. $1,035.00

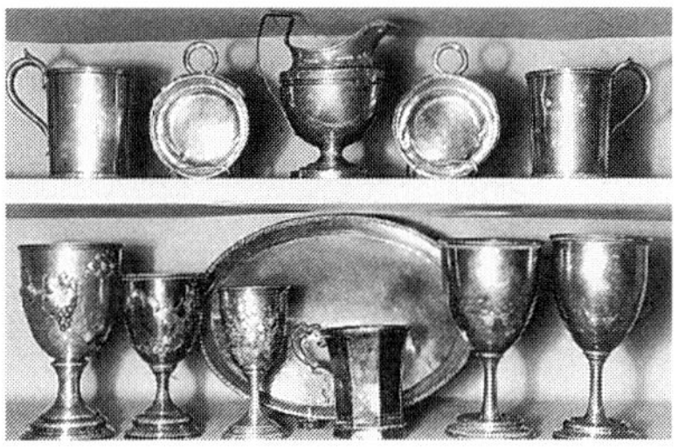

A-OH Jan. 1997 Garth's Auctions

Row 1, Left to Right

Silver Julep Cup, Greek Key border, engr. "Premium Cup M.C.A.S.", mkd. "J.W. King & Co. Coin", 4⅜"H .$302.50

Silver Wine Tasters, pr., Fr., serpent handles, Hallmarks & engr. "Japve Monie", 3⅜" diam. $907.50

Silver Creamer, urn shaped by Joseph Shoemaker, PA, 1798, old soldered repr., 5½" H $302.50

Silver Julep Cup, engr. "Frank Alexander Farnum, June 6th 1858", mkd. "Coin", dents, sm. breaks in silver, 41/8" H $220.00

Row 2, Left to Right

Silver Goblet, w/ chased vintage bowl, unmkd. 6¼" H $192.50

Silver Goblet, w/ chased floral bowl, unmkd. 5¼" H $192.50

Silver Goblet, w/ chased vintage bowl engr. "Fastest Pacing Horse, Decatur Ill, 1864", unmarked., 4⅞" $220.00

Silver Oval Tray, gadrooned edge, engr. "U.S." mkd. "Boudo", S.C., 1825, 10⅜" L $1,650.00

Silver Cup, by Gale & Hayden, NY, 1846, dents & base cracked, 3⅝" H $137.50

Silver Goblets, pr. by Peter L Kreder, PA, 1850, dents & size varies slightly, 6⅜" & 6⅝" H $330.00

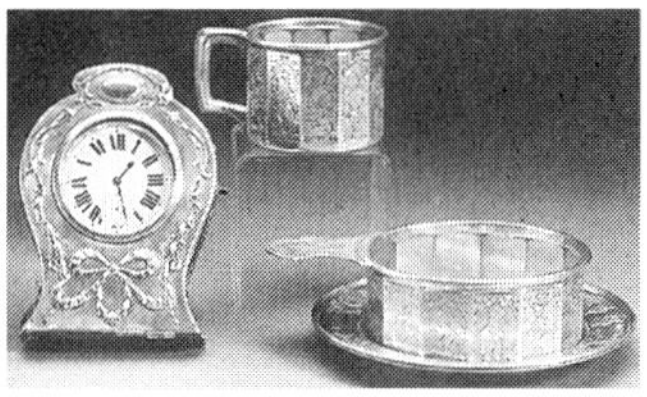

A-MA Sept. 1996 Skinner, Inc.

Left to Right

Watch Case

w/ watch, Eng. silver framed, 1910, S.&B. maker, leather case, eight-day timepiece in nickel case, silver frame 5$5/16$" H $316.25

Children's Tablewares, 3 pcs. sterling, 1920's Kerr breakfast set, cup 2$3/16$" H, bowl 4⅜" diam.; McChesney plate, acid-etched dec., monogram on cup, minor dents on porringer, 6⅜" diam. approx. 13 troy oz. $690.00

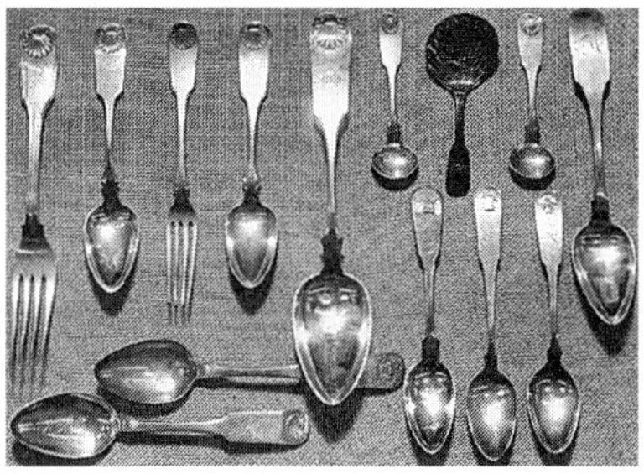

A-OH Jan. 1997 Garth's Auctions

Silver by R & W Wilson, PA 1825-46

Dinner Forks, six, w/ shell handles, engr. "B", one not mkd., 7¾" L $302.50

Silver Teaspoons, twelve, w/ shell handles, engr. "E.M", 6⅛" L . .$275.00

Three Pcs. Silver, luncheon fork, tsp. & tbls., w/ shell handles, various monograms $33.00

Silver Spoons & Caddy, salt spoons w/ shell handles 3⅞" L, & tea caddy w/ shell bowl, all mono. $192.50

Silver Spoons, four, w/ rattail on back of handles, mono., 7¼" L $49.50

Silver Spoons, two mkd. "J.J. Low & Co." w/ flowers on handle, 7¼" L, one w/ shell handle mkd. "E.B. & Co.", engr. "1822" w/ bowl engr. "1890", two mono., 6⅞" L $115.50

Silver Teaspoons, three w/ sheaf & sickle handle, Sibley & Marble, CT, 1801-1806, "L. Lockwood" & Erastus Barton & Co., NY, 1821, 5⅞" L to 6" L $121.00

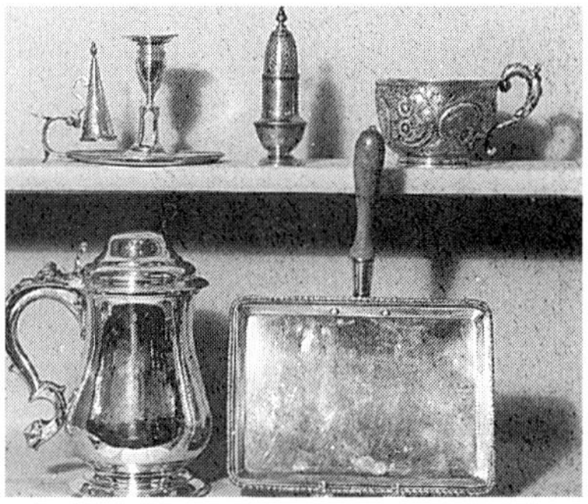

A-OH Nov. 1996 Garth's Auctions

Row 1, Left to Right

Chamber Stick, silver w/ snuffer, London hallmarks for 1786-87, Daniel Smith & Richard Sharp, sm. soldered split, 4" H $660.00

Sugar Shaker, silver, engr. "MW" & mkd. "T. Edwards", 5" H . . .$1,210.00

Coin Cup, silver w/ floral rococo repoussé, "Bailey & Co., Phila", 3⅜" H $110.00

Row 2, Left to Right

Covered Tankard, silver, London hallmarks for 1753-54, John Wirgman, engr. monogram, repr. to hinge, 8" H . .$990.00

Bacon Warming Tray, silver, London hallmarks for 1770-71, Septimus & Jones Crespell, missing lid, 5⅞" x 8⅜", 5¼" handle $302.50

A-MA Jan. 1997   Skinner

Fed. Looking Glass, gilt gesso, labeled Edward Lothrop, Boston, stenciled foliate & star border, minor imper., 13½" W, 30½" H   . . .$1,150.00

A-MA Jan. 1997   Skinner

Fed. Looking Glass, gilt gesso, MA, ca. 1815, eglomise tablet of flower filled urn framed in silver on a white ground, minor imper., 19¾" W, 44" H $1,840.00

A-MA Mar. 1997   Skinner

Fed. Looking Glass, gilt gesso, N.E., early 19th C., eglomise tablet showing battle "Lake Erie", applied foliate devices, 20" W, 35¾" H $920.00

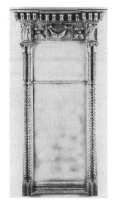

A-MA Jan. 1997   Skinner

Fed. Looking Glass, gilt gesso, NY, ca. 1815, carved drapery, foliate & figural devices, some regilding, 25¾" W, 47¾" H $1,092.50

A-OH Nov. 1996   Garth's Auctions

Q.A. Mirror, walnut veneer on pine w/ gilded liner, ref. & regilding worn & flaked, damage & repairs, old mirror glass, 24¼" W, 39¼" H $3,740.00

A-MA Apr. 1997   Skinner, Inc.

"Vernis Martin" Vitrine, Louis XVI style, giltwood, late 19th C., shaped glass to front & sides, enclosing shelves, raised on cabriole legs, 35" W, 14" D, 71½" H $2,760.00

A-MA Mar. 1997   Eldred's

Two-Part Mirror, Am. Sheraton, cherry w/ rev. painted tablet, 16" W, 34½" H $187.00

A-OH Jan. 1997   Garth's Auctions

Chippendale Mirror, mah. veneer w/ orig. dec. liner in blk. & gold, later brass candle arm at bottom, 48" H, 23½" W $1,430.00

A-OH Nov. 1996   Garth's Auctions

Chippendale Scroll Mirror, ref. mah. w/ gilded compo. eagle & gilded liner, repairs, damage, 14" W, 26¾" H $440.00

A-MA June 1997   Skinner

Fed. Looking Glass, mah. inlaid & parcel-gilt, NY, 1790-1810, inlaid w/ oval reserves, flanked by giltwood drapery, old refinish, regilding, restor. & losses, 24½" W, 62" H . . .$3,105.00

A-OH Nov. 1996   Garth's Auctions

Chippendale Mirror, ref. mah. on pine w/ regilded crest & liner, worn silvering, minor repairs, gilded phoenix flaked, 30½" H $1,430.00

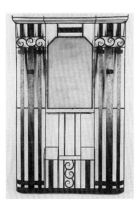

A-MA May 1997   Skinner

Art Deco Hall Rack, metal swirling & textured form surrounding a center mirror w/ glass shelf, 51¼" W, 7" D, 77" H $1,150.00

A-OH Nov. 1996   Garth's Auctions

Chippendale Mirror, mah. veneer on pine w/ old dk. finish, carved phoenix & liner w/ old worn regilding, damage & repr., 21½" W, 39½" H . . .$1,430.00

A-OH Nov. 1996   Garth's Auctions

Architectural Mirror, NY, gilded frame w/ eglomise rev. glass painting, orig. mirror, discolored, glass painting repl., regilding, flakes & repr., 23¾" W, 41¼" H . . .$770.00

A-MA Oct. 1996   Skinner, Inc.

Chippendale Looking Glass, mahogany, New. Eng., c. 1800, glass w/ scrolled frame & molded liner, old finish, 18" H, 11⅛" W $287.50
Q.A. Looking Glass, walnut, New. Eng., late 18th c., scrolled crest & molded frame mirror on a shaped bracket, orig. finish and mirror plate, 23¾" H, 10½" W $920.00
Chippendale Mirror, walnut, New. Eng., c. 1790, w/ orig. condition & surface, 18" H, 12" W $862.50

A-MA Oct. 1996   Skinner, Inc.

Looking Glass, Fed. mahogany inlaid & parcel gilt, prob. N.Y., c. 1790, three inlaid panels & rectangular gilt & string inlaid frame on scrolled bracket, old finish, some regilding, imp., 53" H, 23" W $2,070.00

A-MA Oct. 1996   Skinner, Inc.

Looking Glass, Fed. giltwood, labeled "Parker & Clover: Looking Glass/ and/ Picture Frame Makers/ 180 Fulton Street/ opposite Church Street/ New York," molded cornice w/ applied spheroids, w/ a concave mirror & twist pilasters, 29½" H, 13¾" W $1,840.00

A-MA Apr. 1997   Skinner, Inc.

Sterling Mirror Frame, J.R. maker, rectangular-form, high relief bird & floral design, beveled mirror, 15⅝" W, 19⅝" H $1,150.00

A-OH May 1997   Garth's Auctions

Woven Coverlet, overshot two pc., intricate design w/ sm. scale stars, navy blue, olive, gold & natural white, some wear & moth damage, worn fringe on one end, bare spots where wool is missing, 70" x 92" $220.00

Woven Coverlet, overshot two pc., optical patt. in navy blue & natural white, minor stains & fringe loss, 84" x 100" $247.50

Woven Coverlet, overshot two pc., optical patt. in navy blue & natural white, minor stains & wear w/ tied fringe on one end. 74" x 74" $137.50

Coverlet, double weave two pc., summer/winter snowball & pine tree patt. in navy blue, soft red & natural white, minor wear & repr., 64" x 78" $137.50

Jacquard Coverlet, two pc. single weave, intricate four rose & star medallion center w/ vintage borders & labeled "Made 1858", attrib. to Bucyrus, Crawford County, Ohio, royal blue, teal, red & natural white, wear, stains & fringe loss, top edge is frayed, 65" x 81" $385.00

A-OH Aug. 1996   Garth Auctions

Appliqué Quilt, nine stylized floral medallions, boldly executed date & initials, "1850, L.D." deep sage gr. calico, solid red & yel. & pink calico, well quilted, from Dayton, OH, some overall wear w/ soiling around edges & lt. stains w/ 3" yel. stain in one corner, 76" x 90" $1,265.00

A-OH Oct. 1996   Garth's Auctions

Jacquard Coverlet, two pc. single weave, mkd. "F.B", dk. & lt. olive, red & natural white, aged coloring, stain & wear w/ some missing fringe, 70" x 94" . . .$275.00

A-OH Jan. 1997   Garth's Auctions

Appliqué Quilt, solid yellow & red & brown calico, well quilted, wear, edge damage, stains & 3" L oval patch, 72" x 83" $357.50

A-OH Aug. 1996   Garth Auctions

Pieced Quilt, Irish chain in olive & red on a white ground, very good quilting, initial "CK" in one sq., some wear & lt. stains, 79" x 79" $605.00

Rope Bed, poplar w/ worn reddish br. graining resembling curly maple, orig. side rails, 52¾" W, rails are 71¾" L, 45" H $440.00

A-MA Mar. 1997   Skinner

Tree of Life Quilt, Brodene Perse, Am., 19th C., staining, 112" x 114" $4,600.00

A-OH Aug. 1996   Garth Auctions

Toy Block Obelisk, 6 wooden blocks w/ chromolitho paper covering, worn & blocks have edge damage, 26½" H $423.50

Wooden Figural Blocks, 33 very worn chromolitho paper covering, 5" H $330.00

"Steiff" Donkey Pull Toy, steel frame, worn mohair coat, button eyes, blk. mane & tail trim, & worn red felt blanket, one wheel replaced, "Steiff" ear button, 13½" H $302.50

"Steiff" Elephant Pull Toy, unmkd., steel frame, worn mohair coat, bead eyes & wooden wheels, ring pull voice box is silent, 16" L $275.00

Toy Wooden Barn, w/ chromolitho paper covering & paint, mkd. "R. Bliss", wear & minor damage, new bale of straw, 15" H $308.00

A-MA Sept. 1996   Skinner, Inc.

Studio Giraffe, Steiff mohair plush, mid 20th c., printed mohair, felt ears & mouth, glass eyes, ear & button tag, 98" H $1,035.00

A-OH Aug. 1996   Garth Auctions

Row 1, left to right:

Teddy Bear, articulated limbs, gold mohair w/ white felt trim, glass eyes & embroidered details, silk ribbon, wear & fading, 12½" $71.50

Teddy Bear, articulated limbs, gold mohair, glass eyes & embroidered detail, wear & fading, repairs, paw pads covered & straw stuffing exposed in places, 19" $247.50

Teddy Bear, articulated limbs, gold mohair, bead eyes & embroidered detail, worn, repairs & paw pads recovered, 12½" $49.50

Teddy Bear, articulated limbs, reddish mohair, replaced button eyes, embroidered detail & felt paw pads, worn, repairs, straw stuffing exposed in places & muzzle is limp, 18" . .$71.50

Row 2, left to right:

Teddy Bear, articulated front paws, gold mohair, glass eyes, replaced cloth paw pads & incomplete embroidered detail, wear & repr. w/ straw exposed in places, blue & white check scrap fabric ribbon, 22" $247.50

Teddy Bear, articulated limbs, gold mohair, glass eyes, recovered paw, wear 16" $302.50

Teddy Bear, articulated limbs, gold mohair, button eyes, recovered paw pads & embroidered details, wear & repr., ears have damage $126.50

Teddy Bear, articulated limbs, gold mohair, replaced button eyes & recovered paw pads, very worn w/ patches & holes, red & white candy stripe shirt covers damage, 23" $110.00

A-MA Sept. 1996   Skinner, Inc.

Wind-up Motorcycle, "Hoge Traffic Cycle-Car Delivery", ca. 1930, litho. tin, red w/ gr. delivery body, blue driver, rubber wheels, 10¼" L $3,220.00

A-MA Mar. 1997   Eldred's

Wooden Noah's Ark, handpainted ark w/ a sliding door, dec. w/ windows, siding & a dove on the roof w/ leaf, handpainted & carved figures, incl. six humans & eighty-four pairs of animals from giraffes & polar bears to beavers, anteaters, birds, & spiders, minor damage $7,070.00

A-MA Mar. 1997   Eldred's

Left to Right

Pull Toy Horse, Ger., wooden & compo., without wheels, orig. paint, 10" L, 11" H $77.00

Pull Toy Horses, two Ger., papier-mache, 5" L, & 5½" L $55.00

Logging Sled, wooden model,19th C., old blue & blk. paint, two sets of runners, 7" W, 20" L $132.00

Micmac Basket, painted blue, gr. & ora., 9½" L $88.00

Pull Toy Horses, two Ger., papier-mache, 5" L, & 5½" L $55.00

A-MA Feb. 1997   Skinner

Left to Right

Doll, wax over compo. head, Eng. or Ger., mid 19th C., pink tinted wax, painted mouth, br. glued human hair wig, cloth body, tan leather arms, cracks, 21½" H $230.00

Doll Carriage, early painted wood, mid 19th C., red w/ stenciled body dec., convertible sun shade, some fabric & paint damage, steel rimmed wheels, 36" L, 26¼" H . . . . .N/S

A-MA Feb. 1997   Skinner

Gliding Horse, painted dapple gray, late 19th/early 20th C., glass eyes, horse hair mane & tail, leather ears, red base w/ yel. & blk. striping, remnants of leather saddle, some paint loss, 38¾" L $460.00

A-MA Mar. 1997   Eldred's

Rocking Horse, child's carved wooden, 19th C., worn, 44" L, 35" H $550.00

A-MA Feb. 1997   Skinner

Left to Right

America's Yacht Race Game, McLoughlin Bros., early 20th C., soiled, tears & sm. losses, missing two yachts, 19¾" x 10½" $632.50

Boy Scouts Game, by Milton Bradley Company, ca. 1910, litho. paper, missing playing pcs., minor staining & edge wear, 22" x 10½" $287.50

Jack & the Beanstalk Game, McLoughlin Bros., 1898, good condition, edge wear & minor staining, 19¾" x 10½" $862.50

A-MA June 1997   Skinner

Rocking Horse, carved & painted, Am. 19th C., painted off white w/ leather saddle & reins, repairs, minor losses, old repaint, 27¼" H . . .$920.0

A-MA Jan. 1997   Skinner

Carousel Horse, carved & painted wood, NY Carousel Manuf. Co., late 19th C., orig. paint, old repr., minor imper., 56" L, 39" H $9,775.00

A-MA Feb. 1997   Skinner

Row 1

Steamshovel Truck, "Hercules" Mack, Chein, late 1920's, litho. tin, gr. cab w/ red & blue striping, red shovel w/ gr. roof, boom, & bucket, 27½" L $2,530.00

Row 2

Buddy "L" Dump Truck, ca. 1935, yel. cab, red dump body, electric headlights, 19½" L $287.50

Row 3

Artillery Truck, "Sonny" U.S.A., Dayton Toy & Specilty Co., late 1920's, pressed steel, olive drab, one orig. firestone tire, rust, cannon inoperative, 23½" L .$402.50

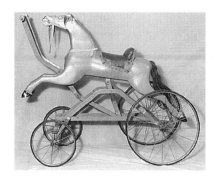

A-OH Aug. 1996   Garth Auctions

Velocipede Horse, steel frame w/ wire wheels & rocking wooden horse, old repaint w/ tan horse w/ glass eyes & blue-green frame, harness & saddle refurbished, some wear, 39" L $550.00

A-MA Jan. 1997   Skinner

Carousel Horse, carved & painted wood, NY, Carousel Manuf. Co, late 19th C., orig. paint, minor losses, paint wear, 60" L 39" H $8,625.00

A-MA Sept. 1996   Skinner, Inc.

Left to Right

Teddy Bear, two, one shown, yel. mohair, fully jointed, Am., excelsior stuffing, felt pads, 14" H; Eng. kapok stuffing, replaced velveteen pads, moth damage 17" H $977.50

Teddy Bear, early Steiff blonde mohair, ca. 1906, fully jointed, excelsior stuffing, spotty fur loss, 10" H $862.50

Teddy Bear, early blonde mohair, prob. Am., ca. 1905, fully jointed tan, beige felt pads, moth & fabric damage, 12" H $460.00

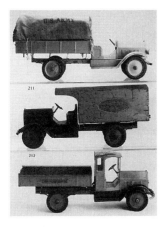

A-MA Sept. 1996   Skinner, Inc.

Row 1

Sturditoy Truck, #20 U.S. Army, ca. 1928, pressed steel, khaki w/ orig. canvas cover, flaking, missing steering wheel, 27" L $920.00

Row 2

Sturditoy Truck, Traveling Store, ca. 1926, pressed steel, blk. cab, ora. body, red frame & wheels, missing back doors, 26" L $747.50

Row 3

Sturditoy Truck, #1 Dump truck, ca. 1929, pressed steel, gr. body, blk. fender, red chassis & wheels, scratches, missing headlights, broken bumper, 27" L $747.50

A-OH Aug. 1996   Garth Auctions

Buckboard Wagon, child size, old worn red & blk. paint, wire wheels have worn & damaged hard rubber tread, bed is 39" L $660.00

A-OH Aug. 1996   Garth Auctions

Pedal Car, child size, sheet steel w/ orig. red & white paint w/ chrome plated trim, mkd. "Fire Ball", & "Murry", some wear & lt. rust, 40" L . .$275.00

A-MA Sept. 1996   Skinner, Inc.

Row 1

Keystone Truck, "Ride-em Dump Truck", ca. 1938, pressed steel, gr. cab, red body, 25" L $316.25

Row 2

Steelcraft Truck, "Hood's Ice Cream", 1930's, pressed steel, red w/ gold decal, 21¾" L $402.50

Row 3, Left to Right

Steelcraft Truck, "Wolf & Dressauer, Northern Indiana's Great Store", 1930's, pressed steel, maroon body, white lettering, batt. operated headlights, scratches to roof, 19" L $690.00

Smith Miller Truck, "Bank of America" Brinks, 1950's die-cast cab, pressed steel body, 14" L $230.00

A-MA Sept. 1996   Skinner, Inc.

Row 1

Buddy "L" Truck, #14 "Standard" Oil Tank, ca. 1934, pressed steel, red cab & tank body, blk. pull rod, scratches, 27" L $4025.00

Row 2

Kelmet "Big Boy" Truck, Aerial Ladder Fire, 1927, pressed steel, white rubber tires, two fire extinguishers, five wooden ladders, minor flaking, 29" L $1,955.00

A-MA Sept. 1996   Skinner, Inc.

Row 1

Buddy "L" Truck, #203A Lumber, ca. 1927, pressed steel, blk. w/ red chassis & wheels, missing two stake sections, 24" L $3,680.00

Row 2

Buddy "L" Red Baby, ca. 1920's pressed steel, cab removed, missing tailgate, 24" L $747.50

Row 3

Sturditoy Truck, #2 Am. Railway Express, ca. 1926, pressed steel, gr. four-panel screen side body, blk. cab, red chassis, missing back door, 26" L $690.00

A-MA Sept. 1996   Skinner, Inc.

Row 1, Left to Right

Britains Egyptian Cavalry, orig. Whisstock box, pre-War, five pcs., one hoof detached, edge wear & end flap torn $115.00

Britains Life Guards Winter-dress, orig. Whisstock box, pre-War, five pcs., one missing leg, edge wear $80.50

Row 2, Left to Right

Britains Royal Scots Grays, orig. box, pre-War, five pcs., missing three horse hooves, bent sword, box has lost side flaps, edge wear, tape repairs .$92.00

Britains 2nd Dragoon Guards, orig. Whisstock box, pre-War, five pcs., missing 2 horse legs, box has lost side flap, tape repairs $80.50

A-MA Sept. 1996   Skinner, Inc.

Left to Right

Four-Seat Brake, rare horsedrawn, Pratt & Letchworth, N.Y., ca. 1890, painted cast iron, 7 orig. figures, one mismatched, front hitch missing, driver wheels missing, detached coachlight, floorboard missing, 28" L . .$18,400.00

Mech. Fire Pumper, horsedrawn, Ives & Blakeslee Co., CT., ca. 1890, painted cast iron, two figures, orig. woodenbox, missing eagle finial, 18¾" L $7,475.00

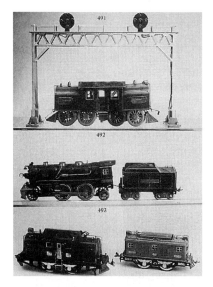

A-MA Sept. 1996   Skinner, Inc.

Lionel Trains

Row 1, Left to Right

Signal Bridge & Panel Board, red base w/ silver bridge, no walkway $258.75

Electric Gauge Locomotive, blk. w/ red window trim, missing two railings $258.75

Row 2

Steam Locomotive & Tender, standard gauge, blk., missing two railings $345.00

Row 3, Left to Right

Electric Locomotive, standard gauge, dk. gr., missing one headlight $201.25

Electric Locomotive, standard gauge, olive gr. $86.25

A-OH Aug. 1996   Garth Auctions

Row 1:

"Lionel" Train, "O Gauge" locomotive 2025 & tender w/ four cars, 2454, 2257, 2452x & 2465, w/ controls & box of track, wear & caboose is damaged $115.50

Row 2, left to right:

"Kenton" Toy, cast iron, "Overland Circus", unused in orig. box, 14¼" L $275.00

"Kenton" Toy, cast iron, "Hansom Cab", unused in orig. box, 15½" L $550.00

"Kenton" Toy, cast iron covered wagon, unused in orig. box, cloth cover in sealed envelope, 15" L $385.00

Row 3, left to right:

Mechanical Bank, cast iron, lion & monkeys, Norman, polychrome paint, trap missing, monkey may be replm., 9½" H $577.50

Mechanical Bank, cast iron, "Darktown Batt.", Norman 2080a, polychrome paint, 9¾" L $1,705.00

Mechanical Bank, cast iron, "Always did 'Spise a Mule", Norman 2940a, mule's tail is missing & back legs are brazed, trap replaced, polychrome paint, 10⅛" L $192.500

A-MA Sept. 1996   Skinner, Inc.

Lionel Passenger set, standard gauge, in mojave, includes electric locomotive, parlor car, dining car, baggage car, observation car, missing 1 panograph, minor wear & scratches $1,955.00

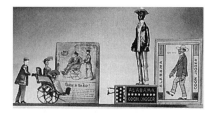

A-MA Sept. 1996   Skinner, Inc.

Row 1, Left to Right

Lehmann "Going to the Fair", E.P.L., Ger. ca. 1889, litho. tin, flywheel mechanism, red fan version, orig. box, some loss to box label, 6¼" L $3,105.00

Lehmann "Oh My Alabama Coon Jigger", E.P.L., Germ. ca. 1910, litho. tin wind-up orig. box & instruction sheet, 10" H $977.50

Row 2, Left to Right

Lehmann "The Balky Mule", E.P.L., Germ., early 20th c., litho. tin, wind-up orig. box, box lid missing three ends, 7" L $488.75

Lehmann "Quack-Quack", E.P.L., Germ., early 20th c., litho. tin, wind-up, orig. box, minor surface rust, box end flap missing, wear, 7¼" L $632.50

Row 3, Left to Right

Lehmann "Climbing Monkey", E.P.L., Germ., early 20th c., painted tin, flocked jacket, orig. box, box edge wear, 7¾" L $184.00

Lehmann "Motor Kutsche Car", E.P.L., Germ., early 20th c., litho. tin wind-up, orig. box, box worn, tears, edge wear, 5" L $747.50

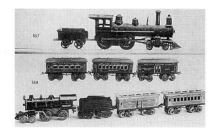

A-MA Sept. 1996   Skinner, Inc.

Row 1

Wilkins Floor Train, Locomotive & Tender, ca. 1890, cast iron, overall loss, top of sandbox & steam dome chipped, 18½" L $431.25

Row 2

Ives Passenger Cars, three, "O" gauge, baggage, chair car, parlor car, gr. w/ gray-green roofs, ...$115.00

Row 3

Ives "Limited Vestibule Express", "O" gauge, wind up locomotive & tender, w/ litho. tin red woodgrained baggage & "Yale" pullman $1,265.00

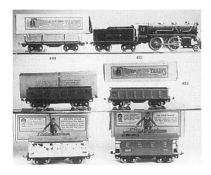

A-MA Sept. 1996 Skinner, Inc.

Lionel Trains

Row 1, Left to Right

Lumber Car, standard gauge, dk. gr., orig. box $115.00
Steam Locomotive & Tender, standard gauge, gr. stripe, build-a-loco motor, orig. box $373.75

Row 2, Left to Right

Gondola, standard gauge, wine, orig. box $115.00
Gondola, standard gauge, peacock, orig. box $115.00

Row 3, Left to Right

Refrigerator Car, orig. box, flaking .N/S
Caboose, standard gauge, gr. w/ red roof, orig. box . . . . .N/S

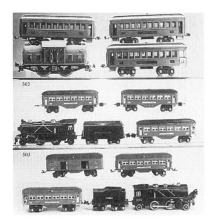

A-MA Sept. 1996 Skinner, Inc.

Lionel Trains

Row 1

Passenger set, standard gauge, including electric locomotive two pullmans, observation in mojave . . .$345.00

Row 2

Passenger set, "O" gauge, including steam locomotive, tender in gun metal gray w/ two pullman cars & observation, red w/ gray roofs & ivory window trim . . . . .N/S

Row 3

Passenger set, "O" gauge, including steam locomotive & tender, pullman, baggage, observation in gray w/ red roofs & ivory window trim, missing five car railings, headlight door latch broken $230.00

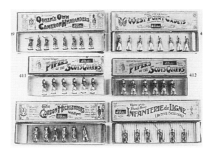

A-MA Sept. 1996 Skinner, Inc.

Row 1, Left to Right

Britains Queen's Own Cameron Highlanders, no pack, pre-War, orig. Whisstock boxes, eight pcs., box has tape repairs & edge wear $143.75
Britains West Point Cadets, orig. Whisstock box, pre-War, eight pcs., box has edge wear & heavy w/ burdens of play $115.00

Row 2, Left to Right

Britains Pipers of the Scots Guards, orig. Whisstock box, pre-War, six pcs., box has torn sides, edge wear . . . . .N/S
Britains Pipers of the Scots Guards, orig. Whisstock box, pre-War, 6-pieces, edge wear $241.50

Row 3, Left to Right

Britains, two pre-War both w/ orig. Whisstock boxes, Gordon Highlanders w/ piper, six pcs., box w/ edge wear & tape repr. & Gordon Highlanders, firing, five pcs., box has tape repairs & edge wear $126.50
Britains Fr. Infantry, pre-War orig. Whisstock box, six pcs. $115.00

A-MA Sept. 1996 Skinner, Inc.

"Home Baseball Game", McLoughlin Bros., 1897, teetotum, 14 wooden disk tokens, half of cover side missing, silverfish damage, 2 tokens missing, 19⅝" H, 10⅜" W, 1" D $2,070.00

A-MA Feb. 1997 Skinner

Row 1, Left to Right

Arcade Sand & Gravel Wagon, double horse-drawn, ca. 1920, repainted hitch & wheels, one horse guide wheel missing, 15" L $115.00
Arcade Contractor's Dump Wagon, horse-drawn, 1920's, painted cast iron, blk. body, yel. wheels, white horses, 14" L $172.50

Row 2, Left to Right

Kenton Army Motor Truck, ca. 1919, cast iron, missing driver, poor condition, 9" L $287.50
Hubley Huber Road Roller, ca. 1930, painted cast iron, gr. w/ driver, some surface rust. 7½" L $345.00
Kenton Jaeger Cement Mixer, ca. 1930, painted cast iron, ora., lt. blue, & nickel plated, 6⅝" L $373.75

A-MA Sept. 1996 Skinner, Inc.

Knickerbocker Krazy Cat, cloth, ca. 1930, blk. velveteen w/ blk. felt ears, white face & hands & yel. felt boots, 10½" H $1,265.00

A-MA Feb. 1997 Skinner

Taxi Limousine, Bing, Ger., ca. 1910, handpainted tin, clockwork, beveled glass windows, nickel-plated carriage lights, rubber wheels, incl. wooden box, minor flaking, missing windshield, driver & rear luggage rack, damage to roof rack, 14¼" L $21,850.00

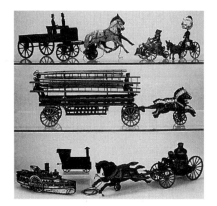

A-MA Feb. 1997   Skinner

Row 1, Left to Right

Carpenter Wagon, double horse-drawn, Harrison, NY, pat. 1881, painted cast iron, animated horses, red wagon w/ blk. striping, removable seat & two flat figures, minor rust, paint loss, 19″ L $2,530.00
Clown on Pig Bell Toy, early 20th C., painted cast iron, 6⅜″ L $862.50
Kenton Foxy Grandpa Nodder, ca. 1910, painted cast iron, 6¼″ L . . .$345.00

Row 2

Ladder Wagon, cast iron, three-horse, early 20th C., red wagon w/ gold striping, blue ladder racks, yel. wheels, wooden ladders, 24½″ L $977.50

Row 3, Left to Right

Wilkins Puritan Side-wheeler, ca. 1900, painted cast iron, some flaking, 11″ L $431.25
"Venus" Steam Locomotive, Fallows, ca. 1880's, painted tin, 6″ L $316.25
Fire Pump, double horse-drawn, Ives & Blakeslee Co., ca. 1890, painted cast iron, one blk. horse, one nickel-plated horse, missing driver, 20″ L . .$920.00

A-MA Feb. 1997   Skinner

Bungalow Dollhouse, yel., 1920's, red gambrel roof, front porch opens, three rooms, assort. wood furniture, some lot damage, 19¼″ W, 10½″ D, 18¾″ H $1,150.00

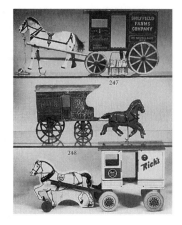

A-MA Feb. 1997   Skinner

Row 1

Dairy Wagon, Sheffield Farms Co. horse-drawn, Rich Toy, ca. 1930, painted wood, w/ six glass milk bottles & tin carrier, 20½″ L $632.50

Row 2

Milk Wagon, double horse-drawn, Converse, lithographed tin, 17″ L $230.00

Row 3

"Rich's" Milk Wagon, Rich Toy, 1930's, litho. tin & wood, 20″ L $287.50

A-MA Feb. 1997   Skinner

Assembled Dollhouse, maple, bedroom setting, most furniture by Gebruder Schneegas, Waltershausen, 1890's, 1-inch scale, some parts missing on furniture, setting contained in an S.S. Pierce wooden case . .$632.50

A-MA Feb. 1997   Skinner

Ger. Carriage House & Carriage, late 19th C., painted wood & lithographed paper, missing loft doors & two gates, 35½″ W, 16½″ D, 25″ H $1,725.00

A-MA Feb. 1997   Skinner

Gottschalk Dollhouse, blue roofed lithographed paper on wood, Saxony, 1870's, elaborate Ger. or Austrian style, two rooms down & up, separate front steps, orig. int. papers, some damage, 26½″ W, 18⁵⁄16″ D, 31″ H $9,200.00

A-MA Feb. 1997   Skinner

Row 1, Left to Right

Schoenhut Elephant, boxed, 1929, standard size, painted eyes, leather ears & tusks, hemp tail, paint wear, damage, 10⅜″ L, lithographed carton, edge wear, 6⅛″ W, 2⅞″ D, 8⅞″ H $632.50
Schoenhut Alligator, painted eyes, leather feet, damage, wear, needs restringing, 12″ L $230.00
Schoenhut Giraffe, painted eyes, leather ears, cotton tail, paint wear, needs restringing, 11⅝″ H . . .$316.25

Row 2, Left to Right

Schoenhut Tiger, painted eyes, cloth tail, paint wear, needs restringing $230.00
Schoenhut Circus Performers, molded & painted heads, bareback rider & ringmaster, cotton & wool clothes, wear & damage, 8″ H & 8½″ H $287.50
Schoenhut Poodle, white, painted eyes, cotton tail, paint wear, needs restringing, 7¾″ L . . . . .N/S

A-MA Feb. 1997   Skinner

Left to Right

Ideal Teddy Bear, lt. yel. mohair, ca. 1905, blk. shoe button eyes, blk. knit fabric nose, embroidered mouth & claws, fully jointed, felt pads, slight pad damage & fur loss, 25" H $13,800.00
Ideal Teddy Bear, lt. yel. mohair, ca. 1905, blk. shoe button eyes, br. knit fabric nose, embroidered mouth & claws, fully jointed, felt pads, some pad damage & fur loss, left ear loose, fur grayed, 25" H $10,925.00

A-MA Feb. 1997   Skinner

Left to Right

Steiff Cinnamon Bear, ca. 1906, ear button, blk. steel eyes, fully jointed, embroidered nose, mouth & claws, felt pads, slight fur loss on muzzle, needs more stuffing, 9" H $2,990.00
Steiff Teddy Bear, lt. yel., ca. 1906, blk. eyes, fully jointed, embroidered nose, mouth & claws, excelsior stuffing, felt pads, button missing, fur & fiber damage, needs stuffing, 12" H $1,725.00
Mini. Windsor Armchair, cream painted chair, 15" H . . . . .N/S
Teddy Bear, yel. mohair, shoe button eyes, embroidered nose, mouth & claws, fully jointed, excelsior stuffing, repl. felt pads, spotty fur loss, top head repr., right ear missing, 14½" H $373.75

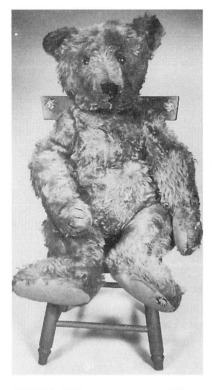

A-MA Feb. 1997   Skinner

Steiff Teddy Bear, golden mohair, ca. 1905, ear button, fully jointed, blk. steel eyes, embroidered nose, mouth & claws, excelsior stuffing, felt pads, moth damage on fur & pads, needs stuffing, 22" H $10,062.50

A-MA Feb. 1997   Skinner

Row 1, Left to Right

Tractor & Access., tin wind-up, ca. 1930, incl. street sweeper, roadroller & dumping trailer, tractor 8" L .$287.50
Strauss Zeppelin, 1930's, tin wind-up, 9½" L $201.25

Row 2, Left to Right

Steamroller, tin wind-up, ca. 1930, 11½" L $230.00
Kingsbury Stake Truck, motor driven, Keene, N.H., ca. 1925, pressed steel, gr., red wheels, repl. rubber tires, 10¾" L $345.00

Row 3, Left to Right

A.C. Gilbert Truck, ca. 1915, tin wind-up w/ driver, 10½" L . .$316.25
Circus Cage Wagon, ca. 1930, possibly Strauss, litho. tin wind-up, articulated walking elephant, hinged opening cages, possibly incomplete $172.50

A-MA Feb. 1997   Skinner

Teddy Bears, three blonde mohair, ca. 1910, poss. Am., blk. steel eyes, embroidered nose & mouth, fully jointed excelsior stuffing, fur loss, repl. pads, 10½" H, 10½" H, & 12½" H $431.25
Teddy Bear, blonde mohair, ca. 1910, blk. eyes, fully jointed, felt pads & straw stuffing, 12" H . . . . .N/S
Teddy Bear, blonde mohair, ca. 1910, blk. shoe button eyes, fully jointed excelsior stuffing, embroidered nose & mouth, repl. pads, extensive fur loss, 12" H . . .$258.75
Teddy Bear, blonde mohair, ca. 1910, blk. steel eyes, embroidered nose, mouth & claws, fully jointed, felt pads, fur loss, damage, 17" H $517.50
Teddy Bears, two, blonde mohair, possibly Am., fully jointed, one has shoe button eyes, embroidered nose, felt pads, spotty fur & pad damage, 15½" H, the other has glass eyes, embroidered nose & mouth, arms & legs are two-piece const., w/o pads, traces of fur, 14" H $345.00
Steiff Teddy Bear, blond mohair, 1950's, glass eyes, fully jointed, excelsior stuffing, embroidered nose, mouth & claws, button missing, fur loss & matting, 13" H $287.50

A-MA Feb. 1997   Skinner

Row 1, Left to Right

Mortimer Snerd's, Hometown Band by Marx, ca. 1930's, litho. tin wind-up, 8¾" L $977.50
Walker "Funny Face", by Marx, ca. 1930's, litho. tin wind-up, orig. box, minor scratches, edge wear on box, 10⅞" H $1,150.00
Lehmann "Oh-My Alabama...", early 20th C., litho. tin wind-up, good condition, wear to top of base, 10" H $402.50

Row 2, Left to Right

Whoopie Car, Marx, 1930's, litho. tin wind-up, orig. box, edge wear, 7" L $747.50
Lehmann Bulky Mule, early 20th C., litho. tin wind-up, 7¼" L $230.00
"Rodeo Joe" Crazy Car, ca. 1930's, litho. tin wind-up, 7" L $201.25

Row 3, Left to Right

Honeymoon Express, Marx, 1920's litho. tin wind-up, 9½" diam. .$172.50
Cowboy Rider, Marx, ca. 1930's, litho. tin wind-up cowboy on horse w/ lasso, orig. box, 7" H $431.25
Wolverine Mystery Car, ca. 1930's, litho. tin, press down on rear to activate mech., red w/ blk. striping, 12¾" L $132.25

A-MA Feb. 1997   Skinner

Walt Disney 1942 Calendar, Morrell's, chromolithograph paper, each of the twelve months shrinkwrapped individually, minor soiling & creased edges,   17¾"   x 8¼" $1,150.00

A-MA Feb. 1997   Skinner

Row 1

U.S. Mail Truck, Keystone Packed, ca. 1926, pressed steel, blk. cab, khaki body, red wheels, rubber tires, overall scratches, 26" L $862.50

Row 2

Dump Truck, Buddy "L" Hydraulic, ca. 1930, pressed steel, dual rear wheels, rubber tires, headlight & bumper, some overpaint, poor condition, 24½" L . . . $1,092.50

Row 1

Dump Truck, Keystone, ca. 1927, pressed steel, blk. w/ red chassis & wheels, overall wear, 26½" L .$345.00

A-MA Feb. 1997   Skinner

Austin J40 Pedal Car, Eng., 1950's, pressed steel, lt. blue, opening hood & trunk, electric headlights & horn, nickel-plated   grille,   bumpers   & hood ornament, surface rust, 61" L $1,610.00

A-MA Feb. 1997   Skinner

Rickenbacker Car, Fire Chief pedal car., Am. National, Toledo, OH, late 1920's, pressed steel w/ wood chassis, red w/ yel. striping, missing front bell, surface rust, poor condition, 42" L $1,840.0

A-MA Feb. 1997   Skinner

Row 1, Left to Right

Schoenhut "Felix" the Cat, 1924, leather ears, decal, trademark, paint wear,   needs   restringing,   8⅛" H $373.75
Schoenhut Circus Animals, painted eyes, hoppo, shown, leather ears & tail, paint good, tooth missing, 10" L, not shown br. horse w/ leather ears, tack & saddle, cotton tail, some leather damage, both need restringing, 9¾" L $345.00
Schoenhut Circus Equip., wire circular cage, 8⅞" H, chair, ball, hoop, barrel, two stools, table, & ladder, some damage $431.25

Row 2

Schoenhut Animals, five & two pcs. of circus furniture, elephant, goat, donkey, br. horse, dapple gray horse, barrel & tub, some damage, 7¼" - 9½" L . .$805.00

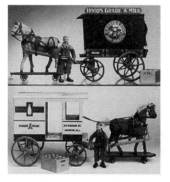

A-MA Feb. 1997   Skinner

Row 1

Schoenhut Dairy Wagon, "H.P. Hood & Sons", early 20th C., painted wood wagon, white cloth covered horse, missing tail, orig. driver, damaged head, wooden crate & seven milk bottles, 25" L $3,105.00

Row 2

Schoenhut Wagon, "Alderney Dairy Co.", ca. 1930, painted wood wagon, br. cloth covered horse, orig. driver, wooden crate & 12 milk bottles, orig. box, 25" L . . . . .N/S

A-PA Mar. 1997   Bill Bertoi Auctions

Left to Right

Donald Duck, Linemar, litho. tin trycycle, w/ rear bell & celluloid Donald Duck, clockwork activates movement & bell ringing, orig. box, 4" L $385.00
Pluto Toy, Marx, copy, 1939, litho. tin, clockwork activates tail which allows Pluto to roll over, orig. box, 9" L .$440.00
Minnie Mouse Knitter, Linemar, Japan, copy litho. tin, clockwork, orig. box, 6½" H $880.00
Ferdinand the Bull, Louis Marx, ca. 1938, litho. tin, w/ cloth flower in mouth & attached bee, clockwork, orig. box, 6" L $578.00

A-PA Mar. 1997   Bill Bertoi Auctions

Row 1, Left to Right

Milk Wagon, Kenton, cast iron, red wheels, blk. horse trimmed in gold & silver, orig. box, 12½" L $495.00
Surrey, Kenton, cast iron, blue overall w/ red canopy, yel. wheels, white horses, orig. box, mkd. Hansom Cab, 12½" L $550.00

Row 2, Left to Right

Bear Cage Wagon, Kenton, cast iron, red overall, white bear, yel. wheels, white horses trimmed in gold, orig. box, 14" L . . .$688.00
Band Wagon, Kenton, cast iron, red overall w/ gold tirm, white horses, yel. wheels, orig. box, 15" L $908.00

A-PA Mar. 1997   Bill Bertoi Auctions

Row 1

Bomber Plane, Fr., litho. tin, hues of br. needs tail fin tab, repainted tail fin, wingspan 20½" 1,155.00

Row 2, Left to Right

Air France Airliner, Arnold, Ger., litho. tin, blue, white & gray, wingspan 19½" $605.00
Air France Airliner, Fr., litho. tin, blue, friction powered, wingspan 20" $990.00

A-PA Mar. 1997   Bill Bertoi Auctions

Row 1, Left to Right

"Lindy" Airplane, Hubley, cast iron, painted gray, emb. wings, nickeled prop, wingspan 10" $1,980.00
"America" Airplane, Hubley, cast iron, nickeled props, two pilots, emb. lettering & stars, wingspan 17" $5,170.00
"Lindy" Airplane, Hubley, cast iron, painted gray overall, nickeled prop, emb. lettering, wingspan 10" $935.00

Row 2, Left to Right

Airplane, Kilgore, cast iron, painted red overall w/ emb. lettering, nickeled wheels & prop, wingspan 7" $1,155.00
"Lindy" Airplane, Hubley, cast iron, painted blue overall, emb. lettering, rubber tires, nickeled prop, wingspan 3½" $743.00
"Spirit of St. Louis" Airplanes, two, A.C. Williams, cast iron incl. prop, painted silver overall, emb. wings w/ lettering, nickeled disk wheels, wingspans 4⅛" & 5⅞" . .$468.00

A-PA Mar. 1997   Bill Bertoi Auctions

Left to Right

Porky Pig, Louis Marx, ca. 1939, litho. tin, 8½" H .$825.00
Cowboy Porky Pig, Louis Marx, litho. tin, includes orig. box, 8½" H $743.00
Porky Pig, Louis Marx, ca. 1939, litho. tin, clockwork, 8½" H $385.00
Donald Duck Toy, Linemar, copy, celluloid figure on metal stand performing acrobatics, clockwork, orig. box, 4¼" W, 6½" H $440.00

A-PA Mar. 1997   Bill Bertoi Auctions

Schoenhut Toys

Mary's Lamb, jointed wood const., white, 7¾" L . . .$330.00
Brown Bear, jointed wood const., hues of br., on hind legs 7½" $248.00
Poodle, jointed wood const., white, 7½" L $440.00
Burro, jointed wood const., gray w/ blk. stripe, 7" L $358.00
Pig, jointed wood const., br. w/ blk., 8" L $248.00
Alligator, jointed wood const., gr. w/ red mouth & white teeth, 13" L $385.00

A-PA Mar. 1997   Bill Bertoi Auctions

Schoenhut Toys

Row 1

Zebu, leather horns & ears 8" L $990.00
Monkey, orig. sales tag, 7¼" H $523.00
Bunny, br., 5¼" L $523.00
Bulldog, br. w/ white, 6" L $550.0
Cat, gray w/ blk. & white, repainted, 4¼" H $303.00

Pig, lt. br., 8" L $165.00

Row 2

Mary's Lamb, white w/ ribbon collar, 8" L $275.00
Brown Bear, hues of br., 7½" H $204.00
Reindeer, br. w/ white, 7" L $220.00
Cow, br., metal bell, 8½" L $275.00
Kangaroo, hues of br. w/ white, w/ extended tail 10½"
L $990.00
Goose, white overall w/ ora. beak & feet, 7" L . . .$275.00

Row 3

Hippo, dk. br., 10" L $209.00
Tiger, ora., striped in br. & white, 8" L $495.00
Camel, hues of br. & blk. hoofs, 7½" L $264.00
Giraffe, realistic natural colors, 11" T $660.00
Camel, hues of br., w/ blk. hoofs, 7" L $275.00
Polar Bear, white overall, repainted, 8" L $358.00

Row 4

Alligator, gr. w/ red mouth & white teeth, 13" L . .$220.00
Leopard, yel. overall w/ br. spots, 7¼" L $413.00
Zebra, lt. br. overall w/ dk. stripes, 7¾" L $248.00
Lion, lt. to medium br., 8" L $385.00
Buffalo, jointed wood const., dk. br., 8" L $193.00
Seal, leather flipper hands, dk. br., 9" L $908.00

Row 5

Horse, br. w/ blk. mane, leather saddle, 9½" L . . .$242.00
Ostrich, jointed wood const., blk. w/ grey & blk., 9½"
T $220.00
Cat, grey w/ blk. stripes & white, 4¼" H $358.00
Bulldog, br. overall w/ white, leather studded collar, 6"
L $550.00
Poodle, white, classic poodle cut design, 7" L $330.00
Felix Toys, two, Sullivan, 1922, blk. w/ W eyes & white face,
4" - 8½" H $660.00

Row 6

Bactrian & Elephant, reduced sizes, Bactrian br. & elephant w/ leather ears $275.00
Burro, grey & blk., 7½" L $220.00
Donkey, olive br. & striped blk., 9½" L $132.00
Pig, lt. br. & blk., 8" L $275.00
Goat, blk. & white overall, 8" L $165.00

A-PA Mar. 1997   Bill Bertoi Auctions

Left to Right

Harley Davidson Motorcycle, Hubley, ca. 1930, cast iron, painted ora. overall, decal on tank, driver dismounts, rubber tires $3,520.00
Popeye Cycle, Hubley, ca. 1938, cast iron, painted red overall, emb. "spinach", rubber tires, 6" L $935.00
Police Motorcycle, w/ sidecar, Hubley, cast iron, red overall, fine casting detail, clockwork, rubber tires, 8½" L $8,250.00

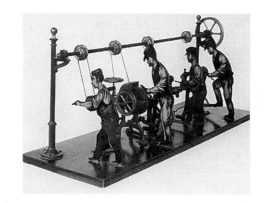

A-IA Mar. 1997   Jacksons

Animated Toy, Ger. tin litho., wood working machines & operators, 13" $2,090.00

A-MA Sept. 1996   Skinner, Inc.

Row 1, Left to Right

Snow White & the Seven Dwarfs, Emerson table top radio, ca. 1939, pressed wood front, two knobs, missing dial, repl. cloth grill, mech. reconditioned, 7¾" H, 7¼" W, 5¾" D $488.75

Pluto the Pup, Geo. Borgfeldt & Co., ca. 1930, wooden body, head & feet, twisted fiber legs & tail, felt ears, orig. box, water stained, 5¾" L $632.50

Walking Mickey Mouse, Japan, early 1930's celluloid wind-up, wire tail, orig. paper inspection label, reglued foot, crack under left arm, 7¼" H N/S

Mickey Mouse Hoop-La Game, Marks Bros., Boston, early 1930's, litho., three wooden rings, orig. box, edge wear, ...$258.75

Row 2, Left to Right

Lil' Abner & His Dog Patch Band, unique art litho. tin wind-up, missing drumstick, 9" L $345.00

Lil' Abner & His Dog Patch Band, unique art litho. tin wind-up, missing one drumstick, 9" L $402.50

A-PA Mar. 1997   Bill Bertoi Auctions

Left to Right

Bubble Blowing Popeye, Linemar Toys, Japan, litho. tin, batt. operated, blows bubbles, orig. box, 11¾" H $1,375.00

Popeye, Chein, litho. tin, clockwork, 6" H $605.00

Barnacle Bill, Chein, litho. tin, clockwork, 6" H $330.00

Popeye Boxer, Chein, litho. tin, celluloid punching bat, 7" H . .$1,118.00

Popeye w/ Parrot Cages, Louis Marx, litho. tin, clockwork, 8" H $303.00

A-PA Mar. 1997   Bill Bertoi Auctions

1928 Lincoln, Tourner Mfg., pressed steel, blue overall w/ blk., br. int., painted disc wheels, 26" L .$2,200.00

A-MA Feb. 1997   Skinner

Left to Right

"Kiddie-Kar-Kid", compo. boy, wooden vehicle, H.C. White Co., North Bennington, VT, pat. 1924, molded head w/ painted features, paint damage, straw-filled cloth body, cotton suit & hat, clothes faded, natural finish car w/ orig. label, red wheels, 9¼" L, 10" H $287.50

Red Riding Hood Set, boxed Freundlich compo., 1934, figures jointed at head, shoulder & hips, molded & painted heads, wolf head on human body, cotton outfits, grandmother damaged, 9" H, 9¼" H, & 9½" H $805.00

Arranbee Dionne Quints, set in a pink low chair, ca. 1936, bent limb compo. bodies, molded hair & features, pastel organdy outfits, repl. diapers & booties, some chipping on Annette face, 6½" H $1,035.00

A-MD Mar. 1997   Richard Opfer, Auc. Inc.

Left to Right

Simon & Halbig Doll, bisque head w/ ball joint body, mkd., old dress & rewigged, 21" H $400.00

Armand Marseille Doll, "Roosebud", bisque head, jointed kid body w/ bisque arms, old wig & clothes, one arm repr., 23" H $165.00

Doll, bisque head, ball joint body, mkd. Made in Germ., old clothes, rewigged, hairline, some body wear, 22" H $160.00

A-MD Mar. 1997   Richard Opfer, Auc. Inc.

Left to Right

Kestner Doll, bisque head w/ ball joint body, mkd. Ger., rewigged, old clothes, torso & neck socket worn, 23" H $575.00

Schoenau & Hoffmeister Doll, bisque w/ ball joint body, mkd. Ger., mouth chip, eyes stationary, rewigged, redressed, body work, 23" H .$225.00

Armand Marseille Doll, bisque head w/ ball joint body, nice body, old wig & clothes, eye flake, 21" H . . .$250.00

A-MD Mar. 1997   Richard Opfer, Auc. Inc.

Left to Right

Daisy Doll, bisque w/ ball joint body, mkd. Ger., dressed & rewigged, slight finger wear, 22" H $450.00

Schoenau & Hoffmeister Doll, bisque w/ ball joint body, mkd. Ger., nice old clothes, eyes stationary, rewigged, body wear, 23" H .$325.00

Doll, bisque head w/ ball joint body, mkd. made in Ger., redressed, rewigged, repainted, all limbs may not be orig. 18" H $250.00

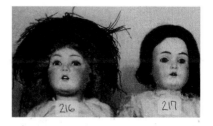

A-MD Mar. 1997   Richard Opfer, Auc. Inc.

Left to Right

Cund & Otto Dressel Doll, bisque doll, ball joint body, redressed, rewigged, fingernail polish added, torso weak at neck & arms, teeth repl., 26" H $475.00
Daisy Doll, bisque head, mkd. Ger., ball joint body, old wig, dressed, some wear, hands repainted, repr., 24" H $325.00

A-MD Mar. 1997   Richard Opfer, Auc. Inc.

Left to Right

Kestner Doll, bisque doll w/ ball joint body, mkd. Ger., old clothes, rewigged, body wear, 27" H $750.00
Heubach Koppelsdorf Doll, bisque child w/ ball joint body, rewigged, redressed, minor repr. to body, 31½" H $600.00

A-MD Mar. 1997   Richard Opfer, Auc. Inc.

Left to Right

Doll, bisque head w/ ball joint body, mkd. Ger., dressed, rewigged, some body repaint, eyes stationary, 20" H $300.00
Armand Marseille Doll, bisque head w/ jointed kid body w/ compo. arms & legs, body label "Dainty Dorothy", redressed, rewigged, fingers chipped $75.00
Doll, bisque w/ ball joint body, mkd. Ger., open mouth, nice old wig & clothes, 23" H $190.00

A-MD Mar. 1997   Richard Opfer, Auc. Inc.

Horse Velocipede, carved & painted wood, orig. saddle, stenciled wheels, 50" L $3,000.00

A-MD Mar. 1997   Richard Opfer, Auc. Inc.

Left to Right

Armand Marseille Doll, bisque head, ball jointed stick body, rewigged & redressed, knee repr. & toe damage, 15" H $100.00
Doll, bisque shoulder plate, jointed cloth body, mkd. Ger., 1900, rewigged & redressed $35.00
Doll, bisque head, five pc. body, illegible marks, redressed, 10" H . .$95.00
Armand Maseille Doll, bisque head, ball jointed stick body, rewigged, redressed, leg repairs, 18" H .$175.00

A-MD Mar. 1997   Richard Opfer, Auc. Inc.

Left to Right

Armand Marseille Doll, bisque head, ball joint stick body, old wig, redressed, hairline, 17" H $110.00
Armand Marseille Doll, bisque head & shoulder plate w/ kid body, old clothes, rewigged, repl. arms 17" H $375.00
Doll, bisque head, ball joint body, old clothes, rewigged, mold flaws on face, torso repr. $80.00
Armand Marseille Doll, bisque head w/ ball joint body, old clothes, rewigged, repl. teeth, 21" H . .$210.00

A-MD Mar. 1997   Richard Opfer, Auc. Inc.

Left to Right

Heubach-Koppelsdorf Doll, bisque head, redressed, rewigged, torso repainted & repr., 26" H $325.00
Armand Marseille Doll, bisque head w/ ball joint body, rewigged, dressed, body repainted, 21½" H $110.00
Doll, bisque head, ball joint body, mkd. Ger., old wig, redressed, hairline, finger repl., 21" H $185.00

A-MD Mar. 1997   Richard Opfer, Auc. Inc.

Left to Right

Floradora Doll, bisque head, five pc. body, rewigged, old clothes, 18" H $85.00
Doll, bisque shoulders & head, kid body, mkd., old clothes, rewigged, missing one arm, 13" H $45.00
Special Doll, bisque shoulders, head & arms, jointed kid body, compo. lower legs, remnants of old wig, dressed, 12" H $65.00
Child Doll, bisque, pink cloth body, compo. hands, mkd. Made in Germ., rewigged, old clothes, 12" H . .$65.00

A-MD Mar. 1997   Richard Opfer, Auc. Inc.

Left to Right

Herm Steiner Doll, bisque head, jointed stick body, rewigged, dressed, thumb missing, 12" H $150.00
Schoenau & Hoffmeister Doll, bisque head, jointed stick body, old clothes, rewigged, glass eye cracked, one leg off, hairline, 14" H $50.00
Armand Maseille Doll, bisque head, jointed stick body, redressed, rewigged, lower leg repl., 11" H $75.00
Armand Marseille Doll, bisque head, five pc. stick body, redressed, rewigged, body worn, 11½" H $75.00

A-MD Mar. 1997 Richard Opfer, Auc. Inc.

Tete Jumeau Doll, bisque head w/ jointed wrist ball joint body, stamped Jumeau, closed mouth, pierced ears, rewigged, old clothes, 21"H $3,600.00

A-MD Mar. 1997 Richard Opfer, Auc. Inc.

Left to Right

Max Handwerck Doll, bisque head w/ ball joint body, rewigged, old clothes, teeth damaged, finger missing, 23" H $160.00
Special Doll, bisque head w/ ball joint body, old wig, dressed, hands damaged, body damage, 22" H $110.00
Armand Marseille, bisque head w/ kid body, bisque hands & old wig & clothes, face cracked, 20" H . .$75.00

A-MD Mar. 1997 Richard Opfer, Auc. Inc.

Character Baby, bisque head w/ five pc. baby body, mkd., old clothes, rewigged, toes damaged, 18" H $500.00
Handwerck Doll, bisque doll w/ ball joint body, mkd. Handwerck body, nice old clothes, old wig, 23" H . . .$900.00

A-MD Mar. 1997 Richard Opfer, Auc. Inc.

Left to Right

Queen Louise Doll, bisque w/ ball joint body, old wig, dressed, 22" H $250.00
Doll, bisque head w/ ball joint body, mkd. Ger., old wig & clothes, neck flake, 23½" H $125.00
Armand Marseille Doll, bisque head w/ ball joint body, redressed, rewigged, some body wear, 20" H $185.00

A-MD Mar. 1997 Richard Opfer, Auc. Inc.

Left to Right

Daisy Doll, bisque head w/ ball joint body, mkd. Ger., rewigged, redressed, two fingers repl. 625.00
C.M. Bergmann Doll, bisque child w/ ball joint body, mkd. made in Ger., redressed, rewigged, finger missing, 22" H $450.00

A-MD Mar. 1997 Richard Opfer, Auc. Inc.

Left to Right

Armand Marseille, bisque head w/ ball jointed body, old wig w/ old clothes, hairline, 15" H $75.00
Morimura Brothers Doll, bisque shoulder head, oil cloth jointed body, mkd. Japan, old wig & old clothes $55.00
Ger. Doll, bisque shoulder & head, cloth body & compo. hands, mkd. made in Ger., old clothes, rewigged, 15" H $95.00
A.M. Doll, bisque head w/ five pc. stick body, prob. orig. clothes, rewigged, 11" H $95.00

A-MD Mar. 1997 Richard Opfer, Auc. Inc.

Left to Right

Am. School Boy, bisque head & arms w/ kid body, redressed, one finger chipped, 10" H $100.00
Heinrich Handwerck Doll, /Simon & Halbig, bisque w/ ball joint body, pierced ears, mkd., old clothes, rewigged, missing two fingers, 15" H $325.00
S. F. B. J. Child Doll, five pc. compo. body, open mouth, prob. orig. wig & hat, redressed, repl. set eyes, one finger missing, 9" H $40.00

A-MD Mar. 1997 Richard Opfer, Auc. Inc.

Left to Right

Doll, bisque head w/ five pc. stick body, mkd. Ger., orig. doll, wig & clothes, no shoes $60.00
Doll, bisque head w/ five pc. stick body, mkd. 7/0, rewigged & redressed, neck chips, finger chip & toes missing, 13" H $45.00
Doll, C.O.D., bisque shoulder head, kid body, & bisque arms, rewigged, old clothes, no teeth, 13" H $65.00
Doll, bisque head w/ five pc. stick body, mkd. G.K., old clothes, rewigged, 10½" H $85.00

A-MD Mar. 1997 Richard Opfer, Auc. Inc.

Left to Right

Simon & Halbig Doll, bisque w/ ball jointed body, mkd., worn body, missing one finger & one repl., redressed & rewigged, 23" H $325.00
Doll, bisque mkd. "DEP", ball joint body, pierced ears, redressed, rewigged, repainted, two fingers missing, 19" H $450.00

A-MA Sept. 1996   Skinner, Inc.

Left to Right

Queen Louise Doll, bisque head, mkd. Queen Louise replaced blonde wig, jointed compo. body, repairs & paint wear, 19½" H $287.50
Handwerck Doll, bisque head, early 20th c., pierced ears, mkd. orig. mohair wig, jointed compo. body, w/ orig. carton, 25" H $862.50
Doll, bisque shoulder head, synthetic br. wig, jointed kid body & legs, 22" H $287.50

A-MA Sept. 1996   Skinner, Inc.

Tinted Parian Doll, turned shoulder head, 1870's, cloth body & limbs, kid hands, period taffeta outfit, left shoulder damaged, 15½" H $488.75

A-MA Feb. 1997   Skinner

Schoenhut Circus, Humpty Dumpty, reduced size, fabric wear & staining, figures need restringing, base 9" W, 8" D $862.50

A-MA Sept. 1996   Skinner, Inc.

Left to Right

Gaultier Doll, bisque swivel shoulder head, pierced ears, mkd. F1G, orig. mohair wig, jointed kid body, bisque hands, kiln imper., 17" H . .$4,887.50
Belton Type Doll, bisque head, 1870-80's, pierced ears, mkd. 1837, orig. mohair wig, straight wrist jointed compo. body, period outfit, imper., 15" H $1,092.50
French Doll, bisque swivel shoulder head, late 19th c., orig. blonde human hair wig, jointed kid body, orig. aqua taffeta outfit, imper., fiber loss, 14½" H $1,955.00

A-MA Sept. 1996   Skinner, Inc.

Left to Right

Simon & Halbig Character Dolls, pr., bisque head, mkd. "Jutta 1914", br. mohair wig, fully jointed compo. body, orig. costumes, needs restringing, missing teeth, 14" H $1,380.00
Armand Marseille Doll, bisque head, mkd. 390, orig. br. mohair wig, fully jointed compo. body, orig. Romanian costume, shoe missing, 20" H . . .N/S
SFBJ Bisque Doll, br. painted, orig. br. mohair wig, br. painted compo. body, jointed at shoulders & hips, orig. costume, needs restringing, glaze & bisque flaking, 16" H $287.50
Armand Marseille Dolls, pr., bisque heads, mkd. 390, orig. br. mohair wigs, fully jointed compo. bodies, orig. costumes, needs restringing, 15" H $488.75

A-MA Sept. 1996   Skinner, Inc.

Left to Right

Shirley Temple Doll, Ideal Compo., mid 1930's, orig. mohair wig, IDEAL 25 mark, orig. outfit, body & limbs crazed, 24" H $201.25
Shirley Temple Ephemera Items, six mid 1930's music sheets; two Saalfield soft cover books; lot in good condition $86.25
Shirley Temple Type Doll, compo. walking, mid 1930's, unmkd., beige mohair wig, jointed at head & shoulders, paint wear, finger damage, 22¾" H $230.00
Shirley Temple Doll, Ideal Compo., ca. 1934, orig. wig, orig. blue sunsuit, minor crazing, fiber loss, shoes missing, 15" H $690.00

A-MA Sept. 1996   Skinner, Inc.

Parian Doll, shoulder head, 1970's-80's, molded lt. br. hair w/ blk. ribbon woven in hair, pierced ears, cloth body & limbs, 17" H $575.00
Parian Doll, tinted shoulder head, 1970's-80's, molded blonde hair w/ blk. ribbon, pierced ears, cloth body, leather hands, 19" H $517.50
German Doll, bisque shoulder head, ca. 1875, molded blonde hair showing ears, mkd. 131-10, cloth body & legs, kid hands, 22½" H $747.50
Parian Dagmar Doll, shoulder head, 1870's-80's, molded pale blonde hair, molded blouse, cloth body & limbs, kid hands, 20" H $690.00

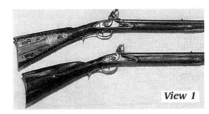

View 1

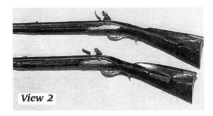

View 2

A-OH Nov. 1996   Garth's Auctions

Flintlock Rifle, VA, curly maple stock w/ old mellow varnished finish, brass hardware, reconverted back to flint, silver thumb pc. inlay, 41½" barrel & forend shortened, sm. repr., engr. "H.B." $3,300.00

PA Rifle, attrib. to W. Haga of the Reading School, 50½" octagon to round barrel, maple stock w/ carving & incised detail, brass hardware w/ flintlock, age cracks & glued repr., patch box lid repl., ...$1,760.00

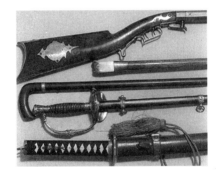

A-OH Nov. 1996   Garth's Auctions

"C. Siebert" Rifle, percussion, OH, engr. nickel silver cap box & hardware, 35" barrel w/ pat. breech, age crack, 54" $1,155.00

Presentation Cane, w/ bone handle, engr. silver band, "... Apr. 7, 1891" $1,045.00

Remington Rifle Cane, 36½" H, gutta percha handle & covering .$2,200.00

Swords w/ Scabbards, two, Shannon, Miller & Crane sword, etched blade, 37½" & Horstmann & Co. Calvary sword, "U.S." etched blade, lt. surface rust on scabbard, not pictured, 38" $1,017.50

Japanese Samurai Sword, w/ scabbard, 26" sgn. blade, temper line, wooden scabbard covered w/ leather $495.00

A-OH Nov. 1996   Garth's Auctions

1836 Flintlock Pistol, Johnson model, .54 caliber, walnut stock, dk. finish, "1837" date on lock, 14" $495.00

Manhattan Revolver, .36 caliber, cylinder scenes & traces or orig. bluing, 1864 pat. date & signature $825.00

Turkish Flintlock, blunderbuss or musket, relief chased dec., gold overlay, walnut stock, carved scrollwork, iron hardware, 15¼" $440.00

Allen & Thurber Pistol, six shot, patented 1837, simple scroll engraving, 7⅛" $357.50

Eng. Flintlock Pistol, 10" barrel, Belgium proof marks, walnut stock, age crack & pieced repairs, 17" .$357.50

Starr Arms Army Revolver, 1858, .44 caliber, double action, stamped w/ signature & pat. date, reblued ..$330.00

Colt 1860 Army Revolver, .44 caliber, serial numbers, surface rust & crack $632.50

Allen & Thurber Pistol, double barrel w/ single trigger, .36 caliber w/ 3" barrels, pitting $192.50

Colt 1855 Revolver, side hammer percussion, reblued finish, 3½" barrel, stamped w/ CT address, .28 caliber $165.00

Savage Navy Revolver, .36 caliber, reconditioned, rebluing, strap shows signature w/ pat. date, 14½" $412.50

A-IA Mar. 1997   Jacksons

Foot Officers Sword, w/ scabbard, US Civil War, 1850, double engr. Ames blade identified to Arthur Mason $1,870.00

A-IA Mar. 1997   Jacksons

Presentation Knife, Ger. WWII, dated 1932, engr. dedication, Alcoso double engr. 15½" blade, silver & gr. portepee $1,100.00

A-OH Nov. 1996   Garth's Auctions

Colt Bisley Revolver, .32 caliber, single action, 4¾" barrel, pat. dates, lt. pitting, not mkd. Bisley model . .$770.00

Bacon Pocket Revolver, cased, .31 caliber, nickel plated metal, fitted wooden case w/ bullet mold, horn, containers & measure, 3¼" x 11" x 6¾" $440.00

Remington-Elliot Derringer, 32 RF, has four shot barrels, ring trigger, 5½" $797.50

Remington Pistol, w/ case, metal cleaned w/ pitting, 3¾" barrel, sgn., mah. case w/ reprs. $417.50

Remington Pistol, 1867 Navy rolling block, .50 caliber, stamped "Remingtons - Ilion, N.Y.", mkd. "H.E.", late fitted case $440.00

Remington Pistol, 1891 cased rolling block target, .22 caliber, 20" round barrel, walnut grip, pat. dates & "P.S." military stamp, lt. pitting $495.00

Frank Wesson Derringer, medium frame w/ 2½" barrels, stamped " Frank Wesson, Worcester, Mass. Pat. applied for" $522.50

Colt Revolver, 1878 Frontier, double action, .45 caliber, reblued finish, needs work $247.50

A.W. Spies Pistol, 6¾" round barrel, walnut handle grip w/ nickel silver inlays, hammer is repr., 11½" L $412.50

A-PA April 1997   Pook & Pook Inc.

Top to Bottom

Percussion Rifle, by "M.C. Clallen, Auburn", w/ octagonal barrel, walnut stock & brass patch box $300.00

Flintlock Rifle, PA, by "J.P. Beck", Lebanon Co., ca. 1790, orig. flintlock condition .N/S

Henry Rifle, PA, late 18th C., w/ brass patch box, flint lock mech., & tiger maple stock $1,900.00

A-OH Nov. 1996 Garth's Auctions

Jacquard Coverlet, two pc. double weave, navy blue, red & natural white, fringe on end only, wear, stains & frays, 78" x 86" $137.50

Hepplewhite Bed, MA, tall post, ref. maple w/ old cherry finish & pine headboard, repl. tester frame, mattress size approx. 50" x 70¾", 75½" H $1,265.00

Country Chest, pine w/ old mellow ref., dovetailed overlapping drawers & one board top, repl. brasses, feet have pieced repairs, 36" W, 37⅜" H $1,100.00

Basket & Footwarmer, woven splint sandwich basket w/ old varnish, some damage, 15" x 19", 4" H plus bentwood handle; punched tin footwarmer in mortised walnut frame, some edge damage & lt. rust, 8" x 9" . . .$220.00

A-OH Nov. 1996 Garth's Auctions

Sheraton Desk, cherry w/ old mellow finish, dovetailed drawers, fitted int. w/ three drawers & seven pigeon holes, one bracket missing, age cracks & replms., pine secondary wood, 29½" W, 22" D, 38" H $770.00

Candle Sconce, PA, tin, sunburst crest w/ star & leaves, 13½" H $1,265.00

Candle Sconces, two tin, sm. w/ sunburst crest, 9" H, & primitive one w/ punched design, pan resoldered & loose, no socket, 13½" H $192.50

Candle Lantern, sheet metal, dec. pierced air holes, old blk. repaint, reputed to have belonged to William Floyd, signer of Dec. of Indep., 17½" H $1,430.00

A-OH Nov. 1996 Garth's Auctions

Fed. Chest, ref. cherry w/ banded inlay, mah. molding, four dovetailed drawers, poplar secondary woods, old brass pulls, 39½"W, 41¼"H .$1,210.00

Creamware Plates, pr., blk. transfer, gr. enameled on "Water", sm. edge chips, worn, 9¾" diam. $440.00

Creamware Plates, eight, w/ reticulated rim, two impr. "Leeds Pottery", chips & stain, two are 10" diam., six are 9⅜" diam. $1,100.00

Creamware Ladle, w/ reticulated bowl, impr. "Wedgwood", bowl has stains & chips, 8⅛" L $165.00

Pearlware Plates, two, King's Rose w/ vine border, 7⅜" diam. & rose dec., 7⅝" diam., both have flaking $82.50

A-OH Nov. 1996 Garth's Auctions

Courting Mirror, wooden frame, painted glass segments, old mirror, damage, section of glass missing, 10⅝" W, 16" H . .$385.00

Hepplewhite Candlestand, ref. cherry, two board top, age crack, 17¼" x 18¼", 28" H $385.00

New Eng. Side Chair, banister back, ref. maple w/ some curl, fish tail crest, cracks, repl. rush seat, 45¾" H $825.00

Pewter Lamp, "Yale & Curtis N.Y. 1" touch, missing snuffers & brass tube loose, 8½" H, plus burner . . .$187.00

A-OH Nov. 1996 Garth's Auctions

Hepplewhite Washstand, NY, mah. & mah. veneer w/ inlay, hinged swivel drawer, dovetailed gallery, damage & repr., 26¼" W, 44¼" H $962.50

Hepplewhite Chair, Martha Washington, ref. cherry & birch, mortised vertical slats, stained varnish fin., worn & soiled gold brocade upholstery, 44¼" H $1,870.00

Figurine, white tin glazed, chips & yellowed repairs, 8½" L $440.00

Delft Wall Pocket, blue & white cornucopia w/ cherub head, sm. edge chips, 7¾" H $1,100.00

Delft Plate, blue & white, illus. from Bible, w/ "MAT: 2.AV.00, 1752", sm. edge chips, 10¼" diam. $770.00

A-MA June 1997 Skinner

Row 1, Left to Right

Blackhawk Weather Vane, molded gilt copper, Am., late 19th C., repr. bullet holes, minor dents & seam splits, 24½" L $2,300.00

Fish Weather Vane, gilt copper, Am., late 19th C., gilt loss, repr. bullet holes, seam splits, 35½" L $3,220.00

Banneret Weather Vane, hand-form gilt copper, Am., late 19th C., gilt loss, bullet holes, minor dents, 26¼" L $1,265.00

Row 2, Left to Right

Cow Weather Vane, molded copper, Am., late 19th C., bullet holes, seam splits, minor dents, 30½" L, 16½" H . .$4,312.50

Weather Vane, scroll banner gilt copper, Am., late 19th C., bullet holes, dents, minor seam splits, 49⅝" L, 37¾" H $1,955.00

A-OH Nov. 1996   Garth's Auctions

Candlestand, wrt. iron, four part base & adjustable candle arm w/ two sockets, pitted, 51½" H $1,265.00
Side Chair, early w/ cane seat & back, red repaint, repairs & replm., 44¾" H $770.00
Brass Bedwarmer, Continental, pierced & tooled lid, turned handle, 43" L $137.50
Cast Iron Rabbit, old white repaint, 12" H $385.00

A-OH Jan. 1997   Garth's Auctions

Hanging Salt Box, ref. pine, dovetailed case & drawer, stains & salt damage, replacements, restored crest, 10¾" L $302.50
Chippendale Mirror, walnut w/ old finish, gilded liner & carved & gilded eagle, orig. glass, worn silvering, repr., 11⅞" W, 22½" H $522.50
Windsor Armchair, cleaned to surface, traces of old finish, 35" H $825.00
Hepplewhite Stand, cherry w/ dk. red paint, dovetailed drawer & two board top, pine secondary wood, 19" x 19⅝", 26½" H $2,310.00
Splint Basket, woven w/ colorful red, yel., gr. & blk., bentwood rim handles, damage & sm. holes, 11¼" x 15½", 8" H . .$220.00

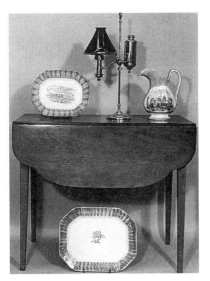

A-OH Jan. 1997   Garth's Auctions

Hepplewhite Table, pembroke, ref. cherry, dovetailed drawer, repairs to joints & legs, pine secondary wood, orig. brasses, 18½" x 35½" w/ 11½" leaves, 28½" H $715.00
Spatterware Platter, blue rainbow, red transfer, sm. rim flakes, 12½" L . .$275.00
Brass Student Lamp, w/ gr. cased shade, labeled "... N. York, sole agent", electrified, roughness on top edge, 21" H $330.00
Spatterware Pitcher, blue transfer of oriental men, faint hairline, 10¼" H $192.50
Spatterware Platter, purple, blue eagle & shield transfer, minor stains, 15½" L $522.50

A-OH Aug. 1996   Garth Auctions

Candle Mold, tin 24 tubes, half candle size, ear handle, lt. rust, 6" H $412.50
Taper Jack, silver-plated, mkd. 5½" H $170.50
Cast Iron Eagle, attrib. to Peter Derr, 1973 printing of 1949 book by James F. Spears is included, 13½" L . . .$247.50
Candle Mold, tin 6 tubes, half candle size, ear handle, rust damage, 6" H . . .$192.50
Grease Lamp, wrt. iron, 5¼" H plus hanger $104.50
Folk Art Wood Carvings, white & gr. owl w/ blk. glass marble eyes, 8"H, & bust of man w/ tie, varnished walnut, 8¼" H, both 20th C. $165.00

"ABC" Plate, tin, "Who Killed Cock Robin...", worn yel. varnish, 8" D . .$27.50
Writing Box, primitive ash & poplar w/ red repaint, fitted int., 10" x 11¼" $27.50
Capstan Candlesticks, two similar mini. brass, some age but not period, 3¾" H $385.00
Hogscraper Candlestick, w/ pushup & lip hanger, lrg. size, 10¼" H .$220.00
Hogscraper Candlestick, w/ pushup & lip hanger, pushup has stamped label, 7" H $165.00
Tôle Food Warmer, worn orig. blk. paint w/ stenciled floral dec. in red, silver, gr., blue & yel., complete w/ burner & pans, 8½" H $220.00
Pewter Desk Set, semi-spherical feet, double hinged lids w/ two glass insert ink wells, minor battering, 5½" x 7½" $291.50
Rockingham Dog, minor chip on base, 9¾" H $93.50
Euro. Treen Salt Box, w/ turned detail & hanging crest, "Wekl", 12½" H $140.50

A-OH Nov. 1996   Garth's Auctions

Hepplewhite Chair, Martha Washington, ref. mah. frame, has repairs & repl. arms & added castors, 43½" H $1,100.00
Chippendale Table, tilt top, ref. mah., one board top, old repairs, latch repl., dk. stains, 30" diam., 27½" H $1,650.00
Delft Plate, blue & white, Dutch inscription on front & back, edge chips, 9" diam. $192.50
Delft Charger, blue & white, floral rim w/ landscape, edge chips, 12" diam. .$467.50
Delft Bowl, blue & white, no table ring, edge chips, 8¾" diam. $2,255.00

A-OH Nov. 1996   Garth's Auctions

Row 1, Left to Right

Snuff Boxes, three, wood w/ curved toe, 3" L; worn blk. lacquer w/ inlaid pewter, 3¼" L; leather & wood, wear, 4½" L $357.50

Snuff Boxes, four, papier mâché, two w/ portraits, one engraving on yel. ground & one floral, wear & damage, 2⅜" to 2¾" $275.00

Snuff Boxes, round burl, w/ tortoise shell int., carved ext. relief scene, mkd. "Party given for the King of Portugal on the Lena, long live Fr." (translation), 3⅜" diam. $220.00

Snuff Boxes, br. gutta percha w/ relief scene, mkd. "Prise d' Yorck 1781", from col. of Gr. Gr. Nephew of George Washington, 2⅞" diam. $742.50

Row 2, Left to Right

Snuff Box, burl w/ inset handcolored engraving, glass cracked, damaged, 2" diam. $49.50

Snuff Box, shaped like ship hull, 5" L $126.50

Snuff Boxes, two round papier mâché, w/ handcolored engrs., one of Gen. Taylor, 3¼" diam., & the other of soldiers, 3" diam., both damaged $1,265.00

Row 3, Left to Right

Snuff Boxes, two round paper mâché w/ handcolored engr. landscape, 3⅝" diam. & wooden w/ decal of chickens "Gratis", 2⅜" L $220.00

Snuff Boxes, three round paper mâché w/ engr. portraits on lids in blk. on deep amber ground, Napoleon 3½" diam.; "LaFayette", 2⅞" diam.; Decatur 3½" diam, all have wear & damage ..$935.00

A-MA Oct. 1996   Skinner, Inc.

Weather Vane, rooster cast & sheet iron, Am., second half 19th c., minor pitting, 32" H, 34" L $4,887.50

A-OH Nov. 1996   Garth's Auctions

Eng. Water Clock, oak w/ chip carving & brass fittings, engr. "John West, 1674, Warwick", not 17th C., 29" H $715.00

Engraving, blk. & white, "MacDonough's Victory on Lake Champlain", stains, edge damage, pinpoint hole, 26½" W, 21½" H, eglomise mat has wear, gilt frame has wear & damage; also a separate framed engraving: "Key to B. Tanner's Print", stains, 11" x 13" ..$2,530.00

Hepplewhite Candlestand, CT, ref. cherry w/ orig. finish on underside of top, one board top, minor age cracks, 15¾" x 16⅜", 27¾" H $1,705.00

Q.A. Chippendale Chair, transitional, attrib. to RI, birch w/ old worn finish, repl. rush seat, feet restored, repairs, 28⅜" H $660.00

A-OH Nov. 1996   Garth's Auctions

Hepplewhite Washstand, Salem, MA., curly maple w/ old finish, dovetailed drawer & high crest, pull has been soldered, again broken, 21" W, 43½" H ...$2,970.00

Delft Bowl, w/ attached strainer, blue & white floral dec., hairlines & old repr., 8¾" diam., 3½" H $467.50

Delft Bottle, blue & white floral dec., lip is chipped, 8¾" H $385.00

A-OH Oct. 1996   Garth's Auctions

Currier & Ives Litho., handcolored "Maple Sugaring", stained, margins trimmed, sm. holes, damaged & edge repr., 14" W, 10" H $412.50

Currier & Ives Litho., handcolored "Squirrel Shooting", stains, sm. hole & edge damage, 13⅞" W, 9⅞" H $357.50

Empire Chest, ref. walnut, dovetailed drawers, pine secondary wood, molding & feet replaced, 20½" W, 32¾" H $1,045.00

Q.A. Side Chair, old blk. repaint, replaced rush seat, 41" H $550.00

Yellowware Pitcher, white bands & dk. br. stripes w/ seaweed dec., stains & wear, 7⅝" H $319.00

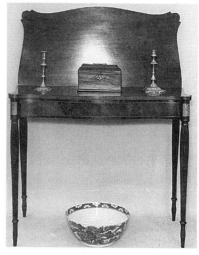

A-OH Nov. 1996   Garth's Auctions

Sheraton Table, ref. mah., attrib. to Salem, MA, 17½" x 36½", 29¼" H $9,350.00

Q.A. Candlestick, brass w/ petal base & pushup, 7⅝" H $935.00

Tea Caddy, mah. w/ old finish, orig. brass bale & escut, some alts, 9" L $495.00

Q.A. Candlestick, brass w/ petal base, poorly resoldered, 8⅛" H $275.00

Imari Porcelain Bowl, blue & white, edge chips, 13½" diam., 5½" H $715.00

A-OH Nov. 1996   Garth's Auctions

Hepplewhite Desk, MA, two pc., ref. mah. w/ inlay, dovetailed drawers w/ applied edge beading, sgn. "Made in the year of our Lord & Savior Jesus Christ 1802, by Thomas R. Williams", minor repairs, pine secondary wood, repl. brasses, 39" W, 20¼" D., 47¾" H $3,850.00
Silver Luster Pots, two, one w/ domed lid, 12¼" H, & one urn shaped, 10⅛" H, both damaged $137.50
Silver Luster Teapot, w/ reeded detail, 5¼" H $137.50
Silver Luster Pitchers, two w/ similar detail, minor wear, 6½", & 6⅞" . . .$181.50
Silver Luster, seven pcs., loving cup, 6⅛" H, creamer; two sugars w/ ribs; pitcher, 7" H; helmet creamer & goblet, 4⅜" H, all have wear & damage $302.50

A-MA Oct. 1996   Skinner, Inc.

Civil War Uniform Jacket, of Elisha Hunt Rhodes, navy blue wool w/ quilt lining & brass buttons w/ tag inscribed "Coat worn by Elisha H. Rhodes, 2nd RI vol. 1869", & on verso "Made by Thomas W. Chace Providence RI", some wear & darned repairs $14,950.00

A-OH Oct. 1996   Garth's Auctions

Row 1, Left to Right
Kugel Ornament, berry w/ silvered amber color, 3¼" D $275.00
Burl Hair Receiver, minor age cracks, 4⅛" diam., 3¼" H $220.00
Scrimshaw String Holder, turned wood w/ ivory feet, repl. brass knob, 4¾" H $110.00
Redware Bowl, w/ beaded tooling & applied handles, wear & chips, 5⅝" H $203.50
Pitcher, blue & white sponge ware, molded ribs & band, 5¾" H . .$220.00

Row 2, Left to Right
Shaker Thread Caddy, wooden w/ worn red pin cushion, mkd. "Sabbathday Lake Shakers, Maine", 5½" H $220.00
Walnut Bank, turned w/ hidden swivel coin slot, damaged, age crack, 6" diam., 6" H $165.00
Mini. Wall Cupboard, slate, 7" W, 6¼" H $49.50
Pease Treen Jars, two, old varnish finish, smaller has chips on finial, both have age cracks, 4" H & 5¾" H $715.00

Row 3, Left to Right
Copper Tea Kettle, dovetailed, dents, 6" H plus swivel handle $82.50
Shaker Sewing Box, ref. mah. w/ recovered pin cushion, lid incomplete, 5⅜" x 7", 6½" H $82.50
Treen Jar, poplar w/ dry patina, 6½" H $93.50
Toy Cook Stove, tin & cast iron w/ old blk. paint & nickel finish, "Venus", two plates of four a missing, 5" H .$99.00

A-MA Oct. 1996   Skinner, Inc.

Jeweler's Trade Sign, gilt & painted metal, double-faced, CT late 19th c., electrified, repl. works, surface imp.,

A-OH Nov. 1996   Garth's Auctions

Turtle Back Bellows, orig. yel. paint w/ stenciled & free hand dec. in red, blk., gr. & gold, brass nozzle, releathered, chips on handle, 17" L $440.00
Mini. Portrait, watercolor on celluloid, wooden frame w/ gilded brass liner, mkd. "Mrs. Gilchrist ...", 5" W, 5⅝" H . . .$467.50
Sewing Kit, tiny gilded in hinged nut case, nut has crack, 1¾" L . . .$220.00
Oriental Netsuke, chick in egg, 2" L $247.50
Turtle Back Bellows, orig. gr. paint w/ red trim & yel. stenciled dec., brass nozzle, leather in tatters, wear, chip on handle, 17" L $165.00
Triptych & Paktong Box, sm. brass triptych, 2" x 3½" open; & paktong box w/ oriental scene on lid w/ figures, 1⅞" L . .$49.50
Tôle Chamber Stick, orig. dk. br. japanning in red, gr., yel. & white, wear, 6½" diam. . . .$1,705.00
Locket, tin type of young woman & swatch of twill from jacket, engr. pale gold filled case, 1⅝" plus ring .$82.50
Snuff Box, bronze w/ dk. patina, angel riding lion w/ "Regent", emb. inscription "In record of the reign of George III", 3" diam. $110.00
Basket & Footwarmer, woven splint sandwich basket w/ old varnish, some damage, 15" x 19", 4" H plus bentwood handle; punched tin footwarmer in mortised walnut frame, some edge damage & lt. rust, 8" x 9" . . .$220.00

A-MA Oct. 1996   Skinner, Inc.

Pine Wall Box, stained, Am., 19th c., old refinish, minor losses, 14½" H, 13" W $546.25
Pine Lidded Wall Box, red painted, Am., late 18th-early 19th c., imp., 20¼" H, 12" W, 6¾" D $1,495.00

A-MA Mar. 1997   Eldred's

Row 1, Left to Right

Wooden Shelf, walnut, 19th C., 31" W, 49½" H . . .$880.00
Wooden Buckets, two, one gr. w/ single wooden handle, 6" diam, 5¾" H,. & similar bucket, stamped "W.C. T3", 9" diam., 10" H $275.00
Duck Pull Toy, w/ noise maker, tail chipped, 12" L $110.00
Wooden Piggin, old gr. paint, 4¾" H $632.50

Row 2, Left to Right

Candle Boxes, two, Am., w/ sliding covers, one painted red containing assort. blocks, one gr., both w/ imper., 8¼" W, 5" L, 4½" H $220.00
Wooden Boxes, two circular, covered, Am., 19th C., gr.-blue, one 9½" diam., 2" H, one 9" diam., 4½" H $330.00

Row 3, Left to Right

Wooden Boxes, two circular, covered, Am. 19th C., one gr., 7¾" diam., 4" H, one gray-blue stamped "J. Burr", 9¼" diam., 5" H $440.00
Brass Lamp, "boat signal", by National Marine Lamp Co., 19th C., orig. kerosene burner $176.00
Two-handled Tub, wooden, old gr. paint, banding, 12" diam., 8" H $880.00

Row 4, Left to Right

Wooden Boxes, two circular, painted, covered, Am., 19th C., one gr., 9" diam., 4" H, & one blue 9½" diam., 5" H $467.50
Wooden Boxes, three painted, covered, 19th C., oval painted red, 2½" H, 6¼" L, 4½" W, one painted lt. gr. stamped "Levi Beal", 3" H, 6½" L, 4¾" W, & a circular painted gr., 3" H, 6½" diam. $495.00
Wooden Buckets, two, one gr. w/ single wooden handle, 6" diam, 5¾" H,. & similar bucket, stamped "W.C. T3", 9" diam., 10" H $275.00

Row 5, Left to Right

Wooden Boxes, two circular covered, painted, Am., 19th C., one red w/ swing handle, 11½" diam., 6½" H, one grain-painted in br., 10" diam., 6" H $275.00

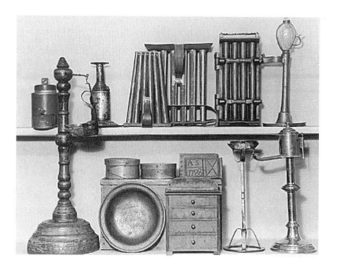

A-OH Aug. 1996   Garth Auctions

Tin Lighting Devices, two, hanging font w/ attached pan, tubular wick support soldered repr., 6" H, & Drummond pat. candle maker & candlestick, filler cap missing, 8" . . .$275.00
Tin Candle Molds, two w/ ear handles, six tubes, 9" H & 12 tubes w/ curved foot, repr., 10" H $165.00
Candle Mold, Fr. cast iron hinged two part, mkd. "Moule Mirabilis Guillon", 11" H $148.50
Time Lamp, pewter w/ glass font, soldered repr., 13" H . .$302.50
Lighting Stand, turned wood w/ holes for inserting lamp, traces of old red & blk. paint, 21¾" H $440.00
Double Crusie Lamp, primitive wrt. iron, 6¾" H, twisted hanger $82.50
Pine Box, w/ worn old greyish paint, 2 section till w/2 drawers, 14" L $60.50
Bentwood Boxes, two w/ finger const. & old finish, round has loose bottom, 4¼" D, oval w/ branded name on lid "B. Sprague", 4⅜" L $247.50
Candlebox, miniature dovetailed, pine w/ old finish, sliding lid has carved designs w/ initials & date "A.S 1788", 4½" L $247.50
Cast Iron dish, 7¾" diam. (pictured); **Jamb Hook,** pitted, 8½" diam., & combo **Door Knocker / Peep Hole** mounted in old wooden board that has age crack & worn damage, pitted, 6¾" x 8" $165.00
Sewing Box, mah. & figured veneer, four dovetailed drawers & pin cushion top, feet added or replaced, 8" H $330.00
Lighting Device, wrt. iron on crown base, four spout open burner, 12¼" H $220.00
Brass Spout Lamp, font w/ spout & wick pick are slightly different color than removable base, soldered repr., 14¼" H $104.50

A-MA Oct. 1996   Skinner, Inc.

Birdcage, paint dec. wood & wire, Am. 19th c., dec. w/ stars & a flowering tree, imp., 17" H $970.00

A-OH Jan. 1997   Garth's Auctions

Mirror, w/ inlaid frame, beveled sides in rosewood & maple, edges mah. veneer w/ applied spool turnings, worn finish, minor edge damage, 11" x 12½" $214.50
Windsor Chair, continuous arm, old worn blk. paint over red, repr. breaks in seat, 33½" H $1,100.00
Hanging Cupboard, pine & poplar, old blue paint w/ gr. door panels, red molding on inside rails & stiles, dovetailed case, int. w/ shelf & two dovetailed drawers, 22½" W, cornice 9½" x 24¼" $1,540.00
Redware Pie Plate, three line yellow slip dec., minor slip flaking, 8¼" diam. $990.00
Redware Pie Plate, three line yel. slip dec., minor wear & edge flakes, 8½" diam. $495.00

A-MA Oct. 1996   Skinner, Inc.

Dress, yel. silk gauze, c. 1810-20, good condition, retains vivid color . .$920.00

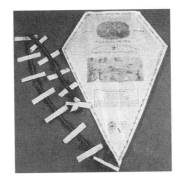

A-MA Oct. 1996   Skinner, Inc.

"A.J. Whitcomb's Indestructible Pocket Kite," patented 1876 Utica, N.Y., yel. glazed cotton w/ engr. dec. & directions, 26½" H, 17½" W . .$1,035.00

A-MA Mar. 1997   Skinner

Checkerboard, painted wood, Am., 19th C., rev. dec. w/ caricature of Zachary Taylor, mustard & dk. br., minor paint wear, staining, 14¼" sq. $2,185.00

A-MA May 1997   Skinner

Left to Right

Arts & Crafts Lantern, gr. hammered glass panels, missing socket & mount, 9" sq. 12½" H . . . . .N/S
Arts & Crafts Copper Clock, New Haven Clock Co., works, deep patina, 6½" sq. 10½" H $488.75
Roycroft Copper Box, geometric dec., orig. patina, minute wear, 10½" W, 6¾" D, 3¾" H $3,450.00
Arts & Crafts Wall Sconce, dec. w/ ceramic circles under blue/green glaze, good patina, 6¼" W, 14½" H $575.00
Roycroft Candlesticks, pr., copper, deep orig. patina, impr. mark, 5" diam., 12¼" H $575.00

A-MA Oct. 1996   Skinner, Inc.

Shaker Items

Row 1, Left to Right

Items, two, three-armed garment hanger, 14½" H, 14" W; cherry fabric form, 18½" L, 6 ⅝" W $460.00
Berry Pails, two, 19th c., loss of finish, other imp. $460.00
Mini. Pail, covered, grain painted, 19th c., stenciled "Pepper", wear, 4½" H $460.00
Items, four, work board 19½" x 14", two tin dust pans, & tape winder, minor imp. $345.00

Row 2, Left to Right

Items, six, brush poplarware box, pin cushion w/ tray & pr. of woven sleeve protectors, breaks $115.00
Rolling Pin, bird's-eye maple, 19th c., 10¼" L $126.50
Lot of Sewing Items, swift, roll of silk satin, stocking darner & five spools $172.50
Swift & Sewing Bird, 19th c., imp., 7" H & 25" H $345.00
Wood & Tin Items, four, 19th c., hanging match safe, & three clothes hangers, one dated 1859 . . . .$488.75

A-MA May 1997   Skinner

Left to Right

Rookwood Plant Stands, pr., iron foliate designs, 54" H . . . . .N/S
Arts & Crafts Umbrella Stand, wooden, orig. finish, 10" W, 17½" H $460.00
Gustav Stickley Bookcase, orig. hardware w/ deep patina, med. br. finish, Gustav decal 54" W, 13" D, 56¼" H $6,900.00
Roycroft Bookrack, carved orb mark & nine asst. vol. of Elbert Hubbard's Selected Writings, orig. finish, 15" W, 6" D, 9" H $488.75

A-MA May 1997   Skinner

Left to Right

Adirondack Rocking Chair, bent oak slats w/ natural timber frame, 21" W, 33½" D, 41½" H $833.75
Adirondack Floor Lamp, center post w/ three legs, half timber slatted shades, 29" diam., 61" H . . .$1,840.00
Adirondack Rocking Chair, bentwood oak slats w/ natural timber supports, 24" W, 32" D, 37" H . .$1,840.00

A-OH Nov. 1996   Garth's Auctions

Garden Bench, cast iron, old blk. repaint, break in seat, 59½" L $825.00
Garden Armchair, cast iron, old blk. repaint, old break in seat, 33½" H .$825.00
Hitching Post, pr., cast iron horse head, old blk. repaint, underground portion repl. on one, 41" above ground $605.00

A-OH Nov. 1996   Garth's Auctions

Pieced Quilt, in red, greyish blue & white, red fabric has gold block printed polka dots, minor stains, 86" x 96" $247.50
Settle Bench, blk. repaint, repairs, 75" L $330.00
Rotary Griddle, wrt. iron, tripod base & shaped handle, 10½" diam., 6½" handle $192.50
Dutch Oven, tin w/ spit, 19" L .$192.50
Griddles, two wrt. iron, 11" diam., & 13½" diam. $220.00

A-OH Nov. 1996   Garth's Auctions

Sheraton Chest, ref. cherry w/ curly maple, dovetailed drawers, burl knobs, repl. top & age cracks, poplar secondary wood, 40¼" W, 44¾" H $1,402.50
Candle Molds, two tin, twelve tube, rounded corners & ear handles, 9¼" & 10¾" H $165.00
Ovoid Jar, redware w/ applied handles, clear glaze, ora. color w/ br., chips & hairlines, 9¾" H $357.50
Candle Molds, four tin, two are four tube, a three tube & a single tube, minor soldered repr., 10½" to 11¼" H $341.00
Candle Mold, twelve tube w/ pewter tubes, brass top plate & tips, stamped "Dyre & Richmond, ... Pat.", missing tube, poplar frame, wear & stains, 5½" x 13¾", 16¼" H $616.00

A-OH Nov. 1996   Garth's Auctions

Chippendale Desk, ref. curly maple, dovetailed case & drawers, feet repl., edge repr. & some replms., 38¼" W, 20" D, 42¾" H $1,980.00
Pewter Tall Pot, "F. Porter, Westbrook", ME, finial wafer missing, 10¾" H $115.50
Pewter Porringer, cast , dents & sm. splits, 5" diam. $148.50
Sewerpipe Dog, simple tooled detail, 10½" H $148.50

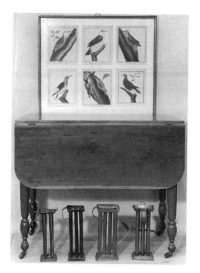

A-OH Nov. 1996   Garth's Auctions

Handcolored Engravings, five, matted & framed, one pen & ink & watercolor of birds, two sgn. "Martinet", pages & mat glued down, 31" W, 26" H $330.00
Drop Leaf Table, ref. cherry, two board top, pieced repr., minor age cracks & edge damage, 19" x 38" w/ 13¾" leaves, 29¾" H $341.00
Candle Molds, four tin, four tube; nine tube & two six tubes, one has old blk. repaint, another has copper wash, 10¼" to 11" H $275.00

A-OH Nov. 1996   Garth's Auctions

Jelly Cupboard, MO, walnut w/ natural finish, dovetailed drawers, pine & poplar secondary wood, age cracks & repairs, 41½" W, 50¼" H $687.50
Oil on Academy Board, still life, surface scratches, repr., 18¼" W, 24½" H, gilded frame $247.50
Coffee Grinder, cast iron, orig. orangish red & blue w/ yel. & blk. striping, "Enterprise Mfg. Co., PA", "Pat. July 12, '98", lid mismatched, 35" H $990.00
Paper Sack Holder, wooden w/ orig. red paint & blk. stenciled dec., 20¼" H $797.50
Wooden Crate, w/ carrying handles, red repaint w/ yel., repaint over another label, 19" L $82.50

A-OH Nov. 1996   Garth's Auctions

Corner Cupboard, one pc., ref. cherry & poplar, added porcelain knobs, panels gouged, cornice repl., 40½" W, 73¼" H $880.00
Biscuit Tin, train engine, worn polychrome dec., "Unica Torino", dents & wear, 23½" L $203.50
Jardiniere Base, pottery, yel., gr. & white w/ gilt, adv. label, mkd. "Sebring", OH, wear & stains, 25" H $440.00

A-OH Nov. 1996   Garth's Auctions

Hepplewhite Huntboard, yel. pine w/ old dk. br. finish & traces of earlier paint, mortised case, dovetailed drawers, locks w/ inlaid escutcheons, sm. repairs, worn surface, 51½" W, 38¾" H $2,530.00
Candle Molds, two tin, nine tube, 11" H & 10½" H $104.50
Candle Molds, two tin, ten tube, leans slightly, 10¾" H, & twelve tube w/ wicks, 9" H $148.50
Candle Molds, two tin, twelve tube, some damaged & soldered repr., 12" H, & six tube, 12" H $115.50
Ovoid Churn, stoneware, impr. "J.C. Smith, Mogadore, OH", w/ flower & "3" in cobalt blue, 16" H $907.50
Stoneware Crock, w/ applied handles, design & "6" in cobalt blue, minor flakes, 13¾" H $110.00

A-OH Nov. 1996   Garth's Auctions

Walking Stick & Spoon, carved stick, age crack, 32½" L; spoon w/ dec. carving, "Mush & milk, Pioneer porridge", natural patina, holes in handle, 14¼" H $214.50
Portrait, watercolor on paper, young man in blue frock, handmade frame, irreg. glass, red & blk. paint, 4¼" W, 5" H $330.00
Wood Carvings, two, walnut pencil box w/ drawer, 6½" L, & natural finish w/ blk. & gold trim, 4⅛" L . . .$77.00
Butter Paddle, curly maple, old finish, hook end, 9¼" L $170.50
Cookie Cutter, tin, heart & hand, handle, lt. rust, 3⅛" L $478.50
Portrait, on celluloid ivory, sgn. "A.B", framed, 3¼" W, 5¾" H $192.50
Pewter Ladle, w/ turned handle, touch mark, 15" L $159.50
Rolling Pin, opal. w/ red, gr. & gold enameling, "Union", 14" L . . .$132.00
Brass Skimmer, wrt. iron handle & tooled initials "A.H.", NY, 21¾" L $192.50

A-OH Nov. 1996   Garth's Auctions

Empire Chest, hardwood w/ flame grain mah. veneer, pine secondary wood, veneer & edge damage, 41¼" W, 46" H overall $1,100.00
Oriental Jars, pewter w/ brass inlay, red stone finials, minor battering of soft pewter, 8¼" H $462.00
Student Lamp, double, brass w/ milk glass shades, orig. burners w/ chimneys, 18" H $605.00

A-OH Nov. 1996   Garth's Auctions

Plantation Desk, ref. pine & hardwood, lift lid, int. pigeon holes, rebuilt base, 28¼" x 44", 78½" H $990.00
Candle Molds, two, tin six tube w/ ear handles, one pc. repl., 11" & 11¼" H $137.50
Candle Molds, three, tin w/ rounded corners, one handle loose, minor soldered repr., 10¾" H $165.00
Candle Molds, three, tin eighteen tube in refin. pine & poplar frame, some mismatched, old pieced repairs, age cracks, 7¾" x 21¾", 16¼" H $495.00

A-OH Nov. 1996   Garth's Auctions

Empire Secretary, two pc., flame grain mah. veneer w/ bird's eye veneer on int. drawers, 43¼" W, 91½" H $1,457.50
Porcelain Tureens, two white, mkd. "H & Co. L", 13" L, 9¾" H $154.00
Ironstone, twelve pcs., sprig dec., not a set, plus lid & four handleless cups . .$330.00

A-MA May 1997   Skinner

Gustav Stickley Costumer, double, orig. dk. br. finish & hardware w/ deep patina, 13″ W, 22″ D, 65½″ H . . .$2,875.00

A-MA May 1997   Skinner

Left to Right

Candlesticks, pr., Heintz Art Metal, foliate silver overlay on bronze base, some patina, impr. mark, 6″ diam., 14½″ H $977.50
Roseville Pottery, Bonita vase, crisp detail w/ gr. glazed ground, paper label, 8″ diam., 10″ H $1,035.00
Stickley Sideboard, orig. hardware w/ deep patina, orig. int., sgn. "The Work of…", 54″ W, 24″ D, 48″ H $4,887.50
Stickley China Cabinet, orig. hardware w/ deep patina, chamfered backboards, int. orig. finish, ext. overcoated w/ good color. 44″ W, 16¼″ D, 62″ H $5,175.00

A-OH Nov. 1996   Garth's Auctions

Roll Top Desk, mah. w/ old finish, seven drawers, brass label "Globe Desk, Chicago, Ill.", 66″ W, 45½″ H . . .$522.50
Brass Andirons, pr., similar fire set all w/ flame finials, dents, 23½″ H $165.00

A-MA May 1997   Skinner

Arts & Crafts Chandelier, brass cross & circle design on border, six gr. slag glass panels, repl. socket, 20″ diam., 10¾″ H $172.50
Silver Coffee Service, Mexican, w/ coffeepot, teapot, tray, sugar & creamer, impr. L.M., sterling, 23″ W, 9″ H . . . . .N/S
Arts & Crafts Dining Table, quartersawn oak w/ med. br. finish, four 9-inch leaves, 48″ diam., 28″ H $1,150.00

A-MA May 1997   Skinner

Arts & Crafts Chandelier, painted metal frame, 12 slag glass caramel colored panels w/ two extended shades, repl. socket, 27½″ W, 14″ H . .$172.50
Fulper Pottery Bowl, dec. w/ smooth mustard color glaze, vertical mark, 10¾″ diam., 3″ H $345.00
Arts & Crafts Dining Table, dk. orig. finish w/ nice quarter sawn oak, minor veneer chip, two leaves, 12″ W, 48″ diam., 28½″ H $575.00

A-MA May 1997   Skinner

Left to Right

Gustav Stickley Armchairs, pr., orig. finish w/ good quarter-sawn oak, Gustav red decal on both, repl. leather, 27″ W, 18¾″ D, 37″ H $3,450.00
Bradley & Hubbard Lamp, base w/ four Aztec animal faces, eight-panel shade w/ reversed painted Aztec design in colors of yel., gr., blue & blk., 21″ diam., 23″ H $1,725.00
Limbert Occasional Table, oak, w/ cutouts, Holland, Michigan, ca. 1912, med/light finish, branded mark, cut down & ref., 30″ diam., 27″ H $1,380.00

A-MA May 1997   Skinner

Left to Right

Stickley Bros. Umbrella Stand, hexagon form w/ hammered finish, orig. dk. patina, 11″ diam., 26″ H .N/S
Gustav Stickley Desk, drop front, orig. dk. br. finish, ink stain to front, Gustav Stickley red mark, missing inkwells, 29″ W, 13¼″ D, 43¾″ H $6,900.00
Tobey Chalet Magazine Stand, attrib., dk. br. finish, orig. tacks, missing leather, 12¾″ W, 12¾″ D, 43″ H $1,265.00

A-MA June 1997   Skinner, Inc.

Marquetry Tea Caddy, ca. 1870, inlay w/ scenes of putti at various pursuits, losses, 4⅛″ H $230.00
Tea Caddy, Victorian, w/ checkerbanded borders, 6½″ L $373.75

A-OH Nov. 1996   Garth's Auctions

Stacked Bookcase, five sections, base & cornice, three sections labeled "...Cincinnati, O." 34" W, 11½" D, 75½" H . .$687.50
Stacked Bookcase, five sections, base w/ drawer & cornice, quarter sawed oak w/ old finish, labeled "...Cincinnati, O", 34" W, 11½" D, 73½" H $1,980.00
Regina Music Box, mkd. "Monopol", walnut case w/ figured veneer & ebonized finish, minor edge wear, ten metal disks, 17" x 19" $330.00
Marquetry Music Cabinet, cherry w/ colored wood veneer, Japanesque carved details, finish worn, 20" W, 13¼" D, 39¼" H $110.00
Pottery Bowl, w/ polychrome rim & floral dec., sgn. "P. Fouitten, Quimper", 11⅝" diam. $1,595.00

A-OH Nov. 1996   Garth's Auctions

Corner Cupboard, one pc., ref. cherry, feet & cornice repl., 48½" W, 77½" H $1,210.00
Turk's Head Molds, redware, two, clear glaze & dk. sponging, edge chips & hairlines, 8" & 8¼" diam. . .$275.00
Two Pcs., cast iron, tea kettle on three short feet, 9½" H, sauce pan w/ iron ferule & long wooden handle, 4½" diam., 29" handle $990.00

A-OH Nov. 1996   Garth's Auctions

Oil on Canvas, landscape, cleaned & restored w/ repr. tears, 18" H, 24¼" W, old gilt frame $495.00
Dough Box, ref. walnut, dovetailed box, lid w/ breadboard ends repl., 21½" x 36½", 29" H $385.00
Noah's Ark, wood w/ orig. white, yel. & gr. paint, br. shutters & red roof, 23 pressed wood animals mkd. "Made in Germany", worn paint & damage, 17¼" L . . .$330.00
Food Mold, sq. tin w/ fruit, 6½" x 6½" $143.00
Baby Cradle, poplar w/ worn lt. blue paint, nailed repr., 10" x 27¼" .$55.00

A-OH Nov. 1996   Garth's Auctions

Colored Etching, girl w/ peacock shawl, sgn. in pencil "Louis Icart", labeled on plate "Copyright 1926...Paris", minor stain under mat, 20½" H, 24"½" W $935.00
Victorian Armchair, walnut frame, old ref. w/ some repairs, reupholstered in mint gr. brocade, 43¾" H . .$247.50
Eastlake Victorian Table, ref. walnut base w/ burl veneer, white marble top, stains & minor chips, 21" x 28¼", 28" H $302.50
Porcelain Platter, w/ matching gravy boat, "Habsburg China, Austria", gr. rim w/ white roses & gilt, 15" L, sm. chip on gravy 8¼" L $92.00
GWTW Lamp, milk glass w/ transfer dec. in red & gr., brass & cast iron fittings, worn gilt, electrified, 26" H$385.00

A-OH Nov. 1996   Garth's Auctions

Victorian Shelves, walnut & rosewood veneer w/ dk. finish, one dovetailed drawer, edge & veneer damage, 40" W, 14" D, 63½" H $660.00
Porcelain, four pcs., handpainted, ewer & jam jar sgn. "Booth", plate w/ ears mkd. "Rosenthale Donatello" 6¾" diam., teapot, roughness, 6⅛" H $220.00
Porcelain Tea Set, five pcs., handpainted, tray mkd. "J.P.L. Fr." & other pcs. are "D&C", yel. & white w/ pastel flowers & gilt, minor damage, tray is 16" L .$165.00
Porcelain Vases, two handpainted, mkd., 9" H & 10¼" H $275.00
Porcelain, three pcs., handpainted, two vases & a pitcher, two are mkd. "Bavaria" one mkd. "Limoges", 10½" H $357.50

A-OH Dec. 1996   Garth's Auctions

Apothecary Case, twenty-four drawers, ref. pine & poplar, early 20th C. wire nail const., backboards replaced, 27" W, top is 12½" x 29", 32" H $550.00
Chippendale Side Chair, hardwood w/ worn finish, replaced rush seat, joints repinned & bottom slat replaced, 37¾" H $148.50
Redware Cat, blk. glaze, impr. "Zaneware, Made in USA", wear & chips, 10⅞" H $104.50
Mirror, cast iron frame w/ traces of bronze finish, 10" W, 12" H . .$49.50
Windmill Weight, cast iron, "Hummer E184" w/ worn blk. & red repaint, wooden base, 9¼" H $330.00

A-OH Dec. 1996   Garth's Auctions

Weather Vane, w/ zinc pig & cast iron arrow, iron has rust, 20¾" L $412.50
Desk, ref. poplar, dovetailed case & gallery, edge damage, 38½" W, 21½" D, 34" H $550.00
Noggin Pitchers, set of three w/ wood & metal handles, ref., minor chips & cracks, 6" to 8⅞" H . .$187.00
Hanging Spice Box, nine drawers, hardwood w/ br. finish, porcelain pulls, wire nail const., age cracks, edge damage, 10¼" W, 19¼" H $192.50
Doll Cradle, dovetailed, ref. cherry w/ pine rockers, 27¾" L $242.00

A-OH Aug. 1996   Garth Auctions

Secretary Bookcase, birch w/ worn mag. finish, lid w/ fitted int., early 20th c., 40" W, 14" D, 74" H $715.00
Ironstone Tea Set, 3 pc., moss rose transfer w/ polychrome enameling & gilt, mkd. "Porcelain Opaque, ridgwood & Son", sm. firing hairline, 8½" H $137.50

A-OH Dec. 1996   Garth's Auctions

Kneehole Desk, ref. walnut, six dovetailed drawers, finish has wear, 23½" x 49", 30" H $440.00
Desk Lamp, polished brass base, gr. cased shade, 24" H $181.50
Table Lamp, brass Art Nouveau base w/ verdigris finish, mkd. "B & H", gr. slag shade, 18½" H $440.00
Desk Lamp, brass base w/ old blk. finish, applied foliage detail, white ruffled shade, 22" H $220.00
Desk Lamp, brass & leather w/ applied brass laurel wreath, 17" H $27.50

A-OH Dec. 1996   Garth's Auctions

Victorian Side Chairs, w/ Duncan Phyfe style drop leaf dining table w/ one leaf, mah. w/ similar finish, 20th C., chairs upholstered in blue crushed velvet, 37½" H, table opens to 39⅞" x 72", 29¼" H, table pads included $467.50
Victorian Parlor Table, Rococo revival, walnut frame w/ rosewood graining, back has wear & damage, white marble turtle top, 26" x 41", 27½" H $1,815.00
Carnival Glass Bowls, two, strawberry in purple, 8½" D, & berry in marigold, 8⅛" D $137.50
Table Lamp, cast iron foot w/ bronze finish, painted & frosted glass base & closed top shade, 15¾" D, 21½" H $1,100.00

A-OH Dec. 1996   Garth's Auctions

Chromolithograph, "The Famous War Engine 'General' of the Western & Atlantic RR", framed 28½" W, 22" H $82.50
Dry Sink, poplar w/ dk. ref. & painted int., one dovetailed drawer, well (covered for display) & crest, minor repr., 35" W, 18¾" D, overall 34½" H $440.00
Stoneware Jars, three w/ lids, two w/ salt glaze, barrel shaped has br. Albany slip, minor chips, 8", 8½" & 9" H $55.00
Chocolate Mold, tin, two part mold w/ separate two part mold for ears & front legs, Germany, 18½" H .$220.00
Bentwood Box, oval w/ laced seams & spring latch lid, ref. w/ traces of blue, 15" L $165.00

A-OH Dec. 1996   Garth's Auctions

Art Deco Clock, lighted & dated 1959, mah. red, cream & gold, working, case has minor wear, 3½" x 5" x 5½" $71.50
Art Deco Lamp, globe of leaded multi-colored glass, blk. stone base & cast metal w/ dk. bronze finish, 14¾" L, 12" H $412.50
Jack-in-the-pulpit Vase, white & yel. irid. w/ deep red int. & dec. in greenish red, mkd. "Czechoslovakia", 12" H $324.50

A-OH Dec. 1996 Garth's Auctions

Plantation Desk, ref. cherry & walnut, two dovetailed drawers, drawers rebuilt, top & base mismatched, 42" W, cornice is 14¼" x 47¾", base is 29½" x 43¾", 76¾" H $770.00

Lace Maker's Pillow, w/ wooden bobbins $165.00

Candle Box, dovetailed, pine w/ stained blue/gr. repaint w/ drapery & foliage scrolls in blue, red & white, lid slides from wide side, 15⅜" L $192.50

Splint Baskets, two woven, oval Woodland Indian w/ swivel handle, 9½" x 11½", 5½" H, round one w/ dk. patina, applied foot has damage, 14" D, 9" H plus handle $165.00

Two Pcs., tobacco cutter w/ horse head blade, 13" L & rush light holder, wrt. iron w/ candle socket counter weight, replaced wooden base, 15" H $165.00

A-MA Dec. 1996 Skinner, Inc.

Left to Right

George III Tea Caddy, inlaid mahogany, late 18th c., inlaid w/ oval reserve of shell, checkered banding & lines, minor losses, 5½" H, 6¼" W, 4" D $460.00

Double Tea Caddy, Regency silver mounted blonde tortoiseshell, early 19th c., rectangular-form, two oval topped int. caddies, losses, no mixing bowl, 5" H, 11¾" W, 5" D . .$1,265.00

George III Tea Caddy, boxwood & harewood inlay, late 18th c., w/ three foliate inlaid oval panels, 5½" H, 6¾" W, 4 -1/2" D $316.25

A-OH Dec. 1996 Garth's Auctions

"Kimball" Pump Reed Organ, oak case w/ Eastlake detail, worn finish, knob labels missing, not working, 43" W, 22¾" D, 74" H $2,750.00

A-MA Dec. 1996 Skinner, Inc.

Jewelry Cabinet, unusual Victorian painted papier mache, mid 19th c., lift top w/ fitted int., two doors enclosing sm. drawers, minor restorations, 12" H, 10" W, 10" D $517.50

A-MA Dec. 1996 Skinner, Inc.

Marble Desk Set, Empire Revival gilt bronze mounted, Verte Antico, late 19th c., letter holder, standish, blotter & weight, foot missing $1,035.00

A-MA Dec. 1996 Skinner, Inc.

Folio Cabinet, ebonized & parcel-gilt, fourth quarter 19th c., 61" H, 40½" W, 6¼" D $1,380.00

A-OH Aug. 1996 Garth Auctions

Empire Ladies Secretary, two pc., mag. veneer, wear & edge damage, missing veneer, three dovetailed drawers & fold down writing shelf, 38¼" W, cornice is 12" x 42¼", base is 18" x 39¾", 59½" H $330.00

Staffordshire Chimney Piece, William Penn & child, polychrome enamel, finial restored & minor enamel flaking, 10¼" H $220.00

Staffordshire Chimney Piece, Scotsman w/ dog & gun, polychrome enamel is flaked, prof. repair, 13½" H $275.00

Staffordshire Chimney Piece, couple w/ flowers, polychrome enamel is flaked, 10¾" H $247.50

Empire Shelf Clock, triple decker by "Seth Thomas, rosewood veneer w/ ref. pilasters, brass works, painted face & weights, pendulum & key, worn paper label, center glass has been replaced, wear & veneer damage, 32½" H $220.00

A-OH Nov. 1996 Garth's Auctions

Eng. Settle Bench, dovetailed drawers, oak & pine w/ old grained repaint, damage, 82½" W, 21" D, 69" H . . .$440.00
Sawtooth Trammel, wrt. iron, pitted, 36½" L $137.50
Hooked Rag Rug, multi-colored animal on br. ground, on stretcher, 41" W, 26" H $302.50
Iron Skillets, two early, wrt. handles, repairs & sm. holes in pan, mkd. handle, 13" diam., 37¾" handle; not pictured, 11½" diam., 14½" handle $104.50
Copper Pans, six, w/ lids, repr., three mkd. "Bazar Francais, New York", 6" to 9½" diam. $302.50
Two Pcs., cast brass kettle w/ wrt. iron bail handle, 9½" diam., & dovetailed copper tea kettle w/ swivel handle, battered, repairs, finial repl., 8½" H $93.50
Balance Scale, cast iron w/ old blk. tin hopper, three weights, 26" H $165.00
Stoneware Crock, "4" & flourish in cobalt blue, chips, 11¾" H . . .$126.50
Cooking Utensils, three cast iron, skillet, 10½" diam.; skillet w/ lid, 13½" diam.; pot w/ lid & ears for handle, 11" diam. .$159.50
Old Iron, six pcs., damage or repr., tin snips, two skillets, tea kettle, sm. tea kettle & trivet w/ fork rest $165.00

A-OH Nov. 1996 Garth's Auctions

Brass Candlesticks, two, similar, one base battered, 5⅝" & 5⅞"$440.00
Staffordshire, hen on nest, polychrome, minor edge wear & chips, 10½" L . .$715.00
Chippendale Chest, mah. w/ old fin. & good figure, four dovetailed drawers, pine secondary wood, orig. brasses, age cracks, 38" W, 33¼" H $13,200.00

A-OH Nov. 1996 Garth's Auctions

Jelly Cupboard, ref. walnut, 42⅜" W, 56½" H $440.00
Hanging Clock, Oak case w/ alligatored varnish, worn paper label "Waterbury Clock Co.", brass works & pendulum w/ key, 19" H $137.50
Country Stand, walnut w/ old finish, dovetailed drawer & one board top, poplar secondary wood, 18¼" x 21", 27½" H $220.00
Gaudy Ironstone, seven pcs. in red, gr., blue & blk. dec., plate 8" diam., six handleless cups & saucers . .$220.00
High Chair, stripped of blk. paint, wear, edge damage & minor repairs, 32" H $225.50
Tin Cake Stand, w/ cover & pan, base w/ four conical legs, 13" diam. $330.00
Pewter Plates, three, pr. mkd. "London" 9¾" diam., wear & scratches, Ger. touch, 9⅜" diam. $214.50
Pewter Charger, Eng., "Made in London", touch, wear & scratches, 16⅝" diam. $247.50

A-PA Apr. 1997 Horst Auction Center

Folk Art, mid 20th C., sgn. hand carved, by Carl Snavely of Lititz, PA, 7⅛" W, 3⅝" D, 7" H $800.00
Folk Art Painting, framed & singed "D. Ellinger", late 20th C., 20⅛" W, 20⅛" H $2,200.00
Folk Art Watercolor, framed & sgn. "D. Ellinger", late 20th C., 9¾" W, 8⅜" H $1,100.00

A-OH Nov. 1996 Garth's Auctions

Chest of Drawers, ref. cherry, three dovetailed drawers & paneled ends, cut down in height, 42¾" W, 34½" H $341.00
Banquet Lamp, cast iron & brass w/ old gilding, white onyx insert in stem, mkd. "B. & H.", electrified & repl. globe, edge damage, 27½" H $330.00
Lamp, peachblow font, swirled ribs & brass base, 11½" H $220.00
Banquet Lamp, cast iron, white metal & brass w/ gold repaint, greyish amber onyx stem, electrified, 29½" H . . .$137.50

A-OH Nov. 1996 Garth's Auctions

Empire Chest, ref. cherry, paneled ends & three dovetailed drawers, top drawer removed, 40¼" W, 39" H $385.00
Cloisonné Plates, pr., polychrome dec. on blue ground, wear & hairlines, scratches in enamel, repr., 12" diam. $247.50
Hepplewhite Mirror, bowfront, mah. veneer on pine w/ inlay, one dovetailed drawer, old repr. on feet, 14¼" W, 7¼" D, 16" H $165.00
Oriental Carvings, three ivory, man w/ monkey & child; man w/ fish & man w/ crane, damage, two w/ wooden stands, 6" to 6½" H $742.50
Cloisonné Vases, Japanese, pr., polychrome flowers & butterflies, 6" H$154.00

A-OH Nov. 1996   Garth's Auctions

Pieced Quilt, maltese cross medallions, gr. & red sateen, edges turned & rebound, some wear, 66" x 84" $247.50

Oak Ice Box, ref., label "Leonard Cleanable Refrigerator", white porcelain int., 35" W, 21½" D, 46¾" H $330.00

Oak Secretary, w/ applied carving, repairs & ref., 36½" W, 11½" D, 68" H $385.00

Ice Box, various hardwoods w/ varnish, weathered surface, 23" W, 15½" D, 40" H $192.50

Oak High Chair, w/ press carved detail, cane seat & back, 39¾" H $275.00

"Edison" Phonograph, in oak case, built in horn w/ grill, recovered in white fabric, working, 31 cylinders, 12½" x 16" $385.00

Mickey Mouse Talkie-Jector, W.D. Ent, in sheet steel case, incomplete but has cord & six rolls of paper film, 13" L ...$137.50

Owen China Vase, pink & white w/ transfer of woman, molded mark, "Swasticka, Keramos", 11¾" H $247.50

Pedal Tractor, sheet steel w/ hard rubber wheels, red & white & blk. "Farmall", wear & some damage, 38" L $88.00

A-OH Nov. 1996   Garth's Auctions

Victorian Étagére, walnut w/ old finish, one dovetailed drawer, minor edge damage, 32¼" W, 16¼" D, 54½" H $550.00

Victorian Shaving Stand, walnut w/ mah. veneer & old fin., some edge & veneer damage, age cracks, repr., 61" H ...$385.00

Porcelain Tea Set, eight pc., molded ribs, polychrome rose dec. & "M" mark in underglaze blue, five cups & seven saucers, chips $412.50

Mantle Clock, ironstone china case, enameling w/ gilt, brass works, mkd. "Ansonia", case mkd. "Mochican", edge flakes, w/ pendulum, 10¾" H $302.50

A-PA Nov. 1996   Pook & Pook Inc.

Store Coffee Grinder, Massive Enterprise Mfg. Co., 19th c., orig. red dec. surface w/ blk. pinstriping & decals, 59" H .$3,750.00

Corner Cupboard, PA, dec., early 19th C., orig. coggle dec. mustard surface, 75½" H $4,250.00

Stoneware Pitcher, PA, w/ blue dec. in tree patt., 7½" H $225.00

Stoneware Ovoid Crock, PA, w/ blue floral dec., chips, 13¼" H $350.00

Stoneware Pitcher, PA, blue dec., repr. to rim, 9" H $275.00

Rocking Horse, Victorian, carved wood & iron, orig. blk. painted surface, 28" H, 34" L $550.00

A-OH Dec. 1996   Garth's Auctions

Chippendale Chest, ref. cherry, four overlapping dovetailed drawers, pine & poplar secondary woods, replaced brasses, feet, repairs, edge damage, 19¾" x 42½" $522.50

Epergene, w/ four trumpet vases, clear & opal. blue w/ threading, minor chips, 17¾" H ....N/S

Pottery Vase, impr. "Doulton Lambeth Faience", sgn. "AS", holly on a deep blue ground, 11½" H ...$275.00

Porcelain Urn, polychrome w/ gilt, scenes by Angelica Kauffman, Potschappel Factory w/ Carl Thieme mark, chips & some edge damage, 21¾" H $1,375.00

A-PA Nov. 1996   Pook & Pook Inc.

Chippendale Desk, PA, Chester Co., cherry slant lid, mkd. "C. Beary" of Coventry Twp. 1797-1833, ca. 1800, 4 beaded edge drawers, restorations to lid & feet, 43½"H, 41¼"W ..$8,500.00

A-MA June 1997   Skinner, Inc.

Pot Cupboards, faux marbelized, early 19th C., paint of later date, 26¾" H $920.00

A-PA Nov. 1996   Pook & Pook Inc.

Pewter Cupboard, N.J., open pine 2-pc., late 18th c., w/ cove cornice, 74½" H, 48" W $2,000.00
Delft Plates, group of 6 blue & white, ca. 1740, damages $200.00
Delft Plates, group of 5 blue & white, ca. 1740, damages $250.00
Delft Plates, group of 4, polychrome dec., ca. 1740, damages $375.00
Delft Plates, group of 5 blue & white, ca. 1740, damages $375.00
Delft Plates, group of 5 blue & white, ca. 1740, damages $425.00
Delft Plates, group 4 blue & white, ca. 1740; polychrome example, damages $500.00
Delft Garniture Set, blue & white, ca. 1750, 2 baluster form jars w/ lids & 2 vases, 8½" H, reprs., dam-ages $650.00
Stoneware Crock, five-gallon w/ blue dec., chip to rim, 12½"H $250.00

A-OH Dec. 1996   Garth's Auctions

Umbrella Stand, cast iron w/ Art Nouveau floral detail, old gr. repaint, 28½" H $137.50
Hitching Post, cast iron jockey boy, polychrome repaint, 37½" H .$357.50
Garden Urn, cast iron on sq. plinth, bolts replaced & bowl is loose, old blk. repaint, 25" H $165.00

A-PA Nov. 1996   Pook & Pook Inc.

Q.A. Looking Glass, mah. veneer, ca. 1730, w/ scalloped crest & molded frame, glass is old replacement 30½" H $600.00
Chippendale Mirror, Eng., mah. veneered, ca. 1770, w/ ornate scalloped crest & gilded phoenix, glass old replacement 39½" H 2,600.00
Chippendale Mirror, PA, mah. veneered, late 18th c., w/ carved giltwood phoenix crest & backboards bearing the Eng. & Ger. label of John Elliott, 37" H $3,750.00
Banjo Form Barometer, Eng. rosewood by D. Fagioli, London, early 19th c., retains orig. gilt dec., 37½" H $750.00
Ship's Barometer, brass gimbaled, early 20th c., 36" H $450.00
George II Gaming Table, mah. w/ leather inlaid round top w/ pockets, acanthus carved knees w/ ball & claw feet, 29" H, 37½" W $2,250.00
Q.A. Bachelor's Chest, Eng., mah., early 18th c., w/ folding top, 30" H, 33" W $3,750.00
Canton Platter, blue & white, hairline, together w/ 7 blue & white **Fitzhugh plates** $950.00
Rose Medallion Vases, four baluster form, late 19th c., some losses, each 10½" H $400.00
Rose Medallion Teapots, ornithological dec., butterfly dec. gold reserve, repr. to handle, 10"H; sm. Chinese export globular form teapot, 6" H $375.00
Chinese Export Teapots, two, late 18th c. w/ 2 export mugs, some repairs $800.00
Chinese Export Teapots, 4 porcelain, late 18th/early 19th c., chips & repairs $375.00

A-PA Nov. 1996   Pook & Pook Inc.

Corner Cupboard, PA., Lebanon Co., grain dec., early 19th c., upper section has 9-light. 83" H, 47" W . . .$4,500.00
Corner Shelf, N.E. folk art grain dec., early 19th c., prob. Maine, 70¾" H $2,000.0
Rocking Horse, Victorian child's calf-skin, orig. leather saddle & red pin stripe dec. base, 31½" H, 46" L $550.00
Kings Rose Deep Dish, 10" diam.. , together w/ 6 plates, 8" diam.$900.00
Staffordshire Teapots, purple grape leaf patt.; teapot w/ purple transfer dec. $350.00
Majolica Teapot & covered sugar bowl in cauliflower patt., repr. to handle of sugar $325.00
Staffordshire Coffee Pots, sepia transfer dec. dome lidded, repr. to spout; Lustre grape leaf ironstone coffee pot $250.00

A-PA Nov. 1996   Pook & Pook Inc.

Chest of Drawers, Am. William & Mary, ca., retains orig. red painted surface, 36½" H, 36" W $1,800.00
N.E. Pine Chair Table, ca. 1740, retains fine old scrubbed surface, 28" H, 53¼" diam.. . . . .$12,000.00
Stoneware Batter Jug, blue dec., mkd. "Cowden & Wilcox, Harrisburg", 2 hairlines, 9" H $800.00

A-MA Oct. 1996   Skinner, Inc.

Stickley Oak Arm Rocker, orig. med.-brn. finish, repl. leather cushions, 31¾" W, 30" D, 42½" H $1,380.00

J.M. Young Bookcase, single drawer w/ twelve mullions, ref., 33¾" W, 14" D, 50½" H $1,725.00

Roseville Futura Jardiniere, crisp mold w/ pink & lavender leaves on a gray ground, 9" diam., 6" H . .$402.50

Gustav Stickley Plant Stand, w/ arched apron, early mark, orig. finish, minor wear, 14" sq., 28" H .$2,415.00

Roseville Vista Jardiniere, strong mold in colors of gr., purple & gray, 12" diam., 10¼" H $546.25

A-MA Oct. 1996   Skinner, Inc.

Stickley Sideboard, ref. & repl. hardware, int. painted gr., 46½" W, 22" D, 45" H $3,335.00

Weller Faience Vase, w/ incised standing rabbits, on a tobacco br. & yel. ground, sgn. Rhead, 7" diam., 9½" H $1,840.00

Weller Faience Vase, white & gr. on a tobacco br. high glaze body, sgn. Rhead, 6½" W, 7½" H $1,840.00

A-MA June 1997   Skinner, Inc.

Traveling Tea Set, Fr. gilt metal cased, early 20th C., by Maquet, w/ two teapots, four spoons, tongs, burner, tea caddy & two Nymphenburg porcelain teacups & saucers .$517.50

A-MA Oct. 1996   Skinner, Inc.

Stickley Desk, double bank, orig. worn finish, minor veneer chips, 59½" W, 33½" D, 30¼" H $3,737.50

School Lamp, Bradley & Hubbard Prairie, painted gold metal frame w/ purple, blue & yel. slag glass, 16" sq., 21" H $1,380.00

Weller Woodcraft Vase, dec. w/ owl & squirrel on a gr. & br. tree trunk, mkd. Weller, 7" W, 18" H $747.50

A-MA Oct. 1996   Skinner, Inc.

Fountain Frog, bright gr. & br. glaze, hole in base & mouth for tube, mkd. "12", 6½" W, 5½" H $632.50

Weller Aurelian Vase, dec. w/ four blossoming irises, sgn. by L.J. Dibowski, mkd. Weller, Aurelian, minor glaze nicks, 13" W, 24½" H .$1,955.00

Floor Lamp, Shop of the Crafters, red, gr., yel. & white leaded glass shade over orig. oil burner lamp, orig. dk. finish & paper label, 24½" sq., 72" H $4,600.00

Straddle Chair, Roycroft, red leather w/ brass tacks, mah., orb & cross mark, 23¾"W, 22"D, 34"H $7,475.00

A-MA Oct. 1996   Skinner, Inc.

Stickley Sideboard, ref. & repl. hardware, int. painted gr., 60" W, 23" D, 45" H . . .$4,600.00

Hampshire Lamp Base, pottery, matte gr. glaze, unmkd. 9" diam., 15" H $2,185.00

Jarvie Candlesticks, pr. brass, orig. patina, incised Jarvie w/ triangle mark, 5¾" W, 13½" H . . . . .N/S

Grueby Pottery Vase, rich deep gr. matte glaze w/ white highlighting, nick, minor glaze imper., 7¾" W, 9½" H $2,415.00

A-MA Oct. 1996   Skinner, Inc.

Stickley Dining Chairs, five, orig. finish, handcraft decal, partial paper label, 19" W, 16" D, 36" H $2,185.00

Stickley Dining Table, four long corbels mounted on pedestal base, two hide-away legs, one leaf, ref., brand mark, 54" diam., 29" H $3,105.00

Roseville Futura Jardiniere, mold w/ pink & lavender leaves on a gray ground, paper label, 12" diam., 8" H $690.00

Chandelier, heavy brass frame containing six caramel colored bent slag glass panels, 19-inches of heavy brass chain & mounting, 25" diam. . .$977.50

A-MA June 1997   Skinner, Inc.

Marble Plaque, Italian inlaid blk., 20th C., depicting the Doves of Pliny, 6¼" L $460.00

Jewelry Box, Italian, late 19th C., stamped C. Roccheggiani, Roma, on bird & foliate feet, 6" W, 5" D, 4" H $4,830.00

A-MA Oct. 1996   Skinner, Inc.

Stickley Sideboard, orig. finish, one drawer lined w/ leather, some veneer loss on doors, 67" W, 24" D, 48" H . .$4,025.00
Art Pottery Tile, dec. w/ landscape w/ moose under a dk. gr. high gloss glaze, 12" W, 6" H $172.50
Art Pottery Tile, dec. w/ landscape w/ birds & a moose in the foreground under a dk. gr. high gloss glaze, 12" W, 6" H $172.50

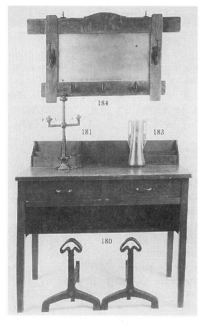

A-MA Oct. 1996   Skinner, Inc.

Stickley Mirror, w/ coat hangers, orig. hooks, ref., 37½" W, 20½" H $632.50
Arts & Crafts Lamp Base, brass, foliate-form under dk. patina, missing mica shades, 11" W, 18" H . . . . .N/S
Fulper Pottery Vase, crystalline gr. glaze, vertical ink stamp & paper label, 4½" diam., 11" H $460.00
Stickley Writing Desk, two drawers over open shelf, orig. finish, sgn. w/ Gustav red mark, loss to seam on top, 39¾" W, 22½" D, 36" H $1,955.00
Stickley Andirons, wrt. iron, each sgn. w/ impr. mark, 13½" W, 18" D, 16" H $9,975.00

A-MA Oct. 1996   Skinner, Inc.

Arts & Crafts Chandelier, yel. & caramel/green slag glass, some damage, 27" diam., 18" H $1,380.00
Pewter Fish Tureen, Old Newbury, hand-hammered finish w/ applied fish handles incl. ladle, impr. mark, 12" diam., 12½" H $460.00
Stickley Dining Chairs, orig. finish w/ old overcoat, sgn. w/ Gustav red mark, 17" W, 16½" D, 39½" H $862.50
Stickley Dining Table, corbel form base, four leaves, orig. finish, sgn., veneer missing, 54" diam. .$3,737.50

A-MA Oct. 1996   Skinner, Inc.

Left to Right

Copper Fire Starter, Old Mission KopperKraft, impr. mark, 8" diam., 9¼" H . . . . .N/S
Arts & Crafts Smoking Stand, copper top w/ pyramid tacks, push button lock, unmkd., 9¼" sq., 25"H $1,092.50
Harden Settee, orig. finish, veneer loss to posts, 54½" W, 24¼" D, 38½" H $862.50

A-MA Apr. 1997   Skinner, Inc.

Mini. Hall Letterbox, Victorian oak, ca. 1880, w/ hexagonal-shaped top & glass inset door, 17" H $3,556.00

A-MA Oct. 1996   Skinner, Inc.

Andirons, ca. 1920, heavy wrt. iron w/ protruding animal faces, 19" W, 28" D, 56" H $2,300.00
Stickley China Cabinet, double-door, 16 panes of glass, one cracked, orig. finish, paper label, 42" W, 15¼" D, 62½" H $5,175.00
Grueby Pottery Jardiniere, deep gr. matte glaze, impr. mark, hairline, 8¾" diam., 5¼" H $690.00
Stickley Reclining Chair, unmkd., orig. cushions, ref., unmkd., 32½" W, 37½" D, 40" H $5,750.00

A-MA Sept. 1996   Skinner, Inc.

Medicine Chest, British brass mounted, mid 19th c., a fitted int. of pigeonholes & drawers, 15" H, 13" W, 7½" D $862.50

A-MA Apr. 1997   Skinner, Inc.

Figural Hall Tree, or umbrella stand, Blk. Forest carved walnut, late 19th C., oiled finish, 84" H $4,600.00

A-PA Jan. 1997   Pook & Pook Inc.

Row 1, Left to Right

Sheffield Candlesticks, two pairs of Adams style, mid 19th C., 11" H, w/ 2 later pairs of silver plated candlesticks, losses $500.00
Sheffield Candlesticks, two pairs of Adams style, mid 19th C.,w/ later pr. of silver plated candlesticks, 11" H $450.00

Row 2, Left to Right

Candelabrum, two similar cut glass, early 20th C, tear shaped prisms above blue & white Wedgwood base w/ brass mounts, 12" H $800.00
Sheffield Candlesticks, pr., 19th C., w/ hurricane globes w/ another pr. & a single, all lacking globes . . .$600.00
Candelabra, pr. of Eng. crystal, ca. 1800, clear prisms & porcelain bases w/ gilt brass mounts, 12" H $1,500.00
Candelabra, pr. of Eng. cut crystal & brass, early 19th C., w/ blue & clear prisms & blue cut to clear base, 10½" H $1,900.00

A-PA April 1997   Pook & Pook Inc.

Dower Chest, Berks Co., late 18th C., lift lid w/ strap hinges, 2 ora. & yel. pots of flowers & heart & floral dec. corners on blue/green ground, orig. brasses, overpainted w/ br. stain, 47" W, 31" H $2,500.00
Storage Box, dome lidded bowfront, early 19th C., overall ochre grain dec., 20½" W, 9" H $700.00
Pitcher, stoneware, 19th C., w/ blue floral dec., 7½" H $300.00
Crock, stoneware mkd. "White Utica", 10½" H, together w/ redware pie plate w/ slip dec., 19th C., 10¼" diam. $325.00

A-PA April 1997   Pook & Pook Inc.

Side Chair, CT, banister back, early 18th C., w/ rush seat & ball & ring turned front stretcher, together w/ another similar chair, worn & damaged $200.00
Band Box, NY City, ca. 1820, damages $650.00
Chest of Drawers, Long Island, walnut, late 18th C., orig. oval pulls, 35" W, 43" H . . . . .N/S
Mini. Bureau, William & Mary style oak, 19th C., w/ 4 drawers, 10" H $450.00
Band Box, NY City w/ view of Castle Garden, ca. 1920, damaged . .$450.00
Stoneware Crock, ovoid, impr. "D. Goodale Hartford", w/ blue floral dec., cracks, 14½" 350.00

A-PA April 1997   Pook & Pook Inc.

Corner Cupboard, mah., southern, ca. 1810, 20-light door, lower section w/ 2 sunken panel doors above skirt w/ line & dart inlay over oval inlaid cartouche, 44" W, 92½" H $11,000.00
Porcelain Service, by Copeland in the Willow patt., ca. 1900, comprising 24 dinner plates, 6 soup bowls, 2 covered sauce tureens, vegetable dish, soup tureen w/ undertray, minor chips $1,150.00

A-PA April 1997   Pook & Pook Inc.

Tavern Table, Lancaster Co. painted pine, ca. 1800, retaining orig. red painted surface, 33" L, 27" H $1,600.00
Tray, New Eng., tole dec., ca. 1800, w/ basket of roses on a blk. ground, 18" x 13½" $1,000.00
Eagle Banks, two, cast iron .$325.00
Doll Cradle, PA, ca. 1800, retaining orig. red painted surface, 19" L $175.00
Windsor Armchair, PA, branded "T. Gilpen", ca. 1750, retains old 19th C. br. varnished surface, branded on the underside $12,000.00
Crock, stoneware by F.H. Cowden, Harrisburg, PA, 19th C., w/ 'baby face' dec., 7½" H $850.00

A-PA April 1997   Pook & Pook Inc.

Q.A. Side Chair, walnut, DL Valley, ca. 1760 . . . .$2,100.00
Q.A. Table, Chester Co., tiger maple, ca. 1770, retains fine old finish, 45" W, 28½" H $9,500.00

Left to Right

Plate, Gaudy Dutch in Single Rose patt., 10" diam. $900.00
Plate, Gaudy Dutch in Zinnia patt., impr. Riley, 8¼" diam. $900.00
Deep Dish & Plate, Gaudy Dutch in the Double Rose patt., 9¾" diam. & 10" diam. $1,300.00
Deep Dishes, two Gaudy Dutch in the War Bonnet patt., 8¼" diam. $1,300.00
Deep Dish & Plate, Gaudy Dutch in the Double Rose patt., 9¾" diam. & 10" diam. $1,300.00
Plates, two, Gaudy Dutch in the Butterfly patt., 7½" diam. & 8" diam. $1,800.00

A-PA June 1997   Pook & Pook, Inc.

Row 1, Left to Right

Oil on Canvas, portrait of a woman, inscribed verso "Anna Burneston wife of Wm. Baker, born Oct. 28, 1757", 36" x 29" $300.00

Lithograph, Am. of various types of racing fire engines, ca. 1880, w/ some hand coloring, minor losses, 40" x 30" $300.00

Row 2, Left to Right

Cupboard, painted pine, ca. 1800, retains orig. blue painted surface, 51" W, 43½" H $2,250.00

Copper Molds, group of 4, ca. 1900, of various forms $475.00

Cooking Molds, four copper, ca. 1900, varous patterns $550.00

Wire Cage, lighthouse form, late 19th C., w/ 3 sm. arched doors, 5' H $500.00

Row 3, Left to Right

Transit, by W. & L.E. Gurley, Troy, NY, in orig. carrying case, damage to case $350.00

Copper Mold, ca. 1900, w/ brass handles, 22" diam. $425.00

Cooking Pots, assembled set of seven graduated copper, ca. 1900, one stamped "L. Barth & Son, NY", 5" to 14½" diam. $450.00

Cooking Pots, three graduated copper, ca. 1900, one stamped "GL" $200.00

A-IA Mar. 1997   Jacksons

Spurs, Hopalong Cassidy, very good condition $198.00

A-PA June 1997   Pook & Pook, Inc.

Watercolor, George Howell Gay (Am. 1858-1931), fall scene w/ country road, sgn. lower right, 14" x 32" $550.00

Windsor Armchair, New Eng., sackback, ca. 1790, w/ scrolled arms, baluster turned legs $1,200.00

Chippendale Table, DL Valley, walnut, ca. 1770, single drawer, 48½" W, 28½" H $2,500.00

Windsor Armchair, New Eng., sackback, ca. 1790, w/ scrolled arms & baluster turned legs, retains old surface, restoration to legs $900.00

Fed. Andirons, pr., brass, ca. 1800 w/ ball tops, octagonal shafts & ball feet, 19½" H $200.00

Fed. Andirons, pr., brass, ca. 1810, 15" H, together w/ later pr. of cast iron andirons of Dutch boy & girl .$225.00

A-PA April 1997   Pook & Pook Inc.

Quilt, Sepia copper plate, two-sided in Bromley Hall patt., ca. 1775, some staining, 77" x 77" $600.00

Windsor Chairs, pr., continuous scrolled arm, ca. 1820, triple gutter carvcd cdgc $1,800.00

Tavern Table, pine & mah., ca. 1800, retains orig. br. painted surface, 19"diam., 25½" H $3,200.00

Crock, stoneware, Remmey type, 4 gal. w/ profuse blue dec., 13" H $250.00

Canister, lidded redware w/ manganese splash dec., chipped, 10" H, together w/ similar sm. canister, 6½" H, redware lid & redware pie plate $250.00

Bean Pot, redware covered, w/ extensive manganese splash dec., together w/ sm. turkshead mold, a stoneware jug mkd. "R.L. Chambers, Newark, NJ", a beanpot & a sm. jug $200.00

A-MA Sept. 1996   Skinner, Inc.

Table Globes, Cary's 12-Inch Terrestrial & Celestial, ca. 1830, the terrestrial corrected to 1827, the celestial to 1800, to top meridian 18" H $4,140.00

A-MA Sept. 1996   Skinner, Inc.

"Franklin" Globe, Am. 6-Inch Terrestrial, by Merriam, Moore & Co., Troy, N.Y., ca. 1852 . . . .$2,415.00

A-MA June 1997   Skinner, Inc.

Terrestrial Globe, Regency, 12" by Bardin of London, corrected to 1817, w/ ebonized four leg stand, losses, 16" H $1,380.00

A-MA Apr. 1997   Skinner, Inc.

Celestial Table Globe, Am. 6-Inch, by Gilman Joslin, ca. 1840, on a cherrywood stand, minor abrasions $4,025.00

A-PA Jan. 1997   Pook & Pook Inc.

Dutch Cupboard, PA, ca. 1800, two 6-light doors, w/ plate rails & spoon rack, 52" W, 20¾" D, 83¼" H $7,500.00
Mountain Goats, pr. of Blk. Forest carved groups, painted white, 27" H $2,750.00
Bentwood Boxes, oval Shaker type, w/ a Shaker swift & a ballot box $450.00
Bentwood Boxes, three Shaker, together w/ another similar example .$1,000.00
Sugar Bowl, blue & white Leeds canister form, together w/ another example lacking lid & 2 other Staffordshire sugar bowls, lids by association $425.00

A-PA Jan. 1997   Pook & Pook Inc.

Windsor Side Chairs, pr. of child's squirrel cage w/ bamboo turnings $1,000.00
Redware Charger, PA, early 19th C., w/ 4-slip trailing line & swag design, 13⅛" diam. . . . . .N/S
Redware Charger, early 19th C., inscribed yel. slip "Lafayette", minor chips, 12" diam. $2,600.00
Redware Charger, PA, early 19th C., w/ extensive 3-slip line & swag dec., 12¾" diam. $2,000.00

A-PA April 1997   Pook & Pook Inc.

Dower Chest, PA, Berks Co., salmon painted background & the date "Anno 1804", panels w/ blk. & gr. flowers, corners dec. w/ gr. hearts w/ white, 50" W, 24" H $2,100.00
Jelly Cupboard, child's, mid 19th C., retaining orig. red painted surface, 19" W, 29½" H $950.00
Hanging Cupboard, walnut, Lancaster Co, ca. 1750, orig. rat tail hinges & escut., lower portion of base reduced, 25¼" W, 14¼" D, 33½" H $1,300.00
Windsor Rocker, PA, child's w/ orig. br. & stencil dec. $275.00
Stoneware Crocks, two blue dec., late 19th C. w/ floral dec. . . .$325.00
Doll Furniture, 19th C., Victorian dropleaf table, wicker side chair, losses, & a cane seat rocker $325.00

A-PA April 1997   Pook & Pook Inc.

Pitcher, stoneware, 19th C., w/ blue leaf & wriggle work incised dec., 6" H $400.00
Pipe Rack, mah., early 19th C., together w/ walnut hanging pipe box $425.00
Mini. Portrait, attrib. to Charles Wilson Peale, oval of a lady in a blue dress, 2" x 1½" .N/S
Grotesque Bank, Southern stoneware, 20th C., some chips, hole in base, 8" H $300.00
Tea Caddy, Eng. apple form fruitwood, ca. 1790, lacking stem, escut. $800.00

A-PA June 1997   Pook & Pook, Inc.

Chippendale Secretary Desk, New Eng., cherry oxbow, tambour door w/ inlaid prospect door, lower section w/ flip top writing surface over 4 long drawers, molded base, 41½" W, 48" H . . . . .N/S
Canton Water Pitcher, Chinese export blue & white, repr., 14" H $325.00
Canton Pitcher, Chinese export blue & white, 9¾" H $1,150.00
Canton Pitcher, Chinese export blue & white, 8½" H $900.00
Canton Pitcher, Chinese export blue & white, 7¾" H $950.00
Canton Pitcher, Chinese export blue & white, 6" H $950.00
Cut Out, PA, mid 19th C., w/ a central serrated heart flanked by birds, sm. swans etc., 8¾" x 7" $250.00
Crewelwork Picture, silk, lion, 18th C., w/ fruit tree, losses, 11½" x 8½" $2,700.00
Canton Vase, Chinese export blue & white, w/ Ming leaf dec., 12½" H $1,100.00
Banjo Clock, Fed. mah. by Stephenson, Howard & David, Boston, ca. 1849, eglomise throat panel w/ gilt & floral dec. on a yel. ground, repaint, lacking weights, 33½" L . . . . .N/S
Canton Charger, Chinese export blue & white, sm. chip, 16¼" L $600.00
Candlestand, Fed. mah., w/ oblong cut corner top w/ reeded edge, brass castors, 26" L, 27" H $2,100.00
Canton Pitcher & Bowl, Chinese export blue & white, 16" diam., 13" H $2,900.00

A-MA Apr. 1997   Skinner, Inc.

George III Tea Caddy, fruitwood apple-form, ca. 1790, golden yel. color, foil lined int., 4½" diam., 4½" H $1,150.00

A-PA Jan. 1997   Pook & Pook Inc.

Corner Cupboard, PA, paint dec., ca. 1810, w/ overall tiger grained yel. & ochre surface, 12-light door, over base w/ 2 paneled doors & short bracket feet, 85" H $4,750.00

Grotesque Mug, Am. stoneware, 20th C., w/ overall br. glazing, by Marie Rogers, GA, 5" H $275.00

Redware Mold, Am., early 19th C., w/ swirled body & manganese splash dec., 7" diam., w/ slip dec. earthenware bird house $325.00

Pitcher, earthenware w/ manganese stripes & yel. slip heart w/ date "1879", 8" H, together w/ sm. redware pitcher w/ yel. slip swags centering on manganese splash dots, repar to sm. pitcher $400.00

Staffordshire Tureen, blue & white transfer dec, repr., together w/ platter, early 19th C., w/ hunting scene, impr. "Adams", 18½" L $900.00

Octagonal Plate, redware slip dec. & molded w/ cross hatch slip dec. & relief tree design, repr., 8½" diam. $200.00

Tall Case Clock, PA, mah., ca. 1800, turned rosettes & free standing columns, 8-day works w/ white painted face inscribed "David Weatherly, PHILAD", orig. turned feet, 96½" H $7,000.00

Spinning Wheel, maple, late 18th C., w/ ivory mounts, losses, 34½" $400.00

Am. Redwood Mold, early 19th C., w/ swirled body & manganese splash dec., 7" diam., w/ slip dec. earthenware bird house $325.00

Carved Figures, two folk art, 20th C., incl. reclining bathing beauty, polychromed relief sgn. "S.L. Jones" $475.00

Victorian Sleigh, Am., child's push sleigh, w/ red & gilt pinstriped dec. $600.00

A-PA Jan. 1997   Pook & Pook Inc.

Pembroke Table, PA, mah., ca. 1790, patched leaves, 31½" W, 28" H $1,800.00

Chippendale Side Chair, DL Valley, cherry, ca. 1770, pierced splat, reeded stiles, repairs $4,000.00

Q.A. Basin Stand, mah., ca. 1790, 29½" H $950.00

Silver Water Pitcher, Am., by McMullen, PA, ca. 1820, w/ vase shaped body & die-rolled borders, 26 oz. total weight, repr., 10¼" H $500.00

Silver Waste Bowl, by Wiltberger, ca. 1795, w/ a beaded edge rim & sq. base, 15 oz. total weight, 6⅜" diam., 5⅝" H $1,200.00

A-PA Jan. 1997   Pook & Pook Inc.

Tall Case Clock, PA, late 18th C., 30-hour works & white face inscribed "Henry Hahn Reading", feet restored, 91" H $3,500.00

Q.A. Highboy, upper section w/ 4 drawers & base w/ long drawer over shell carved center drawer, married, 37¼" W, 77½" H $3,750.00

Canterbury, mah., ca. 1815 w/ single drawer & brass castors $1,800.00

Still Life Apples, oil on board, late 19th C., 8" x 10" $550.00

Still Life Fruit, oil on canvas, sgn. lower right "SCRS '92", in orig. gilt frame, sm. tear, 9½" x 22½" .$500.00

A-PA Jan. 1997   Pook & Pook Inc.

Mini. Cupboard, PA, walnut, ca. 1810, w/ molded edge top, 18½" x 11¾" . . $350.00

Pitcher & Bowl, transfer dec. ironstone, mkd. "Correla, B & S" .$300.00

Candlestand, walnut, PA, w/ round tilting dish top, 21" diam., 30½" H $1,600.00

New Eng. Settee, ca. 1820, dec. w/ stenciled back on gr. background, painted rush bowfront seat, 45" W, 33¼" H $2,100.00

Rockingham Humidor, 3-pc., w/ dolphin & shell dec. lid, relief dancing figures on main body, losses .$175.00

Batter Jug, "Cowden & Wilcox, Harrisburg, PA", w/ blue floral dec., 9" H N/S

Redware Urn, two-handled by Jacob Medinger w/ manganese splash dec., repairs, 11" H $450.00

Flower Pot, Shenandoah Valley redware, attrib. to Bell Pottery, seaweed patt. $350.00

Fraktur Marriage Cert., PA, dated 1828, w/ gr., yel. & red pin prick tulips, 13" x 8½" $1,200.00

A-PA Nov. 1996   Pook & Pook Inc.

Chippendale Side Chair, DE Valley, mah., ca. 1770 w/ foliate carved crest rail, gothic splat, slip seat . .$4,000.00

Pembroke Table, PA, mah., ca. 1780 w/ dropleaf top, single drawer retaining orig. brasses, blocked marlbrough legs joined by arched cross stretchers, 29" H, 22" W., 30" L $7,500.00

Q.A. Spice Chest, PA, Chester Co., walnut, ca. 1760, panel doors enclosing 14 sm. drawers, alterations to base 32½" H, 20¾" W. $11,000.00

A-PA April 1997   Pook & Pook Inc.

Oil on Canvas, portrait of gentleman, sgn. indistinctly verso & dated "1762", sm. tear, 33" x 24¾" $1,100.00

Huntboard, Midatlantic states, walnut, 19th C., 35" W, 44" H . .$2,500.00

Pitcher, cut glass, late 19th C., in star patt., 9" H $65.00

Boule Clock, J.E. Caldwell, poor condition, w/ a Waltham sterling silver dresser clock w/ foliate engr. frame, 10" H $550.00

Vase, cut glass, late 19th C., swirling diamond patt., 19½" H $475.00

Chippendale Clock, tall cherry case, dated 1792, 8-day works w/ painted dial & moon phase sgn. "Seneca Lukens fecit Jacob Meva 1792", 19½" W, 11" D, 93" H $13,000.00

A-PA June 1997   Pook & Pook, Inc.

Pitcher & Bowl, rainbow spatter, w/ blue & red dec., 19th C., 11½" H $700.00

Child's Bureau, PA, Hepplewhite mah., ca. 1810, w/ 4 drawers on Fr. bracket feet, 25" W, 28½" H $2,500.00

Q.A. Tall Chest, New Eng., tiger maple, ca. 1770, retains orig. brasses & surface, 36" W, 59" H $12,500.00

Fraktur, attrib. to Gustav S. Peters, ca. 1827-1847, 12" x 15" $350.00

A-PA April 1997   Pook & Pook Inc.

Spatterware Cups, two, red peafowl, & saucers, 19th C., sm. chips to rim of one cup $625.00

Spatterware Creamer, striped purple & br., 3¾" H, w/ gr. peafowl handleless cup & saucer & a blue star spatter cup & saucer, all 19th C., roughness .$750.00

Chest of Drawers, tiger maple, ca. 1800, fan inlaid corners, herringbone inlaid borders, restored straight bracket feet, 40" W, 39" H $4,100.00

Carved Eagle, Am. full bodied, late 19th C., 22¾" H $550.00

Dome Lidded Box, w/ orig. polychrome dec. panels, late 19th C. $425.00

Windsor Armchair, PA, combback, ca. 1760, w/ carved ear crest rail, retains old finish $4,000.00

Jacquard Coverlets, pr. of red, blue & gr. w/ roosters & floral patterns, each sgn. "John Smith 1836", made for "L. Walder", & "H. Walder" .$2,500.00

A-MA Mar. 1997   Maritime Auctions

Chronometer, marine, 56 hour, Russian origin, working condition $800.00

A-PA April 1997   Pook & Pook Inc.

Cupboard, PA, pine Dutch, ca. 1840, two arcaded 6-light doors, 59½" W, 93½" H $2,600.00

Following Six Items 19th C.
Amish Snow Flake Patt.

Bowls, eight, two impr. "SB", 9½" diam. $750.00

Coffee Service, comprising coffee pot, 9½" H, creamer, covered sugar, waste bowl & 12 cups w/ saucers $2,200.00

Plates, ten, 8¾" diam. $500.00

Ironstone, group comprising sm. pitcher, bowl, serving dish, nine 6½" diam. plates & four 7½" diam. plates $1,000.00

Platter, oval, 13¼" L $350.00

Platter, oval, 16¼" L $2,600.00

Stoneware Crock, 19th C., by Jas. Hamilton & Co., Greensboro, PA w/ eagle & floral dec., 24" H . .$1,900.00

Stoneware Crock, PA, blue floral dec., cracked, 16" H $200.00

A-MA Apr. 1997   Skinner, Inc.

Left to Right

Regency Tea Caddy, tortoiseshell sarcophagus-shaped, 19th C., two lidded wells in int., losses, 12¼" L $1,265.00

Regency Tea Caddy, tortoiseshell, 19th C., cushion-shaped, two int. lidded compartments, losses, 8¼" L . . .$1,265.00

A-PA June 1997   Pook & Pook, Inc.

Chippendale Desk, walnut, DL Valley, ca. 1800, slat lid opens over 4 long drawers, 40" W, 43" H $3,900.00

Silhouettes, pr. of hollow cut boy & girl, mid 19th C., period gilt frame $300.00

Rogers Pitcher, historical blue transfer dec., "State House Boston", 19th C., 8½" H $650.00

Rogers Bowl, historical blue transfer dec., "State House Boston", 19th C., 9¾" L $550.00

Platter, historical blue transfer decor, "Washington", 19th C., 16½" L $3,000.00

Clews Platter, historical blue transfer dec., "Landing of Gen. Lafayette", 19th C., minor rim flake, 19" L $1,100.00

A-PA Nov. 1996   Pook & Pook Inc.

Bass Parade Drum, by Horstman of PA, 19th c., w/ eagle & banner dec. on blue field & red bands, orig. leather & roping, 27" diam.. . . . .$7,000.00

Q.A. Child's Side Chair, New Eng., banister back, ca. 1740, retains early blk. surface w/ gold highlights, 31" H $2,600.00

Tavern Table, PA. pine & poplar, ca. 1780, w/ battened top, 29" H, 39" W . $1,600.00

Cased Waterline Model of the Maratania, 8½" H, 19" L $250.00

Canadian Goose Decoy, ca.1930, w/ cork bodied decoy & canvas back decoy $225.00

Wooden Churn, w/ vivid red & blk. grained surface $550.00

A-PA April 1997   Pook & Pook Inc.

Mirror, giltwood, ca. 1800, ebonized panel w/ raised gilt lattice work, lacking some backboards, 23¾" W, 48" H $1,400.00

Tea Table, DL Valley, ca. 1770, underside of top restored, cherry battens may not be orig., 35½" W, 29" H $1,500.00

Porcelain Bowl, Tucker, w/ floral dec. & gold banding, 8" diam. $1,300.00

Toby Jug, form of old woman, repairs, 11" H $125.00

Mirror, giltwood girondole, ca. 1820, w/ eagle & dolphin pediment, 30" W, 39" H $8,000.00

Hepplewhite Drawers, CT, mah., ca. 1790, minor repr. to inlays & skirt, 39¼" W, 33" H $3,750.00

Bowl, coin silver footed by Lownes, 5¾" H $500.00

Whale Oil Lamps, pr., amber, late 19th C., w/ etched dec. $275.00

Shaving Mirror, GA, ca. 1770, bowfront base w/ line & crosshatch inlays, ivory ball feet, 21" W, 23" H $750.00

A-MA Mar. 1997   Maritime Auctions

Scrimshaw, sperm whale teeth, 6" L $1,500.00

A-PA Nov. 1996   Pook & Pook Inc

Q.A. Side Chairs, pr. of N.E. yoke back maple, retains fine old patina, . .$1,200.00

Q.A. Highboy, N.E. figured maple, ca. 1750, base restored, 62" H, 34" W $3,500.00

Stoneware Crock, mkd. "Harry Remmey Stoneware, Philadelphia", 19th c., w/ blue floral dec. & applied handles, 14" H $550.00

Earthenware Potty, ca. 1830 w/ strap handle & vibrant blk. manganese splash dec., 6¼" H $600.00

A-PA Nov. 1996   Pook & Pook Inc.

Chippendale Lowboy, DE Valley, walnut, ca. 1770, w/ oblong notched corner top, top restored, 30½" H, 32" W $9,000.00

Chippendale Armchair, PA, mah., ca. 1780, w/ foliate carved crest rail gothic splat, slip seat, retains orig. seat frame & blocking . . . . .N/S

Georgian Knife Boxes, pr., mah., ca. 1780, w/ elaborate interiors, orig. brass latches & side handles, resting on claw feet, 14" H $4,500.00

Georgian Candlesticks, pr., brass base, mid 18th c., converted to electric, 9" H $1,300.00

Chinese Export Soup Tureen, blue & white Fitzhugh, w/ gilt finial, hairline, 10" H, 14" L $650.00

A-MA Mar. 1997   Maritime Auctions

Chelsea Clock & Barometer, mounted in a ship's wheel, clock is working & strikes proper ship's bells $700.00

A-PA Jan. 1997   Pook & Pook Inc.

Left to Right

Candlemold, 24 tube sgn. "Mithinbridge, VT", 19th C., together w/ an 18-tube & two 12-tube tin candlemolds . $300.00

Candlemold, 33 tin tube, 19th C., together w/ 24-tube candlemold $350.00

Lighting Devices, two northern Europ. wooden table-top, late 18th/early 19th C., both w/ polychrome dec., adjustable double-light arm, screw form shaft & circular bases w/ ball feet, 31½" H & 33" H $1,300.00

Candlemold, wood & pewter 24-tube, 19th C., each tube sgn., 22½", W18" H $1,100.00

Candlemold, wood & pewter 18-tube, 19th C., 22" W, 16" H . . .$750.00

Lighting Bracket, Am. wooden hanging, mid 18th C., w/ lollipop form back & wrt. iron pricket holder & 2 hooks, 20½" H $600.00

Gimbaled Oil Lamps, three Near Eastern brass reticulated globe form, 18th/19th C., 7½" diam., 4" diam., & 3" diam. $350.00

Pricket Stick, table-top, 17th C., w/ hexagonal dished rim, swedged baluster & faceted ball shaft, 20" H, w/ iron side-ejector candlestick, 18th C., w/ wall spike $1,500.00

A-MA Mar. 1997   Maritime Auctions

Sewing Stand, wood w/ whale bone & ivory fittings, 9½" H $5,600.00

A-PA Jan. 1997   Pook & Pook Inc.

Left to Right

Windsor Side Chairs, pr., PA, ca. 1790, w/ bamboo turnings .$2,000.00

Brass Transit, manuf. by W. & L.E. Gurley, Troy, NY, late 19th C., w/ leather case & tripod $750.00

William & Mary Table, oak, ca. 1710, w/ oblong thumb molded edge top, single molded front drawer, 29¼" W, 26½" H $1,500.00

Q.A. Candlesticks, pr., Eng., ca. 1740, 7" H, together w/ 3 single Georgian brass candlesticks $1,300.00

Candlesticks, pr., 19th C., 10½" H, w/ pr. of northern Euro. brass candlesticks, 18th C., w/ ball shafts & sq. bases w/ turned feet, 9" H, & pair of brass chambersticks, 20th C. $1,300.00

Boot Scraper, wrt. iron, early 19th C., in form of deer $450.00

Early Lighting, group of 3 table-top candleholders, rush light & spiked triple pan light $1,100.00

Oil on Masoniste, portrait of gentleman, dated 1755, 16" x 12½" .$450.00

A-PA June 1997   Pook & Pook, Inc.

Windsor High Chair, PA, ca. 1800, retains traces of old red paint, one arm restored $650.00

Dower Chest, PA, dec., inscribed "Gorgi 1813 Ruhl", w/ a lift lid, gr. stippled sides, front w/ a cartouche w/ name & date, ora. stippled panel flanked by two 12-pointed blk. & ivory stars, feet early replacements, 50½" W, 23½" H $2,800,00

High Wheeler, bicycle, late 19th C., w/ hand brake & pneumatic tire, 57" H $750.00

Barber Pole, folk art, ca. 1900, retaining orig. polychromed surface, 51" H $1,700.00

Doll Carriage, Victorian . . .$175.00

A-PA Jan. 1997   Pook & Pook Inc.

N. Euro. Box, lift lid, early 19th C., orig. polychromed decor, 9" x 16¾" $700.00

Wagon, child's wooden & paper dec., titled "United States & Canada Express" $350.00

Gumwood Kas, NJ, ca. 1750, w/ bold ogee cornice above 2 double raised panel doors w/ H-hinges, orig. bat wing brasses, 60" W, 76½" H $5,000.00

Windsor Armchair, folk art carved, early 19th C., w/ bowback, bamboo turnings, human form arms & white & gold dec. $1,100.00

Jacquard Coverlet, blue, red & gr., mid 19th C., manuf. by Clochman, Hamburg, PA, 1842 . . . .$250.00

A-MA Mar. 1997   Maritime Auctions

Pastry Wheel, of whalebone, 5¾" L $525.00

A-MA Mar. 1997   Maritime Auctions

Double Sailor's Valentine, w/ saying "Forget Me Not", 9" x 18" $2,100.00

A-VA Apr. 1997   Ken Farmer Auction

Eng. Wardrobe, oak w/ mah. banding, 19th C., 87½" x 61½" x 20½" $1,375.00

A-MA June 1997   Skinner, Inc.

Spanish Baroque Vargueno, iron mounted walnut, bone inlaid & parcel-gilt, 44½" W, 16" D, 62" H $10,925.00

A-OH May 1997   Garth's Auctions

Garden Table, cast iron w/ round reticulated top & four legs, old white repaint, 40" diam., 26" H $110.00

A-VA Apr. 1997   Ken Farmer Auction

VA Stand, walnut w/ poplar secondary, beveled nailed drawer over 2 beaded drawers, chip carved sides & back, turned legs, ref., 29½" x 16¾" x 16¾" $550.00

A-MA Mar. 1997   Eldred's

Row 1, Left to Right

Iroquois Beaded Bag, w/ br. velvet ground, 8" x 6½" H $220.00
Needlework Purse, 19th C., inscribed "L.P. Ransom Cambridge KY", floral dec.,10½" x 9" $852.50

Row 2, Left to Right

Needlework Purses, two, one in red, lt. blue, ora. & other colors, 5½" x 6" one in blues, white & dk. red, 4½" x 3½" $495.00
Beadwork Bag, 19th C., in gr., white & red, beadwork inscription, "M. Pope Dec 1 1834", 4¼" x 3" $330.00
Needlework Purses, two, one in red, lt. blue, ora. & other colors, 5½" x 6" one in blues, white & dk. red, 4½" x 3½" $495.00

A-PA Nov. 1996   Pook & Pook Inc.

Top to Bottom

Blunderbuss, Eng. walnut, ca. 1837, engr. "T. Blissett" w/ brass barrel, engr. trigger guard, butt plate & fixed bayonet $1,200
Flintlock Long Rifle, PA., tiger maple, ca. 1820, stock w/ bird dec. brass patch box, inlay crescent, incised C-scroll carvings and cross hatching $2,200.00
Flintlock Long Rifle, English, early 19th c., sporting pc. w/ checkered stock & brass trigger guard . .$550.00
Brown Bess Flintlock Rifle, English ca. 1800, w/ walnut stock . . .$850.00
Short Artillery Sword, 1833 model w/ leather sheath & belt, lacking part of buckle $700.00
US Army Colt 45 cal. 6-shot revolver, Peacemaker, pat. 1872, single action, ...$4,500.00
US Navy Colt revolver 36. cal., 1862 model $650.00
Cival War Officer's Sword & Scabbard, Model 1851, company grade, together w/ "Puppy Paw" Cival War "US" belt buckle $650.00
1858 Percussion Model 1842 Marshall Pistol, together w/ Waters percussion Marshall pistol (overcleaved) & musket bayonet, ca. 1812 . . . .$500.00

A-PA April 1997   Pook & Pook Inc.

Gumwood Kas, Hudson Valley, massive cornice, 2 door upper section, single drawer base, rear feet & drawer back restored, 60½" W, 73" H $4,000.00

A-MA June 1997   Skinner, Inc.

Linen Press, Dutch mah. & marquetry, late 18th C., w/ three int. shelves, 63″ W, 21″ D, 87″ H $9,200.00

A-PA Jan. 1997   Pook & Pook Inc.

Top Left

Sampler, PA, Chester Co. Westown School silk on linen, initialed "M.C. 1824", by Mary Carmelt, 11¼″ x 8½″ $1,400.00

Top Right

Sampler, PA, Chester Co., silk on linen by Lydia A. Dowell, dated 1834, 20¾″ x 20¾″ $1,100.00

Bottom Left

Sampler, PA, Chester Co., silk on linen by Ann Longacre, dated 1797, 17¼″ x 8¼″ $900.00

Bottom Right

Sampler, PA, Chester Co., silk on linen by Sarah Walter, dated 1798, 15¾″ x 14½″ $8,000.00

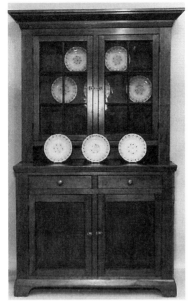

A-OH May 1997   Garth's Auctions

Wall Cupboard, two pc., ref. cherry, dovetailed drawers in base, old glass, orig. brass thumb latches, poplar secondary wood, cornice 14½″ x 58″, shelf is 21½″ x 52″, 89″ H $4,070.00
Spatterware Plates, set of eight, red & gr. design spatter border & center, 9½″ diam. $660.00

A-PA June 1997   Pook & Pook, Inc.

Corner Cupboard, PA, ca. 1780, upper section w/ a flat & reeded cornice above 2 arched lighted doors, base w/ 2 short drawers over 1 deep long drawer, 92¼″ H $5,500.00

A-MA June 1997   Skinner, Inc.

Dutch Desk, walnut & floral marquetry, late 19th C., minor veneer loss, 51″ W, 24″ D, 30¾″ H $2,760.00

A-PA April 1997   Pook & Pook Inc.

Left to Right

Q.A. Highboy, CT, ca. 1760, 3 short drawers, minor lip repr., brasses & drops repl., 37¾″ W, 68½″ H $7,500.00
Cast Bronze, Roman on horseback, 19th C., resting on marble plinth, 23″ H $1,700.00

A-MA Jan. 1997   Skinner

Tavern Sign, painted & gilt, N.E., ca. 1800, blk. painted frame, sides painted dk. gr., "Independence" in red, 31″ W, 41¼″ H $17,250.00

A-MA June 1997   Skinner

Girandole Mirror, giltwood carved, Eng. or Am., 19th C., w/ eagle, regilded, 22" W, 40" H $920.00

A-MA Oct. 1996   Skinner, Inc.

Gustav Stickley Bench, orig. leather, orig. worn finish, 41½" W, 24" D, 36" H .$1,955.00

A-MA Jan. 1997   Skinner

Screw Candlestand, painted maple & pine, prob. N.E., late 18th C., painted apple gr., imper., 11" diam., 40" H $2,300.00

A-OH May 1997   Garth's Auctions

Garden Settee, cast iron, vintage design, one back foot repl., white repaint, 57" L $165.00

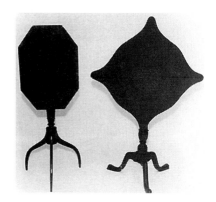

A-NH Mar. 1997   Northeast Auctions

Fed. Candlestand, New Eng., mah. inlay, urn turned standard, 21" L $1,250.00
Am. Candlestand, mah., serpentine top above a vase turned pedestal, top 22" sq., 28" H $400.00

A-PA Nov. 1996   Pook & Pook Inc.

Q.A. Candlestand, N.E. maple, ca. 1760, retains old red wash, 26" H, 15¼" W . $250.00
Candlestand, grain dec., early 19th c., 25½" H, 18½" diam.. . . . .$1,000.0
Candlestand, N.E. birch, ca. 1790, retains orig. red washed surface, 21½" H, 16½" diam.. . . . .$350.00
Q.A. Candlestand, N.E. maple, 18th C., 25½" H, 17½" diam.. . . . .$200.00

A-NH Mar. 1997   Northeast Auctions

Fed. Candlestand, New Eng., mah. inlay, urn turned standard, 21" L $1,250.00
Am. Candlestand, mah., serpentine top above a vase turned pedestal, top 22" sq., 28" H $400.00

A-VA Apr. 1997   Ken Farmer Auction

VA Blanket Chest, VA, early to mid 18th C., dovetailed const., orig. hardware & shoe feet, old dry finish, feet slightly reduced, slight warpage, 24½" x 51" x 20½" $3,300.00

A-VA Apr. 1997   Ken Farmer Auction

Blanket Chest, over two drawers, ca. 1810-1815, cherry w/ birch & curly birch secondaries, old ref., 3 board top, scratch-beaded drawers over turned feet, 33" x 49½" x 21½" $770.00

A-PA Mar. 1997   Bill Bertoi Auctions

Yawning Pup Doorstop, 7"x5" $385.00

A-OH May 1997   Garth's Auctions

Row 1, Left to Right

Mocha Shaker, blue band, blk. stripe & earthworm dec. in br., blk. & white, blue top, repr., 4⅞" H $330.00
Mocha Mustard Pot, w/ lid & ribbed handle, tan band w/ blk. stripes & earthworm in white, yel. & blk., chip on rim & lid has sm. repr., 2½" H $605.00
Mocha Shaker, tan bands, br. stripes & blk. seaweed dec., chips, 4⅛" H $220.00
Mocha Salt, gray band, blk. stripes & white wavy lines, stains in foot & hairline in rim, 3" diam., 2⅛" H . .$330.00
Mocha Shaker, blue bands & blk. stripe, stains, 4¾" H . . . . .N/S

Row 2, Left to Right

Mocha Jar, covered, pale blue band w/ blk. stripes & earthworm & cat's eyes in white, blk. & blue, repairs & hairline in lid, 5" H $495.00
Mocha Milk Pitcher, dk. bluish gray band, blk. stripes, emb. band w/ gr. & blk. seaweed, leaf handle, wear & painted over flake on spout, 4⅝" H $440.00

Row 3, Left to Right

Mocha Mug, dk. br. band & stripes w/ earthworm in blue, white & tan, leaf handle, hairlines, 3¾" H $550.00
Mocha Bowl, gr. band on a canary yel. ground, earthworm in yel. & blk. impr. "CL & Mont", chips & repairs, missing handle 4¾" diam., 3½" H $110.00
Mocha Waste Bowl, orangish tan band & dk. br. stripes w/ emb. gr. band & earthworm in blue, white & dk. br., repairs, 5⅝" diam., 2⅞" H $550.00

A-MA Mar. 1997   Maritime Auctions

Castle, whale bone by POW, intricately carved w/ open work const., 12" W, 9" D, 11½" H $8,250.00

A-OH May 1997   Garth's Auctions

Row 1, Left to Right

Bank, pottery cat head, white clay w/ gr. glaze, 3" H $275.00
Child's Mug, canary, reddish br. transfer "My Son, if sinners entice thee...", leaf handle, sm. lip flakes, 2⅜" H $412.50
House Bank, yellowware, molded detail picked out in blk., roof has "For My Dear Girl", firing crack, 3⅝" H $660.00
Child's Mug, canary, flower in red & gr., leaf handle, 2¼" H . . .$192.50
Bank, pottery dog, white clay in dk. gr. glaze, flake at coin slot, 2½" H $110.00

Row 2, Left to Right

Mocha Shaker, stripes in blk., tan & blue, 4⅞" H $330.00
Garniture Set, three pc., canary, br. stripes & flowers & foliage in red, br. & gr., wear, repr. & dec. varies slightly, 4¼" & 4⅞" H $1,430.00
Mustard Pot, blue feather bands & leaf handle, lid has hairline & flake on inner flange, 3⅝" H $55.00

A-PA Mar. 1997   Bill Bertoi Auctions

Left to Right

Popeye Flex Doll, ca. 1935, King Features Syn., jointed wood const., compo. head, 10" H $1,155.00
Popeye Flex Doll, ca. 1935, King Features Syn., jointed wood const., compo. head, 13½" H $330.00
Pinocchio Doll, Ideal Toy Co., jointed wooden arms & legs, compo. head & body, orig. decal on chest, 8" H $105.00
Pinocchio Doll, Ideal Toy Co., jointed woode arms & legs, compo. head & &body, orig. decal on chest, 8" H $105.00

A-MA Apr. 1997   Skinner, Inc.

George III Dining Chairs, set of 10, mah., w/ two armchairs, beige faux leather upholstery, 37¾" H   . . .$5,750.00

A-PA April 1997   Pook & Pook Inc.

Windsor Side Chairs, set of 6, PA, each branded "MOON",
ca. 1800, repairs to one chair $15,000.00

A-PA April 1997   Pook & Pook Inc.

Chippendale Dining Chairs, set of 8, PA, mah. each branded "Wallace Nutting" w/ tassel & leaf carved crest rails, nee-
dle-point slip seats $8,500.00

A-MA Apr. 1997   Skinner, Inc.

Rococo Rosewood Settee, ca. 1850-60, minor restora-
tions, 67" L, 41" H $2,070.00

A-MA May 1997   Skinner

Left to Right

Gustav Stickley Chairs, two, child's armchair in orig. finish, Gustav red decal, 18¼" W, 14" D, 26" H, side chair overcoated, Gustav
red decal, 14" W, 13" D, 23½" H $1,035.00
Gustav Stickley Trestle Table, orig. finish, paper label & Gustav red decal, child's, 36" W, 24" D, 22½" H $2,185.00

A-NH Mar. 1997   Northeast Auctions

George III Chairs, set of twelve, mah., w/ carved Prince-of-
Wales plume, molded edge & spade feet $32,000.00

A-PA Nov. 1996   Pook & Pook Inc.

Chippendale Side Chairs, pr., DE Valley, mah., late 18th
c., w/ slip seats $2,100.00
Federal. Breakfast Table, PA. mah., ca. 1810, attrib. to
Henry Connelly, two drawers retaining orig. lion's head pulls,
brass paw castors, 29" H, 23½" W, 43" L $5,500.00

A-MA Sept. 1996　　　　Skinner, Inc.

Lamp Bases, pr. of Fr. cobalt blue ground porcelain & gilt metal, late 19th c., gilded surround, 16″ H $431.25

A-MA Oct. 1996　　　　Skinner, Inc.

Cameo Glass Lamp, Mt. Washington, shade & fluid font composed of opal white opaque glass overlaid in bright rose-pink acid etched dec., mounted upon silver plated metal fittings, impr. "Pairpoint Mfg. Co. 3013 ", electrified, needs rewiring, 10″ diam., w/o chimney 17″ H $3,105.00

A-MA Oct. 1996　　　　Skinner, Inc.

Left to Right

Handel Desk Lamp, gr. textured surface, mkd. "Mosserine Handel 6010", adjustable bronzed metal base w/ threaded label on felt liner, 8″ L, 15″ H $1,380.00
Desk Lamp, Bradley & Hubbard panel glass, adjustable tilt shade w/ narrow ribbed panels, rev. painted w/ gr., blue, br. arts & crafts border motif, mounted on single socket metal base, 8½″ W, 13″ H $460.00

A-MA Jan. 1997　　　　Skinner

Left to Right

Whalebone Handled Whip, 19th C., losses to leather, crack, 24¼″ L $172.50
Three Measures, whalebone, ivory & exotic wood, 19th C., one inscribed "WH", minor imper., 14⅞″"6″ L $345.00
Whalebone Yardstick, 19th C., 35⅞″ L $488.75
Three Measures, whalebone, ivory & exotic wood, 19th C., one inscribed "WH", minor imper., 14⅞″"6″ L $345.00
Pointer, whalebone & ivory, 19th C., w/ carved eagle's head handle & exotic wood spacers, minor cracks, 24¼″ L $977.50
Two Pointers, whalebone, ivory & baleen, 19th C., one w/ baleen inlay on knob, finial missing, minor cracks, 29-35½″ L $345.00
Walking Stick, baleen & shark vertebrae, 19th C., vertebrae & baleen spacers, cracks, 33⅞″ L $373.50
Walking Stick, ivory, whalebone & inlaid ebony, 19th C., brass finial, inlay loss, minor cracks, 36″ L $345.00
Walking Stick, inlaid ivory & whalebone, 19th C., scribe line dec., whalebone shaft w/ ivory inlay, minor cracks, inlay loss, 35¼″ L . .$1,150.00
Walking Stick, carved& inlaid ivory & whalebone, 19th C., ivory sailor's knot knob, baleen spaces, whalebone shaft inlaid w/ figural & geometric motifs done in tortoiseshell, mother-of-pearl, baleen & exotic woods, minor inlay loss & replm., minor cracks, 37″ L $2,185.00

A-MA May 1997　　　　Skinner

Tiffany Student Lamp, bronze, fine patina on single burner lamp, urn-form font, orig. vented chimney, opal cased gr. damascene irid. favrile glass shade inscribed "LCTif", 7″ diam., 21″ H $9,200.00

A-PA Mar. 1997　　　　Bill Bertoi Auctions

Row 1, Left to Right

1950 Hudson, Dealer Promo car, plastic model, blue-green overall, teal sides, Hudson hubcaps, 12½″ L $385.00
1939 Desoto, Kingsbury, pressed steel in ora. overall, sliding moon roof, chrome hubcaps, 14″ L $578.00

Row 2, Left to Right

1937 Chrysler, Cor-Cor Mfg., pressed steel, red overall w/ blk. roof, chrome hubcaps, 16½″ L $1,155.00
1933 Graham, Cor-Cor Mfg., pressed steel, aqua gr. w/ blk., electric headlights, emb. "Cor-Cor Toys", 20″ L $1,375.00

A-PA Mar. 1997　　　　Bill Bertoi Auctions

Row 1

Flat Bed Truck, Kelmite, "White", pressed steel, blk. overall w/ red trim, wood flat bed body, 26″ L . . .$990.00

Row 2, Left to Right

Dump Truck, "Buddy L", pressed steel cab, blk. overall, dump body red, electric lights, rubber tires, emb. spokes orig. box, 20½″ L $1,485.00
Motor Truck, Marklin, pressed steel parts, red cap w/ sim. stake side body, gr. accent, clockwork, orig. booklet, 15½″ L $1,760.00

A-MA Mar. 1997　　　　Skinner

Q.A. Dining Table, maple, prob. MA, ca. 1760, old ref., repr., 44½″ W, 45″ D, 28⅛″ H $2,300.00

A-MA Jan. 1997   Skinner

Left to Right

Jagging Wheel, ivory figural, 19th C., inlaid eyes & nostrils, minor losses, 7⅛" L $4,600.00
Jagging Wheel, ivory, 19th C., open carved handle, minor cracks & chips, 6¼" L $920.00
Jagging Wheel, pierced carved whale ivory, 19th C., minute losses, 5¾" L . . .$2,875.00
Jagging Wheel, engr. ivory, 19th C., dec. w/ Am. flag & vines, 7¼" L .$517.50
Jagging Wheel, ivory, 19th C., pistol handle & baleen spacer, cracks, old repr., 7¼" L $230.00

A-PA Mar. 1997   Bill Bertoi Auctions

Large Dog Doorstop, 12" x 9". $550.00

A-PA Mar. 1997   Bill Bertoi Auctions

Doorstops

Left to Right

Dachshund, sgn. "Taylor Cook", 5½" x 7¼" $1,540.00
Parrot, sgn. "Taylor Cook", 10½" x 4⅞" $413.00

A-PA Mar. 1997   Bill Bertoi Auctions

Cosmos Doorstop, Hubley, pastel flowers, 17¾" x 10¼" $2,090.00

A-MA Oct. 1996   James D. Julia Inc.

Art Deco Lamp, silver plated bird w/ blk. & white marble base & Italian Millefiori glass globe, 9" W, 11" H $250.00
Handel Desk Lamp, bronze & gr. glass, orig. gr. patina, cloth label on base, shade diam. 6", 11" H .$800.00
Desk Lamp, art nouveau, br. caramel blown out glass panels w/ metal overlay, metal base & shade, base w/ two inkwell holes, missing, overall 15" H . $400.00
Desk Lamp, electric brass lamp, socket & harp pivots 200°, unsgn. butterscotch shade, overall 12½" H $250.00

A-MA Oct. 1996   James D. Julia Inc.

Handel Lamp Base, sgn., w/ glass ball dec. in yel. & blue, bronze stem on mottled round onyx base, 22½" H $275.00
Table Lamp, art nouveau, three arm w/ set of three cut & painted lamp shades, dk. metal finish on base w/ frosted & deep apricot shades, shade diam. 3¾", overall 21" H $400.00
Table Lamp, hand painted rev. Jefferson type, w/ bronzed base, blue & yel. ground, pink roses, replaced finial & cap, shade diam. 14½", overall 24" H $350.00
Jasper Urn, blue & white, medium blue & white w/ several cherubs in design, modern base & cap, 16" H $75.00

A-PA Mar. 1997   Bill Bertoi Auctions

Persian Cat Doorstop, Hubley, 8½" x 6½" $193.00

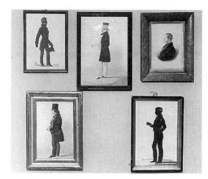

A-OH Jan. 1997   Garth's Auctions

Row 1, Left to Right

Silhouette, full length, cut figure w/ white highlights, sgn. "J. Blackburn, King St. Manchester, 1827", minor stains, 7" W, 9⅜" H $247.50
Portrait, full length profile, watercolor on paper, framed 8⅝" W, 11¾" H $742.50
Portrait, profile bust, watercolor on paper, lt. br. hair & blk. frock coat, minor stains, bird's eye veneer frame, 8¼" W, 10¼" H $192.50

Row 2, Left to Right

Portrait, full length, gentleman w/ top hat, watercolor on paper w/ good detail, old gilt frame, 8⅝" W, 11⅝" H $797.50
Silhouette, full length, youth w/ book, cut paper w/ gilt detail, emb. label, framed, 8" W, 11¼" H $632.50

A-MA Jan. 1997   Skinner

298-Walebone & Ivory Items, 13 pcs., 19th C., incl. set of three napkin rings, handform napkin ring, two knives, fork, mini. goblet, glove stretcher, glass cutter, mini. boat, a club, & an articulated erotic figure, minor losses .$805.00
295-Wngraved Whale Pan Bone, 19th C., double sided engravings, three-masted ships under sail, crack, gouges, 2¼" x 3¼" $373.75
302-Whalebone, Whale Ivory & Wood, 19th C., incl. ivory pickwick, quiver-form needle case, hand-form stud, Maltese cross-form dec., whalebone clothespin, carved wood clothespin w/ heart & geometric dec., inscribed "MP", mini. clamp & numerous spools $575.00

A-PA April 1997   Pook & Pook Inc.

Oil on Canvas, English ships, 18th C., 22" x 28½" $3,500.00
Chippendale Drawers, PA, ca. 1770, 4 lipped drawers w/ orig. bail & rosette brasses, restorations, 39" W, 33½" H . $7,500.00
Chinese Teapot & Mug, blue & white, early 19th C., together w/ later baluster form lidded jar $350.00
Platters, two Imari fish form, early 20th C., 15" & 11" L $400.00
Chippendale Mirror, mah., oval inlay leaves on gr. reserve, 14" W, 34" W . . N/S
Candlestand, PA, walnut, round dish top, 18½" diam., 27" H $750.00
Chinese Vase, ovoid form, ca. 1900, w/ polychrome scenes of warriors on ivory ground, 13½" H $200.00

A-?? Feb. 1997   Thomas Hirchak Co.

Marbles

Left to Right & Top to Bottom

End of Day Cloud, 1⁷⁄₁₆", mica .$264.00
Swirl, 1¼", white latticinio core . . .$82.50
Swirl, 1⁹⁄₁₆", yel. latticinio core . . $77.00
Swirl, 1⅛", yel. latticinio core . . $82.50

A-?? Feb. 1997   Thomas Hirchak Co.

Marbles

Left to Right & Top to Bottom

Swirl, 2¼", white latticinio core . .$82.50
Swirl, 2¼", yel. latticinio core . . .$148.50
Swirl, 2⁷⁄₁₆", white latticinio core . .$170.50
Swirl, 1⅞", white latticinio core . . .$88.00

A-MA Oct. 1996   Skinner, Inc.

Shaker Items

Row 1, Left to Right

Woodenware, five items, 19th c., cheese box, horsehair sieve, dipper, dry measure & cheese cutter said to have been used at Canterbury $345.00
Sieve, horsehair, 19th C., 8" H, 8⅜" Diam. $345.00
Sewing Carrier & Covered Oval Box, carrier relined, age crack . .N/S
Boxes, two, 20th c., sewing carrier, lacks lining, & covered oval box, 9- 9½" L . . . . .N/S
Box, oval, 13½" L $805.00

Row 2, Left to Right

Peg Rack & Carrier, divided oval, 20th c., rack 69" L, carrier 10½" L $575.00
Sewing Carrier, covered, lacking lining, 12" L $546.25
Box, gr., repainted, 5½" L . . . . . .N/S

Row 3, Left to Right

Joined Double Bin, 19th c., each 4½" Diam. $115.00
Sewing Carrier, covered, lacks lining, 31½" L $632.50
Box, red, repainted, minor age cracks, 8¼" L . . . . .N/S
Boxes, two, 20th c., sewing carrier, lacks lining, & covered oval box, 9- 9½" L . . . . .N/S

A-OH Jan. 1997   Garth's Auctions

Row 1, Left to Right

Mini. Book Boxes, three, leather w/ gilt: "Pearl Buttons" 3"; "Anden Ken 1898", w/ metal clasp, 3" & match box, 1⅞" $302.50
Gum Boxes, three sm., walnut w/ line inlay, 2⅜"; cherry w/ marquetry inlay, 3"; & chestnut w/ prominent nail heads, 2⅝" $247.50
Gum Box, multi-colored inlay, w/ checkerboard inset & gold ends, shiny varnish, 3⅞" $176.00
Gum Box, Chip carved pine w/ old varnish & gold paint, 4" $203.50

Row 2, Left to Right

Gum Box, rosewood w/ inlay dec. both sides, 5⅞" $412.50
Gum Box, poplar w/ br. & blk. graining, minor wear & age crack .$247.50
Gum Box, old blk. paint w/ yel., red & br., revarnished, age cracks, 4⅞" L $137.50
Gum Box, chip carved pine w/ simple inlay, olf varnish & gold paint, minor edge damage, 5" L $192.50
Gum Box, chip carved pine w/ old varnish, mkd. "Made by Blaney Lewis on Geore's Bank 1838", 5" . . .$330.00
Gum Box, pine w/ inlay & old varnish, 5" $192.50

A-PA Jan. 1997   Pook & Pook Inc.

Fruit Baskets, pr. of Tucker reticulated, ca. 1830 w/ gilt highlighting, 8½" H, 9" diam. . .N/S
Blk. Forest Pipe Rack, late 19th C., in form of 2 bears, 13½" H $800.00
New Eng. Highboy, William & Mary burl veneered, ca. 1730, herringbone inlays & engr. brasses, base restored, 39" W, 21½" D, 69½" H $5,500.00
Tall Case Clock, w/ broken arch bonnet, painted white moon-phase dial & 8-day works, 88½" H $4,500.00
Dome Lidded Box, dated 1872, w/ bird & star dec., 14" L, 9¼" H $300.00

A-MA Oct. 1996   Skinner, Inc.

Left to Right

Quezal Desk Lamp, glass & brass, gold ird. shade w/ gr. & white pulled feather dec., inscribed "Quezal", 14½" H $575.00

Quezal Art Glass Lamp, dec. by five gr. feathers w/ gold irid. outlines, inscribed "Quezal", 5¼" diam., 4½" H . . . . .N/S

Quezal Art Glass Vase, dec. opal body w/ gold feather below gr. hooked elements w/ medial gold band, gold irid. surface, inscribed "Quezal 490", 4⅝" H $2,070.00

Quezal Vase, gold & opal, dec. by five pointed gold irid. feathers on opal white body, inscribed "Quezal", 4¾" H $575.00

Am. Art Glass Lamp, opal vasiform base w/ pulled & looped gold dec. shaped glass shade w/ gold & gr. pulled feather dec. in the Quezal style & technique, unsgn., 10" diam., 20" H . . . . .N/S

Quezal Mini. Lily Vase, pinched quatraform rim on slender transparent golden bud vase w/ five gr. spiked feathers, lrg. partial label covers pontil, 5" H $1,035.00

Quezal Vase, floriform Jack in the Pulpit, gold irid. blossom rim on ribbed glass body dec. by five gold outlined gr. pulled leaf-forms, base inscribed "Quezal", 8" diam., 9" H . . . . . . .N/S

Quezal Lamp Shades, two, art glass, bell-form gold irid. ribbed shades w/ gr. & white pulled feather design, each inscribed "Quezal" on rim, one w/ chip, 2⅛" diam., 5¼" H $345.00

A-?? Feb. 1997   Thomas Hirchak Co.

Marbles

Left to Right & Top to Bottom

20 Count Set, Comics, Peltier Glass Co., w/ orig. box $2,970.00

A-OH May 1997   Garth's Auctions

Row 1, Left to Right

Mini. Basket, woven splint, eight melon ribs w/ woven strips of splint in multi-colors, 2¼" diam., 1⅜" H, plus bentwood handle $115.00

Buttocks Basket, sm. woven splint, 22 ribs, old thick blue paint, 4¼" x 5", 2¼" H, plus bentwood handle . .$577.50

Melon Rib Basket, woven splint w/ red, 14 ribs, Berk's County, 6" x 6¾", 3¼" H, plus bentwood handle . . .$165.00

Row 2, Left to Right

Buttocks Basket, woven splint w/ painted floral dec. in red, ora. & gr., 30 ribs, minor damage, 10" x 10½", 5" H, plus bentwood handle $440.00

Round Basket, woven splint w/ 30 ribs, applied foot & red, blk. & yel. color, 10" x 11", 6¼" H, plus bentwood handle . .$110.00

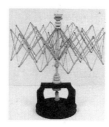

A-MA Mar. 1997   Maritime Auctions

Yarn Winder, whale bone w/ turned whale ivory base clamp & top pin cushion, mid 19th C., 16" H $1,400.00

A-Feb. 1997   Thomas Hirchak Co.

Marbles

Left to Right & Top to Bottom

Lutz, ¾", Onionskin $440.00
Lutz, ¾", Onionskin $187.00
Lutz, ¾", banded, blue base .$176.00
Lutz, ¾", Onionskin $132.00
Lutz, ¹¹⁄₁₆", Onionskin $132.00
Lutz, ⅝", Onionskin $187.00
Lutz, ⁹⁄₁₆", banded, semi-opaque, white base $170.50
Lutz, ⁹⁄₁₆", banded, semi-opaque, blue base $308.00

A-?? Feb. 1997   Thomas Hirchak Co.

Marbles

Left to Right & Top to Bottom

End of Day, ¹⁵⁄₁₆", Onionskin .$99.00
End of Day, ¹⁵⁄₁₆", Onionskin .$60.50
End of Day, ¹³⁄₁₆", Onionskin .$49.50
Mica, ¹⁵⁄₁₆", green $88.00
Mica, ⅞", amber $27.50
Indian, ¾" $49.50
Indian, ¹¹⁄₁₆" $38.50
Slag, ¾", orangeade $11.00
Agate, ¹¹⁄₁₆", lemonade oxblood, .$88.00
Akro Agate Co., ¹¹⁄₁₆", egg yolk oxblood $33.00
Solid Core, 1" $44.00
End of Day, 1 of 2, Onionskin. .$49.50
End of Day, 1 of 2, ¾", 2 of 2, ¾". .$49.50
End of Day, 1 of 2, ¾" $49.50

A-?? Feb. 1997   Thomas Hirchak Co.

Marbles

Left to Right & Top to Bottom

China, 1 of 2, ⅞", crows feet, 2 of 2, 1", crows feet $99.00
China, lot of 6, various $38.50

A-?? Feb. 1997   Thomas Hirchak Co.

Marbles

Left to Right & Top to Bottom

Sulphide, 1¾", fox $143.00
Sulphide, 1¾", hen on nest . . .$231.00
Sulphide, 1⁹⁄₁₆", sitting bear $137.50
Sulphide, 1⁹⁄₁₆", rooster $154.00
Sulphide, 1¾", standing dog . .$148.50
Swirl, 1⁹⁄₁₆", solid core $60.50
Swirl, 1³⁄₁₆", four band divided core .$27.50
Swirl, 2", four band divided core .$154.00

A-NH Mar. 1997   Northeast Auctions

Q.A. Wing Chair, New Eng., walnut & maple, ogival wings & outscrolled armrests, loose cushion, 48" H $25,000.00

A-MA Jan. 1997   Skinner

Fed. Easy Chair, mah. upholstered, prob. N.E., ca. 1800, in white damask, 44" H $1,265.00

A-MA Mar. 1997   Skinner

Chippendale Chair, mah., MA, ca. 1780, restored, 37½" H $1,495.00

A-MA June 1997   Skinner, Inc.

Fauteuil Chair, walnut, Italian, upholstered w/ needlepoint, 47" H $1,495.00

A-OH Jan. 1997   Garth's Auctions

Row 1, Left to Right

Burl, two pcs., napkin ring, 2" diam., & sm. shaker jar, minor age cracks 2¾" H $110.00
Turned Box, w/ lid, old dk. worn finish, 3⅛" diam., 3⅛" H $165.00
Burl, two sm. pcs., bowl, 2⅝" diam. 1⁷/16" H, & flat jar w/ lid, sm. chip, 2⅝" diam. 1⁷/16" H $181.50

Row 2, Left to Right

Burl Footed Salt, turned & good figure, minor age crack, 3" diam., 3⅛" H $165.00
Burl Bowl, turned, sm. hole & wear, shiny finish, 4½" diam., 2⅝" H$214.50
Burl Jar, turned, keg shaped, turned rings, 4⅝" H $286.00
Burl Gum Box, book shaped w/ sliding end, one pc. of wood, 3¾" L....................$275.00

Row 3, Left to Right

Burl Chalice, turned in three pcs., minor age cracks, 4¼" diam., 5" H $71.50
Burl Box, beveled edge, brass knob, age crack, 5¾" L $352.00
Burl Bowl, naturally shaped, mkd. "WS" & scratch carved date "1840", 5½" x 7", 2½" H $275.00

A-OH Jan. 1997   Garth's Auctions

Chippendale Armchair, mah. frame w/ old finish, legs have some edge damage, foot w/ pieced repr., 44¾" H $2,090.00

A-OH Jan. 1997   Garth's Auctions

Chippendale Lolling Chair, cherry frame w/ old refinish, reupholstered in forest gr. velvet brocade, wear & edge damage, steel braces added to seat frame, 39¾" H $1,430.00

A-OH Jan. 1997   Garth's Auctions

Hepplewhite Armchair, mah. base, branded "J. Davis", stretchers repl., 45" H $2,530.00

A-OH Nov. 1996   Garth's Auctions
Oriental Rug, Kazak w/ multiple
borders in dk. red, lt. blue & ivory on
dk. red ground, 4'2" x 6'2" . . .$1,100.00

A-OH Nov. 1996   Garth's Auctions
Oriental Rug, Armenian Kazak dated
1936, lt. blue & ivory borders on dk. red
ground, 3'8" x 6'6" $1,210.00

A-OH Nov. 1996   Garth's Auctions
Oriental Rug, Kazak w/ animals, lt.
blue border on red ground, double
fringe w/ wear, 4'5" x 8'7" . . .$1,760.00

A-OH Nov. 1996   Garth's Auctions
Oriental Rug, Shirvan w/ reddish border
on dk. blue ground, worn areas, primarily in br. color, 4'2" x 9'5" $1,540.00

A-MA Mar. 1997   Skinner
Hooked Rug, geometric, Am. late
19th C., repairs, 84" x 50" . .$2,990.00

A-MA Mar. 1997   Skinner
Flatweave Rug, Sweden, early 20th
C., in red, ivory, gold & red-brown on
the blue-green field, border of similar
coloration, sm. rewoven areas, 4' 6" x
4' 6" $345.00

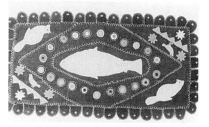

A-PA May 1997   Aston Americana Auction
Penny Rug, wool applique w/ fish,
birds & beaver motif $1,733.00

A-OH Jan. 1997   Garth's Auctions
Oriental Rug, Heriz, midnight blue
border & ivory spandrels on salmon
ground, 6'5" x 8'8" $4,290.00

A-OH Jan. 1997   Garth's Auctions
Oriental Saddle Bag Face, Quash
Quai Shiraz, floral design in gr.,
browns, ivory, blues & brick red, w/
ivory border & midnight blue ground,
pile has wear, 2'6" x 2'10"   .$4,400.00

A-OH Aug. 1996   Garth Auctions
Hooked Yarn Rug, gold, red, grey tan,
br., gr. etc., some minor damage &
attached to a larger pc. of wool felt, 25"
x 40½" $165.00

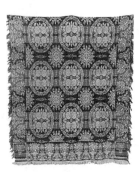

A-OH Oct. 1996   Garth's Auctions
Jacquard Coverlet, one pc., single weave,
mkd. "Made by D. Cosley, Xenia, Greene Co.
Ohio 1848", red, gr., navy blue & natural
white, minor wear & lt. stains, missing
fringe, 82" x 94" $275.00

A-OH Jan. 1997   Garth's Auctions

Row 1, Left to Right

Treen, two pcs., cup w/ old varnish, age crack, 2½" H, & dish w/ chip carved rim, worn dk. br. patina, age crack, 3¾" diam. $93.50

Pig Bottle, pottery, dk. br. Albany slip, mkd. "Good Old Rye in a hogs", attrib. to Anna Pottery, IL, chips, 7¼" L $880.00

Burl Bowls, two w/ some figure, 4" diam, 1¼" H, & 3⅛" diam., 1⅛" H $165.00

Row 2, Left to Right

Round Box, w/ sliding lid, chip carved surfaces, wood peg const., minor edge damage, 3½" diam., 2¾" H $154.00

Double Bowl Chalice, burl w/ dk. patina, floral dec. int. w/ carved "IXC", 3¼" diam., 4" H $60.50

Buttocks Basket, sm. woven splint, sixteen rib w/ faded gr. bands, 4½" x 5", 2¾" H plus handle $357.50

Bentwood Box, oval w/ no lid, chip carved, worn natural patina, openings for spring clips, 6" L $22.00

Row 3, Left to Right

Bent Bark Boxes, two w/ dec. overlapping bands, larger has whittled wooden lid, br. finish, 6" H, sm. has hinged pewter lid, 2¼" H $60.50

Euro. Burl Bowl, relief carved design, men spearing fish, 8" diam., irregular 4" H $137.50

Treen, three pcs., mah. gum box, 3¼" L; turned sander, sm. age crack, 3⅛" H, & three part turned box, 5½" H $187.00

A-PA Apr. 1997   Horst Auction Center

Trinket Box, dated 1870, Lancaster County, PA, paint dec. slide lid, dovetailed box, sgn. by Folk Artist "WC", 7⅛" L, 3¾" W, 2⅝" H $1,150.00

A-OH Jan. 1997   Garth's Auctions

Row 1, Left to Right

Book Box, w/ inlay & ink designs, crest on lid w/ flags & sun, "Recuerdo Centenorio 1910", secret locking device, 9½" L $203.50

Book Box, w/ ink punch Roman numerals, secret compartment in base, 7¾" L $137.50

Row 2, Left to Right

Book Box, Marquetry inly, ref. w/ gold repaint on page ends, spine pulls out as drawer, 5⅝" L $220.00

Book Box, pine w/ chip carving & old tan varnish, made from one pc. of wood, ends slide open, corner chipped, 7" L $137.50

Book Box, marquetry inlay, one pc. of oak w/ walnut & other inlaid wood, sliding lid warped, glued repr. & loose trim, locking device, 7½" L . . .$77.00

Book Box, marquetry inlay, yel. painted "Cora", made from cigar boxes, spine pulls out, "AD" on inside drawer, 6¼" L $99.00

Row 3, Left to Right

Book Box, marquetry inlay, spine pulls out as drawer, worn finish, 8" L $220.00

Book Box, marquetry inlay w/ "Heidelberg", hinged lid, velvet lining, worn finish, 9" L $71.50

Book Box, mah. w/ inlay, ends slide off revealing divided drawer, wire nails in drawer, minor damage, 10⅞" L . .$264.00

Book Box, walnut w/ brass wire inlay w/ hinged lid, lacquer finish, 9⅝" L . . .$82.50

A-MA Oct. 1996   Skinner, Inc.

Shaker Box, lrg. oval, New Lebanon, N.Y., 19th c., w/ orig. pumpkin paint, six finger, w/ remnants of paper label inscribed "soap," minor surface imp., 7¾" H, 15" L $8,050.00

A-OH Jan. 1997   Garth's Auctions

Row 1, Left to Right

Sauce Pans, three sm. copper, cast iron handles, worn tin lining, 2⅝", 3¼" & 4" diam. $38.50

Sauce Pans, two brass, cast w/ wrt. iron handle, 5" diam., 6½" handle; hammered w/ dovetailed seams & conical handle, 6" diam., 4" handle $60.50

Row 2, Left to Right

Eng. Tankards, three in brass or bronze alloys, color varies, "Pint" engr. "W.G.F.", 5¼" H & "1/2 Pint", 4" H $330.00

Eng. Tankards, three in brass or bronze alloys, color varys, one has silver plating "1/2 pint", 4" H, & two "Gill", 3¼" H $49.50

Eng. Tankards, four, two "1/2 Gill" in bronze, 2⅜" H.; "Quarter Gill" in silver finish, 2⅛" H, & smallest in pewter, 1¾" H $82.50

Row 3, Left to Right

Candleholders, two, similar brass spring loaded, one emb. "Cornelius & Baker, PA", 9½" H $110.00

Tankard & Bowl, Eng. copper tankard, soldered repairs, 6¼" H, & brass footed bowl, 5½" diam., 5" H, both traces of silver plate $99.00

Tea Kettles, two brass, large oriental, 4¾" & 5¼" H, plus swivel handles . . .$137.50

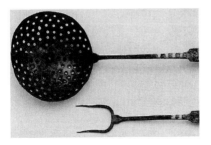

A-PA June 1997   Pook & Pook, Inc.

Strainer & Fork, PA, inlaid, ca. 1828, w/ brass & copper inlays, punched dec., each dated 1828, strainer w/ initials "JD", 22" L $2,500.00

A-PA Mar. 1997   Bill Bertoi Auctions

Circus Mechanical Bank, Shepard Hardware Co., pat. 2/8/1887, Hegarty Collection $11,550.00
Clown on Globe Mechanical Bank, J & E Stevens Co., pat. 5/20/1890 . . . .$1,540.00
Trick Dog Mechanical Bank, Shepard Hardware Co., red & lt. gr. base $2,970.00
Elephant & Clowns Mechanical Bank, J & E Stevens Co., pat. 8/28/1883, cracked at base $1,320.00
Trick Dog Mechanical Bank, Hubley Mfg. Co., ca. 1906 . . . .$825.00

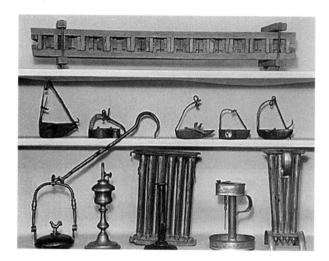

A-OH Oct. 1996   Garth's Auctions

Row 1

Candy Mold, to produce twelve house shapes, 29½" L . . .$77.00

Row 2, Left to Right

Lighting Devices, two, wrt. iron, double crusie, 6" H & hanging pan lamp, 4¾" diam., 13¼" H $159.50
Betty Lamp, wrt. iron, mkd. "J.B Wurtz" on crest, 3½" H $165.00
Betty Lamps, two wrt. iron, one w/ chicken finial, battered & rust damage, 5" H, no hanger, & one w/ hanger but no pick, 3½" H $148.50
Betty Lamp, wrt. iron, 5" H $110.00

Row 3, Left to Right

Hanging Lamp, iron w/ brass time incl. brass bird finial, 8" H plus hanger $115.50
Fr. Brass Lamp, w/ single spout, mkd. "Gardon...", 9½" H $93.50
Candle Mold & Candlestick, tin, twelve tubes, damaged, 10¼" H, & Hog Scraper w/ push up & lip hanger, blk. repaint, mkd. "Shaws", 7" H $82.50
Betty Lamp, on elevated base, has wick pick on chain, 7¼" H $220.00
Candle Mold, tin, eight tubes, 10⅞" H $258.50

A-PA Mar. 1997   Bill Bertoi Auctions

Hen & Chick Mechanical Bank, J & E Stevens, pat. 10/1/1901 . . . .$2,145.00
Magic Mechanical Bank, J & E Stevens Co., pat. 3/7/1886 . . . .$1,870.00
Mule Entering Barn Mechanical Bank, J & E Stevens Co., pat. 1/6/1880 . . . .$2,860.00
Speaking Dog Mechanical Bank, maroon base, Shepard Hardware Co., pat. 10/20/1885 . . . .$2,530.00

A-PA Mar. 1997   Glass Works Auctions

Row 1, Left to Right

Shaving Mug, Am., ca. 1885-1925, tailor shop scene, "made in Ger.", 3¼" H $400.00
Shaving Mug, Am., ca. 1885-1925, horse drawn coal wagon, "Germany", 3⅞" H $3,500.00
Shaving Mug, Am., ca. 1885-1925, pharmacy scene, 3⅞" H $1,850.00
Shaving Mug, Am., ca. 1885-1925, horse drawn funeral hearse, "Leonard Vienna Austria", 4⅛" H $1,050.00

Row 2, Left to Right

Shaving Mug, Am., ca. 1885-1925, man shoveling coal, "T & V Limoges Fr." $950.00
Shaving Mug, Am., ca. 1885-1925, cabinet maker planing a board, "T & V Limoges Fr.", 3⅝" H $400.00
Shaving Mug, Am., ca. 1885-1925, mkd. "T & V France", 3⅝" H $1,100.00
Shaving Mug, Am., ca. 1885-1925, caboose w/ letters "B of RT", 3⅝" H $625.00
Shaving Mug, Am., ca. 1885-1925, man photographing a woman, "T & V Limoges Fr.", 3⅝" H $975.00

A-NH Mar. 1997   Northeast Auctions

Chairs, set of six, New Eng. yellow-painted thumbback, w/ vintage dec. $2,400.00
Farm Table, Am. Sheraton red-painted, rectangular top w/ two short drawers, top 59½" x 36", 30" H $1,000.00

A-MA June 1997   Skinner

Sampler, "Mary Pollard born July 7th 1809...", minor staining, fading, 23⅝" x 17½" $2,415.00

A-MA June 1997   Skinner

Samplers, pr., "Elizabeth H. Moore 1826" & "Martha A. Moore 1826", PA, toning, very minor losses & staining, 25½" x 21" $19,550.00

A-OH Aug. 1996   Garth Auctions

Sampler, silk on linen homespun, birds & trees w/ verse & "This made by Hannah Francia 1817", vivid unfaded colors in shades of gr., br., blk., white yel., blue etc., minor stains, framed 18½" H, 17½" W $962.50

A-MA June 1997   Skinner

Sampler, "Wrt. by Eliza Ann Hayward Aged 12 April 24th 1827", minor staining, 17⅜" x 13¾" $2,875.00

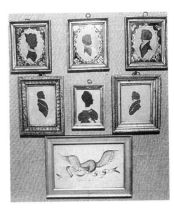

A-OH Aug. 1996   Garth Auctions

Hollow Cut Silhouettes, set of three w/ blk. paper backing & pen & ink w/ simple watercolor detail, matching gilt frames w/ eglomise glass, minor stains & blk. paint on glass is flaked, 5¼" H, 4½" W $693.00

Hollow Cut Silhouettes, pr. of gentlemen, blk. cloth backing is faded to a brownish grey color, stains, matching gilt frames, 6" H, 4⅞" W & 6" H, 5⅛" W $99.00

Hollow Cut Silhouette, of a young woman in ink detail, dress & collar cut from emb. pale gr. paper, blk. ink detail & coloring, old gilt frame, 4⅝" H, 3⅝" W $247.50

Spencerian Pen & Ink, calligraphy on lined paper, banner in blk., red & blue ink w/ "Horace Spencer" beneath, minor stains, framed, 6⅝" H, 9⅝" W $522.50

A-OH Nov. 1996   Garth's Auctions

Sampler, silk on linen homespun, "Abigail Cook born Feb. 6th, 1796...", pristine, gr., blue, pink, rust red, white, 14¼" H x 14¼" W $2,145.00

Edouart Silhouette, cut paper profile, "Lydia Harris" by "Aug. Edouart fecit 1842", w/o frame, 8⅞" W, 10⅞" H ...$2,310.00

A-OH Jan. 1997   Garth's Auctions

Row 1, Left to Right

Silhouette, man reading, cut figure w/ ink detail on background, sgn. "Aug. Edouart fecit 1826", faded background, edge tear, framed, 8¾" W, 12⅛" H $330.00

Silhouette, man in chair reading, cut paper, sgn. in ink "Aug. Edouart fecit 1828", age stains, 9" W, 10" H $1,210.00

Silhouette, man walking, cut paper w/ inkwash ground, sgn. "Augustin Edouart fecit 1826", framed 7" W, 10⅜" H $990.00

Row 2, Left to Right

Silhouette, gentlemen w/ top hat, cut paper w/ gilt detail, inkwash ground, sgn. "F. Frith", oak veneer frame w/ gilded liner, 10⅝" W, 13¼" H $330.00

Silhouette, man in chair, cut paper w/ gilded detail, inkwash ground, sgn. "S. Metford fecit", minor stains, Ogee frame, 9½" W, 11¾" H $440.00

A-OH Oct. 1996   Garth's Auctions

Wool Sheet, homespun, two pc. const. natural white & red & blue stripe, minor damage, 72" x 81" $93.50

Whaling Harpoon, wrt. iron, 45" L $275.00

Candle Mold, tin w/ four oversize tubes, soldered repr., 30½" H $137.50

Lighting Trammel, wooden, adjusts from 38" L $220.00

Baton or Cane, wooden carved horse head w/ ball in cage, dk. finish, age cracks, 40" L $137.50

Pen & Ink, drawing on lined paper, "Little Birds, Home" dk. br. ink, lt. stains, framed, 14½" W, 12½" H $93.50

Candle Mold, twenty tin tubes, pine frame, rust damage & old dk. finish, 5¾" x 26¼", 12½" H $467.50

Candle Mold, tin, single tube, foot scrolled braces, minor resoldering, 21¼" H $220.00

Armchair, various hardwoods, old br. finish, repl. rush seat, minor repairs & feet ended out, 41½" H $220.00

Candle Mold, tin, twenty four tubes w/ double ring handles, one handle loose, 9¾" H $82.50

A-OH Aug. 1996   Garth Auctions

Hanging Spice Box, poplar w/ old red, dovetailed drawer, lift lid, divider replaced & crest, repr. in lid, 10½" W, 7" D, 14¼" H $550.00

Painting on Velvet, by David Ellinger, 20th C., PA folk artist, unsgn. but orig. backing sgn. "D.Y. Ellinger", orig. dec. frame, 7¼" H, 8¾" W $1,210

Drop Leaf Stand, two pcs., cherry w/ old dk. ref., two dovetailed drawers, top is old replm., has added surface nails, leaves may be orig., poplar secondary wood, 18" x 22" w/ 10¾" leaves, 28¾" H, & a repro. **Hepplewhite Style Table** w/ sq. tapered legs, pine w/ mellow finish, 17" x 22", 21¾" H, not pictured .$440.00

Arrowback Side Chairs, set of four, dec., worn orig. br. brushed graining w/ yel. & gr. striping, floral design on crest, bamboo turnings, plank seat & rabbit ear posts, 34" H $770.00

Stoneware Jar, w/ applied handles, impr. label "N.Y. Stoneware Co. Fort Edward, N.Y. 2", design in cobalt blue quill work, hairlines & sm. flakes, 11" H $275.00

Kentucky Rifle, flintlock, curly maple stock, incised carving, brass hardware, stamped "Norris & Co. Warrented", 42" barrel, 57" L, restoration $1,045.00

Wall Sconces, pr., brass, w/ candle sockets, threads stripped on one, 9½" from wall $1,265.00

Burl Butter Paddle, good figure throughout, soft patina, 6" diam., 6" L ...$605.00

Moon Dial, painted steel, from clock, church & ships, 8½" diam. $720.50

Walking Sticks, three, carved hand, shown, 25¼" L; sapling w/ crook root, 38" L; simple carving & inscrip. "Made Oct. 1896 ...", 35½" L, all have worn finish .$165.00

Trigger Guard, cast & engr. w/ good detail, 13" L................$60.50

Walking Stick, ebony w/ carved ivory lion handle, age cracks, 35½" $330.00

A-OH Jan. 1997   Garth's Auctions

Engravings, 2 blk. & white, "Andrew Jackson" & DeWitt Clinton", not a pr., stains, 7⅞" W, 9¾" H, frames w/ gold & blk. paint, matching $550.00

Blanket Chest, walnut w/ old finish, dovetailed feet & drawer, till lid repl., repairs , 28" W, 11¼" D, 13" H $1,100.00

Windsor Arm Chair, old dk. br. finish, mkd. "I. Samler, N-York", 36" H $3,520.00

Hepplewhite Table, walnut w/ old finish, repr., Eastham, MA, 7¾" x 18" w/ 5" leaves, 12¾" H $550.00

Burl Bowl, ash w/ striped figure, good wear & color, 12" diam. 4⅜" H $1,155.00

A-OH Oct. 1996   Garth's Auctions

Currier & Ives Litho., handcolored, "The Narrows. NY Bay from Staten Island", foxing, tears, 16¼" W 12⅛" H $93.50

Country Stand, ref. cherry & maple, dovetailed drawer & one board top, 28" H $302.50

Q.A. Side Chair, CT, maple & poplar w/ old ref., replaced paper rush seat, 41¾" H $770.00

Pewter Soup Plates, two Continental, "T. Holster 1808" 9½" diam. $187.00

Ovoid Jar, stoneware, misshapen, repr., 14½" H $110.00

A-OH Jan. 1997   Garth's Auctions

Tobacco Box, Dutch, brass, engr. scene, 4¾" L $374.00

Burl Tinder Box, carved hinge, missing pin, old finish, edge damage, steel strike, 4" L $181.50

A-OH Aug. 1996   Garth Auctions

Pastel Portraits, pr., gentleman & lady in oval gilt frames, repr., 18¼" H, 16" W $165.00

Hooked Rag Rug, bright yel. cats on a red ground w/ blue border, some damage & rag missing or loose, not too old, 21" x 39" $275.00

Side Chairs, pr., ref. curly maple, one foot ended out & other pieced repairs, old rush seats have damage & strips of wood on seat sides replaced & one pc. is missing, 33¼" H $220.00

Lectern, ref. walnut, 42" H . .$220.00

Windsor Stool, old blk. repaint, shaped seat, scars & age cracks, legs slightly askew, 15" H $357.50

Rag Dolls, four in printed cotton, one in white dress, one in blue dress w/ shoes, wear & repairs, one mkd. "Art Fabric Mills, N.Y. patented 1900", 16½" H, 23" H, 24" H, 25" H $550.00

Doll Carriage, folding steel frame in painted blk. w/ br. leatherized fabric covering, wheels replaced, 22" H $49.50

A-OH Aug. 1996   Garth Auctions

Chippendale Desk, birch, pine & poplar w/ red repaint, dovetailed case, four overlapping dovetailed drawers, horizontal scroll work bracket has unexplainable nail holes, pine feet appear orig. but have been skillfully ended out, lid hinges & hardware replaced, edge wear & damage to drawer overlap, 33½" W, 17½" D, 38¼" H, 30¼" writing height $3,740.00

English Pewter Plates, four, soup plate by "Townsend & Compton", 8" D; partial touch 9¾" D; "H. Little" 9¼" D & "Samuell Ellis", 8¾" D, all have wear $220.00

Candle Mold, tin six tubes w/ conical feet & ear handles, some rust damage & resoldering, 11¾" H $385.00

Pewter Charger, crowned rose touch w/ "P.D.B", wear & corrosion, 13¾" D $275.00

Toaster, wrt. iron w/ scrolled detail, 18" W, 16" L $286.00

Hutch Table, pine & birch cleaned down to old red, seat in base, oval three board top, two feet have damage & arms reinforced at hinges, crack in top, 44½" x 53½", 29¾" H $2,090.00

Pease Jar, turned, old worn dk. patina & wooden handle w/ wire bail, drilled ¾" hole in center of bottom, age cracks in lid & bottom, 12" D, 9½" H $627.00

Pease Jars, two, turned, wooden handles w/ wire bails, one has old finish w/ age crack in bottom & no lid, 9" D, 7¼" H, & one has old ref. w/ uneven color & age crack in base, 8" D, 8" H . .$407.00

Pease Jars, three lrg. turned wooden, old finish, one w/ wooden handle & wire bail, age cracks & chip on lid, 5¼" H, one w/ age crack in side, 5½" H, & one that is 4¾" H $561.00

A-MA Mar. 1997   Eldred's

Bulbs & Ornaments, Christmas collection, early 20th C., w/ two Santa figures, approx. twenty-three pcs. .$385.00

A-MA Mar. 1997   Eldred's

Tin "Pepper" Canisters, two painted, 19th C., Am., Can Co. NY, gilt dec., repl. blk. knobs, 7¾" W, 7" D, 9" H .$440.00

A-OH Jan. 1997   Garth's Auctions

Engravings, seven, handcolored, bird prints by "George Edward", dates 1740's to 1750's, six w/ old gilt frames, one unframed has dk. stain, some edge damage, 10½" W, 12½" H . . .$885.50

Q.A. Mixing Table, maple w/ worn dk. red finish, mortised & pinned apron slate insert, tray top repl., leg repr., 21" x 30¾", 28½" H $2,200.00

Blown Demi-John, olive gr., not pontiled, applied lip, 15¼" H $247.50

A-OH Aug. 1996   Garth Auctions

Oil on Canvas, by contemporary folk artist "Janis", sgn. lower right, 24" H, 36" W, framed, 30" H, 42" W .$275.00

A-OH Aug. 1996   Garth Auctions

Dovetailed Blanket Chest, pine w/ old reddish br. finish, wrt. iron strap hinges, 52½" W, 22" D, 19½" H . . $220

Candle Mold, 18 pewter tubes in pine frame, old worn patina & steel rods for tying wicks, cast label "W. Webb N.Y.", minor cracks, 6¼" x 22", 17½" H $825.00

Drying Rack, w/ shoe feet, pine w/ old dk. finish, screws added to mortised & pinned joints, 25" W, 34¾" H $82.50

Candle Mold, tin 12 tubes, extra long, ear handle, 16½" H $187.00

Candle Mold, round tin 12 tubes, punched conical finial, some battering & old splits, 12" H plus ring $495.00

Candle Mold, tin 12 tubes w/ curved base & ear handle, old blk. paint, 11½" H $220.00

Candle Mold, tin 16 tubes, 9¼" H $110.00

Wooden Box, oblong w/ laced seams & spring loaded lid, pine w/ worn old red, 23" L $385.00

Candle Mold, tin 26 tubes, w/ ear handle, 20¾ L, 11¾" H $253.00

Ovoid Jug, stoneware w/ applied handle, impr. label "I. Seymour Troy", cobalt blue at label & quill work "3", minor firing lines, 15¼" H . . . $192.50

A-OH Aug. 1996   Garth Auctions

Banjo Clock, mah. veneer case w/ gilded facade, brass works w/ weight, pendulum & key, replacements, regilded surface flaking, rev. painted glass panels are replaced, 40½" H . $880.00

PA Chippendale Scroll Mirror, mah. w/ old finish, repr. breaks in two bottom ears, mirror replaced, 28⅜" H, 15½" W $770.00

English Barometer, mah. veneer w/ inlay, silvered dial is mkd. "Scurr Thirsk", 38¼" H $660.00

Sheraton Card Table, ref. birch w/ figured mah. & bird's eye maple veneer on apron, repr., 17" x 35", 28¾" H . $2,090.00

Canterbury, walnut w/ old finish, dovetailed drawer, wire nail const., replaced brasses, 16" x 22¾", 23½" H $550.00

A-OH Aug. 1996   Garth Auctions

Painted Bin, poplar w/ old red paint, divided int. w/ double hinged lid, holes in lid & holes in divider cut in & filled w/ orig. pc., 68½" W, 17¾" D, 20" H . $440.00

Candle Mold, tin w/ 24 removable tubes in a carrier w/ band, soldered repr. & tubes are mismatched, 7¾" x 11½", 16¼" H $220.00

OH Ovoid Churn, stoneware w/ applied shoulder handle, impr. "T.P. Mead", cobalt blue at handle & label, chips, 14¾" H $110.00

Candle Drying Rack, eight rotating arms, each w/ rack that hold 32 candle wicks, hardwood w/ old gr. paint, one arm is ended out, 39" H . $770.00

Stoneware Cooler, w/ double ear handles, cobalt blue quill work w/ flourish, wooden spigot, stains & minor chips, 22¾" H $220.00

A-OH Aug. 1996   Garth Auctions

Painted Windsor Chair, old worn white repaint w/ blue striping & polychrome rose dec. on crest, age cracks in seat, 33¾" H $110.00

Country Stand, ref. curly maple w/ good figure & color, rounded drawer front & two board top, dovetailed drawer has poplar secondary wood, 21¾" x 22¼", 28¼" H $1,375.00

Decorated Box, poplar w/ orig. red paint w/ blk. trim & blk. & yel. striping, lid has holes from removed handles, 13" L $302.50

A-OH Oct. 1996   Garth's Auctions

Pie Safe, poplar w/ worn old red & punched tin panels, dovetailed drawers, edge damage, missing lock, pulls replaced, 53" W, 48" H $1,650.00

Tin Candle Mold, thirty-six tubes, soldered repairs & handles battered, 14¾" H $137.50

Round Box, stave const., with laced wooden bands, old worn gr. repaint, 12½" diam. $330.00

Tin Candle Mold, six pewter tubes in pine frame, tubes have removable threaded tips, 16¾" H $825.00

Windmill Weight, Cast Iron Horse, made by Dempster Mill Mfg., Beatrice, NE, old repaint, 16½" L, 17" H . . . $302.50

A-OH Aug. 1996   Garth Auctions

Blanket Chest, dec., poplar cleaned down to old red graining w/ traces of later blk. paint, dovetailed case, applied base & lid edge moldings & till w/ lid, 44" W, 21¼" D, 25¾" H $440.00

Candle Mold, w/ wooden frame & 20 tin tubes, missing foot & screw broken, rust damage, 28" H $137.50

Candle Mold, w/ 16 pewter tubes in a pine frame, frame has old patina & tubes have old silver paint, 8½" x 12½", 14" H $880.00

Copper Tea Kettle, dovetailed copper, has stamped initials "D.M.D." minor dents, old patina, 14" H$159.50

Ovoid Jar, stoneware w/ applied handles, impr. "I.M. Mead & Co. Portage Co., Ohio", cobalt blue at handles & label, hairlines, lid w/ cutout hand grips, minor lid edge chips, different color than jar, 14" H $187.00

A-OH Jan. 1997   Garth's Auctions

Fraktur, w/ Eng. text, ink, pencil & watercolor, in red, yel., blue & blk., "George Baker's Age Paper", faded, fold lines & rprs., w/o frame 14½" W, 12¼" H $715.00

Crib Quilt Top, applique chintz on white cotton, floral in shades of red & blue, dk. stains, 37" x 41" . . .$715.00

Fire Bucket, leather, old blk. paint w/ yel. & red "G. Manent 1789", wear & handle damaged, 13½" H . .$1,210.00

Fire Bucket, leather, gr. paint w/ traces of dec., very worn, handle missing, 11¾" H $330.00

Q.A. Corner Chair, walnut w/ old ref., restoration, prob. orig. potty chair, 30½" H $660.00

A-OH Oct. 1996   Garth's Auctions

Currier & Ives Litho., handcolored, "Am. Homestead Winter", minor stains, 10" H, 14" W $467.50

Chippendale Scroll Mirror, mah. w/ old finish, top of bottom crest restored, 11¾" W, 21½" H $192.50

Windsor Armchair, old bluish gr. repaint, repairs, 37½" H $467.50

Sheraton Stand, cherry & maple w/ some curl in legs, dovetailed drawer, 16¼" x 20½", 30 " H $660.00

Chocolate Mold, tin, two-part, rabbit mkd. "Ger." edge clips repl., 20" H . .$170.50

A-OH Oct. 1996   Garth's Auctions

Hanging Mail Box, walnut w/ old finish, locking compartment, screw const., 9¼" W, 21¼" H $104.50

Candlemold, tin, ten tubes, hinged top w/ notches for wicks, old dk. pitted finish, 10¾" H $275.00

Pen & Ink Watercolor, on paper, yel., ora., gr. & blue, stains, paper dk., w/ beveled pine frame 11" W, 9" H . . .$82.50

Country Stand, pine w/ old red finish & blk. grid, one board top, repl. drawer, dk. stain, 17" x 19", 28¾" H $99.00

Windsor Side Chairs, set of three, dk. varnish, one repr. seat, legs ended out, size varies, 36½" H, 37" H, 38" H $660.00

A-OH Oct. 1996   Garth's Auctions

Cupboard w/ Pie Safe Base, stepback one pc., poplar cleaned down to old red paint, hardware replaced, chewed mouse holes on top doors, 48" W, 83" H .$2,310.00

Candle Mold, tin twelve tubes w/ rim handles, 11½" H $93.50

Candle Mold, tin w/ twelve pewter tubes w/ brass top plate & tips in a poplar frame w/ worn patina, 15¾" H $990.00

Candle Mold, w/ ten oversize tubes, minor damage, 15"H $148.50

Ovoid Stoneware Jug, w/ applied strap handle & mkd. "S.S. Perry & Co. W. Troy", cobalt blue dec., stains, 16" H . . .$220.00

A-OH Oct. 1996   Garth's Auctions

Bucket Bench, OH, poplar w/ old gr. paint, attrib. to Fairfield County, 37¾" W, 9⅜" D, 36" H $440.00

Doorstop, cast iron pointer, worn orig. paint, lt. rust, 15¼" L . . .$165.00

Stoneware, two pcs., cobalt blue stenciled labels crock "Hamilton & Jones", 7" H & jar "Jas. Hamilton & Co", 8¼" H $247.50

Doorstop, cast iron Boston Bull dog, worn orig. paint, lt. rust, 9¾" H $137.50

Stoneware, two pcs., jug w/ white glaze & cobalt blue label "Riedel & Hill... NY", lip flakes, 16" H & jug, pebbled tan glaze, w/ impr. label "Maurice Knight, ...Ohio", 14½" H $110.00

A-MA Mar. 1997   Eldred's

Wooden Flagon, Am., 19th C., old gr. paint, four iron bands, carved handle & cover, 16" H $1,320.00

A-OH Aug. 1996   Garth Auctions

Empire Chest, ref. cherry w/ curly maple veneer trim, paneled ends, four dovetailed drawers & crest, poplar secondary wood, 41" W, top is 21½" x 42", 49½" H, plus crest 57½" H over-all $522.50

Stoneware Jugs, two w/ tin lids & wooden handles w/ wire bails, leaf ears & white glaze, 10" H, & br. Albany slip, impr. "White & Wood, Binghamton, N.Y. 6", spout lid missing, 9½" H, both have minor chips $198.00

Redware Pitchers, three w/ applied handles, clear glaze w/ br. splotches, wear & chips, 7¼" H, blk. glaze, 6¾" H, & clear glaze w/ br. flecks, wear & chips, 5½" H $132.00

Wall Cupboard, child size step back, pine w/ old worn reddish br. finish, paneled doors, 24½" W, 12¼" D, 25¼" H $935.00

Bentwood Box, Shaker round w/ lid & swivel handle, copper tacks, varnish finish, 7¼" D $137.50

A-OH Jan. 1997   Garth's Auctions

Oil on Canvas, primitive portrait, rebacked on artist board, cleaned & repairs, back of canvas inscribed "Mehitable Hoobler painted in Peoria, Ills", 23" H, 19" W, old molded frame $660.00

Chippendale Tea Table, Eng. tilt top, mah. w/ old finish, one foot ended out, repairs to base, cleats & hinges, top replm., 29" diam., 27¾" H . . .$495.00

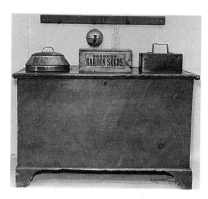

A-OH Aug. 1996   Garth Auctions

Shaker Peg Board, pine & cherry w/ old patina, one peg is missing, 38¾" L $49.50

Shaker Blanket Chest, pine w/ orig. red paint, dovetailed case, some wear & edge damage, reattached feet & one back foot replaced, stenciled label "H.B. Bear" attrib. to Ohio Community, 48½" W, 23¾" D, 29½" H $770.50

Shaker Warmers, two, oval tin 12½" L & rectangular sheet steel w/ riveted const. & worn bluing w/ lt. rust, 11¼" L $115.50

Seed Box, unfinished pine w/ blk. & white paper label "Shakers' Garden Seeds, raised at New Lebanon, N.Y.", leather hinges broken, 14¾" L $1,100.00

Shaker Pieces, one tin spherical herb infuser 5" D, & one aqua medicine bottle "Shaker Digestive Cordial, A.J. White, New York", 5⅝" H $49.50

A-OH Jan. 1997   Garth's Auctions

Row 1, Left to Right

Bronze Mortar, mismatched pestle, mortar has old dk. patina, 4¼" diam., 3½" H $49.50

Iron Strong Box, early w/ key & bale handle, 5⅝" L $220.00

Brass Mortar, & pestle, 4½" D, 3" H $49.50

Row 2, Left to Right

Capstan Candlestick, early brass, minor wear, 5⅜" H $1,210.00

Iron Strong Box, early, reinforced corners, internal lock repl. w/ hasp, 7¼" L $412.50

Brass Candlestick, early sq. base, color varies, base & stem soldered, sm. hole in base $82.50

Capstan Candlestick, early brass, sm. solder filled hole in base, 5⅛" H $1,320.00

Row 3, Left to Right

Lafayette, bronze bust, 7⅜" H $330.00

Brass Pieces, three, goblet, 5½" H, jar w/ hinged lid, 3" H, & muffin-eer $60.50

Iron Strong Box, early safety deposit box, w/ key $49.50

A-OH Aug. 1996   Garth Auctions

Drop Leaf Table, ref. curly maple, reconst., top is 22¾" x 38", 29¼" H $550.00

Strong Box, dovetailed w/ wrt. iron strapping & lock, walnut w/ old ref. & holes, dated "1645", crack in top, 16" L .$467.50

OH Stoneware Jug, w/ strap handle & br. Albany slip, impr. "P.H. Smith 2", 12½" H $71.50

A-OH Oct. 1996   Garth's Auctions

Two Textiles, pieced quilt, trees in red & sage gr., overall wear, 76" x 78", & fish scale rug (not shown) 22" x 38" $390.50

Hepplewhite Table, cherry & pine w/ red stain finish, dovetailed drawer & breadboard top, repairs, back apron & top repl., 32" x 44", 28" H . .$588.50

Sheraton Side Chair, dec. youth size, orig. red & blk. graining w/ yel., rush seat, wear, 29" H $440.00

Apple Tray, pine w/ old worn pumpkin colored paint, edge damage & age cracks, 17" x 25¾", 4" H $247.50

Washing Machine Model, working, oak w/ natural finish & mkd. "The Double Washer", 17½" L $247.50

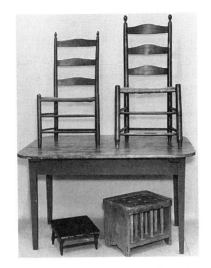

A-OH Aug. 1996   Garth Auctions

Shaker Hepplewhite Work Table, hardwood base w/ old red & pine top w/ old scrubbed finish, two board top & rounded corners, attrib. to Enfield, N.H., 37½" x 48¾", 27¼" H . .$935.00

Shaker Ladderback Chair, orig. dk. finish w/ "Mt. Lebanon, N.Y." label, "3" impr. on top slat, repl. seat in blue & grey, 33½" H $467.50

Shaker Ladderback Chair, old dk. finish & woven split cane seat, turned finials, attrib. to South Union, Kentucky, 38" H $82.50

Shaker Foot Stool, worn orig. dk. finish w/ "Mt. Lebanon, N.Y." label, edge wear & minor corner damage, 11½" x 11¾" $302.50

Candle Mold, 16 pewter tubes in a pine frame, worn patina, 12¼" x 15½", 13¼" H $770.00

A-OH Jan. 1997   Garth's Auctions

Q.A. Lowboy, maple w/ dk. red finish, dovetailed overlapping drawers w/ beveled top edges, edge damage, insect damage, repl. brasses, pine top, 35" W, 34¼" H $2,200.00

Candlesticks, pr., turned wood, mah. w/ worn red paint over blk., scratches & glued break, 9⅞" H $412.50

Burl Bowl, ash w/ tight figure & worn varnish, minor age cracks, 11" diam., 3¾" H $495.00

Andirons, pr., wrt. iron knife blade, brass trim, repairs & restorations, one stamped "D & W", 29½" H . . .$577.50

A-OH Oct. 1996   Garth's Auctions

Sleigh Bells, twenty-one metal on new leather strap, 86" L $385.00

Ladderback Side Chair, hardwood w/ old br. finish, rush seat tattered, front rung repl., 43½" H $93.50

Pie Safe, poplar w/ red repaint, rehinged door, may be from another safe, 21¼" W, 48¼" H $440.00

Peel, wrt. iron, 37½" L $137.50

Redware, two pcs., both w/ wear & chips, apple butter jar w/ flecked glaze & strap handle, 7⅝" H, pitcher w/ dk. br. glaze & white slip int. w/ banded lip detail & strap handle, 10½" H . . .$110.00

A-OH Oct. 1996   Garth's Auctions

Water Bench, pine w/ yellowish wash, 33¾" W, 12" D, 42¼" H $440.00

Row 1

Candle Molds, three, tin, old soldered repr., sixteen tubes, 11¾" H; twelve tubes, 10½" H; eight tubes, 10" H 247.50

Row 2

Candle Molds, four, tin, four tubes, 10½" H; three tubes, 10¼" H; four tubes, crimped pan battered, 10½" H; four tubes, 13" H .$247.50

Row 3

Stoneware, two pcs., jug w/ strap mkd. "2", chips, 14½" H, & ovoid jar, blue stenciled label "Eneix & Frankenbery, New Geneva, Pa. 2", hairlines & stains, 11½" H .$82.50

Candle Molds, four, tin, four tubes, handle loose, 10¾" H; six tubes, handle loose, 10½" H; four tubes, some damage, 10¼" H; & five tubes w/ handle, old soldered repr., 10½" H$220.00

A-OH Aug. 1996   Garth Auctions

Lighting Stand, or drying rack, turned hardwood w/ old worn red & gr. paint, late 19th C., 39" H $137.50
Braceback Windsor Chair, w/ added rockers, old dk. reddish br. repaint, breaks in bow & some slight variation in turnings w/ some possible old replm., 35" H $165.00
Candle Mold, tin 12 tubes w/ lrg. ear handle, 8⅛" H $275.00
Candle Molds, two tin w/ ear handles, six tubes & three tubes, 10½" H $137.50
Candle Molds, two tin w/ oversize tubes, one tubes is 16¼" H & four tubes is 20¼" H $220.00

A-OH Aug. 1996   Garth Auctions

Decorated Chest, poplar w/ orig. flame graining in imitation of mah., paneled ends & four dovetailed drawers, damage, 19⅞" x 41¾", 64" H .$247.50
Toy Firehouse, wooden w/ colorful polychrome paint, 13½" x 18", 17½" H $159.50
Footstool, hexagonal w/ applied wooden thread spools, pine w/ old varnish, wire nail const., 14½" D $27.50
Whirligig, wooden w/ polychrome paint, 20th C. folk art, 17" H . .192.50
Blocks, 26 wooden w/ die stamped emb. designs & colorful screen painted designs $82.50

A-OH Aug. 1996   Garth Auctions

Jelly Cupboard, cherry w/ dk. ref., two dovetailed drawers & top w/ removable gallery that has scrolled crest, dovetailed const., feet have water & edge damage, repairs, yel. pine secondary wood, gallery may be an old addition, 46¼" W, 22" D, 48¾" H, plus gallery, 57½" H overall . .$880.00
OH Ovoid Jar, stoneware w/ applied handles, impr. "I.M. Mead & Co. 2", cobalt blue at handles & label, hairline in rim, 11¾" H $165.00
OH Ovoid Jug, stoneware w/ applied handle, impr. "I.M. Mead & Co. 2", cobalt blue at handle & label, chip on base, 13¼" H $165.00
OH Ovoid Jar, stoneware w/ applied handle & incised lines, impr. "I.M. Mead & Co. 4", cobalt blue & handles & label, chips & crow's foot hairline, 14" H $165.00
OH Ovoid Jar, stoneware w/ applied handles, impr. "I.M. Mead & Co." cobalt blue at handles & label, chips & rim hairline at label, 14" H $115.50

A-MA Jan. 1997   Skinner

Left to Right

Decoy, Eider Drake Am., early 20th C., cracks, paint wear, minor losses to bill, 14" L $258.75
Decoy, blk. duck drake hollow core, Am., late 19th/early 20th C., cracks, repaint, 18½" L . . . . .N/S
Decoy, golden eye drake, Am., 20th C., losses to tail, cracks, paint wear, 13½" L $4,025.00

A-OH Aug. 1996   Garth Auctions

Hanging Candlebox, tin, 11" L . .$357.50
Hepplewhite Work Table, pine & poplar w/ old red, two nailed drawers & two board top, edge damage & age cracks, drawer runners replaced, 23¼" x 38¼", 29" H $880.00
Candle Mold, 36 tin tubes in pine frame w/ old red paint & blk. stenciled label "J. Walker, E. Bloomfield", recessed top is lined w/ tin & has wire rods for tying wicks, 11" x 13¼", 11" H $2,255.00
Hanging Salt Box, primitive, ref. poplar, one drawer, lift top compartment & crest, edge damage & old repairs, lid replaced, 13" W, 7¾" D, 24½" H $357.50
Candle Mold, 36 tubes in a cherry frame, old dk. worn patina & wire rods for tying wicks, ends have ghost lines & nail holes indicating some other attachments at one time, 14" x 23", 16" H $1,540.00

A-OH Oct. 1996   Garth's Auctions

Jacquard Coverlet, one pc. single weave, red, blue, gr., br. & natural white, minor wear, 81" x 84" $302.50
Settle Bench, dec., dk. from layer of br. varnish, floral dec. & striping, one rung broken, 80" L $660.00

A-OH Aug. 1996   Garth Auctions

Empire Chest, ref. cherry w/ mah. veneer facade, four dovetailed drawers, top is orig., back overhang cut off & low crest added, poplar secondary wood, replaced brasses, minor veneer damage & feet are replaced, 41¼" W, top is 20½" x 41½", 46" H . . .$445.50
Victorian Candlesticks, pr. brass w/ pushups, 8¾" H $99.00
Pewter Teapots, two of similar design, one mkd. "H.C. Wilcox & Co.", 8½" H, unmkd. on has repairs & added brass bottom, 9" H $220.00
Continental Pewter Plates, similar pr., angel touch, wear & dents, 9½" D $110.00
Pewter Charger, incomplete touch marks, English or Continental, wear & scratches, 15" D $302.50

A-OH Aug. 1996   Garth Auctions

Chromolithographs, 3 from early nursery catalogue, minor damage, good color, 8½" H, 5¼" W, cherry frames, 12⅜" H, 9⅞" W $82.50
Hutch Table, pine w/ old br. repaint, top w/ 3 boards w/ rounded corners, lift lid seat in base appears to be an old addition, 35" x 53½", 28¾" H . .$935.00
Dome Top Box, dec. dovetailed, pine w/ worn orig. br. vinegar graining on yel. ground, repr. cracks on lid, lock is missing hasp, 24" L $165.00
Stoneware Jug, w/ strap handle, impr. label "N.A. White & Son, Utica, N.Y. 2", bird in cobalt blue slip, sm. flakes, 14¾" H $495.00

A-OH Oct. 1996   Garth's Auctions

Jacquard Coverlet, two pc. double weave, navy blue & natural white, corners dated "1850", minor wear, 78" x 92" $550.00
Q.A. Work Table, PA, walnut w/ scrubbed finish, mortised & pinned apron, dovetailed drawers, removable three board top, repr. foot, drawers replm., 34¾" x 65¾", 28½" H .$440.00
Desk Box, dovetailed , ref. poplar, 17½" x 19½", 7" H $192.50
Blanket Chest, dovetailed, end feet ended out, lid edge restored & lid molding repl., hinges loose, 35½" L $302.50

A-OH Aug. 1996   Garth Auctions

Whirligig Model, non-working, balsa w/ polychrome, contemporary folk art, minor damage, 36" L, 34¼" H . .$220.00
Hepplewhite Work Table, maple base & poplar top w/ old yel. paint over red, two board top w/ one replaced board that has age cracks, 35" x 50", 27⅜" H $544.50
Stoneware Crock, w/ applied handles, cobalt blue quill work design & "4", minor chips, 11½" H $220.00
Stoneware Crocks, 2 w/ applied handles, cobalt blue quill work "3" w/ flourish, 10⅜" H & 11" H $330.00
Horse Pull Toy, wood w/ blk. fabric covering, wooden base has worn red edge stripe & cast iron wheels, restored & repr., legs loose, 24" H $440.00

A-OH Oct. 1996   Garth's Auctions

Currier & Ives Litho., two, hand-colored "The Children in the woods", damage & stains, framed 14½" W, 18½" H, & "The Barefoot Boy", stains & surface damage, framed 12¾" W, 16⅜" H $165.00
French Map, handcolored engr., of N. & S. Am., "L'Amerique", printed in Paris in 1762, stains, framed 20¼" W, 14½" H $192.50
Wooden Sleigh, orig. varnish & red paint w/ blk. & white striping, bird in blue & gr., some wear & edge damage, 32" L $770.00
Spinning Wheel, hardwood w/ red stain, considerable repr. & replm., 34" H $220.00
Baby Cradle, dovetailed, ref. curly maple, all surfaces are ref., 42½" L $660.00

A-OH Aug. 1996   Garth Auctions

Pieced Quilt, & appliquéd, yel. & white w/ fruit appliqués on deeper yel. & gr., stains & sm. holes, 66" x 82" $275.00
Rope Bed, poplar w/ worn old blk. paint, orig. side rails, 56¼" W, rails are 71" L, 39" H $275.00

A-OH Oct. 1996   Garth's Auctions

Hanging Pie Safe, attrib. to Berks County, PA, poplar w/ old dk. finish w/ "F.W. Sanner Hardware, Tremont, Pa" on both ends, 39" W, 36" H . .$1,320.00

Stoneware Cooler, w/ applied shoulder handles & tooled lines, impr. "3", cobalt blue brushed floral dec., 13½" H $220.00

Bentwood Box, round w/ decorative brass upholstery tacks, crack in edge, 13¾" diam., 6½" H $165.00

Ovoid Stoneware Jar, cobalt blue brushed & stenciled "Hamilton & Jones, Greensboro, Pa.", filled rim chip, 9⅜" H $137.50

Stoneware Jug, w/ applied handle, cobalt blue quill work mkd. "Bernhardt Bros...Buffalo, N.Y.", 13" H $192.50

A-OH Oct. 1996   Garth's Auctions

Empire Jackson Press, ref. cherry, dovetailed drawer & gallery, feet & molding repl., 41¾"W, 56"H $1,155.00

Empire Shelf Clock, mah. veneer, carved eagle crest missing top, mkd. "Riley Whiting, Winchester, Conn", has pendulum & key, one weight missing, 29¼" H $192.50

A-OH Oct. 1996   Garth's Auctions

Penny Rug, colorful wool felt applique on canvas, unused, 30" x 53" $132.00

Wooden Sled, old worn red & blue paint w/ blk. striping, 35" L . .$357.50

Dry Sink, OH, sm., pine & poplar w/ old worn bluish grey repaint, 14½" x 25¾", overall 35¾" H $632.50

Doorstop, cast iron, Boston bulldog, orig. paint has minor wear, 8¼" $93.50

Doorstop, cast iron, Boston bulldog, orig. paint has minor wear, 9¾" H $137.50

A-OH Oct. 1996   Garth's Auctions

Diorama, w/ ship, wood compo., sgn. "Kenneth Walcott", gold painted frame, 18¼" W, 15¾" H $280.50

Windsor Side Chair, old worn blk. repaint, bamboo turnings in base & spindles, 35½" H $440.00

Sheraton Stand, ref. cherry, mortised & pinned apron, two board top, repl. top & rebuilt drawer, 18¾" x 22¼", 28¼" H $357.50

Knife Box, dovetailed w/ four sections, ref. walnut, 12½" x 14½" $93.50

Windmill Weight, cast iron horse by Dempster Mill Mfg., Beatrie NE, old repaint is read & gr., 18½" H .$412.50

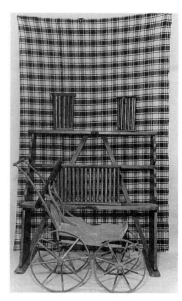

A-OH Oct. 1996   Garth's Auctions

Wool Blanket, homespun two pc., blue & white, edge damage & sm. holes, 72" x 76" $165.00

Shelves, pine w/ worn layers of red & br. paint, age cracks, 39" W, 22" D, 39" H $467.50

Candle Molds, two, tin, fifteen tubes, some resoldering, 11¼" H & ten tubes, 10½" H $137.50

Candle Mold, forty-eight tubes, top edge battered, 4" x 19", 11" H $330.00

Baby Carriage, doll size, wood w/ steel fittings, worn orig. red paint w/ blk. & yel. striping, sun shade in blk. leatherized cloth, worn paper lining, 33" L . . .$357.50

A-OH Oct. 1996   Garth's Auctions

Dry Sink, ref. ash & poplar, early 20th C., w/ wire nail const., cast iron latch repl., 46½" W, 18½" D, 42½" H . . .$605.00

Pitcher, blue & white sponge ware, 8¾" H $341.00

Pitcher, blue & white sponge ware, minor chips on spout, 8¾" H .$165.00

Pitcher, blue & white sponge ware w/ flower, chips on rim, 9" H . . .$269.50

Pitcher, blue & white sponge ware, chips, 8¾" H $357.50

A-OH Oct. 1996   Garth's Auctions

Ackerman Lithos. set of four, London, Rowlandson's "Doctor Syntax", handcolored in red & blue, minor damage, framed 11⅛" W, 8⅛" H $220.00
Country Stand, weathered pine & poplar w/ reddish br. stain, 12" diam., 22½" H $38.50
Windsor Rocker, combback, worn blk. repaint over red, mkd. "A. Hagget, Charlestown", repairs & broken spindles, comb crest damaged, 45¾" H . .$330.00
Candle Molds, two, tin, four tubes w/ ear handle, 8½" H, & six tubes w/ ear handle, battered, 6¾" H, both soldered repr. $121.00
Bentwood Box, mkd. "W.E. Sawyer", old finish, copper tacks, stains & edge damage, 14¾" diam. $71.50

A-OH Aug. 1996   Garth Auctions

Row 1, left to right:
Lehnware Covered Jar, polychrome strawberries on a pink ground, 5⅛" H $962.50
Lehnware Blanket Chest, miniature, pine & poplar w/ red wash over a pink ground w/ yel. striping & polychrome floral dec., dovetailed case & molded edge lid, lock w/ key, 8½" L $6,380.00
Lehnware Covered Jar, footed, polychrome flowers on a peach ground w/ strawberries on lid, 5" H $715.00

Row 2, left to right:
Lehnware Vessel, footed, polychrome flowers on a peach ground, 2⅝" H $880.00
Lehnware Mush & Milk, polychrome & floral decals on a deep pink ground, wear $660.00
Lehnware Vessel, footed, polychrome strawberries on a pink ground, 2¾" H $880.00
Lehnware Vessel, footed, polychrome strawberries on a peach ground, old repr. to foot, 1⅞" H $1,100.00

A-OH Aug. 1996   Garth Auctions

Carved Panel, primitive relief w/ gargoyles, oak w/ old soft finish, some edge damage, 8" x 27" $148.50
Wall Pocket, figured walnut w/ old finish, carved foliage detail, damage, 26¾" H, 15¼" W $247.50
Decorated Rocker, orig. red & blk. graining w/ red flame graining on seat & arms, yel. striping & stenciled design on crest in polychrome & gilt, wear & glued cracks on seat, 40¼" H $137.50
Country Stand, ref. curly maple, two dovetailed drawers & one board top, poplar secondary wood, 18¾" x 18¾", 30¾" H $1,265.00
Candle Molds, circular w/ 12 tubes & conical finial w/ ring handle, rust damage, 14½" H; six tubes w/ oval bottom & top, handle missing, 11" H; 12 tubes in a single row, damage, soldered repr. & blk. repaint, 10½" H, 14½" L $478.50

A-MA Jan. 1997   Skinner

Row 1, Left to Right
Sewing Box w/ Swift, whalebone & ivory inlaid mah., 19th C., repr. to screw, missing finial, minor cracks, 13" W, 8" D, 15" H $1,840.00
Mini. Obelisk, inlaid mah., 19th C., abalone & ivory, minor losses, minute cracks, 13⅜" H $805.00
Watch Hutch, baleen & ivory inlaid walnut, 19th C., in form of clock, minor losses, 13¾" H $4,025.00

Lantern, whalebone, 19th C., repl. glass, minor loss, 10½" H . .$1,380.00

Row 2, Left to Right
Doll's Bed, whalebone, tall post, 19th C., minor cracks, 7⅞" W, 10⅝" D, 10⅜" H $3,737.50
Dipper, coconut, whale ivory & rosewood, 19th C., w/ baleen spacers, cracks to ivory, repr. to handle, 14¼" L $488.75
Sewing Carrier, reticulated whalebone & pine, 19th C., repr., minor cracks 7" L, 6⅞" H $1,150.00
Watch Hutch, whalebone, 19th C., minor cracks, 5" W, 3¾" D, 7½" $8,625.00
Wood Sewing Bird, ivory inlaid, 19th C., inlay loss & replm., 4⅛" $1,150.00

Row 3, Left to Right
Oval Ditty Box, whalebone, 19th C., single finger const., 5⅞" L . $1,150.00
Crimper, inlaid whalebone, 19th C., w/ baleen & abalone inlay, old repr. to handle, 9 - 14" L $977.50

A-OH Oct. 1996   Garth's Auctions

Pieced Quilt, in pink & gold cotton crepe, 73" x 73" $165.00
Mammy's Bench, w/ baby guards, shiny blk. repaint, weathering & age cracks, 79" L $330.00
Rocking Horse, carved wood, old dapple grey paint, flaking & touch up repr., glass eyes, leather saddle & worn horsehair main & tail, 52½" L $632.50